Library of
Davidson College

ENLIGHTENING ALLEGORY

Theory, Practice, and Contexts of Allegory
in the Late Seventeenth and Eighteenth Centuries

Edited by
KEVIN L. COPE

AMS Press
New York

Library of Congress Cataloging-in-Publication Data

Enlightening allegory: theory, practice and contexts of allegory in the late seventeenth and eighteenth centuries/edited by Kevin L. Cope.
   (AMS studies in the eighteenth century; no 18)
   Includes bibliographical references and index.
   ISBN 0-404-63518-0 (alk. paper)
   1. English literature — 18th century — History and criticism — Theory, etc. 2. Allegory. 3. English literature-Early modern. 1500-1700 — History and criticism — Theory, etc. 4. English literature — Early modern, 1500-1700—History and criticism. 5. English literature — 18th century — History and criticism. 6. Enlightenment — Great Britain. I. Cope, Kevin Lee. II. Series.
   PR448.A44E55 1993   91-75412
   820.9 15—dc20   CIP

All AMS Books are printed on acid-free paper that meets the guidelines for performance and durability of the Committee on Production Guidelines for Book Longevity of the Council on Library Resources.

Copyright © 1993 by AMS Press, Inc.
All rights reserved.

AMS Press, Inc.
56 East 13th Street
New York, N.Y. 10003

Manufactured in the United States of America

For the Little Champion

CONTENTS

List of Illustrations vii

Acknowledgments xi

Preface xiii

Part I
Presentations: Theories, Speculations

HAZARD ADAMS, *University of Washington*
Reynolds, Vico, *Blackwell*, Blake:
The Fate of Allegory   3

THOMAS MARESCA, *SUNY—Stony Brook*
Personfication vs. Allegory   21

JOHN SHAWCROSS, *The University of Kentucky*
Allegory, Typology, and Didacticism:
Paradise Lost in the Eighteenth Century   41

THOMAS A. VOGLER, *University of California—Santa Cruz*
The Allegory of Allegory: Unlockeing
Blake's "Crystal Cabinet"   75

GRANT HOLLY, *Hobart and William Smith College*
The Allegory in Realism   131

KEVIN L. COPE, *Louisiana State University*
Directions to Signify: Exploring the
Emblems of Enlightenment Allegory   171

Part II
Presences: Acts, Events

NANETTE LE COAT, *Trinity University*
The Language of Revolution: Allegory in
Volney's *Les Ruines*   221

DEBORAH ANN JACOBS, *Prestonsburg Community College*
   The Plot in a Dream and Dreams of a Plot:
   The Lessons of Occasional Allegory   241

CONNIE CAPERS THORSON, *University of New Mexico*
   Allegory in Minor Restoration Theatricals:
   Anti-Papist Rhetoric and Propaganda   255

JANET WOLF, *Le Moyne College*
   Political Allegory in the Later Plays of
   John Gay   275

Part III
Representations: Texts, Talks, Tales

NEIL SACCAMANO, *Cornell University*
   Knowledge, Power, Allegory:
   Swift's *Tale* and Neoclassical
   Literary Criticism   299

DUSTIN GRIFFIN, *New York University*
   The Visionary Scene: Vision and
   Allegory in the Poetry of Pope   323

VERONICA KELLY, *De Paul University*
   "Embody'd dark": The Simulation of
   Allegory in *The Dunciad*   351

PETER WALMSLEY, *McMaster University*
   Guardian #39: Berkeley's
   Allegory of Mind   373

Index   391

LIST OF ILLUSTRATIONS

Denis Diderot, *Encyclopédie (Planches)*, 3	144
Denis Diderot, *Encyclopédie (Planches)*, 3	145
Denis Diderot, *Encyclopédie (Planches)*, 11	146
Denis Diderot, *Encyclopédie (Planches)*, 8	147
Denis Diderot, *Encyclopédie (Planches)*, 9	148
Denis Diderot, *Encyclopédie (Planches)*	149
Denis Diderot, *Encyclopédie* (Planches), 1	154
Denis Diderot, *Encyclopédie* (Planches), 1	155
Denis Diderot, *Encyclopédie* (Planches), 4	156
Denis Diderot, *Encyclopédie* (Planches), 2	157
Denis Diderot, *Encyclopédie* (Planches), 3	158
Denis Diderot, *Encyclopédie* (Planches), 3	159
Denis Diderot, *Encyclopédie* (Planches), 1	160
Denis Diderot, *Encyclopédie* (Planches), 3	161
Exemplary Imaginary Map	165
Engraving from Benjamin Cole, *Select Tales and Fables*	183
Engraving from Benjamin Cole, *Select Tales and Fables*	184
Engraving from Benjamin Cole, *Select Tales and Fables*	185
Emblem from Nathaniel Crouch, *Delights for the Ingenious*	186
Emblem from Nathaniel Crouch, *Delights for the Ingenious*	187
Emblem from Nathaniel Crouch, *Delights for the Ingenious*	188
Emblem from Nathaniel Crouch, *Delights for the Ingenious*	189
Emblem from Nathaniel Crouch, *Delights for the Ingenious*	190
Frontispiece, George Henry Millar's *New and Universal System of Geography*	201
Frontispiece, Frederic Watson's *New and Complete Geographical Dictionary*	202
Map of Greenland, Edward Pellham's *God's Power and Providence*	203
Map of Derby, from *London Magazine* (1752)	204
Map of Shetland, from *London Magazine* (1752)	205
Anonymous, *A General Map of the Discoveries of Admiral De Fonte*	209
From Robert Gillet, *The Pleasures of Reason*	210

AMS Studies in the Eighteenth Century, No. 18

ISSN: 0196-6561

Other titles in this series:

1. Modern Language Association of America, *Proceedings of the 1967-68 Neoclassicism Conferences.* Edited and with a Selected Bibliography, 1920-68, by Paul J. Korshin. 1970.
2. Francesco Cordasco. *Tobias George Smollett: A Bibliographical Guide.* 1978.
3. Paula R. Backscheider, ed. *Probability, Time, and Space in Eighteenth-Century Literature.* 1979.
4. Ruth Perry. *Women, Letters, and the Novel.* 1980.
5. Paul J. Korshin, ed. *The American Revolution and Eighteenth-Century Culture.* 1986.
6. G. S. Rousseau, ed. *The Letters and Papers of Sir John Hill (1714-1775).* 1982.
7. Paula R. Backscheider. *A Being More Intense: A Study of the Prose Works of Bunyan, Swift, and Defoe.* 1984.
8. Christopher Fox, ed. *Psychology and Literature in the Eighteenth Century.* 1987.
9. John F. Sena. *The Best-Natured Man: Sir Samuel Garth, Physician and Poet.* 1986.
10. Robert A. Erickson. *Mother Midnight: Birth, Sex, and Fate in Eighteenth-Century Fiction (Defoe, Richardson, and Sterne).* 1986.
11. Malcolm Jack. *Corruption and Progress: The Eighteenth-Century Debate.* 1989.
12. Christopher Fox, ed. *Teaching Eighteenth-Century Poetry.* 1990.
13. Robert J. Dircks, ed. *The Letters of Richard Cumberland.* 1988.
14. John Irwin Fischer, Hermann J. Real, and James Woolley, eds. *Swift and His Contexts.* 1989.
15. Kenneth W. Graham, ed. *Vathek and the Escape from Time: Bicentenary Revaluations.* 1990.
16. Kenneth W. Graham. *The Politics of Narrative: Ideology and Social Change in William Godwin's Caleb Williams.* 1990.
17. Richard J. Dircks. *The Unpublished Plays of Richard Cumberland.* 1990.
18. Kevin L. Cope, ed. *Enlightening Allegory: Theory, Practice and Contexts of Allegory in the Late Seventeenth and Eighteenth Centuries.* 1992.
19. O M Brack, Jr. *Writers, Books, and Trade: An Eighteenth-Century English Miscellany for William B. Todd.* 1992.
20. Malcolm, Jack. *William Beckford: An English Fidalgo.* 1992.

ACKNOWLEDGMENTS

Hercules, a favorite subject among Augustan allegorists and a remarkably persistent fellow, had a hard time finishing up his seven labors. Indebted to twice-seven contributors and obliged to countless colleagues and intermediaries, this less-then-divine editor stands little chance of completing the formidable task of recognizing everyone who has helped with *Enlightening Allegory*. Suffice it to say that I shall always remain indebted to the profession of "eighteenth" (and seventeenth, too!) century studies and to all the wonderful, sometimes eccentric, and always affable people who belong to it.

Some kindnesses have been so great that they require special commendation. For generously supporting my research expeditions I owe thanks to Louisiana State University, especially to William E. "Bud" Davis, Carolyn Hargrave, David Harned, and the LSU Foundation Fund for Special Projects. My research travels took me to Wolfson College, Oxford, and to McMaster University, Ontario, Canada, where I received unremitting hospitality and useful advice. Especially helpful at Oxford were Wolfson President Sir Raymond Hoffenberg, Keeper of the Printed Books Julian Roberts, Wolfsonian Christine Ferdinand, seminarian Michael Suarez, and all-around scholar Patricia Brückmann. The American Society for Eighteenth-Century Studies and McMaster University provided me with a grant in support of my studies in Canada. While visiting McMaster and its neighbor institutions, I profited from the conversation and assistance of Peter Walmsley, David Blewitt, Elaine Rheim, Eleanor Ty, Richard Morton, Brian John, and Kenneth and Erika Graham. Charlotte Stewart–Murphy, Carl Spadoni, and Margaret Foley patiently guided me through my wanderings in the "Mac" Division of Archives and Research Collections. Cynthia Wall, of the University of Chicago and the Newberry Library, retrieved and expedited the processing or many of the visuals in this book. For expert technical advice and friendly encouragement I thank Jim Springer Borck; for administrative aid and cheerful collegiality, I am grateful to John R. "Jack" May, certainly a personification of the tradition of humane letters.

The boundary between personal and professional appreciation is one that ought to be crossed—both ways—more often. For happy and informative "e-mail" discussions, I acknowledge Paula R. Backscheider. For stirring my spirits and enacting many an allegory, I applaud the LSU Athletic Department, from its groundskeepers and its secretaries to its players, coaches, and administrators. For an example of courage in scholarship, I thank Ward Parks; for long-term support of my projects, I thank James Engell, Connie Capers Thorson, and James "Jim" Thorson. For plain old fun and ever-renewing wisdom, I give special praise to my wife, Susan Kotler–Cope.

PREFACE

Allegory has always been the phantom in the opera of late seventeenth-and eighteenth-century scholarship. It won't go away, but neither will it come forward for inspection. Rather, it remains in the rafters, in occasional disputes over Bunyan's type-characters, Fielding's interpolated stories, or Blake's visionary outbursts. Nominally associated with that *bête noir* of sophisticated critical speculation, "the other," allegory sports with its interpreters. Seeming to accommodate hard truth to mean capacities, it ends up making accommodation itself problematical. When compounded with that all-too-familiar de-familiarizing process of historical change (and educational depletion) that has made any and all early texts seem difficult and inaccessible, the putative "otherness" of allegory takes on a formal, political, and social as well as a semiotic interest. As its name implies, allegory is eminently public, a part of the *agora*. Yet, despite its prime location amidst the hurly-burly of the marketplace, this multivalent form vanishes into its own clouds. Like some over-spectated Notre Dame (or under-appreciated Sears Tower), it recedes into fogs rising from its boggy foundations, to the great disappointment of touristic voyeurs. Seen by many but seized by few, glimpsed as it gets away, allegory invites explication while it mystifies with its multiplicity.

The evanescence of allegory belies its monumentality. Despite attempts by Augustan critics to depreciate its fantasticality, opacity, gothicity, and all-around orotundity, despite complicity by modern critics in this long-term campaign of neglect, allegory and its retinue of critical questions continue their often unwanted visitations. By resisting reduction to simple critical formulae, this most enigmatic of forms resists exclusion from critical controversy. The problems and pleasures of allegory are especially acute in that allegorically vague discipline, "eighteenth-century studies" (1649–1836?), as well as in our own puzzlingly post-deconstructed, post-new-historicist culture: milieux in which mysteries, uncertainties, and occultations may put off audiences eager for clarity.

The peripheralization of Enlightenment allegory results partly from its unwieldy multidisciplinarity. Scholars cannot hope to tackle the subject without mastering a dozen disciplines, from art history (for explicating images) to zoology (for bestiaries and emblems). Fortunately, the forces of professionalization are providing the solution to, as well as creating the problem of, informatic overkill. Easy-access data systems, especially computerized resource bases with high-speed retrieval capacities, can help to reconstruct the enormous array of ideas, influences, and prejudices that played upon both vulgar and sophisticated readers, writers, and audiences as they encountered allegories and engendered interpretations. The increasing accessibility of these vigorously diverse materials is now making possible a "holistic" understanding of allegory that could only have been the dream of its pioneering modern critics of the genre, whether the meditative C. S. Lewis, the psychoanalytic Edwin Honig, or the systematic Northrop Frye. No one should vaunt to scholarly swamihood by conjuring up long-gone authors, artists, and audiences in the vain hope of knowing their "mentalities." Scholars should, however, take full advantage of our enlarging critical apparatus to survey the range of allegorical experience—especially if such a survey permits an escape from overly specific academic disciplines.

The study of allegory has a bad habit of ascending from facts into abstract speculations, but its strange history offers far more than generalized theories. Turbulently multiplexed, allegory supports a lively network of specific, recurring, and indeed canonical critical questions. A synopsis of criticism from several millennia would explode this preface into a book, but it is not too dangerous to compile a brief, provisional list of the classic issues treated by critics old and new.

That scion of contemporary allegoricians, Angus Fletcher, moves allegory from the fixed category, "genre," to the protean category, "mode." He continues the longstanding debate over whether allegory is either of these, both, or neither. Is "allegory" restricted to allegories, or are there allegorical moments in comedy, tragedy, poetry, and song? Fletcher, moreover, re-discovers the constructively divisive tendencies of allegorical productions. Allegories abound with "segmented" characters, incomplete alter-egos who hop, skip, and jump through evocatively elliptical episodes. Emblematically detailed but sublimely expansive, Fletcher's criticism is among the first to champion Enlightenment allegory. It ranks Cowper's *Task* above Langland's *Piers Plowman*, discovering in the eighteenth century a palette of partitioned poems "overwhelmed" by modernizing, erratic, and most of all "usurping commentary."

The fractive character of allegory points up its intractable heterogeneity. Jon Whitman and Clifford Gay are only the youngest sons of a veritable genealogy of critics dedicated to the etymological explication of this form. Whitman, Gay, and their ancestors explore the paradox (or at least the oddity) of "speaking of the other in the public market." They contemplate the cacophonous but codified disclosure of secret information from the capitol steps. An important sub-issue within what could be called the "exosemantic problem" concerns the tendency of allegory to comment on itself. Reifying its apparent "self-sufficiency," the average, garden-variety allegory incorporates both the "other" and the audience, both reading and interpretation, by giving hints of its proper interpretation or of the right method for its appreciation. Allegory, in other words, has a way of turning into explicative allegoresis—into something other than itself.

The exegetical inclinations of allegory allow allegorizing authors to indulge in the nasty habit of defeating their interpreters. In the *Dunciad*, Alexander Pope dead-ends his readers in vast compilations of stupefying (and commentary-eliciting) allusions. The major editions of Samuel Butler's *Hudibras* contain many, many, many times more commentary than text. Critics from Dante to Hazard Adams and Carolyn Van Dyke have puzzled over this simultaneous convergence and divergence, in allegory's cybernetically overpopulated texts, of implied meanings and the historical exemplifications of those meanings. C. S. Lewis's attempt to differentiate sacramentalism from allegory, to create an awkward distinction between the allegorical projection of men's minds and the historical enactment of God's ideas, is but one example of this de-literalizing literalism. Writers from Quintilian to Rosemund Tuve wonder whether allegory, an "extended metaphor," might just prove to be more extended than the capacities of allego*ret*ical criticism.

One classic problem that holds special interest for our own age of political re-alignment and confused allegiances is that of the doubly defiant character of allegorical forms. Formalist critics, from the ancient neo-Platonics to our own post-structuralists, have linked allegories to classical "pre-texts" on which allegories comment and expand. This reliance on a pre-text seems to suggest a reactionary, fundamentalist foundation for allegory, yet, throughout history, allegory has proved both conservative and revolutionary, both zealous for the repetition of tradition and clever with its subversive re-interpretation. The genre has worked equally well both for revolutionaries like William Langland or John Bunyan and for conservatives like John Gower or Henry Fielding. For that matter, it has also performed admirably in textless pictures, text-critiquing pageants, and text-antecedent oral traditions. Anyone who has scanned the ESTC knows that popular tradition might have offered as many or more semi- or anti-authoritative "pre-texts" as did the great tradition. Antiquity, modernity, precedent, and innovation conspire to complicate authority/author/audience relations. Classical in heritage, Christian (or at least gnostic, Neo-Platonic, and hermetic) by historical association, elusive allegory wraps itself in the air but not the substance of authority. It helps yet also exasperates both sincere millenarians and apparatchik propagandists. It refuses to depreciate either authority or innovation. Allegorists like Samuel Johnson, Thomas More, and the *Pearl* poet know exactly what they want to say. They explode Paul de Man's scheme to aerate allegory into a meta-allegory for the displacement of signs by other signs. Yet they also look askance at such overconfident projects as Northrop Frye's stark (and surprisingly artless) portrayal of allegory as "thematic counterpoint."

Conservatively defiant allegory asserts its traditional indeterminacy. Critics in the school of Louis MacNeice are often disappointed in their efforts to distinguish allegory from such allegorizing forms as parables, tales, and emblems. Their essentialized allegory is permanently expelled from the "great divide" between the "anchored" allegories of Spenser and the "drifting" parables of Coleridge and Shelley. Maureen Quilligan goes so far as to bruit the "Augustan end of allegory." Yet those "Augustan" allegorists who have been plunged into this dividing darkness, whether the eminently damnable Bernard Mandeville or the post-purgatorial author of *The Pleasures of Reason*, persist unrepentantly in designating their works as "allegories" and in offering theoretical affirmations of the flexibility of their favorite term.

Whatever its merits, the squabble between rigidifiers and flexibilists bends into a more useful discussion of the status of the complex personality—as well as that of its less complex counterparts (caricatures, personifications, abstractions, and characters)—in allegorical writings. Investigations into the flexibility of allegory likewise encourage evaluations of the relation of allegory to subsidiary forms, whether visions, emblems, satire, or cartography. Tireless, Dame Allegory delights in congenial controversy.

These big, classic questions hint of the many entertainments, fascinations, and fancies that arise when critics of the allegorical heritage move from theory to practice and from library carrel to historical context. *Enlightening Allegory* designs to involve its reader in some small part of this emanative process. Part I, "Presentations: Theories, Speculations" advances essays concerned with theorists from, theoretically provocative works in, or theoretical implications of the allegorical tradition of the Enlightenment. Spanning a globe of theories and temperaments, Hazard Adams reaches back to the mythic fundamentals of allegorizing language. He acquaints us with the energetic speculations of Henry Reynolds, Giambattista Vico, and Thomas Blackwell. Thomas Maresca and John Shawcross try to unriddle, in theory and practice, the relations between allegory and personification. Maresca's cheeky riposte to the sloppy nomenclature of hit-or-miss theorizers discovers unrecognized allegories everywhere throughout our period—especially where we least expect it! Shawcross wings through the Miltonic firmament, gliding past Sin, Death, and critical theory to land on the *terra firma* of a practical theory of personification. Thomas Vogler unlocks Blake's *Crystal Cabinet* with his cultural-epistemological key to allegorical visions from the later eighteenth century. Entering Diderot's encyclopedia, Grant Holly steps from the worn shoes and the dead feet of the ancients into the automated world of playing-card manufacturers, slipping from allegoresis and narrative into a delightfully paradoxical, playfully modern, and even dutifully Darwinian theory of allegorizations. Cued by Holly, Kevin L. Cope explores the daring annexation of worlds of meaning into flat, easy, and outright funny emblems, maxims, and maps, in the hope of discovering a non-mystical, immediately available source of allegorical communication.

Part II, "Presences: Acts, Events" brings the theory of allegory into a sharper resolution. It focusses on the implementation of allegory in pageants, processions, and other historical events. The papers in this segment examine the possibility of extra- or non-literary, participatory and even involuntary, allegorizations. Nanette Le Coat thrills her readers with a lively, dramatic, and yet theoretically sophisticated analysis of French Revolutionary pageants. Deborah Jacobs and Connie Capers Thorson revise the opinions of prominent but theory-bound allegoricians by probing into the shamefully amusing propaganda, prevarications, and processions of the Popish Plot era. Janet Wolf contextualizes John "Hilarius" Gay's political plays and fables, with special reference to both Gay's own *oeuvre* and to the semiotically supercharged popular traditions of Gay's allegory-obsessed society. Wolf shows that allegorical skullduggery continued well into the realism-loving eighteenth century.

Part III, "Representations: Texts, Talks, Tales," offers refreshingly uninhibited readings of familiar, "canonical" texts as well as of new entries in the allegorist's shelflist. Like the whale that sports with Swift's tub, Neil Saccamano tumbles, splashes, and overturns all the old prejudices about the linkage of ethics and allegory in Swift's *Tale of a Tub* and other works. Active, even imperialistic, Saccamanoan allegoresis limits the textual instabilities and ethical uncertainties implied by allegorical elusiveness. Unnesting the wasp of the toilette, Dustin Griffin withdraws Alexander Pope's literary career from the embroidered pockets of critical dandies, dressing it anew in the seamless, durable gown of visionary verse. In the process, he repairs the rents dividing allegory from vision and visionary from mainstream. Terrifying but reformative, Veronica Kelly's exploration of Pope's incest imagery takes us on a stately, tragically sublime march along an infinite regression, from allegories into simulations upon simulations of allegories. Peter Walmsley investigates the literary habits of conversational philosophers. He bypasses disciplinary bounds to behold Bishop Berkeley's philosophical allegorizations of sensual experience. Walmsley rounds out the allegoricians' conversation by uncovering a chest full of delightfully taboo buried critical treasures, from God and meaning to authorial intention.

Inquiry into historically localized segments of the tradition of allegory is just now opening up. Although preceded by millennia of general theorizing, although already subjected to three centuries of on-and-off critical scrutiny, the late seventeenth-and eighteenth-century explorations of the genre remain uncharted. The canon of allegorical texts from the Enlightenment cannot be revised, for it has not yet been set. There is no better time than our information-abundant but belief-deprived era in which to re-stock this enormous silo of hidden meanings. *Enlightening Allegory* aims to initiate a dialogue on its immense, if not infinite, topic, to instigate a new tradition of critical adventure—and, perhaps, of interpretative ecstasy.

Part I

PRESENTATIONS

Theories, Speculations

REYNOLDS, VICO, *BLACKWELL*, BLAKE
The Fate of Allegory

Hazard Adams

At the expense of oversimplification, we can consider allegory in two ways. The first way is to treat it strictly as a literary device of the sort we find in Spenser's *Faerie Queene*. As a device it was, of course, variously used: to protect the author against censorship and political revenge, to give density to a work by creating various levels of meaning, to delight the reader, who is amused and satisfied to come upon or unlock a hidden significance, and to join abstract ideas to particular images, thereby giving to such ideas a delightful intimacy, visible presence, and animation.

The second way is to treat allegory as a tendency of language over a broader range of usages, considering its role in theories of the origin of language, religion, and learning, with particular reference to its connection with mythology. It is this second way that concerns me here, though, of course, the two are intertwined; in most important ways the second precedes and includes the first. Consideration of myth, language, and allegory was almost an obsession with certain eighteenth-century intellectuals; and the turn that speculation about these things took is particularly important to, though often ignored by, the history of criticism. If "allegory" was a term used honorifically, or at least neutrally through much of the eighteenth century, it began to take on a pejorative sense late in the age, partly because of conflicts difficult to resolve in the implied theories of scholars of mythology. It is in this context that the work of Thomas Blackwell (1701–1757) has its major interest, for Blackwell, a shrewd and learned scholar, professor of Greek in Marischal College, Aberdeen, stands somewhere between the many conventional students of myth of his day and later theorists with radically different epistemological assumptions.

In the eighteenth century, the question of allegory in the second aspect I have mentioned was tied to questions about the origins of human beliefs and understanding, if not the nature and origin of wisdom itself. This connection was mediated by theories of mythology. We can look at most of the scholars of myth and archeology in this period as naive antiquarians who worked from inadequate principles of etymology and archeological evidence to false conclusions, theorists limited in perspective either by traditional religious assumptions based on a literal reading of the Bible or by deistic and rationalistic biases. Or we can read them as unintentional inventors of speculative mythological works, predecessors of later, much more self-conscious artists who produced their own so-called fictive "systems." William Blake was one of these, and it is with Blake that I shall end, though the story I begin to tell certainly does not end with him.

In order to follow this story through the work of Blackwell, I shall look briefly at the position Henry Reynolds (fl. 1627–1632) took toward myth in his defense of the ancients a century before, and I shall proceed to imply a parallel and contrast between the theories of Giambattista Vico (1668–1744) in *The New Science* and those of Blackwell. Vico was known neither to Blackwell nor to Blake, and this was perhaps unfortunate for Blackwell in that Vico offered a theory that, even if it might not have been entirely satisfactory, could have been an indication to Blackwell that there were ways to escape from the contradictions he expresses in a theory of language and tropes. In *The Marriage of Heaven and Hell* (1792), completed forty-four years after publication of Blackwell's last book, Blake found a somewhat different intellectual climate in which to exhibit tendencies present in Vico and, under some stress, in Blackwell.

II

Henry Reynolds's "Mythomystes" (c. 1632) is an attack on the lack of learning and shallow writing of the moderns. Reynolds argues that the moderns are trivial and the ancients were profound. The latter expressed what we would now call occult wisdom in allegories that were deliberately hidden from vulgar minds. The allegorical truth hidden in a work was for Reynolds its body—a body of reason, while the exterior sense was but the external covering, clothing, or "bark" (C, 196).[1] All matters of rhetoric, including of course tropes, are relegated to this surface, which hides from vulgar minds that are likely to corrupt the truth of the "real form and essence," or the message (C, 196). The truth so hidden is a holy "mystery." The first savants were "those old, wise Egyptian priests [who searched out] the mysteries of nature (which was at first the whole world's only divinity)" (C, 201). Their medium was the hieroglyph, their manner *dissimulanter,* and their matter "high and mystical matters" (C, 202). The dissimulation was to protect truth from vulgar interpretation by the "profane multitude" (C, 202). Presumably a pure language lay behind the protective device of allegory. It is not surprising that Reynolds identifies this language with number, as it is in Platonic thought. A true knowledge of number would "unlock and explain...mystical meanings to us" (C, 203), because God "through his wisdom disposed all things as in weight and measure, so likewise in number" (C, 202). Following Josephus Picus, Reynolds regards the Mosaic law of the Pentateuch as a container of hidden meaning. He calls it an "interpretation," indicating that the truth lies originally behind the text to be recovered there. One has to suppose that it is ideally prior to language, as number is the source and meaning of nature, which emanates from it. This original truth Reynolds seems to identify with Jupiter, the source of the "golden chain of Homer, that reaches from the foot of Jupiter's throne to the earth" (C, 209). The connection of the Greek chain of being with the Pauline movement from invisible truth to visible signature leads to a connection between Greek and Biblical myth, the Greek figures being at least parallels to Biblical personages, and Moses and the Greeks both having learned from the Egyptians, though Moses was "inspired so far above them with the immediate spirit of Almighty God" (C, 210). Since the days of these ancients the fables have been further and further corrupted, and so there must be an act of recovery.

Allegory, for Reynolds, begins with the priestly creation of fables to protect high truth from vulgar corruption. This truth is prior to language; it is number, which one might say the world of appearance copies. In the course of history the original fables holding a mystical connection to truth became degenerate, corrupted, and trivialized by modern writers and misunderstood by modern scholars.

III

Some of these not unusual views came down to Blackwell (the notion of the invention of allegory in Egypt, for example); but before I consider Blackwell's work, I want to look at Blackwell's contemporary Vico. From among the legions of occultists, euhemerists, deists, Anglicans, and rationalists of his time who studied myth, only Vico has emerged to command our attention and respect. His work came relatively early in the century, *The New Science* having first appeared in 1720. It was importantly revised in 1730 and 1744. Vico's book has been amazingly fertile for a number of reasons: it includes a theory of the origins of language and thought attractive today to poets and critics because it grounds language and myth in tropes (a nonground some would say today, but that is part of its interest); it offers a theory of history based on a *ricorso* of rise and fall again attractive to poets; it offers a secular theory, carefully independent of Church doctrine; and finally, it offers a provocative distinction between "imaginative" and "abstract" universals. I shall emphasize this last point, because Blackwell lacked such a theory; though obviously skeptical of the Reynoldsian sort of Platonism, which privileged the pure abstraction of mathematics (belonging to Vico's "abstract universal"), Blackwell could never quite develop a notion of tropes that would emancipate his views from the threat of the Platonic.

Like Reynolds, and like Blackwell, Vico believed that many fables have come down to us in corrupted and even obscure form, but he entirely rejects any piety of the sort we find in Reynolds. For him, the Egyptian hieroglyphics do not contain mystical truth, nor do the Greek myths contain high philosophical allegories out of which a priesthood can extract original revelation derived from Egypt. About the Bible he is deliberately silent. However, Egyptian antiquity did bequeath two "great remnants" to us:

One of them is that the Egyptians reduced all preceding world time to three ages; namely, the age of gods, the age of heroes, and the age of men. The other is that during these three ages three languages had been spoken, corresponding in order to the three aforesaid ages: namely, the hieroglyphic or sacred language, the symbolic or figurative (which is the heroic) language, and the epistolary or vulgar language of men employing conventional signs for communicating the common needs of their life. (N, 69)

But for Vico, none of these languages has the authority of mystical truth, nor does it hide such truth. All are strictly secular human creations. Indeed, the earliest is a direct product of primitive reaction to natural phenomena by crude and savage people who did not have the power of reason, that is, the power to form "abstract universals":

The first men, the children, as it were, of the human race [we note that the farther back we go the younger the human race becomes, while for Reynolds the very opposite is the case], not being able to form intelligible class concepts of things, had a natural need to create poetic characters; that is, imaginative class concepts or universals, to which, as to certain models or ideal portraits, to reduce all the particular species which resembled them. (N, 74)

This is the purely secular and strictly linguistic source, for Vico, of "poetic allegories, which gave the fables univocal, not analogical, meanings for various particulars comprised under their poetic genera" (N, 75). Mystical interpretations were impositions on these purely naturalistic expressions of "poetic logic," often corrupted in the passage of time and change of custom. Here there is no incursion of truth from some higher realm of being, no revelation—at least for the Gentile nations. Rather, these primitive people "imagined the causes of the things they felt and wondered at to be gods" (N, 116). Human beings begin with a "wholly corporeal imagination" (N, 117). Everything emanates from the body—all passions, all ideas of the gods. Vico attacks the idea of the superiority of the ancients, even though he argues that the ancients did produce poetry that has never been surpassed in sublimity. The so-called wisdom of the ancients was the vulgar wisdom of the lawgivers who founded human society, not the esoteric wisdom revealed to venerable philosophers.

The poetic logic of the ancient poets proceeded in a way entirely opposite to the human reason as we know it. Indeed, poetic logic was, for Vico, possible only by virtue of the deficiency of reason in the first men. Poetic logic, making imaginative universals, created animate divinities with particular imaged characteristics. Human reason, by contrast, privileges the abstract, imageless universal as the real and then produces "personifications, to which we refer all the causes, properties, and effects that severally appertain to them" (N, 128). Poetic logic maintains the image in and as the universal. Human reason establishes the abstract universal: "...when we wish to give utterance to our understanding of spiritual things, we must seek aid from our imagination to explain them and, like painters, form human images of them. But these theological poets, unable to make use of the understanding, did the opposite and more sublime thing: they attributed senses and passions...to bodies, and to bodies as vast as sky, sea, and earth" (N, 128). There set in, however, a gradual reduction of these personifications to "diminutive signs," as the power of abstraction grew (N, 128). Soon the original meaning and sublimity were lost.

Vico concludes from this history that originally tropes, which were "fables in brief" (N, 129), formed mythologies, and these mythologies he calls "allegories":

> Allegory is defined as *diversiloquium* insofar as, by identity not of proportion but (to speak scholastically) of predicability, allegories signify the diverse species or the diverse individuals comprised under these genera. So that they must have a univocal signification connoting a quality common to all their species and individuals (as Achilles connotes an idea of valor common to all strong men, or Ulysses an idea of prudence common to all wise men). (N, 128)

Vico reaches a number of important conclusions: *Tropes are fundamental to language.* As a result, one can't claim them to be merely decorative or persuasive. Later they were so used, but only after the dominance of the abstract universal. *Poetry preceded prose.* It can hardly be regarded as improper. It seems likely that *writing in the form of hieroglyphic preceded speech,* but hieroglyphic was not invented by a priesthood to protect wisdom from vulgar distortion. *All later so-called discoveries of esoteric wisdom attributed to the ancients are false.* It was vulgar wisdom generated as it was in the absence of reason.

Vico concludes further that poetry is imitation. Here he clearly means the expansion of particular images, taken from life, into imaginative universals rather than deduction of particulars from universal ideas as in the Aristotelian syllogism (N, 168). He offers as an example of an imaginative universal the figure of Homer. A real fable always enlarges the "ideas of particulars" (N, 312). Homer received the earliest fables, in distorted forms. But this does not imply an original, lost "literal" history—events transferred bodily into a perfectly representational language. The original form was itself a fabulous form, the expansion of tropes into fabulous stories. But then distortion set in. The figure of Homer himself is a product of tropological thought. There was no one Homer. Rather his works are the product of the Greek people, and he is an imaginative universal created by their poetic logic.

The story Vico tells combats explanation of mythology as an esoteric allegory deliberately hidden by ancient wisemen. It also argues against the notion that language has a rational source in pure ideas rather than a poetic source in vulgar images and things (Vico's "imitation"). It opposes the Platonic notion that all language has always aspired to the condition of mathematics, which in its perfect abstraction most closely reaches the idea. There is no suggestion that language fell from some Edenic condition of abstraction. In other words, Vico turns the rationalist conception of language inside out.

But in historicizing and secularizing language, Vico ended up privileging the abstract universal over poetic logic after all. He thought of the invention of the abstract universal as progress, even as he valued poetry for its sublimity. Perhaps this is because of his sense of distance from those early human beings who thought in poetic logic. In writing *The New Science* he says that he "had to descend from these human and refined natures of ours to those quite wild and savage natures, which we cannot at all imagine and can comprehend only with great effort" (N, 100). Or perhaps Vico thought that there was no need to defend poetry beyond remarks like the following about sublimity: "The most sublime labor of poetry is to give sense and passion to insensate things" (N, 71); or, "it was deficiency of human reasoning power that gave rise to poetry so sublime that the philosophies which came afterward, the arts of poetry and of criticism, have produced none equal or better, and have even prevented its production" (N, 120). Thus Vico sides with the ancients, but for reasons entirely different from those of Reynolds.

IV

Vico's *New Science* is not a defense of poetry. Its interests are in the nature of history and culture. Later writers like Croce and Cassirer carried on some of Vico's ideas into theories of art with implied defenses. Thomas Blackwell was a defender of Homer and of Greek mythology. Heir to the kind of interpretation of myth represented by Reynolds, he brought a somewhat different perspective to the role of the ancients by secularizing their thought, as did Vico. Yet Blackwell, without Vico, proceeded without a theory of poetic language that might have given his discourses greater consistency. Still, we see in him the defense of poetry only latent in Vico. Blackwell's *Enquiry into the Life and Writings of Homer* (1735) is a work of literary criticism, that ranges broadly into the relation of Homer to his culture. His *Letters Concerning Mythology* (1748) states as its aim "to explain the religious opinions of the ANCIENTS and their consequent Practice" (L, A). He offers a theory that tries to avoid various reductionist interpretations or explanations of the source of myth.

The book on Homer can be fairly described as a work of historical and relativistic criticism. Blackwell, who apparently believed in the existence of a real individual named Homer, describes the poet as having had the good fortune to be born when and where he was. He saw and learned "the *Grecian* Manners at their true Pitch and happiest Temper for Verse: Had he been much sooner, he would have seen nothing but Nakedness and Barbarity: Had he come much later, he had fallen in the Times either of wide Policy and Peace, or of General Wars, when private Passions are buried in the Common Order, and established Discipline" (E, 35). Homer, therefore, escaped perpetrating the incongruity we feel in Virgil between Virgil's refined language and the events he portrays (E, 47) As a result of this and of Homer's ability to present homely detail, we come to believe that all he tells us is true (E, 290). Homer characteristically employs "natural" machinery; and except where he uses Egyptian and Orphic allegories, "which he usually puts in the Mouths of his Gods," he pretends to write in "the *prevailing Language* of the Country" (E, 46). Few people understand that the prevailing language at that time wore a "metaphorical habit," that Homer's language, as in Trojan times, "retained much of the *Eastern* cast; their Theology was a *Fable* and their moral Instruction an allegorical Tale" (E, 47).

Having said this, Blackwell sometimes does, sometimes does not presume that this theology, moral instruction, and allegorical presentation were originally esoteric wisdom deliberately expressed darkly so as to hide truth from the vulgar. On the one hand, he holds, as did Reynolds that "allegorical religion" originated among the Greek priesthood in secrecy. On the other, it became arcane only when a priesthood attempted to establish and maintain its authority, by hiding doctrine (E, 83–84). Fable was "the first Form in which Religion, Law, and Philosophy (united originally) appeared in the World" (L, A3). Myth developed from the boisterous speech of primitive peoples. The allegorical element of myth is coincident with its flowering. Allegory and fable were the learning of Homer's day as they were in Egypt (E, 100). Mythology became debased when it became intermixed with history and accounts of actual people (he agrees here with Vico), and was further distorted in superstition, which takes representations for things, in corrupted transmission, and in the adoption of abstruse symbolical mannerisms (L, 171–8). The meanings of ancient myths are not reachable by euhemerist methods, though presumably those methods might help to erase the corruptions. But he holds that there are few myths that we cannot understand at all (L, 189) and these principally because of corruption, priestly secrecy, or the disappearance of traditions that fostered understanding (I, 189). Most is recoverable because "Symbols carry natural Marks that strike a sagacious Mind, and lead it by degrees to their real Meaning" (L, 204). At the same time, he argues that to be "entertained with this allusive shadowy way of writing" and to "discover the Art of an ingenious fiction and truly judge of its Propriety and Elegance" requires a "peculiar Cast of Mind" (L, 213). Furthermore, there is a paradox in the obscurity of fable: "The Veil of Fable...*magnifies* the objects which it covers; It shows them in a grander Light, and invites the Eye to contemplate them more eagerly than if they were open and undisguised" (E, 326), but vulgar eyes will not grasp the meaning. The image of the veil, like that of clothing and bark in Reynolds, tends to work against Blackwell's desire to treat allegory and fables as original and natural ways of language. His remark that the ancient Egyptians were a people "addicted to *Metaphor* and *Allusion*," however, leaves it unclear just how Blackwell felt about this, since addiction suggests something unnaturally compulsive. Still, the rest of the statement seems less concerned with the unnatural. "Their very *Method of Writing* or *Sacred Scripture* was a complete and standing System of *Natural Similes*" (E, 169). Hieroglyphic was for the Egyptians uniquely capable of merging abstract and concrete. Blackwell's desire to connect Homer closely with Egypt and even to call him an *"Egyptian* mythologist" (E, 168) is closely related to his interest in the concrete quality of Egyptian expression. Here he edges up to the Vichean imaginative universal.

Like Vico, Blackwell grounds his discussion of myth on the trope. Of the various species of mythology he mentions, the fundamental one "flows from pure untaught Nature; a Similitude, a Metaphor, is an Allegory in Embryo, which extended and animated will become a perfect piece of full grown Mythology" (L, 70). Here he parallels Vico's notion of the trope as a "fable in brief" (N, 129). Both seem to imply a synecdochic relation between trope and fable. As did Vico, Blackwell anticipated the views of Rousseau on the fundamentally tropological nature of early poetry.

For Blackwell, fable is the "truest species" of poetry (L, 310). Knowledge in Homer's day was "wholly fabulous and allegorical" (E, 100). The Hellenes described everything by means of some analogy and resemblance to human actions, this being their science. Blackwell denies that allegory came on the scene late. Rather, it was, with trope and myth, the earliest mode of knowledge and expression, "understood and receiv'd from the Beginning" (L, 212).

Although Blackwell refers to "sacred scripture," whether of the Egyptians or others, he never attributes supernatural authority to it. Like Vico, he reads the gods of mythology as human creations meant to explain and domesticate the natural world. Mythology is for him, as for Vico, a mimetic art and has its source in nature (L, 69). Religious utterances seem in his view to be attempts to conceptualize the world. He privileges no particular position. The ancient poets made gods of the "Principles of Being" as they were able to express them tropologically (L, 180) from the parts composing the universe (L, 409). Poetry and philosophy were one; only later were they separated, at which point poetry began to descend to the level of mere entertainment.

This means that the ancient myths are in some way instructive, but at the same time they are expressive of passions. Vico identified passion with poetic logic because it meant for him absence of reason. Blackwell, no doubt, thought along these lines, but he never quite draws the line between reason and primitive thought, as did Vico. Instead he holds on to the notion that the ancients combined reason and passion in their fables. Thus there was still instruction, identified with reason, in them. It is apparently poetry now that is purely passionate (mere entertainment?). At the same time, Blackwell insists that the ancient myths are pliable to the interpreter, at least insofar as there may be a sophisticated and learned interpretation, an interpretation of common sense, and a vulgar one. These correspond to three classes of readers: the wise and knowing few, the middle sort of reader of good sense, and the unthinking multitude.

Before I examine this shift to a readerly perspective and admission of the possibility, nay the inevitability, of multiple meaning, it is worthwhile to note a distinction Blackwell makes between "cool" and "sudden and flashy" myth:

> *Mythology,* Taken in the largest Sense, must be distinguished into two sorts: the one *abstracted* and *cool*; the Result of great Search and Science: "Being a Comparison of the Harmony and Discord, the Resemblance and Dissimilitude of the Powers and Parts of the *Universe.*" It often consists of their finest *Proportions* and hidden *Aptitudes* set together and personated by a Being acting like a *Mortal*. "The other, sudden and flashy; rapid Feelings and Starts of a Passion not in our Power." The first of these may be called *artificial,* and the second *natural* Mythology; the one is a Science [where obviously reason governs but does not suppress passion], and may be learn'd; the other is the Faculty that for the most part, if not always, invents and expresses it. This cannot be learned; but like other natural powers admits of *Culture* and *Improvement.* (E, 161–2)

There is, for Blackwell, nothing occult or divine about this power; it is "natural." According to him, Homer acquired the first power and improved the second. It is the cool element that Blackwell tends to identify with allegory, though its source seems to be in the "sudden and flashy." His treatment of metaphor and simile follows the same division, one hot and one cool, or, better, cooled: "Metaphor is the Language of *Passion*; as Simile is the Effect of a *warm Imagination*; which when *cooled* and *regulated* explains itself in diffuse Fable and elaborate Allegory" (L, 71).

The distinction seems to suggest a temporal or historical movement, with "natural" metaphor regarded as the origin of both hieroglyphic and speech. It "cools," though paradoxically it expands into fable and allegory. When Blackwell comes to defend myth, he does so on the grounds of the virtues of the "cooled," for the criterion seems to be the traditional one of delightful instruction: "Mythology in general is *Instruction* conveyed in a Tale. A Fable or meer Legend without a Moral, or if you please without a Meaning, can with Little Propriety deserve the Name" (L, 70). The recourse to instruction and its identification with reason or something like reason is difficult to identify with Blackwell's theory of the ambiguity of metaphor and the pliability of mythic meaning. One would think that moral instruction required a single clear sense. The following two remarks are central:

1. A Metaphor is a *general Pattern,* which may be applied to many Particulars: It is susceptible of an infinite number of *Meanings*; and reaches far because of its Ambiguity. (E, 317)

2. But there is still another Conveniency in this Method of Instruction by *Fable* and *Allegory,* that must effectually prevent any Fallacy, or hazard of being deceived: I mean its *Condescension* and *Pliableness* to all sorts of Subjects, and Aptness to illustrate indifferently various or even opposite Opinions. For Mythology confines you to no Creed, nor pins you down to a Set of Principles, beyond which, you must either not take a step, or lose her Company. On the contrary, she permits, nay assists, you to contemplate at ease. (L, 120)

In (1) above, Blackwell describes metaphor as if it were a Vichean imaginative universal but then goes on to deny the univocality Vico gave to it. In (2) above, Blackwell means to extend the idea of "general pattern" to show that fable and allegory have numerous applications to particulars, again as in the imaginative universal; but the passage ends by describing a situation of instability. This problem surfaces elsewhere:

Mythology leaves us at liberty to think and reason as we list; and therefore can lead us no further astray than we ourselves have a mind to follow. You have seen how variously it represents the Rise of Things, according to the different Opinions of the Sages concerning them; like a Mirror that reflects whatever Object is held before it, and in the Colours it wears, whether genuine or not. (L, 130–131)

The pliability theory seems to lead toward a pure critical impressionism; Blackwell is aware of the difficulty: "You ask first, whether the Meanings we ascribe to ancient Fables be not for the most part *Conjectures* of the Moderns, who admire every thing that is ancient, merely because it is so, and torture their Brains to find out Meanings and Mysteries which the Authors or the Contemporaries never thought of?" (L, 186)

On the other hand, Blackwell insists on meaning: "the old Sages imposed no particular Person or Character upon their primary Gods, nor interwove those Characters in a tale, without a meaning" (L, 93). The resolution for him lies in his distinguishing literal belief from apprehension of meaning. Writing of a myth of Venus and Cupid, he remarks,

> Cou'd any body, do you imagine, take it into his Head after reading this Allusion, That the Author of it actually believed the little fluttering Thing he has so exquisitely described to be a real divine Person, and wou'd worship him accordingly as *a God?* One shou'd think *not:* Especially as this very Parable has been taken for an Argument of his Unbelief...Or, on the other hand, wou'd it not be as absurd to say, that it had *no meaning at all?* It must be a strange Turn of Mind that cou'd lead to either: "For to believe it literally, or to condemn it for Want of Ingenuity, are equally preposterous." (L, 10)

Clearly here, what Blackwell comes around to attacking is a *literal* reading. For this literality he substitutes his notion of levels of understanding. After a discussion of a myth of Vesta, he remarks;

> The emblems are explained. What more is to be done? To moralize—and draw Inferences from the Explication—? No—but only to observe a strange sort of Likeness between ancient and modern Superstition.—A passion diffused thro' all Ages and Generations, and acting uniformly, however its Objects may be varied. The

> Circumstance of the preceding Allegories that makes me say so is this: The Gods of the Ancients, you see, appear in a Double Light; as the Parts and Powers of Nature to the Philosophers, as real Persons to the Vulgar...Has not the same thing happened in modern Religious Matters? (L, 62)

The range is from allegorical to literal. Also, because myths have come down to us frequently distorted, their surface literality often has no meaning, yet they "point at some latent Truth" (L, 119).

Blackwell strives, against its Reynoldsian implications, to hold on to the term "doctrine" in connection with allegory, no doubt thinking it a valuable counter in a defense of mythology. Here the idea of different classes of readers comes in, but now myths have different aspects appealing to these classes as if deliberately so intended. This is perhaps finally the extent of myths' pliability:

> They fall naturally into *three* Classes, and had Worshippers suited to them of *three* different Characters. I. The PARTS and natural POWERS of the Universe, called out of *Chaos,* said the Poets; formed in *Chaos,* said the Philosophers, by an all-wise MIND that first regulated and still keeps them in order. II. GENII, or spiritual abstract Substances, supposed to exist in, or preside over these Powers, and III. HUMAN creatures deified. (L, 246)

As we move down this scale, interpretation becomes simpler but cruder. The idea moves us back to the old idea of myth as a conveyor of secret mystical doctrine, probably supralinguistic and Platonic, guarded by a priesthood.

To be consistent with his own bent of mind, Blackwell should not be talking about the pliability of myths or even classes of readers but about their evasiveness to any mind wishing to interpret them willfully, any mind desiring to discover abstract, not imaginative, universals *behind* them. Yet if he *does* do this, he must then call in question the instructive quality of myth (if, as his age insists, it must be identified with reason) and undo the defense he has mounted for it. At this point he has left to him only the formula *dulce et utile,* which too easily divides myth into instruction and decoration. So we see him undecided over whether myths are allegories of reason (particulars standing for abstract ideas), whether myths are so pliable as to have no meaning and therefore are usable to personal ends by anyone, or whether myths speak their own language, not really pliable to the interpreter, but challenging the reader with an inexhaustible meaning or the illusion of a meaning always beyond reach.

Blackwell wished to build a concept of mythological wisdom which was neither that of the science he knew nor that of occult Platonism. He wanted his theory to be secular. Fleeing from these obvious choices, choices that continue to be brought before us today under various new guises, he found himself unhappily reduced to that last refuge of critics, the *Je ne sais quoi*:

> if ever the *Je ne sais quoi* was rightly applied, it is to the *Powers* of Mythology, and the *Faculty* that produces them. To go about to describe it, would be like attempting to define *Inspiration,* or that *Glow of Fancy* and *Effusion of Soul,* which the poet feels while in his *Fit.* (E, 151)

But we cannot leave him there, because he never quite stays there. He never provides literary criticism with a language derived from his equation of myth and poetry, though his work certainly implies that the greatest poetry—that which does not merely please but is identical with philosophy in the sense of its ancient practice—is mythological and allegorical. He seems to have been struggling through the terminology of eighteenth–century criticism to a secular idea of mythic and poetic expression as a mode with its own laws. In this, Vico's secular notion of poetic logic and the imaginative universal might have been of use to him. Anticipating in his distinction between fiery and cool allegory the distinction of Schiller between naive and sentimental poetry, Blackwell seems to have seen myth as a mode of expression of human sympathetic identification with nature. The tools his age gave him were inadequate. A more sophisticated theory of language, and especially of tropes, was necessary. He was given the concept of hidden meaning that had to be driven back to mathematical "truth" or to the abstract universal on the one hand or attributed to divine intervention and/or poetic madness on the other.

The problem is perhaps best symbolized by a remark Blackwell makes just after he has argued that language is fundamentally in its very nature metaphorical: "few People imagine that the *Ordinary* Language wore this metaphorical Habit at that time" (E, 47). Here, in typical rationalistic fashion (later, positivistic fashion), the trope is relegated to outer clothing, not to the body itself. The image combats the very point Blackwell tries to make. It is this split between language and metaphor (taken in the sense of tropes in general) that generated the revolt against the term "allegory" which began late in the century and continued even into modernism, for in this figure "Habit" connotes decoration and triviality. "Allegory" came to be identified with a prettying over of what Vico called abstract universals. This meant that poetry was merely the prettification of what was regarded as the essence of language—pure abstraction.

V

William Blake is one of the last in the century to employ "allegory" in an honorific sense, but it is significant that he finally came to use it, for the most part, pejoratively. It is pejorative usage that tended to win the day as the word "symbol" came to be opposed to "allegory" and favored by poets and critics from Goethe to Yeats. Blake, however, did not employ the term "symbol"; rather, he came to oppose it with the word "vision." It is possible that "symbol," with its suggestion of the concept of the eucharist, implying a miraculous embodiment of a bodiless mystery, was anathema to a painter who, though many thought his work unworldly, insisted, "I know that This World Is a World of Imagination & Vision. I see Everything I paint In This World, but Everybody does not see alike" (B, 702). For Blake, the miraculous symbol would be no different from allegory.

In 1792 in *The Marriage of Heaven and Hell,* Blake told his story of the making of language and like Vico attributed it to the "ancient poets," his own imaginative universal for the inventors of poetic logic:

> The ancient Poets animated all sensible objects with Gods or Geniuses, calling them by the names and adorning them with the properties of woods, rivers, mountains, lakes, cities, nations, and whatever their enlarged & numerous senses could perceive [sic]. (B, 38)

But there set in a gradual abstraction of these "mental deities," that is, invented gods, from their natural objects. Priesthood began when those who sought to gain and maintain power created a mystery around these deifying words. Blake claims that thus "forms of worship" grew up out of "poetic tales" and men "forgot that All deities reside in the human breast." Religion became the worship of an abstract mystery behind the veil of language and appearance. This situation Blake came to identify with allegory, though first he divided allegory into two kinds, favoring an allegory addressed to intellect, which he tended to identify with a creative imagination, over one addressed to the understanding:

> Allegory addressed to the Intellectual powers while it is altogether hidden from the Corporeal Understanding is My Definition of the Most Sublime Poetry. (Letter to Thomas Butts, July 6, 1803, B, 730)

Blake's definition here does not imply a priesthood of interpreters hiding meaning from a vulgar multitude. He is writing about two attitudes or sets of assumptions to be met by the work of art. It is the "corporeal understanding" that divides things into body and spirit, primary and secondary qualities of experience and then proceeds to reduce everything real to number and measurement. Blake employs "corporeal" in a way directly opposite to Vico's. For Blake corporeality is the notion of matter so abstracted from itself as to have no image. It is this that paradoxically creates a "reality" of pure abstraction behind a veil of "appearances." The intellectual powers, for Blake, do not make this separation but instead oppose it, as did Vico's "poetic logic."

Seven years later, Blake had changed his mind about the word "allegory." He now identified it totally with the "corporeal understanding." The contrary term had become "vision":

> The Last Judgment [He is describing his painting by that name] is not Fable or Allegory but Vision. Fable or Allegory are a totally distinct & inferior kind of Poetry. Vision or Imagination is a Representation of what Eternally Exists. Really and Unchangeably. Fable or Allegory is Formed by the Daughters of Memory. Imagination is surrounded by the daughters of Inspiration who in the aggregate are called Jerusalem. Fable is Allegory but what Critics call The Fable is Vision itself. The Hebrew Bible & the Gospel of Jesus are not Allegory but Eternal Vision or Imagination of All that Exists. Note here that Fable or Allegory is Seldom without some Vision Pilgrims Progress is full of it the Greek Poets the same but Allegory and

vision ought to be known as Two Distinct Things. (*A Vision of the Last Judgment*, 1810, B, 554)

Thus, in Vichean terms, "allegory" had slipped from a term identified in his own work and in Blackwell's with "imaginative universals" to a figure of speech in which an "abstract universal" is represented by an image. This practice is what Wordsworth inveighs against in his preface to the second edition of *Lyrical Ballads* (1800), calling the result "personification of abstract ideas," admissible occasionally, but "utterly rejected as an ordinary device to elevate the style, and raise it above prose" (C, 435). The century closes with the most important critical document of the time not merely eschewing allegory explicitly; it does not mention it at all.

NOTE

1. Quotations within this essay are taken from the following texts and are identified within the text by a letter code ("C") followed by a page number: David V. Erdman, ed., *The Complete Poetry and Prose of William Blake* (Garden City: Anchor Books 1982) ("B"); Hazard Adams, ed., *Critical Theory Since Plato* (New York: Harcourt Brace Jovanovich, 1971) ("C"); [Thomas Blackwel], *Enquiry into the Life and Writings of Homer* (London: 1735) ("E"); [Thomas Blackwell], *Letters Concerning Mythology* (London: 1748) ("L"); Thomas Goddard Bergin and Max Harold Fisch, trs., *The New Science of Giambattista Vico* (Ithaca: Cornell University Press, revised translation of the Third Edition [1744], 1968) ("N").

PERSONIFICATION VS. ALLEGORY

Thomas E. Maresca

In the more than two decades since Rosemond Tuve documented the simple fact that personification and allegory are not the same thing[1], almost no one engaged in criticism or scholarship seems to have taken any notice of the profound importance of that distinction[2]. The briefest glance at any handbook or dictionary of literary terminology will confirm this: Whatever definition of allegory is given—usually some variant of the etymologically-based "saying one thing and meaning another"—the first example cited is invariably *The Pilgrim's Progress*. Most people, scholars and civilians alike, simply have no idea of what allegory could be if it isn't personification. The only shift in the notion of allegory that even the most up-to-date critics seem to have made is its expansion to include a deconstructionist, specifically de-Manian, meaning. In Restoration and eighteenth-century studies, the identity of allegory and personification stands totally unchallenged.

This condition doesn't reflect as badly on our sensitivity to important differences as its bare statement may at first blush seem to indicate. A good part of the reason students of the Restoration and eighteenth century don't often distinguish between allegory and personification is that, quite simply, the period—at least in England—was largely responsible for popularizing their confusion in the first place[3]. In fact, it is highly possible that the text so often cited as an example of allegory—Bunyan's *Pilgrim's Progress*—was itself a center for the dissemination of that particular confusion.[4] But that is only one of many confusions that have plagued the discussion, and the history, of allegory.

II

From its earliest appearances, allegory has been subject to contrary pulls, tides of understanding that have run in opposite directions for the creators of allegory on one hand and for the analysts of allegory on the other. The construction of allegory *conceals* meaning, but the interpretation of allegory—or the interpretation of works as allegories—reveals it. These are not merely differing directions: They are radically different purposes as well. The conscious allegorist who veils his meaning beneath a puzzling or deceptive fiction is employing a rhetorical device (and one that the rhetoricians have a great deal of trouble talking about) for actively anti-rhetorical purposes, to conceal meaning rather than convey it, to hinder understanding and agreement rather than to expedite it.[5] The conscious allegorist is insisting that each reader/hearer must work through the allegory personally, must get it or fail to get it through his or her own efforts and intellect: He who has ears to hear, let him hear. The after-the-fact allegorist defeats that artistic and technical goal: whether or not the text explicated is or isn't truly allegorical, the simple fact of explication opens the shrine to the profane, reveals the secrets to the uninitiated, gives a free ride to the lazy. So from its earliest days, allegory is dogged by both difficulties of definition and by the more serious—and all the more serious for being innocent or unconscious—opposition or resistance of the critics and commentators, who wish to make explicit what author and text have chosen to make at least implicit and at most puzzling.

The psychology of all this is fascinating: the commentators and their readers want answers. Presumably the authors and at least some of their readers were content with questions or conundrums or problems. It's clear that the vast majority of readers cannot tolerate that: from the *post-hoc* allegoresis of Homer forward, a large part of the history of allegory consists of the discerning or imposing of meanings on "sacred" texts of various kinds in order to resolve or remove problems—most often, in order to preserve their "orthodoxy" and their canonicity. Allegoresis (the term I prefer for the explication of allegory, especially as it is practiced on texts that were not necessarily written as allegories) is the process of removing difficulties, eradicating confusions, reducing the complex to the simple. All of the various "keys" to the *Tale of a Tub* or *The Rape of the Lock* or *Gulliver's Travels*, even Swift's own parodic notes to the *Tale* and the satiric Scriblerian variorum notes to *The Dunciad*, are examples—least common denominators, in fact—of this reductivist tendency. Even in the highly developed area of Scriptural exegesis, this same broad tendency holds true: while St. Augustine's famous admonition that we read Scripture for its "kernal of charity" may generate subtle, learned, or complex readings of Biblical texts, it is in its essence a counsel to reject difficulties of a textual and logical nature in favor of an "acceptable" reading, one that guarantees the orthodoxy and thereby the canonicity of the troublesome text by removing, through re-interpretation, the aspects of it that trouble.

For most readers of the Middle Ages and Renaissance, basic ideas about the workings and ways of meaning of allegory would come from the practice of Biblical commentators and the by-and-large parallel practices of commentators on canonical profane texts such as *The Aeneid* or Ovid's *Metamorphoses*. Despite all the counter-indications to be found in the writings of grammarians and of the secular poets themselves, most of whom insist on allegory's slipperiness and complexity, the intermittency and irregularity of its mode of signifying, those two influential sources would reinforce the notion of allegories as yielding essentially simple readings, even univocal readings. One can readily see this process at work in, for instance, Bunyan's adaptation of most of the key words of Scriptural allegoresis to describe his own text, a work that is in fact an almost pure personification narrative with a single, readily apparent—in fact transparent—meaning.

That Bunyan himself thought he was writing an allegory there can be no doubt. What he thought an allegory was is more problematic. Bunyan was not a learned man, not "literate" in the Renaissance's sense of that word: trained in Latin, and particularly in the tradition of Latin grammar, rhetoric, and literature. Consequently, it should hardly be a surprise that Bunyan's use of literary terminology is imprecise. I would argue, however, that Bunyan's handling of critical terms in the materials prefacing *The Pilgrim's Progress* goes well beyond imprecision and betrays fundamental confusion about the natures of and distinctions between the various figures and tropes he names to explain his undertaking. His "Author's Apology for His Book"[6] tells us that the "mode" (139) practically forced itself upon him, and he subsequently describes it by almost all of the terms available to denote figurative speech. He

"Fell suddenly into an Allegory" (139). He writes "dark" and "feigning words" (141). He speaks "By Metaphors" (142). He uses "parables" (142), "dark and cloudy words" that like the "Dark Figures, Allegories" of Scripture "hold/The Truth, as Cabinets inclose the Gold" (142). Scripture frequently resembles "this method, where the cases/Doth call for one thing to set forth another" (144). Finally, the whole tale is told "in the similitude of a dream."

You will search long and hard to find all these dark devices in Bunyan's fiction. The "similitude of a dream" is the barest frame device, quickly forgotten by the reader and all but forgotten by Bunyan himself, except for one rather pointless waking and immediate return to sleep. The dreamer has no developed character and a negligible role, even as witness of the action. Metaphors of any sort scarcely appear at all, and Bunyan's "Dark Figures" have always been transparent to all but the most literalist readers. Christian, Faithful, Hopeful, Vanity Fair, the Delectable Mountains, the Valley of the Shadow of Death—all are and do what their names proclaim. When, toward the end of the "Author's Apology," Bunyan offers to "shew the profit of my Book," what he states as its moral meaning, the kernel of significance it contains, is in fact a synopsis of his narrative, a fact that demonstrates conclusively, if any demonstration is needed, the utter transparency of all the "dark figures" he employs. Here are Bunyan's words:

> This Book it chaulketh out before thine eyes,
> The man that seeks the everlasting Prize:
> It shews you whence he comes, whither he goes,
> What he leaves undone; also what he does:
> It also shews you how he runs, and runs,
> Till he unto the gate of Glory comes. (144)

Christian flees the City of Destruction to seek the Celestial City. That is not metaphor but a literal narrative statement, and it does not figure anything significantly other than what it says. In the context of Bunyan's specific belief or in any broadly Christian context, the use of the words "City of Destruction" for the physical world is no figure of speech stronger or more complex than synonym. That is certainly true as well for the central narrative notion of human life as pilgrimage. Whatever Bunyan thought he was doing—and his "Apology" indicates that in literary terms, as opposed to theological terms, he had no clear idea of his undertaking—he wrote univocally in *The Pilgrim's Progress*.

The serious issue Bunyan's "Apology" seems designed to engage—its deep content, if you like—really appears to be the discrepancy between the narrative events of Bunyan's book and the most literal-minded version of truth. The dream frame has no artistic function in the work[7]: It seems designed exclusively to allow the historical John Bunyan to avoid accusations of writing a total fiction—that is, a lie, an accusation to which he shows some sensitivity in the text.[8] Because there is literally no such physical place as the Valley of the Shadow of Death, in England or the Bible (though, of course, the Bible gives Bunyan the name), Bunyan must defend his presentation of it as figurative. For a believer like Bunyan, the authority for figurative writing lies in Scripture. Figurative writing in Scripture appears most often as "allegory" (typology for example) or parable.[9] Ergo, the narrative of *The Pilgrim's Progress* must be described as allegorical and/or parabolic. I doubt the equivocal example of Spenser in this regard (characters like Despaire, or Defetto, Decetto, and Despetto, who bear the names of but do not necessarily enact the role of personified abstractions) played much part in Bunyan's choice of terminology. His language seems almost entirely dictated by the prestige of Scriptural terms, despite their inappropriateness to his actual enterprise. The wonder is not that Bunyan called his work an allegory but that the term has stood unchallenged so long. What, after all, is the "other meaning" conveyed or shadowed by his narrative?

Allegory, at a very minimal definition, involves saying one thing and meaning another. It is a device of indirection, and indirection is the last thing either Bunyan or his book are interested in. The sustaining device of *The Pilgrim's Progress* is personification, which works the very opposite way, to define, to make precise, to make explicit. Insofar as personification concretizes the abstract and the general, it is the device *par excellence* of explicitness, which is why it is the darling tool of didacticism and propaganda of every school, Enthusiastic Christianity not excluded. Its directed explicitness accounts for our inability, in reading *The Pilgrim's Progress*, to pinpoint all that darkness Bunyan makes so much of.

Another important Restoration and eighteenth-century notion/phenomenon also contributed strongly to the propagation of the idea that allegories yielded univocal and consistent meanings. This was the idea of historical allegory, the reflecting of contemporary events or of topics of contemporary interest in narratives, either historical or fictional, of past events. Dryden's *Absalom and Achitophel* is probably the crowning achievement in this vein, and the readiness with which the central characters (Absalom, Achitophel, David) of its pseudo-Biblical story can be identified as the protagonists (Monmouth, Shaftesbury, Charles) of a very real Restoration political drama serves as a kind of model of our readerly expectations of such sorts of works.

Alan Roper has recently and correctly reminded us that the Restoration much more frequently spoke of such kinds of writing by using the terms "parallels" and "applications" than by calling them allegories. And Roper has also shown the difficulty of discerning the limits of such parallels in Restoration texts. His final advice, that we "proceed with caution when arguing for the topical reference of literature,"[10] can stand—*mutatis mutandis*—as a general *caveat* for reading all "allegorical" works. Even in a text such as *Absalom and Achitophel*, which seems to our hindsight almost a paradigm of "historical allegory," we should have been amply warned against seeking for consistent one-to-one parallels by the built-in difficulties of the text (for example, Dryden's obvious suspension of the outcome of the Biblical Absalom narrative, his alteration of Achitophel's role, his introduction of characters from other Biblical times and events). Nevertheless, such examples and ideas, along with the kinds of confusion exemplified by the chasm between Bunyan's terminology and his practice, all worked throughout the Restoration and eighteenth century to propagate the by-now dominant attitude that allegories are entirely personification or nearly so, that they consistently work by means of one-to-one correspondences, and that they respond to critical inquiry of a reductive, give-me-a-one-word-answer sort: "What is this an allegory of?"

III

The distinctions that the Restoration and eighteenth century blurred for us are amply clear in earlier texts, both of the grammarians and of the poets. For instance: Most early texts—this is true through the Renaissance—treat prosopopoeia in a totally different class of figures from those which have anything to do with allegory.[11] Personification belongs to the class of figures whose characteristic trait or behavior is transferral: the shifting, *on the basis of an underlying likeness*, of an attribute of some part to the whole or whole to the part or the gifting of one thing with some attribute or attributes of another. Allegory, on the other hand, belongs to a whole class of devices which share two traits: They work *by an exploitation of difference* rather than likeness, and they deliberately pursue obfuscation rather than clarity. The "figures"—if they can legitimately be called that—that allegory is most closely associated with are irony and enigma or riddle, both of which, like allegory, are extreme and often puzzling ways of saying one thing and meaning another. Here is George Puttenham's distinction between metaphor and allegory, from *The Arte of English Poesie*:

> As figures be the instruments of ornament in euery language, so be they also in sorte abuses or rather trespasses in speach, because they passe the ordinary limits of common vtterance, and be occupied of purpose to deceiue the eare and also the minde, drawing it from plainnesse and simplicitie to a certain doublenesse, whereby our talke is the more guilefull & abusing. For what els is your *Metaphor* but an inuersion of sence by transport; your *allegorie* by a duplicitie of meaning or dissimulation vnder couert and darke intendments; one while speaking obscurely and in riddle called *Aenigma*; another by common prouerbe or Adage called *Paremia*; then by merry skoffe called *Ironia*; then by bitter tawnt called *Sarcasmos*.[12] (III: vii)

Similarly, Abraham Fraunce defines metaphor as "when the like is signified by the like; so then a metaphor is nothing but a similitude contracted into one word." Allegory, on the other hand, he associates with irony, "that by naming one contrary intendeth another," and which "continued maketh a most sweet allegory."[13] In the traditional grammarians, the separation between allegory and personification is always this firm and this clear, unlike the shadowy and shifting lines between allegory and irony or allegory and enigma. Prosopopoeia is a device of specificity whose primary purpose is to underline and clarify meaning, to direct attention univocally to its object. A successful personification grounds and makes concrete the abstract in such a way that there can and should be no question about its meaning: it always means exactly what it says. Conversely, allegory is rooted in the concrete and works toward multiplicity of meaning: this is where all that shadowy figuration about which Bunyan's "Apology" so worries genuinely comes into play. Cibber asleep in the lap of Dulness does not signify just one thing; none of the things that that *gestalt* signifies is the same as what is conveyed by Cibber's crowning, two books earlier. Even when allegory borders on personification, the personifications it employs or seems to employ are usually deeply flawed, and by virtue of their flaws as personifications begin to give rise to allegory. To put it another way: the factors that confuse the status of a personification and the factors that upset the conventional expectations of readers are major contributors to the creation of multivalent allegory. Mr. Allworthy is not in fact entirely worthy (he makes several very blameable errors), nor is Sophia always perfectly wise, and those ironies in action are indeed capable of making "a most sweet allegory."

Not just English grammarians insist on the complexity and difficulty of allegory. English poets do as well, and specifically the poet universally agreed to have produced the most significant allegory in the language. Spenser's letter to Raleigh offers us a classic allegorical document, a purported guide to his long and convoluted poem that, exactly in the manner of Dante's similar letter to Can Grande della Scala, in fact gives nothing away, offers no real help whatever in understanding the particulars of the poem. Just as the letter to Can Grande misapplies the terms of Scriptural allegory to its own contents (all of the content of the "allegorical" levels of Scripture forms the literal level of the *Commedia*), so the letter to Raleigh garbles Aristotle (and even Homer: does anyone actually believe that the Agamemnon of *The Iliad* is an "ensample" of "a good gouernour," or the "Vlysses" of *The Odyssey* is an "ensample" of "a vertuous man"?[14]). Spenser's letter spends the great bulk of its time and space—again like the letter to Can Grande—talking about things that aren't in the poem, for the most part purely narrative events such as Arthur's pre-textual history, the convocation at Gloriana's castle, the assignment of specific missions to individual knights, etc.

Spenser even comes very close to declaring overtly that he won't explicate his own poem. In the opening sentence of the letter, after reminding Raleigh how difficult allegories are to understand and that he (Raleigh) directly commanded the writing of this set of crib notes, Spenser announces that he will "discouer...the general intention and meaning...*without expressing of any particular purposes or by-accidents therein occasioned*" (II: 485; my emphasis). That is to say, I'll tell you the broad aim of my work but absolutely nothing about any particular aspect of it. Now, this is disingenuous to say the least: surely not even the most malicious of Spenser's detractors ever thought that his goal was ignoble and his plan to debauch. If the objects of Raleigh's command and of this letter's putative revelations were to avoid "gealous opinions and misconstructions" and to prouide "for your better light in reading," then surely it was, as it still is, the poem's "particular purposes" and "by-accidents" that create obscurity and uncertainty of meaning, and not the over-all intention or design of the poem. Yet, quite politely but quite clearly, that is exactly what Spenser refuses to cast any light upon, while still insisting on the darkness of his "conceit."

Crucially for our understanding of traditional allegory, Spenser emphasizes variability of signification in these remarks to Raleigh. First, he distinguishes two separate significations in Gloriana: "In that Faery Queene I meane glory in my generall intention, but in my particular I conceiue the most excellent and glorious person of our soueraine the Queene, and her kingdome in Faery land." Then, he distinguishes two persons in Elizabeth, which are reflected in different persons of his narrative: "And yet in some places els, I doe otherwise shadow her. For considering she beareth two persons, the one of a most royall Queene or Empresse, the other of a most vertuous and beautifull Lady, this latter part in some places I doe express in Belphoebe." (II: 486). Putting aside the knotty questions raised by Spenser's suggestion that England is "shadowed" in Faery Land, I would call your closest attention to Spenser's distinction between his general and particular intentions and what he implies about their simultaneous/overlapping/successive presences in the same figure. Note too his careful "in some places," applied to the figure of Belphoebe: the implication clearly is that signification is not the only one that Belphoebe bears, nor does she bear it consistently. Taken *in toto* with his remarks about the varying significations of Arthur and the practices of predecessor poets (Homer, Virgil, Ariosto, Tasso) in merging or separating the qualities of "a good gouernour and a vertuous man" in single or multiple heroes, these comments have to be understood not as authorizations for univocal readings of the "Una is the Protestant Church" sort but rather as calls for their opposite, for very flexible, multivocal understandings of the persons of the poem. Among the few particular directions that the *Letter to Raleigh* actually gives for reading *The Faerie Queene*, Spenser's warning against seeking one-to-one correspondences between the *figurae* of his fiction and abstract ideas or historical personages certainly looms largest—though this has not deterred scholars from doing exactly that. It would seem that the (putatively) consistent "parallels" and "applications" of Restoration and eighteenth-century historical poems and plays have engendered expectations of the same sort of analogies in earlier and very different works. In effect, they have retrospectively colored readings of *The Faerie Queene*'s topical material, sending generations of readers scurrying about in search of Philip and Mary and lesser personages of all sorts. And in the unending Mobius strip that is criticism, such ideas about *The Faerie Queene* may have ultimately reinforced the attitudes that generated them, sending scholarship happily about the business of finding one-to-one correspondences for the images and events and characters of Restoration and eighteenth-century poems, since the uncontested conventional view was that was how allegory worked.

Whatever particular problems the letter to Raleigh creates for our understanding of *The Faerie Queene* (though they are in their kind illuminating about the difficulties of all allegories), we are more concerned here with what the letter to Raleigh actually tells us about allegories in general. A very few broad characteristics are discernible. First, allegories are difficult to construe, "dark" and "clowdy"—genuinely so, with complexities of narrative and signification well beyond any of Bunyan's similarly advertised but purely doctrinal cruxes. Second, signification in allegory is unstable, perhaps intermittent, perhaps multi-modal and overlapping, most certainly multivalent. Arthur, for instance, is an "image of the twelue priuate morall vertues" (whatever they are), but he also sets forth "magnificence in particular" and appears in each book under the guise of the presiding particular virtue of that book. Gloriana has at least two significances, glory in general and Queen Elizabeth, but Elizabeth is elsewhere in the poem "shadowed" in different guises—Belphebe for one, and Belphebe clearly cannot, in many of her actions, be taken as figure for Elizabeth without making gibberish of the poem.

Spenser speaks in this letter only of a few characters out of the many that crowd *The Faerie Queene*, and he speaks of no actions at all of the endless stream of action that is the poem. Nevertheless, a clear set of directions emerges from the remarks he does make: multivalency, intermittency, overlapping of significations and/or roles. Such "help" as the letter to Raleigh offers works first to engage and reassure the reader on the most naive and simple level—yes, Arthur embodies an abstract value—and then to pull the rug out: Arthur also embodies other, different values, and he also sometimes appears in this guise, or this, or this. The end result is to leave naive and/or unnoticing readers reassured that they can read the poem univocally, as personification, which is the way most interpreters of allegory like it, and to leave percipient readers thoroughly puzzled—which is pretty much how writers of allegory prefer it.

Swift and/or his narrator play a similar game with the reader in "The Preface" to *A Tale of a Tub*.

> Sea-men have a Custom when they meet a *Whale*, to fling him out an empty *Tub*, by way of Amusement, to divert him from laying violent Hands upon the Ship. This Parable was immediately mythologiz'd: The *Whale* was interpreted to be *Hobs*'s *Leviathan*, which tosses and plays with all other Schemes of Religion and Government, whereof a great many are hollow, and dry, and empty, and noisy, and wooden, and given to Rotation. This is the *Leviathan* from whence the terrible Wits of our Age are said to borrow their Weapons. The *Ship* in danger, is easily understood to be its old Antitype the *Commonwealth*. But, how to analyze the *Tub*, was a Matter of difficulty; when after long Enquiry and Debate, the literal Meaning was preserved.[15]

Any reader who emerges from that short course in allegorical dyslexia confident about the mode of figuration of *A Tale of a Tub* is either preternaturally percipient or naive in the extreme. First, there is that Bunyanesque piling up of critical terms: parable, mythologize, interpret, antitype, analyze, literal meaning. And they are, in the conglomerate, as little coherent as Bunyan's terminology. For example: To "mythologize" a "parable" is at least formally redundant. The juxtaposition of topical reference (*Leviathan*) and cliched metaphor mislabelled "antitype" (the ship of state) is a logical and methodological horror. Even the apparently simple personification (anthropomorphosizing?) of the whale miscarries grotesquely (see his "violent Hands"). The whole "allegorizing" enterprise collapses into futility, dwindling to an ironically intact literal meaning that immediately doubles the irony by turning out not to be literal at all. The tub whose "literal Meaning was preserved" becomes the metaphor or figure or ground for the whole book. It becomes, in fact, *A Tale of a Tub*'s figure of all figuration, the container that contains the whole tale and sets the boundaries for its imagistic syntax—a tale of a tub indeed. The only assurance about the workings of the *Tale*'s allegory that a reader can take away from such a simultaneously charged and short-circuiting figurative field is that whatever grows from it simply will not, cannot, conform to conventional readerly expectations. There is surely allegory in *A Tale of a Tub*, but it equally surely will not occur in the transparent (at least in its broad outlines) parable of Peter, Martin, and Jack that so attracts and entraps the "terrible wit" of the narrator, becoming thereby—just as he said it would[16]—the tub that diverts *him*.

Examples like these show clearly enough that allegory needs to proceed neither consistently nor singlemindedly nor simplemindedly, nor need it be susceptible of interpretation either single or simple. Context is crucial, and this too is a major generic difference between allegory and personification: Not the characters themselves but their actions and their circumstances generate their allegorical significance. Christian is always christian, Hopeful always hopeful. But in the precincts of allegory our interpretations of the very same character can vary widely, depending on the total context in which he makes his appearance—a fact about allegory that at least in part illuminates why readers who see Gulliver as a constant have so much trouble with the "allegory" of *Gulliver's Travels*, just as it paradoxically provides a consistent explanation of or rationale for the startling shifts of opinion executed by the narrator of *A Tale of a Tub*.

IV

What all this implies for Restoration and eighteenth-century studies is fairly straightforward. We have been laboring under a serious handicap: We've been working with a major misnomer which has disguised from us a whole dimension of our period. Taking personification for the whole of allegory has caused us to overlook a large and important aspect of the literature with which we deal. The fact that the phenomenon, prosopopoeia, usurped the label "allegory" doesn't mean that writers stopped creating allegories: They just thought of them as something else, and called them that something else or called them nothing at all. The years and the writers that fall between 1660 and 1798 are as linguistically and methodologically sophisticated as any before or since: It is not to be believed, without overwhelming evidence, that traditional allegory—works of complex, multivalent meaning, created out of multiple, perhaps competing, meaning systems, and exploiting, sometimes exploding, conventional modes of signification and figuration—simply dropped out existence.

Rather than dropping out of existence, works of this kind proliferated throughout the period. Look simply at the modulation of formal devices by which Swift moves into the complex "personifications" of *The Battle of the Books*: A fable—the republic of dogs—explained by a parable—the quarrel of the Ancients and Moderns about possession of the highest peak of Parnassus—leads to a metaphor—ink as weapon, books as trophies—explained by a fact—books are stored in libraries—and all offered, in the context of a newspaper report, as an explanation of the outbreak of an actual battle in the Queen's library. The animated, leather-bound books of Swift's fiction are first of all literalizations of a figure of speech—for example, "I'm reading Virgil"—so commonplace that for most people it has entirely lost its figurative dimensions. That sort of expression, in its turn, originates in just such a sense of the author's personality or spirit being distilled in his book. It serves, in *The Battle of the Books*, as the "literal" and "factual" explanation of the vitality of what remain, physically, merely bundles of bound paper. Are they then personifications, or are they synecdoches? Is it fact or fiction to say that "Virgil survives in his works"? Further: How then are we to construe an "allegorical" or "personification" figure who, like Aesop, in the middle of an "allegorical" work, "allegorizes" the supposedly "factual" encounter of a spider and a bee? And does so, moreover, in exactly the same manner that the "historical" Aesop employs in similar beast fables? Is that the extreme of fantasy or simple psychohistorical realism? Precisely these sorts of de-stabilized relations of fact to fiction and figure to thought provide the basis of Swift's allegory, which depends far less on one-to-one correspondences than it does on the reader's awareness of the shifting boundaries of realism and fantasy, reality and metaphor, the nature of the world and the terms in which we agree to talk about it—all of which is, of course, the battle of the books.

In a very similar vein, consider as well Dryden's conglomeration of discursive and/or linguistic systems—Scriptural, epic, dramatic, topical, sexual, historical, prophetic—in *MacFlecknoe*, or Aphra Behn's multiplication of genres and their concomitant expectations—romance, history, epic, biography and autobiography or memoir, heroic drama, scientific report, pastoral, oratory—in

Oronooko, or Sterne's obsessive examination of how (many) languages convey meaning in *Tristram Shandy* and *A Sentimental Journey*, or the webs of ambiguous signification—psychological, political, religious, moral, philosophical—Fielding weaves around the characters of all his novels. Allegory, in the sense the term had for Spenser and the generations before him, is all over the eighteenth century, but because *they* didn't call it that, *we* haven't looked for it—or at it.

That, of course, is what is important about taxonomy. Terms direct our attention—and I would argue (I hope I have been arguing) that it's time we in Restoration and eighteenth-century studies directed our attention to some of the terms we use all too glibly. Our period perpetrated or perpetuated a major taxonomic confusion, and we have so far allowed it to stand. It's time enough now to clean up, if not our whole act, at least our terminology.

This won't be as easy to do as it is to say. The great weight of the historical evidence shows that for most of us—lay readers and critics alike—allegory is just too much trouble, too much work. Most readers want to cut the Gordian Knot and untangle the difficulties. They—we—want the quick fix, the easy answer, the simplest, clearest statement to use on the exam. Think of the most common form of the basic question "we" ask about allegory: "What is this an allegory of?" Well, Johnny, it's an allegory of salvation. "We" want to take a whole work and reduce it to a single noun. Wham bam thank you ma'am: next allegory please. Genuinely allegorical works can be made to respond to this sort of treatment only by the wholesale amputation of facets and aspects, by the reinterpretation of irregularities and unorthodoxies as the blandest, least offensive conventionalities. That, ironically, is the work of allegoresis: to preserve canonicity and "orthodoxy" by removing the troublesome parts of a work—in the case of allegory, by eliding all the ambiguities, uncertainties, and multivalences, all the traits that make a work an allegory in the first place. Allegoresis undoes allegories.

As a starting place for the reconsideration of allegory in the Restoration and eighteenth century, I offer the following brief, definitely not exhaustive, set of definitions of some of the major meanings of the word allegory that we need to be aware of. Most readers will be able to provide more, and more particularized, definitions from their own experience—but this is at least a beginning.

Personification vs. Allegory

The word allegory should be understood as having at least five separate senses:

1. A broad term embracing nearly all figurative uses of language, including symbol, metaphor, and personification: in this sense, "allegorical" is equivalent to the broadest uses of terms like "symbolic," "metaphoric," "figurative," and so forth. This use of the term is widespread in the eighteenth century (for example, Swift's narrator's reference to "the Allegory of the Coats" [4]).

2. A specific term designating after-the-fact interpretation, usually or essentially for purposes of establishing the presence of orthodox or acceptable morality or philosophy or doctrine, such as the texts of Homer, Virgil, and Ovid have been subjected to. For this sense, "allegoresis" would be a more exact usage.

3. A specific term designating both the methods of interpreting the Bible widely employed by Medieval and Renaissance exegetes and the kinds of interpretations engendered by such readings, exemplified by (but not necessarily confined to) typology and the fourfold levels of "allegorical" explanation. For this sense, normal and accurate usage should say "scriptural allegory," or "the allegory of scripture," or "the allegory of the theologians."

4. A general term covering the sort of readings generated by deconstructionist analysis. Allegory in the deconstructionist sense (specifically in the destructionist theory of Paul de Man) is really a misnomer: what is referred to there is actually a particular species of irony, wherein the duplicity of language itself betrays all intention and control. Close reading always reveals a text's unreadability, which unreadability is always the "allegory" of every text.

5. A specific term designating a narrative or drama of multiple, complex, perhaps incompatible, often overlapping, and therefore non-paraphrasable meaning(s), a story or play whose words and events are simultaneously metaphors of and veils of its meaning(s). This sense of allegory is its

oldest and newest, because allegory is a term in evolution. The means by which its multiple apprehendable-but-unstatable significances are achieved alter with the conditions of each culture in which allegory is attempted. Allegories of the Middle Ages and the Modern Period are alike in their achievement, in their "saying other"; they differ markedly in the ways in which they manage to establish that "other."

This fifth sense of allegory is both the most important and the most difficult. In that it comes closest of the five to the sorts of ideas about allegory that seem to underlie both Spenser's letter to Raleigh and the actual practice of *The Faerie Queene*, it precludes the identification of allegory with personification or any other single device and insists rather on a multiplicity of signifying means or figures and a consequent multivalence of signification. It restricts personification and related devices of specificity to subordinate roles within the literary construct, roles which may often enough actually violate the normally consistent behaviors of such tropes. Allegory in this fifth sense should not be confused with deconstructionist allegory, which, for all its verbal pyrotechnics, renders only univocal readings (indeed, always the same univocal reading). Full-fledged allegory, on the other hand, recognizes the same "duplicity" of language that propels deconstructionist theory, but allegory rejoices in it, finding in it a source of connection and a mine of undiscovered meaning. To put it another way: for deconstruction, all language puns, and all puns are disjunctive, driving the mind to disparate and intolerable extremes and rendering meaningful communication impossible. For allegory, all puns are conjunctive, weaving the universe together in ways that we the readers apprehend and comprehend according to our abilities. The "nunnery" in Hamlet's "Get thee to a nunnery" lives in a totally different linguistic cosmos from the "Ignorance" or "Hopeful" of *Pilgrim's Progress*.

Conjunctive punning makes a fair metaphor for the way allegory says one thing and means another. Just as a pun releases its meaning instantly or not all, so too allegory. Just as a pun cannot be paraphrased and still exist as a pun, so too allegory. In allegory, even actions and characters pun and are puns. A very small example: that Parson Adams, for instance, marries Joseph and Fanny is true in at least two ways (that he performs the ceremony and that he is—narratively, figuratively, "ideologically"—wedded to them) and he himself "is" at least two people ("Mr. Adams at church with his surplice on, and Mr. Adams without that ornament, in any other place, were two very different persons")—as are, of course both Joseph (thought Andrews, actually Wilson) and Fanny (thought Goodwill, actually Andrews). All of these changes of name are not merely nominal, but indicative of far larger and more important changes of perspective and role for the characters and perspective and value for the readers.

This is all important, but in novels as much as in literary theory, taxonomy is only a tool. As Rosemond Tuve reminded us 25 years ago, allegory isn't a "changeless essence," and the proper task of scholarship and criticism isn't to grant or deny poems and plays and novels admission to its exclusive category. Rather, our proper work is, by accurately identifying the phenomena we're dealing with, to discover what "was involved in reading allegorically...at a given time" (33), and from that, in turn, to learn whatever we can not only about the specific texts we choose to read allegorically but, more generally and more usefully, whatever we can about how to read—period.

NOTES

1. In *Allegorical Imagery: Some Mediaeval Books and Their Posterity* (Princeton: Princeton University Press, 1966), 24ff., Tuve argues there very persuasively for the distinction between allegory and personification on the basis of *function*, what each does or is supposed to do. Following her lead, in my "Saying and Meaning: Allegory and the Indefinable" (*Bulletin of Research in the Humanities* 83 (1980): 248-61) I tried to make the distinction even firmer: I argued there, on the basis of the history and overall purposes of the two tropes (if tropes they be), for their ideological opposition—that their entire thrust and orientation are directly opposite. This is not say, of course, that allegories do not employ personifications, though it is very firmly to declare that no personification ever used an allegory.

2. The major works on allegory before (Angus Fletcher's *Allegory: The Theory of a Symbolic Mode* (Ithaca: Cornell University Press, 1964)) and after (Maureen Quilligan's *The Language of Allegory* (Ithaca: Cornell University Press, 1979)) Tuve's book, while both quite acute about other aspects of allegory, nevertheless treat personification as either a central mode (trope?) of allegory or the basis of the whole trope (mode?).

3. This confusion, though dominant in the modern period, is by no means a modern invention. Rather, it has quite deep roots, as Tuve indicates: "Modern descriptions of works often seem to proceed on the assumption that prosopopoeia is identical with allegoria. This is quite as uninformed when sixteenth-century men, better trained rhetorically, are sometimes caught thinking it. The popular tag "personification allegory,"

usually used pejoratively, is especially useless to make the needed discriminations; the simple glove-girl Idleness is as much a personification as are Grace-Dieu and Caritas, yet the first is an idle person doing idle things, the latter two convey various niceties of theological doctrine. As usual, *function*—how it operates in the fiction—truly defines the form of an image, and thence comes its classification." Rosemond Tuve, *Allegorical Imagery*, 177.

4. See my "Saying and Meaning," 258–61.

5. For a very full discussion of the idea of allegory as veil or initiation, see Michael Murrin, *The Veil of Allegory: Some Notes toward a Theory of Allegorical Rhetoric in the English Renaissance* (Chicago: University of Chicago Press, 1969).

6. The text of Bunyan quoted here and throughout is *Grace Abounding to the Chief of Sinners and The Pilgrim's Progress*, ed. Roger Sharrock (London: Oxford University Press, 1966). Page numbers are cited parenthetically after quotations.

7. The final lines of Part I of *Pilgrim's Progress* could serve one purpose, a very unorthodox deconstructionist one unforeseen or unplanned by Bunyan. "So I awoke, and behold it was a dream" as thoroughly "authorizes" a counter-reading of Bunyan's narrative as Aeneas's notorious gate-of-horn exit from the Underworld does of Virgil's.

8. From the "Apology":

> "Well, yet I am not fully satisfied,
> That this your book will stand, when soundly tried."
> "What, what's the matter?" "It is dark." "What though?"
> "But it is feigned." "What of that? I trow
> Some men by feigning words as dark as mine
> Make truth to spangle and its rays to shine."

And later:

> "Sound words, I know, Timothy is to use,
> And old wives' fables he is to refuse;
> But yet grave Paul him nowhere doth forbid
> The use of parables, in which lay hid
> That gold, those pearls, and precious stones that were
> Worth digging for, and that with greatest care."

9. Scriptural allegory, and what that term may mean, is a whole vexed subject of its own, and anyone curious about it should consult the work of, among others, Pere Henri de Lubac (*Exegese medievale*, Paris, 1959) and Beryl Smalley (*The Study of the Bible in the Middle Ages*, New York: Philosophical Library, 1952). But ideas about the allegory of Scripture, particularly about the notorious four levels of interpretation (literal, allegorical, anagogical, tropological) have little or nothing to do with the allegory of the poets.

10. Alan Roper, "Drawing Parallels and Making Applications in Restoration Literature," in *Politics as Reflected in Literature* (*Papers Presented at a Clark Library Seminar, 24 January 1987*, ed. Richard Ashcroft and Alan Roper (Los Angeles: William Andrews Clark Memorial Library, 1989), 29–65. See especially 31 and 51–52.

11. For a good and representative example of this, see the so-called *Rhetorica ad Herrennium*, long thought to be by Cicero: *Ad C. Herrennium De Ratione Dicendi*, ed. and tr. Harry Caplan (London and Cambridge: William Heinemann and Harvard University Press, 1954), IV.liii.66. Also see Cicero, *Orator*, xl: 137-8.

12. Quoted from O. B. Hardison Jr., *English Literary Criticism: The Renaissance* (New York: Appleton-Century-Crofts, 1963), 177-8.

13. Quoted from *The Arcadian Rhetoric* I: 6 and I: 7; *The Renaissance in England*, ed. Hyder E. Rollins and Herschel Baker (Boston: Houghton Mifflin, 1954), 635.

14. The text of Spenser quoted here and throughout is *Spenser's Faerie Queene*, ed. J. C. Smith, 2 vols (Oxford: Clarendon Press, 1909; rpt 1961), II: 485.

15. The text cited here and throughout is *A Tale of a Tub, The Battle of the Books*, and *The Mechanical Operation of the Spirit*, eds. A. C. Guthkelch and D. Nichol Smith (Oxford: Clarendon Press, 1958), 40.

16. "And it was decreed, that in order to prevent these *Leviathans* from tossing and sporting with the *Commonwealth*...they should be diverted from that Game by a *Tale of a Tub*. And my Genius being conceived to lye not unhappily that way, I had the Honor done me to be engaged in the Performance" (40-41).

ALLEGORY, TYPOLOGY, AND DIDACTICISM
Paradise Lost in the Eighteenth Century

John T. Shawcross

It is commonplace to observe a difference between the sense of allegory in the earlier seventeenth century and the later. The earlier continues to harken back to medieval allegoresis,[1] and the later narrows to a so-called "naive" allegory which demands unmistakable continuous allegoric elements developing a sustained allegoric fiction.[2] The contrasts between William Langland's *Piers Plowman* and John Bunyan's *Pilgrim's Progress* define the change, and Edmund Spenser's *The Faerie Queene* aided in effecting the transition. By employing allegoresis, particularly in such parts as Book I, "The Legend of the Knight of the Red Cross, or of Holiness," and by partially subverting it to emphasize a philosophic concept, as in the jousting tournament arranged by Satyrane in Book IV, "The Legend of Cambel and Telamond [that is, Cambell and Triamond], or of Friendship,"[3] Spenser becomes the inflection point of change. It is a change developed further by Milton in *Paradise Lost*, though not understood by critics of Spenser and Milton in the eighteenth century.

Cambell and Triamond, it will be remembered, are only one pair exemplifying friendship and appear only in Cantos ii–iv. The development of their friendship is a narrative of action which can be reenacted by others in other contexts; the magical dimensions of the fiction (Cambell's magic ring, Cambina's rod of peace and cup of Nepenthe, the transmigration of the souls of Priamond and Diamond) not only do not allegorize but rather put an Ariosto-like romantic veneer on an otherwise potentially realistic episode. On the other hand, the three-day tournament opposing the Knights of Maidenhead to other champions takes on anagogic meaning by the success of Satyrane, then of Cambell and Triamond, and then of the newly arrived and disguised Artegall, whose name implies "the equal of Arthur." But balance is restored between the forces of romantic love and more "natural" carnal love by the Knight of the Ebon Spear's unhorsing of Artegall: This is Britomart, hero of Book III, of Chastity, reviving thus the philosophic concept of chastity (with, in turn, its remembrance of temperance and the golden mean of Book II). Despite allegoric and especially romantic elements, this episode becomes in perspective an example of the need for balance rather than a statement of "darke conceit."[4] The upsetting of the Christ-like achievement of Artegall on the third day of the tournament tends to deny an anagogic/allegoric reading, ignores any tropological/allegoric dimension, and posits instead a generalized metaphor of the precedence of chastity as an example of temperance. We have begun to move from allegory to mimesis.

Generally the allegorical can be seen as opposite to the mimetic. In both earlier and later modes of the allegorical (if we consider Spenser's and Milton's works as the point of contrast), figures, personifications, or abstract qualities explore an idea or ideas which are set forth by an action. Involved, thus, are analogies and correspondences. The eighteenth-century dissociation of personification and agent, however, has imposed a distinction not required by medieval allegoresis. Knapp (63) quotes Samuel Johnson ("*Discord* may raise a mutiny, but *Discord* cannot conduct a march, nor besiege a town"[5]) in conjunction with his analysis that eighteenth-century criticism differentiated "producing an effect and conducting an action." In Spenser and Milton this differentiation does not exist: personification and agent exist side by side, or as one; the personification acting as an agent adds further and more complex allegory. A main contributor to a combined personification/agency lies in what Fletcher analyzes as Spenser's generation of the double: "Each partial aspect that has been generated out of the main character is now available to the author for its development parallel to every other partial aspect...[T]he creation of a double plot line enforces an allegorical interpretation" (195). That is, to use Fletcher's example, the personification of Sir Guyon's good and bad characteristics not only is a fictional correspondence to a virtue or vice but is the means of developing plot as Sir Guyon fights identical wars against each evil. In *Paradise Lost* such doubling can be seen in Beelzebub as an aspect of Satan, or indeed in Sin as an aspect of Satan. Both generations exhibit Satan's ego and allow Satan to produce effects and conduct actions.

This fusion of effect and action in Spenser, as well as doubling, is evident in the Red Cross/Sansfoy/Sansjoy episode in Book I. Sansjoy both stands for Despondency, which Red Cross overcomes by defeating him (Cantos iv–v), and initiates the duel with the knight upon recognizing the slayer of his brother Sansfoy. Red Cross's slaying of Sansfoy (Faithlessness) surmounts Despondency (Sansjoy) and leads to Pride in his second victory. The allegory is clear, though it cannot stop at this point because such pride enlists him in the service of Lucifera. The continued narration of Red Cross's experiences will impose a moral allegory concerning pride, its source, its manifestations, and the means to conquer it. Perspective on the episode delineates "effect" but at the same time the mimetic dimension of the duel is provoked by the "action" of an avenging brother. Thus the figure, personification, and quality are set forth by an action created by an agent which they define. They and the action each represents something other than just itself.

The something else represented may involve moral meanings, a historical or actual person/event, or a broad mythic or psychological substruct, and we find all these elements and readings in *The Faerie Queene*. At times such elements are focussed and individual (like the wedding of the Thames and Medway in Canto xi of Book IV), although the wider view can see such specific "conceits" as representing another version of the more pervasive allegory (just as the wedding of the rivers figures forth the wedding of Marinell and Florimell and all other male/female unions of friendship/love). For the most part as we proceed in time allegoric writers like Bunyan disallow the focussed and individual and instead sustain a closed and singular allegory, which creates a separation of personification and "mimetic" action, with the personification only remaining.

Allegory may be built on narratives which provide semblances of a realistic action by persons who, though fictional, take on appearances of being "real."[6] The abstract narrative allows an exchange of some or all of the attributes whereas the mimetic implies little beyond itself: the sign is the signified. The Restoration and eighteenth century, accepting the allegoric but rejecting in allegory a truly mimetic dimension, saw the equation of, say,

Christian with a christian (all christians, that is), who meets Obstinate and Pliable, who signify obstinacy and pliability and nothing more. They represent that in Christian which is or is potentially his own obstinacy and its opposite, pliability. The allegoric figure delineates a person's predilection toward one or the other, and implies the moral preference for some position in-between, the same message we find in the second book of *The Faerie Queene*. The narrative offers a seemingly mimetic action except that that action represents something else, a philosophic and ubiquitously significant lesson. The personifications do not act; they equate what they signify only.

This kind of "surface" allegory occurs frequently in Spenser, as when Disdain and Scorn beset Mirabella, who has exhibited these attitudes in the past, in Book VI, Cantos vii and viii. But the allegory in Spenser (or earlier writers) does not stop there: Disdain is a giant (adding another "message"), who levels abusive language at her (adding still another element), and Scorn is a fool (adding further meaning), who keeps whipping her mount, an ass, which always represents humility in the epic (adding thus another precept, both that humility always suffers at the hands of fools and that the source of scorn lies in self-centeredness). Mirabella's champions, Arthur and the Salvage Man, would have killed Disdain and Scorn respectively, signifying the type of person who would not experience such negative attitudes, except that she stops them, for her past actions have demanded a penance of enduring these beings. The moral point is clear, but it is more than just the surface meaning, the only kind of meaning pervading *Pilgrim's Progress*. On top of all this is further allegory, that which is the sustained metaphor of which this episode just recounted is but a part: Book VI concerns the legend of Courtesy, and Mirabella has been most discourteous in the past and must suffer the consequences for her acts. In the past this court beauty was so proud that she disdained all suitors to her hand in scornful words. The didactic lesson is that not all suitors were necessarily acceptable for her, but they should not have been treated so discourteously, and perhaps some may have been acceptable except that her discourteous attitude did not allow her to realize this. The episode reflects the code of courtly love. It leads us to realize that the sign is sometimes the signified but that it also may signify many things, sometimes localized, sometimes a part of a much larger whole. Localization of allegoric components (like the wedding of the Thames and Medway) may be a mimetic statement: the two rivers do merge;

and the multiple relationships of allegoric components (like Discord and Scorn with Mirabella and contrastingly with Arthur) raise mimetic dimensions and create allegories which are not "naive" or "surface." It is the localization (or specificity) of allegory with its mimetic underpinnings that is generally missing in later seventeenth-century and eighteenth-century literature as well as the multiple ambiguities of the sign.

The relationship of "typology" and "didacticism" to allegory complicates understanding of the mode and reading of the allegories of *Paradise Lost*. Typology arose through Biblical reading and belief in the Christ, creating the words "antitype" and "type" for persons and events recorded in the two testaments. The antitype (which does not imply in any way "the opposite of a type," despite frequent misuses of the word in that sense) is the person or event or symbol in the New Testament which was read to provide a closure for persons or events or symbols in the Old Testament. That is, the person (like Moses in his role in effecting the Exodus through the Red Sea; Exodus xiv) or the event (like David's defeat of Goliath; 1 Samuel xvii) or the symbol (like the rainbow shown to Noah; Genesis ix: 12–17) foreshadowed something in the New Testament concerned with the life of Jesus, the Christ: his prophetic role as he walks on the sea (Matthew xiv: 22–33), his defeat of Satan through the crucifixion, the brief eclipse, and the resurrection (Matthew xxvii: 36–xxviii: 10), and the ark (tabernacle) of the new covenant, which is the bequest of the New Testament itself (Hebrews viii: 6–13, ix: 11–28). The Old Testament is seen as shadowing forth, but it is thus incomplete, perhaps inexact or ambiguous as to message, generally localized and delimited. The symbol may be replaced, like the conflagration of 2 Peter iii: 10 foretelling the Second Coming and replacing the rainbow, or revised into a broader concept, like the ark, which, though symbol, represents the presence of the Christ who is to be imitated, not like the rainbow which is a sign delimited to a reminder of covenant.[7]

The point is significant in the critical analysis of *Paradise Lost*, for typological understanding does not relate to Adam and Eve until the protevangelium is pronounced (X: 179–81) and the narrator establishes the antitypes of the Son and Mary when he remarks, "So spake this Oracle, then verifi'd/When *Jesus* son of *Mary* second *Eve*/Saw Satan fall" (X: 182–84).[8] And what is important for the present study is the lack of relationship or correspondence between allegory and typology in the poem. They are separate ways of viewing. Paul J. Korshin is careful to talk of prefigurative techniques and to delineate the secular applications of the typological way of thinking. Emphasis in typology is on figuralism, and it works in the secular world to provide order or pattern or correspondence between seemingly unrelated things through its parallelism. In the secular world, it drops its biblical signification and emphasizes parallelism and often the didactic lesson of imitation of the good and avoidance of the bad. It has also been viewed as a redemptive process of history as humankind attempts to emulate the antitype, each type perhaps proceeding to a closer imitation. Thus in a work like *Paradise Regain'd* the Son has been seen not only as the antitype of the New Testament narrative but the exemplar to be imitated. As I read that poem, however, the latter part of that statement misrepresents what Milton is doing: he is not establishing an exemplar to be followed although that is implied in the typological thinking of the antitype for post-Messianic periods; rather he is presenting "one man whose rite of passage has shown how to live one's life," how to achieve a spiritual inner being which will guide when example or precedent seems lacking.[9] While the Son is the antitype and someone like Melchizedek or Spenser's Prince Arthur can be seen as types, the thesis of Milton's poem involves definition of true heroism and its achievement, an analysis of what this antitype is. The wide difference from allegory should be clear: Milton is not concretizing a figure or character qualities with an implied didactic message; he is offering a mimetic picture of the "sign."[10]

Although the difference between typology and allegory seems clear, it has not been so to commentators. Maureen Quilligan thinks that "one dimension of allegory" is "that of Biblical typology," calling *Paradise Lost* Milton's "great typological poem." "Spenser, relying less solidly on a typological foundation throughout, must remind his reader when to read typologically." For her, the language of the epic is "almost designedly unallegorical" until the Fall when "it falls into punning ambiguity; it falls into 'allegory'." Milton as Puritan, she argues, would stress "plain style" and would suspect "continued metaphor." Thus she quotes Anne Davidson Ferry approvingly, "He chose consistently to limit his allegory to parts of the poem relating only to fallen experience."[11] Somehow or other, apparently, the Father, the Son, the various good angels, and even Adam and Eve before the Fall are antitypes or types in biblical terms. Aside from the chronological confusion that that makes within the poem, no foreshadowing of the Christ and his experience, the central point of typology, exists in the poem until the Fall. Not even Abdiel is a type of Christ, though he serves a didactic purpose, representing both how one may be led by fraud into near disobedience and a lack of faithfulness and love and how one may see through such fraud for what it is. That he recognizes Satan finally for what he is and rejects disobedience does not make him a Christ figure, even though that seems to be the way he is treated in some recent critical examinations of the episode. We can see Abdiel, at the center of the poem, as "the pattern of the 'one just man,'" as "an exemplum both to Adam and the reader" of the potential fall by fraud and of the self-sufficiency of freedom of will. (The correspondence with Eve who falls through fraud and with Adam who falls through his unhappy exercise of free will has not generally been observed, however.) In this Abdiel may represent a type to the reader, that is, one like "the whole series of such individual triumphs in the final books (Enoch, Noah, Abraham, etc.)."[12] This view of Abdiel involves the secularization of typology, the figuralism and parallelism which can lead one to a didactic lesson (or a warning): this is what I (the reader) should or should not do. *Paradise Lost* is in this way a "great typological poem," as Quilligan writes, and so "contributed to the continuity of this figural mode," as Korshin records. Yet within the poem this angel that Milton makes up (thus not a biblically "real" character) can be seen to concretize an idea as much as Sir Guyon does.

The poem offers typologies, but this, we should note, is a reader-generated view: within the poem itself someone like Uriel and his not at first recognizing Satan and his hypocrisy is a preparation for, and an exoneration of, Eve's not recognizing Satan and his deceit. The artistic *use* of what a reader can classify as a typology, in other words, is in a different realm of being "typology," and although it is the author who has so ordered his work as to sustain typological interpretation, the typology may not be within the work itself—Eve cannot know of Uriel's experience though for the reader it has proleptic significance for Eve's dream and the temptation, nor does she know of Abdiel's action. When Bunyan creates Christian, however, the allegoric figure takes on certain aspects of a secular type and the two otherwise disparate modes begin to coalesce. What a reader may see as Milton's types remain only types without the allegorization that someone like Giovanni Pico della Mirandola had applied to Bible characters and events in the *Heptaplus* (1489). The realm of allegory may involve some of these same *interpreted* types and events, but in *Paradise*

Lost it does not coincide with that of the interpreted typology. The function of Uriel as narrative element and as one who is pure yet incapable of discerning hypocrisy is neither typological nor allegoric: he is included to direct Satan and then warn Gabriel of Satan's escape from hell and entry into Eden, and to make the significant point that hypocrisy may at first be unrecognized. While Abdiel becomes a part of the narration, his *function* is not as a narrative element but as an allegoric element in the panorama of the poem.

Milton perceived the paradox in the story of the rebellion of Satan and its ensuing effects. God the Father's great prescience foresaw that he had to provide the Son as one who would, in his Incarnation, demonstrate the means to true love (obedience and faith with their rewards, salvation) for humankind, since humankind would fall through the deceit of Satan. Humankind had to be created to replenish Heaven after the expulsion of the rebellious angels, who, led by Satan, revolted against the begetting of the Son, misunderstanding his Godhead and believing that a revision in hierarchy had been created. The Providence that is Eve's and Adam's guide as they leave Paradise is allegorically that Spirit of God which would be incarnated through the Son's sacrifice years hence.[13] The foreseen revolt of Satan is paradoxically caused by the begetting of the Son, who is begotten because of his future role as Redeemer of those created to replace the apostates. The ascent of the Son in the Paternal Chariot on the third day of the War in Heaven is an analogy to the ascent of the incarnated Son Jesus on the third day of what should be the end of the War on Earth, defeating Satan and Sin and Death. The dialogue in Heaven in Book III reviews the foreseen divine and human action after the expulsion of the apostates from Heaven, with that aspect of God, the Son, manipulating a different aspect of God, the Father,[14] announcing the graciousness of the Son as Redeemer, though it is only the Father, we know, who has omniscience and foresees the Crucifixion, unnamed here but in each reader's consciousness. The War in Heaven and the War on Earth look forward eschatologically to that time when God will again be all in all (1 Corinthians xv:28), the *creatio ex Deo* being reversed and the army of Michael being reduced "Under thir Head imbodied all in one." (Michael, like the Greek Hermes, was conductor of the dead to the afterlife, and "reduced" puns on the etymology "to lead back" and the physical reduction of beings into a composite whole, the saved becoming the body to the head, who is God.)

The "continued metaphor" is overwhelming in its completeness and thoroughness and expansiveness. But what this story and its paradox make clear is that God the Father foreknew that Satan would rebel under some circumstances, a thought that verges on Manichaeism and God as the creator of sin. It is a problem that Carl Jung wrestled with often and especially in *Answer to Job*.

The biblical typology that is referred to in the poem by the narrator in various places does not exist until after the protevangelium (though such referents be cited prior to this point in the poem) and the expulsion from Eden, and that which is offered for Adam's education, good types leading up to the antitype and bad types, appears only in the post-Edenic world of Books XI and XII. The examples offered to Adam by Raphael—good, Abdiel; bad, Satan—are not couched in typological language, nor would Adam understand a "system" of types at this time. The types of Books XI and XII in no respect show allegoric substance: they are "real" figures from the Bible who act in certain ways. One can derive lessons from the recounting of their stories but there is no concretizing of an idea or quality.

If we can separate in our thinking the allegorical and the typological, we can consider the matter of didacticism. Typology involves prefiguration and sets up a view of matters in parallel. When the antitype is viewed by the observer (or reader) as an ideal to be emulated, implying that failings of the types that have not reached that ideal should be shunned, typological thinking has picked up a didactic dimension. But in itself it is not didactic, nor does it present allegory with a concretization of idea through a personification which represents an abstract quality. In a literary work we can learn to follow or not to follow an ideal or its incomplete parallel if authorial expectation (the didactic) has been injected or is read as being present. Such authorial expectation would occur when typology is *used* (as in a literary work), not when only analysis of its existence is offered as a way of looking at something (as in the Bible; for example, Elijah as a type of the Christ offers no didactic concept).[15] But allegory has as a main thrust a learning process particularly in moral or ethical realms. The authorial presence in allegory is all-important but what seems to be the intent of that presence is crucial to the degree of didacticism that may be attached to the allegory. Such intent may range from mere observation to inculcation of an attitude or an action. Thus, differences of critical opinion are manifest in viewing a piece of literature according to the critic's reading of an author's presence and intent and that critic's acceptance of the didactic. Perhaps an eclectic reading of a work of literature on different levels is best: as intrinsic work, as work capable of offering something to be learned by different readers at different times, as a work that may be doctrinaire. Critical evaluation will rest not only on how and how well the work of literature presents the intrinsic work and the lesson (or lessons), but also on the critic's appreciation of a work that may be more than just mimetic and the acknowledgment that an authorial presence exists in a work even after it has left the author's hand.[16] Allegory presents a world that *is*, but it looks toward a world that should be (through the didactic).

Didacticism requires an authorial intent, which, as I have said, may range from mere observation to inculcation of an attitude or an action. That didacticism may be presented through concretized ideas embodied in a figure, a personification, or an abstract quality, thus making allegory the vehicle for a moral or ethical lesson. The didactic raises both the lesson to be learned and those aspects of the context to be rejected. When the didactic stresses a moral precept to be followed, it is affirmative and constructive; but it implies the obverse of the precept or its constituencies which is to be shunned, though becoming negative and destructive. Yet even when the didactic stresses the negative, it implies the constructive. The "meaning" therefore, in its fragmentary form when the text stresses *a* lesson, does not necessarily equate the intent of the author, whose intent may lie in the obverse and/or in the fully developed set of lessons to be learned.[17]

Allegory, thus, is "attenuated semiosis" with the authorial manipulation intending to instruct, whether simply as "naive" or "surface" allegory or as a sustained and constantly developing lesson—a lesson which may hold negative as well as positive advice. What Milton does in *Paradise Lost* is employ typology, naive allegory with its didactic dimension, and sustained allegory with its didactic dimensions: recognizing them and their distinctions therein is the burden of this essay.[18] For the Restoration and eighteenth century, the lack of distinction led to rejection of some of the allegoric substance of the epic and to nonrecognition of other allegoric narratives, with accompanying misreadings.

My own way of looking at the didacticism in the epic is as follows. The first half of the poem leads up to Raphael's advice:

> let it profit thee t' have heard
> By terrible Example the reward

Of disobedience; firm they might have stood,
Yet fell; remember, and fear to transgress.
(*PL* VI: 909–12)

But advice is meaningless, it seems, without experience, and the thrust of the first half is nullified by the second half. Adam and Eve (apparently informed of the gist of Raphael's narration) have not internalized this advice and have not remembered the "terrible Example" when they are in a position to stand or fall. The allegoric and didactic, engaged here in the negative, are also present in positive ways, though few critics have seen the positive allegory (for example, in Abdiel). The second half leads up to the antitype, providing an exemplar, and types of the exemplary action precede, as when Eve and Adam "in lowliest plight repentant" stand "praying" (the ending of Book X and beginning of Book XI). But exemplars have limitations in creating followers, as the negative types of Books XI and XII manifest. Milton came to realize by a question put to him by his friend Thomas Ellwood that exemplary action and actors are not always recognized, let alone imitated. And so *Paradise Regain'd* with its mimetic presentation of the "one greater Man."

The two different approaches of didacticism in *Paradise Lost*, advice and imitation, should but do not create reflexive action ("Thou" and "I" are always distinct); needed is first "reflective" understanding (in which "Thou" and "I" can be seen as interrelated) and then "refractive" action (in which the "I" has achieved an independence emulating the "Thou"). *Paradise Lost*, seeking the origins of humankind's actions, analyzes didacticism and allegorizes both reflexive and reflective action; *Paradise Regain'd*, a result of Milton's recognition of the failure of the didactic and allegoric where people are involved, presents the means to refractive action. Only by a superimposition on the part of the reader of an allegorical mode on such episodes as the banquet in Book II or of didactic interpretation of the rejection of earthly glory does the brief epic move into the realm of allegory. Authorial intention here is to eschew deliberate allegory and to manifest didacticism only through mimesis. While Satan concretizes concepts of evil and thus of adversarial action to Jesus's selfhood, he does not represent a naive allegory of personification but rather a generalized metaphor of evil and adversarial action. The received text of *Paradise Regain'd*, produced in the Restoration, has turned its back on allegory, showing no signs of the morality play as *Paradise Lost* does in retentions of Milton's first thoughts on the latter work as recorded in the Trinity MS. This view of the brief epic may supply a basic reason for the lack of attention paid it by most critics in the eighteenth century (who would say, in effect, we know the message since it is about "Christ," the exemplar) and a powerful reason why it was so admired and influential in the Romantic age.

II

For the eighteenth century, as well as our own times, the allegory of *Paradise Lost* is the treatment of Sin and Death, especially in Book II, though, of course, the bridge which they build and traverse to Earth in Book X is also significant in discussions. The concretizations of the idea of Sin and of Death, abstract concepts though their effects are graphic enough, were the kind of figures the age had come to recognize as allegoric and had come to expect allegory to provide. Little else seems to be considered allegorical in the poem.[19] The first part of John Hughes's definition makes clear the delimited understanding of the allegorical: "An Allegory is a Fable or Story, in which, under imaginary Persons or Things, is shadow'd some real Action or instructive Moral...it is that *in which one thing is related, and another thing is understood.*"[20] Only these two characters fit the requirement, for all other personages in the poem have the "reality" of the Bible or religious belief. God is God, the Son is the Son, there is a Satan, there were Adam and Eve, there are angels, and so forth. Now, Milton believed this too, but just as in "Lycidas" where the mythic constructs and employment of classical materials which so offended Samuel Johnson are the substance of the interiorization of doubts and their defeat, Milton believed in the monomyth as truth: the Christ and St. Peter did walk upon the waters and so too may Lycidas and the uncouth swain. The metaphor of the poem is sustained throughout it: it is allegoric in that one thing is related and another is understood, though not for Milton a "fable," if what is meant is untruth; its persons and things are both "imaginary" (like Hippotades) and not imaginary (like the Pilot of the Galilean lake), yet they stand for something more than themselves in the world of the poem; and the possibility of real action in the future and the instructive moral are implicit in the "fresh woods, and pastures new." Milton's manner of intertwining the classical and the modern, the real (whether old Damoetas or the grim wolf) and the fabulous (like Arethuse or Mincius or Camus), or the direct

Allegory, Typology, and Didacticism 53

lesson (such as Fame's being "that last infirmity of noble mind") or indirect (that involving the "fatall and perfidious bark/Built in th' eclipse"), is not very different in *Paradise Lost*. What has withheld recognizing this in the epic is the religious belief of the critic; what has withheld it is the shock, and thus avoidance, of the thought that Milton could believe in God and yet employ the figure of God as a character with metaphoric dimensions. These "real" personages and what happened in the basic biblical account of the Fall (Genesis) and the revolt in Heaven (Revelation) cannot have allegoric meaning.

Not understanding the point of the preceding paragraph, some early commentators condemned Milton's epic for just this confounding of truth and fable, Charles Leslie, for example, in 1698:

> This was one reason why I have endeavoured to give a more serious representation of that War in Heaven, and I hope I may say much better founded than *Milton*'s groundless supposition, who, in the fifth Book of his *Paradise Lost* makes the cause of the revolt of *Lucifer* and his Angels to have been, that God upon a certain day in Heaven, before the creation of this lower World, did summon all the Angels to attend, and then declar'd his Son to be their Lord and King...The folly of this contrivance appears many ways...But if Mr. *Milton* had made the cause of their discontent to have been the Incarnation of *Christ*, then, at that time, reveal'd to the Angels; and their contesting in such manner as hereafter told for the dignity of the angelical above that of the human Nature, his contexture had been nearer to the truth, and might have been much more poetical, in the severe and just measure of Poetry, which ought not to exceed the bounds of probability, not to expatiate into effeminate romance, but to express Truth in an exalted and manly improvement of thought.[21]

The inclusion of the Sin and Death episode was for Hughes two decades later also "romantic" since it appears in a poem with a moral stance; indeed, allegory should exist "without the Bounds of Probability or Nature." The first fundamental and unpardonable flaw in the poem for John Clarke in 1731 was:

> The Poem is founded upon a very absurd Supposition, that has not the least Appearance of Probability; but on the contrary, seems utterly impossible, *viz.* The Rebellion of Angels against God, with a Design to dethrone him; a Design that could never enter into the Thoughts of any created Being, especially of exalted Knowledge, as the Fallen Angels are every where represented by the Poet.

If we combine this statement with Hughes's, we can conclude that the rebellion is allegoric since not probable and indeed absurd (fabulous). Clarke's fourth defect is even more to the point:

> The Introducing of God, and the Son of God, as Actors in his Poem, and delivering themselves in long Speeches, is, in my Mind, an unpardonable Boldness. A Poet may contrive Scenes of Action, and find Speeches for his Fellow-Mortals of the highest Degree, because if he trips in his Judgment, and does not well suit their Characters, no Harm is done. But shall a Man, a poor short-sighted Creature, dare to bring down the most High into a Scene of Diversion, and assign him his Part of Acting and Speaking, as if he was a proper Judge of what is fit for him to do, and to say, upon any Occasion, wherein, to serve the Ends of his own Vanity, or Amusement, he has a Fancy to introduce Him, Him whose Judgments are a great Deep, and whose Ways are past finding out.[22]

Soon after this a controversy emerged in the *Gentleman's Magazine* over Milton's "Arianism," a charge leveled on the basis of this last "defect."[23] "Theophilus" argued that "he has certainly adopted the *Arian* Principle into his *Paradise Lost.* This suiting his Religion to the Occasion of Entertainment, has made me often think, that he as little believed the Religion of his Country, as *Homer* and *Virgil* did that of theirs." In rebuttal "Philo-Spec." declared that Milton "had not only a very few Circumstances upon which to raise his Poem, but was also obliged to proceed with the greatest Caution in every thing that he added out of his own Invention. And indeed notwithstanding all the Restraints he was under, he has filled his Story with so many surprizing Incidents, which bear so close an Analogy with what is delivered in holy Writ; that it is capable of pleasing the most delicate Reader, without giving offence to the most scrupulous." But he continues,

"If *Milton*'s Majesty forsakes him any where, it is in those parts of his Poem, where the Divine Persons are introduced as Speakers," though he approves the representation in Book III of "all the abstruse Doctrines of Predestination, Free-will and Grace, as also the great Points of Incarnation and Redemption (which naturally grow up in a Poem, that treats of the Fall of Man)."[24]

We can thus comprehend the attitudes toward Milton's inclusion of the allegory of Sin and Death: it directly fit the expectation of what allegory is and it was out of place in a poem dealing with great truths. But we should also comprehend that continuing attitudes toward God blind readers to other allegories within the work. Joseph Addison was a major contributor to these attitudes, asserting that Milton "has brought into it two Actors of a shadowy and fictitious Nature, in the Persons of Sin and Death, by which Means he has wrought into the Body of his Fable a very beautiful and well-invented Allegory. But notwithstanding the Fineness of this Allegory may atone for it in some Measure; I cannot think that Persons of such a chimerical Existence are proper Actors in an Epic Poem; because there is not that Measure of Probability annexed to them, which is required in Writings of this Kind" (*Spectator*, No. 273, 12 January 1712). It was Voltaire, however, who received most opprobrium for his remarks of similar nature, because of outright condemnation of Milton the poet without the sufficient amelioration of the allegory's sublimity to excuse it:

> The Fiction of *Death* and *Sin* seems to have in it some great Beauties and many gross Defects...We must first lay down that such shadowy Beings, as *Death*, *Sin*, *Chaos*, are intolerable, when they are not allegorical. For Fiction is nothing but Truth in Disguise. It must be granted too, that an Allegory must be short, decent, and noble. For an Allegory carried too far or too low, is like a beautiful Woman who wears always a Mask. An Allegory is a long Metaphor; and to speak too long in Metaphor's must be tiresome, because unnatural. This being premis'd, I must say that in general those Fictions, those imaginary Beings, are more agreeable to the Nature of *Milton*'s Poem, than to any other; because he hath but two natural Persons for his Actors; I mean *Adam* and *Eve*. A great Part of the Action lies in imaginary Worlds, and must *of course* admit of imaginary Beings.

He finds Sin's generation "a beautiful Allegory of Pride," but he disapproves of the invention of Satan and of Sin's sex; the whole episode is intolerable because of "its Foulness." "But what is more intolerable, there are Parts in that Fiction, which bearing no Allegory at all, have no Manner of Excuse. There is no Meaning in the Communication between Death and Sin, 'tis distasteful without any Purpose; or if any Allegory lies under it, the filthy Abomination of the Thing is certainly more obvious than the Allegory." Further, Satan and Death's quarrel, the section involving Chaos, Night and Discord, and the Bridge all seem without purpose, or too common.[25] Voltaire proceeds from limited views of allegory, from religious precepts, and from moral indignations. Knapp summarizes the three major objections to Sin and Death for the century: "they are too 'romantic,' too 'improbable,' and, as shadowy, artificial persons, too active to be admitted to the properly historical genre of the epic" (64).[26]

Of allegory Thomas Parnell wrote:

> This way of Writing is not only very engaging to the Fancy whenever it is well perform'd, but it has been thought also one of the first that the *Poets* made use of. Hence arose many of those Stories concerning the *Heathen Gods*, which at first were invented to insinuate Truth and Morality more pleasingly, and which afterwards made *Poetry* it self more solemn, when they happen'd to be receiv'd into the *Heathen Divinity*.[27]

Its aim is instruction ([vi]), or as Hughes delineated it, "It is a kind of Poetical Picture, or Hieroglyphick, which by its apt Resemblance conveys Instruction to the Mind by an Analogy to the Senses; and so amuses the Fancy, whilst it informs the Understanding. Every Allegory has therefore two Senses, the Literal and the Mystical; the literal Sense is like a Dream or Vision, of which the mystical Sense is the true Meaning or Interpretation" (xxi–xxii). The "Moral contained in" Sin and Death results from metaphor extended to simile which is extended to allegory ("an Assemblage of Similitudes drawn out at full length") (xxii). There are two kinds of allegory[28] that of Sin and Death being of the second type: "Story is fram'd of real or historical Persons, and probable or possible Actions; by which however some other Persons and Actions are typify'd or represented" and "that in which the Fable or Story consists for the most part of fictitious Persons or Beings, Creatures of the Poet's

Brain, and Actions surprising, and without the Bounds of Probability or Nature." The first is sufficient without a moral and instruction; the second is not. Therefore in the second type "Virtues and Vices, acting divine, human, infernal" are used in fictions for their moral sense, yet such as these "are to be excluded from the Action in Epick Poems" (xxxi). Another problem has reared its head for the eighteenth-century critic: while the allegory of Sin and Death is built on "an Assemblage of Similitudes drawn out at full length" and while it is morally instructive and has moved beyond "the Bounds of Probability," it appears in an epic and that creates a mixed genre. "Tho the Epick Poets...have sprinkled some Allegories thro their Poems, yet it wou'd be absurd to endeavour to understand them every where in a mystical Sense" (xxxvi). Under these restrictions one can appreciate (though not agree with) Johnson's dislike of this allegory because it comprises neither human actions nor human manners as an epic is supposed to and we can understand his distinction between the allegoric actor and allegoric action. "The employment of allegorical persons," he confesses, "always excites conviction of its own absurdity; they may produce effects, but cannot conduct actions; when the phantom is put in motion, it dissolves" (187). Sin and Death and that allegoric Bridge never dissolve.

Sin and Death present an allegory, therefore, conforming to Duff's and Hughes's second type. It was consistently looked upon as sublime, by Edmund Burke for example, and by Thomas Green, who concluded, "The scene betwixt Satan, Sin, and Death, in the 2d. Book, is transcendantly sublime: the Allegory, to which Addison objects, is lost amidst such force and vividness and majesty of description, as, I think with Atterbury, renders the grandest passages in Homer and Virgil comparatively feeble and dwarfish."[29] The objection, as we have noted, was its inclusion in an epic poem, just as "romantic" matter was to be rejected from it. Richard Hurd addressed the problem without coming down explicitly on either side of the argument: Milton relinquished "his long-projected design of Prince Arthur, at last, for that of the *Paradise Lost*; where, instead of Giants and Magicians, he had Angels and Devils to supply him with the *marvellous*, with great probability. Yet, tho' he dropped the tales, he still kept to the allegories of Spenser. And even this liberty was thought too much, as appears from the censure passed on his *Sin and Death* by the severer critics."[30] To be noted is the probability that Angels and Devils allow.

The overall analysis of these eighteenth-century critical positions we have been citing indicates the taxonomy that is repeatedly sought, an absolutism of categorization on the basis of that taxonomy, and the apparently unrealized assumptions dictating the schema and the placement. Defining epic as dealing with the probable disallows anything "romantic" or "allegoric"; defining "allegory" as fabulous disallows an allegoric agent, since an agent would exhibit mimetic action; and assuming angels and devils and divine personages and the "two natural Persons" as not "imaginary" (they are thus "agents") no place in the schema of allegory is possible for these characters or their actions. Judgment levelled against a literary work depended in the eighteenth-century upon its agreement or disagreement with such taxonomies. But such an attitude at the same time can lead to misreading (both by commission and by omission). The literary work commented upon and judged in such a situation is the reader's literary work, not necessarily the literary work written by the author. We might say the presence of the author has been dismissed from the work, becoming a strange forerunner of some twentieth-century literary theory. It is also, therefore, clear why allegory has had such a negative treatment in recent years, for it demands an authorial intent (or didacticism) be acknowledged.

Two recent excellent treatments of the allegory of Sin and Death are nonetheless delimited by their confinement to what is supposedly the rare uses of allegory in *Paradise Lost*, to iterate Murrin's words and to recall Ferry's influential remark. What we should unfortunately constantly do in working out our own critical readings is to reexamine anew all the material we may be dealing with, not simply employ someone else's critical stance as if it were absolute. (One might mention as other critical failings resultant from assumption of critical clichés the frequent reading of Shelley as effusive "romantic" rather than controlled author, or of Shaw as always doctrinaire.) Kenneth J. Knoespel shows that Eve's creation account "transforms the fable [of Narcissus] from a narrative about love to a narrative about understanding"[31] and is thus "warning" rather than "deception." Milton's "dramatizing Satan's intellective pride...psychologizes self-love and prepares for the psychological setting of Eve's creation scene" (80). One concurs with the conclusion that "Through the allegorical account of Sin's conception, Milton expands the meaning of Narcissus to include the deceptive nature of thought itself" (83). But a further sentence indicates a basic acceptance that Eve and Satan are indeed "real" people in the poem and partially denies allegoresis: "By assuming that all fable recounts the action of actual figures, euhemerism not only provides an alternative to allegorical criticism but urges the psychological amplification of ancient fable" (96). I do not deny that euhemerism may exist in the poem or that it helps explain the speaking and action of the divine persons that people like Clarke objected to. But at the same time the conception of Sin *is* presented allegorically and the experience of Eve has the didactic purpose (though unheeded, unrecognized) of indicating what could happen should excessive pride prevail. The voice (God) does give her identity and purpose (IV: 467–75), but like Duff's first kind of allegory the "warning" "attempts to instruct by the invention of a series of incidents strictly probable."

Knoespel referred to Echo as a "symbol of God's spirit" and the warning voice as a "symbolic manifestation of the Echo motif" (97–98, n11). Regina Schwartz also stresses repetition but specifically in those episodes involving Satan, Sin and Death.[32] Milton risks the kind of negative criticism he received in the eighteenth century "because only in allegory could the fundamental logic of compulsive repetition be fully addressed. Allegorical characters are projections of the self, and Satan's incestuous self-reproduction graphically illustrates that the issue of such repetition is not a new creation, but Death" (99). Further agreement with Knoespel's analysis is recognized by her very significant comment that "Doubling is the spatial form of temporal repetition, and its source, according to both Freud and Otto Rank, is narcissism" (99).[33] Narcissism leads to Death as allegorically shown in the Satan/Sin/-Death story, but, I would point out, also in the account of Eve, should she not heed the warning voice, as she does not when the issue arises. In the first stage of the Fall, as "she pluck'd, she eat" "Earth felt the wound, and Nature from her seat...gave signs of woe,/That all was lost" (IX: 781–784). The wound has prepared the way for death (to pursue the analogy) if it is not treated in such a way as to lead to recovery, and the woes possible have been "signed." In the second stage of the Fall, Adam in his own display of narcissism, "Flesh of Flesh,/Bone of my Bone" (IX: 914–915), scruples "not to eat/Against his better knowledge, not deceav'd" (IX: 997–098). "Earth trembl'd from her entrails...and Nature gave a second groan" and the "mortal Sin/Original" is completed. It is Adam, of course, who is undeceivedly disobedient, not Eve who is disobedient through fraud; their "mortal tast/[has] Brought Death into the World, and all our woe" (I: 2–3). And thus we can understand that in Book IX repetition and echo have occurred, a similar kind of narcissism and a similar kind of allegory where "real" representations depicting potential virtues and vices have been used for their moral sense. There is a doubling of Adam in his view of Eve, and there is an exercise of free will similar to Satan's and dissimilar to Abdiel's. The birth of sin is accompanied by the groans of Nature; the pair engorge the false Fruit and vent their lust, allowing death (IX: 993, 1167, and thus enclosing this episode) to come into being. Through the birth of Sin and Death, the parallel equates Adam *and* Eve in their acts with Satan.

The correspondence between Eve and Satan, and between Adam and Satan, and the potential one between Eve and Adam and us describes an allegory which "attempts to instruct by the invention of a series of incidents strictly probable," one which "is fram'd of real or historical Persons, and probable or possible Actions: by which however some other Persons and Actions are typify'd or represented," one in which Truth and Morality are more pleasingly insinuated. The allegory, like some of those in *The Faerie Queene*, presents what may be seen as a mimetic action, expanding upon the minimalization of the biblical account, and at the same time what may be understood to represent a potential narrative of humankind. "Sin" as representation of sinfulness and "Satan" as representation of adversarial being to God and what God is certainly function in commonplace allegoric terms. "Eve" as representation of the gullible who sin through deceit, "Adam" as representation of wilful sinners do not function differently. The allegoric message that perspective yields is that the way into sin and hence death (of the soul) is through deceit and through will; and significant is the preparation that deceit affords for the wrong exercising of will. The implied constructive precept underscores wariness and right reason as the means to stand against the assaults of the adversary to God.[34]

The objection to this paragraph (both in the eighteenth century and today) is that Eve and Adam were real people and their experience was a non-fictional event, for the Bible has so recorded it, and the aim is not analogy by which the reader will say, "there but by the grace of God go I." It is an account of the real occurrence of the past by which life as we have known it came into being, an example of what did happen, although as a typology it may provide a lesson. The critical difficulty is whether or not we accept Murrin's belief that Milton was cut off from the language of analogy (its "tradition" cannot possibly be conceived as

Allegory, Typology, and Didacticism 61

limiting Milton) and whether he truly was only literal in reading scripture (that is, beyond *De doctrina christiana*, which supplies Murrin's evidence for his statement). Frequently Milton in this poem about the origins of things presents metaphoric statements to lead readers to understand and to order their lives, a lesson though perhaps not didactic. How scripturally literal is the Creation in Book VII? It is interpretation of what appears in Genesis, and the thrust of *De doctrina christiana* is the interpretation of the Bible necessary to guide humankind. Is not, however, the metaphoric statement in the echo of the "Darkness profound" which covers the Abyss and the "brooding wings" of "the Spirit of God outspred" "on the watrie calm" (VII: 233–35, and see I: 19–22), derived from the moving of God upon the waters in Genesis i: 2, present because it offers a lesson? Is it not a "dark conceit," for surely it is not mimetic (particularly when we remember the original Aramaic and acknowledge the sexual content of Milton's metaphors)? Is not Milton presenting (perhaps in nontraditional language of analogy but nonetheless in analogy) the creative act by which humankind may become dove-like creatures, creatures like the Holy Spirit, the "white" coming from the "dark," the goodness coming from whatever may appear not good?—a creative act of internalization, generating the dove-like self.

Eve's narcissism has got out of control through the deceit of Satan playing upon "The Organs of her Fancie," just before she partakes of the fruit: "Fairest resemblance of thy Maker fair...[unseen] one man except...who should'st be seen/A goddess among Gods, ador'd and serv'd/By Angels numberless"; "Empress of this fair World, resplendent *Eve*...no Fair to thine/Equivalent or second...[I] worship thee of right declar'd/Sovran of Creatures, universal Dame." The word *gaze* appears in this section five times within eighty-eight lines (from IX: 524, to IX: 611), each with Eve or the Tree as object.[35] Its echoing occurs as Satan ends "his words replete with guile" and "Fixt on the Fruit she gaz'd" (IX: 733, 735). Immediately she debates with herself, reacting to "his perswasive words, impregn'd/With Reason," concluding nothing hinders to reach. "So saying, her rash hand in evil hour/Forth reaching to the Fruit, she pluck'd, she eat" (IX: 780–81). The "Smooth Lake" that she sees in Book IV seems another sky, she bends to look, the shape bends in answering looks, and "There I had fixt/Mine eyes." Correspondences in extended contexts and in words (though not yet *gaze*) link the scenes. She draws back from the lake rather than extend her hand; she hesitates and then reaches forth as the temptation proceeds. Had the warning voice not intervened, she would have "fixt" her "eyes till now, and pin'd with vain desire"; but in that place "where no shadow staies" (directing the reader to the metaphor of God as Sun, directly shining forth and dispelling all darkness) she will receive an identity. Yet the self that is potential in the fixing of eyes and pining in desire (a self that all humankind—men, not only women—have) has only been made latent. In the temptation scene the latency is dissolved by the transference of satanic gaze and satanic desire, and the potential self is actualized. Negative narcissism has triumphed. With Adam negative narcissism leads to transference of self to the Other: "to loose thee were to loose my self" (IX: 959).[36]

The analogy with the Christ, who loses his divine self for humankind, is made explicit as Eve rhapsodizes: "O glorious trial of exceeding Love,/Illustrious evidence, example high!" (IX: 961–62). The parodying of the angelic chorus's hymn to the Son's offer to redeem the fallen, "O unexampl'd love,/Love no where to be found less then Divine!" (III: 410–411), as well as the human view of the antitype, "O goodness infinite, goodness immense!...Taught this by his example whom I now/Acknowledge my Redeemer ever blest" (XII: 572–73),[37] lays bare the allegoric nature of these interrelated sections of the epic. Eve does not offer Adam as a type of the Christ but as what (*we* recognize) would become under positive circumstances the antitype. We understand that the Christ becomes the Second Adam; but as Dennis Danielson has lamented, it is too bad for the world that the First Adam was not the First Christ.[38] Milton's dramatic presentation sets up the possibility, and faith in God should have allowed some "miraculous" way out of the dilemma.[39] But Adam puts self, a narcissistic self, first and does not maintain faith. Of course, scripture could not be overturned on this issue but recognition that *within the poem* the possibility exists tells us why *Paradise Lost* is not simply a greatly amplified version of Genesis and Revelation along with other parts of the Bible. This kind of recognition is the key to the "continued Allegory" and the somewhat hidden extended metaphor.

III

If then we accept allegory to be of two types, one is demonstrated by the personifications of "imaginary" beings like Sin and Death, as well as Chaos and Old Night, who do act as agents, despite restrictions against agency in the Restoration and eighteenth century.

Allegory, Typology, and Didacticism 63

They encompass a lesson for the reader to draw which is "clear and intelligible," "consistent with itself," "lively, and surprising," apt "in the Fable to the Subject on which it is employed" (Hughes, xxxiv–xxvi). In the allegoric understanding of things supplied by Chaos, we recognize an obverse to God and what he is and what he connotes. "*Chaos* Umpire sits" (II: 907) contrasts with God's guide for humankind, "My Umpire *Conscience*" (III: 195); his "decision more imbroils the fray/By which he Reigns" (II: 908–89), in contrast with the Son's decision so that the redeemed may return to God the Father

> to see thy face, wherein no cloud
> Of anger shall remain, but peace assur'd,
> And reconcilement; wrauth shall be no more
> Thenceforth, but in thy presence Joy entire.
> (III: 262–65)

In the imaginary persons are shadowed real action and instructive morals concerning the workings of the not-good, of the dark, and of the not creative. Next to Chaos "high Arbiter/*Chance* governs all"; God, of course, orders things through Providence. Satan promises Chaos to "reduce" "that Region lost...To her original darkness and your sway" (II: 982–84), and Milton plays on what was, but for the reader what will be, Michael's action at the end of the War in Heaven (which we have already noted). God has created (in Book VII) and Satan as apposite will "uncreate," turn all things back to their original confusions. Milton again has supplied a concept that will echo for the astute reader as Adam in his last words before his fall says,

> Nor can I think that God, Creator wise,
> Though threatning, will in earnest so destroy
> Us his prime Creatures, dignifi'd so high,
> Set over all his Works, which in our Fall,
> For us created, needs with us must fail,
> Dependent made; so God shall uncreate,
> Be frustrate, do, undo, and labour loose.
> (IX: 938–44)

The personifications of Chaos, Old Night, Chance, have been invented to insinuate Truth and Morality more pleasingly; the moral is contained in the metaphor extended to simile extended to allegory ("an Assemblage of Similitudes drawn out at full length"); the "Virtues and Vices, acting divine, human, infernal" have been used in fictions for their moral sense.   Clearly the relationship of God the Father and God the Son to this allegoric fiction places them in some other position than simply "real" because they exist. God and his actions (and he surely is an agent) take on meanings beyond their "reality." While God is not allegorical, he encompasses that which may be presented and viewed allegorically, and with particular significance he is the paradigm against which the allegories operate. Duff's first type of allegory can be recognized as well as Hughes's. For the believer in God the story is framed of real or historical persons, and probable or possible actions, and the correspondence for humankind lies in their emulating what God connotes and what God does: will humankind create or uncreate? be guided by Providence or Chance? exhibit charity or more embroil the fray (whether directly against God like Satan in the War in Heaven or indirectly like Nimrod in the War on Earth)? is humankind aligned with Faith, and Vertue, Patience, Temperance, and Love or with Rumor and Chance and Tumult and Confusion and Discord?

The personification of Providence seems not to have been understood in the past. But Providence is a guide, not really differently conceived from Christian's Faithful or Hopeful, encouraging those of wandering steps and slow through the Valley of the Shadow of Death. The aim of *Paradise Lost* is to "assert Eternal Providence," meaning not only to express and affirm, but to join to oneself, as its etymology makes clear. Providence as Adam and Eve's guide is joined to them as they leave Paradise; the existence (and potential enjoinment) of Providence justifies God's ways toward men. Milton can only hope that his laying forth of what Providence is will justify to men God's ways. We have here that "in which one thing is related, and another thing is understood." The analogy of Satan's passage through Chaos and Adam and Eve's passage through the world upon their expulsion is firmly set forth in Satan's address to Chaos:

> I come...by constraint
> Wandring this darksome Desart, as my way
> Lies through your spacious Empire up to light,
> Alone, and without guide, half lost, I seek
> What readiest path leads where your gloomie bounds
> Confine with Heav'n.

Allegory, Typology, and Didacticism 65

(II: 970–77)

The allegory of guide, scene, and moral should be clear once we disallow that such "real" beings as Satan and Adam and Eve cannot be employed allegorically.

Earlier I argued for the allegoric status of Eve and Adam as representatives of humankind whose experiences figure forth the experiences of the world, offering lessons of wariness and exercise of free will conditioned by right reason. I have implied that the War in Heaven (which the eighteenth century very often alluded to positively for its sublime truths, but which has seemed to some in the twentieth century a comic interlude of tin soldiers) likewise is allegoric, representing, that is, the effects of negative narcissism, envy, pride, and demagoguery, and their confutation by positive narcissism (of the Father and Son), agape, fortitude, and obedience. The figure who persists through all these fictions is Satan, generally dismissed from discussions of the allegory of Sin and Death because of his "reality," diminished star that Lucifer had become. The play of creativity and uncreativity we have just looked at and the generational metaphors/similes/allegories of the narcissism and Falls of Eve and Adam and Satan constitute the most basic allegory of the poem, developing "attenuated semiosis," "a continued Allegory," "localized" elements that fit into a whole with its multiple ambiguities. The technique descends from Spenser's allegory in Book VI.

The Spirit that has been present from the first of time

>   with mighty wings outspread
> Dove-like satst brooding on the vast Abyss
> And mad'st it pregnant

is recalled when

>   Into this wild Abyss,
> The Womb of nature and perhaps her Grave,
> Of neither Sea, nor Shore, nor Air, nor Fire,
> But all these in thir pregnant causes mixt
> Confusedly...Into this wild Abyss the warie fiend
> Stood on the brink of Hell and look'd a while,
> Pondering his Voyage.
>   (II: 910–19)

The dialectic of positive generation and of nongeneration underscores Satan's function as apposite to God, adversary, yes, but even more an obverse of all that is God. In the unfallen world of Book IV (497–502) Adam

> in delight
> Both of her Beauty and submissive Charms
> Smil'd with superior Love, as *Jupiter*
> On *Juno* smiles, when he impregns the Clouds
> That shed *May* Flowers; and press'd her Matron lip
> With kisses pure.

but in the fallen world of Book IX "in Lust they burn," they "play," his sense is enflamed "With ardor to enjoy" her, her eye darts "contagious Fire" and she goes "nothing loth" to a "shadie bank," where "they thir fill of Love and Loves disport" become "wearied with thir amorous play" (1015–1045). In Book IV the possibility of impregnation and birth is within a context of heavenly realms; in Book IX there is non-generation, only lust and "play" (the word signifies sexual intercourse as in Exodus xxxii: 6, "and rose up to play") in shadow. Satan is not an "antitype" of all the evil personages or nonfaithful to God; he is rather an allegoric figure personifying evil and all its constituents, its ramifications; he is a generator only of "a formidable shape," "a Serpent arm'd/With mortal sting," and of a "shape...that shape had none," the two beasts of Revelation xiii: 18. These two shapes beget Hell Hounds whose kennel is their mother's womb. The allegoric implication leads us to see that all those who are children of Satan and who thence couple with Sin are like Hell Hounds that hide in their mother's womb, not like Flowers that grow out in the open where the Sun (Truth) and rain (Mercy, note the cloud image before suggesting not only rain but respite from constant heat) will generate other Flowers.

As allegoric figure Satan should not be advanced as hero of the poem, as Dryden, Batteux, Godwin, Shelley and Blake most notably have done. As allegoric figure he is example of the other type of allegory, "fram'd of real or historical Persons, and probable or possible Actions; by which however some other Persons and Actions are typify'd or represented." Leslie would not allow that the revolt in Heaven was possible; if it is not, then the fiction which Milton produced has meaning symbolically, allegorically. It stands for all kinds of rebellion against Godhead, and its causes lie in morally reprehensible traits of character and thoughts such as Satan exhibits. As allegoric figure, Satan cannot be the kind of epic hero meant by Dryden although his main point is that any kind of similar negative action against the Godhead is not heroic.[40] Satan can be epic hero for Shelley only in equation with Prometheus or a rebel against tyranny, but both readings make him allegoric, which Shelley did not intend. The idea that the Son is the hero of *Paradise Lost* offers religious belief, not literary analysis; and the idea that Adam and Eve (or humankind) constitute the hero can be dismissed on various counts, but at least because of their allegorical dimension. They are the protagonists (and Milton makes this single) just as Christian is.

The criticism of allegory and specifically of *Paradise Lost* in the eighteenth century and carried through the twentieth century has been conditioned by prescriptive taxonomies of "allegory," "agent," "epic poem," "hero" and the like; by a lack of recognition of the "real" characters as allegoric figures, as a result of religious convictions and concepts of sacrilegiousness; and by lack of understanding of medieval/Spenserian allegory which underlies *Paradise Lost* even while its author produced something "unattempted yet in Prose or Rime." Psychologically Milton has given us an analysis of Self and Other, a self with propensities toward good and with propensities toward evil; the projections of both selves can be seen in the allegoric figures of the poem—Satan, Abdiel, Adam, Eve. The Other involves both that which one is not but wishes to be and that which one is but may wish not to acknowledge. The allegories establish various fusions of Self and Other: that which brings forth Death; that which is "connubial Love," "wedded Love, mysterious Law, true sourse/Of human ofspring"; that which conquers the evil propensities; that which will bring forth both the good (Abel) and the evil (Cain), a generation without end.

NOTES

1. A recent collection of essays, *Allegoresis: The Craft of Allegory in Medieval Literature*, ed. J. Stephen Russell (New York: Garland, 1988), instructively reviews and extends concepts of medieval allegory and its literary examples. Russell remarks: "allegory was 'attenuated semiosis,' the authorial manipulation of signs that differ from other writing only in its being completely self-conscious and deliberate" (xii). The essays present "reflective" directions (where allegory manifests thought process, the signature of the writer) and "refractive" directions (where allegory and signifying are interdependent, the work itself limiting the signifying).

2. An indispensable study of allegory is Angus Fletcher's *Allegory: The Theory of a Symbolic Mode* (Ithaca: Cornell University Press, 1964), to which should be added Michael Murrin's *The Veil of Allegory: Some Notes Toward a Theory of Allegorical Rhetoric in the English Renaissance* (Chicago: University of Chicago Press, 1969), Maureen Quilligan's *The Language of Allegory: Defining the Genre* (Ithaca: Cornell University Press, 1979), Stephen A. Barney's *Allegories of History, Allegories of Love* (Hamden: Archon Books, 1979), and Steven Knapp's *Personification and the Sublime—Milton to Coleridge* (Cambridge: Harvard University Press, 1985).

3. The variation in name may be an error due to the compositor or copyist, but the singling out of only one pair as "hero," as example of friendship, without some modifying phrase strikes one as strange when there are a number of pairs.

4. In the prefatory letter of the first edition of Books I–III (1590), Spenser spoke of the poem as being "a continued Allegory, or darke conceit," by which he seems to stress the maintenance of allegory (with similarities among the allegories of the individual books) and a somewhat hidden extended metaphor. The tournament (like other episodes such as the return of Pastorella to her discovered parents, Bellamour and Claribell, in Book VI) presents a reduced allegoric sense and an increased romantic narrative. Comparison of such sections with *The Romance of the Rose* underscores the reduction of allegory in Spenser, despite the similar theme of courtly love.

5. Samuel Johnson, *The Lives of the Most Eminent English Poets* (London: 1781), "Alexander Pope," IV: 3–240; see 187.

6. William Duff, in *An Essay on Original Genius* (London: 1767), distinguishes two kinds of Allegory: one, "like the Epic fable, attempts to instruct by the invention of a series of incidents strictly probable" and one "in which there is very little regard shewn to probability. Its object also is instruction; though it does not endeavour to instruct by real or probable actions; but wrapt in a veil of exaggerated, yet delicate and apposite fiction, is studious at once to delight the imagination, and to impress some important maxim upon the mind" (173–74). In the latter category he places *The Faerie Queene*; its deceit "lasts no longer than the perusal," and "we never admit as true what is not strictly probable" (174–75). In the former category he places "the beautiful and striking ALLEGORIES contained in different parts of the Sacred Writings" (173). We shall return to this distinction later.

7. For a major and thorough study of typologies (for there are various kinds), see Paul J. Korshin, *Typologies in England 1650–1820* (Princeton: Princeton University Press, 1982), especially his discussion of Milton, 70–71, and *passim*. As he states, "Milton's

typology becomes more elaborate and difficult to interpret over the course of his entire career. But more central to the scope of this chapter is the way in which Milton's typology contributed to the continuity of this figural mode in the seventeenth and eighteenth centuries" (71).

8. See my study "Milton and Covenant: the Christian View of Old Testament Theology" in *Milton and Scriptural Tradition: The Bible into Poetry*, ed. James H. Sims and Leland Ryken (Columbia: University of Missouri Press, 1984), n43, 188–89. William Madsen's investigation of the topic errs, I believe, in numerous ways because of non-recognition of this turning point in the epic; see *From Shadowy Types to Truth* (New Haven: Yale University Press, 1968). It should be evident that typology is a system of thinking devised by human beings to order the materials of the two often conflicting testaments and thereby impose a divine rationale on biblical history. Of course, some fundamentalists will argue that the divine rationale was from the mind of God and was only discovered by humankind. In *Paradise Lost* Milton is trying to get to a rational statement of the origins of things, and thus we have the narrator valorizing the origin of the divine rationale of typology at the point when it begins with the protevangelium. Books XI and XII are a record of some of the positive and negative future types, continuing up to the existence of the antitype (XII: 465). This is followed by the rapturous significance of the antitype, the Christ (XII: 466–551), after which the epic rapidly moves to completion in the present time of the poetic narrative (XII: 552–649).

Quotations from *Paradise Lost* are from *The Complete English Poems of John Milton*, ed. John Shawcross (Garden City: Anchor, 1963).

9. See my *Paradise Regain'd: 'Worthy T' Have Not Remain'd So Long Unsung'* (Pittsburgh: Duquesne University Press, 1988), 83.

10. See Mary Ann Radzinowicz, *Milton's Epics and the Book of Psalms* (Princeton: Princeton University Press, 1989), 60–61, for discussion of the typologies within the Psalms that contribute to the Son's inference of messiahship, involving how one should live and who the Messiah is. As to allegory within the poem, a reader may look upon the temptations and their rejection as constituting a fable "in which one thing is related, and another thing is understood" (Hughes, see n20), and so I used the term of the brief epic in *Paradise Regain'd*, 66. But the word is misleading in its implications. Rather, the poem becomes a "parable by which Man learns how to remove himself from the secured existence of the paternal—primarily maternal—home in order to face and conquer the wilderness of life" (67).

11. The quotations come from Quilligan, 179, 119, 119, 179, 181, 182, and 181 respectively. Reference is to Anne Davidson Ferry, *Milton's Epic Voice: The Narrator in Paradise Lost* (Cambridge: Harvard University Press, 1963), 131. (Quilligan's quotation and reference are not quite exact. Her belief that punning exists only after the Fall and only in connection with Satan is simply wrong; see later for one example.) For a full study of the alteration of language in the poem see Kathleen M. Swaim's *Before and After the Fall: Contrasting Modes in Paradise Lost* (Amherst: University of Massachusetts Press, 1986).

12. The quotations come from Joseph H. Summers's *The Muse's Method: An Introduction to Paradise Lost* (London: Chatto and Windus, 1962), 112.

13. Joseph Priestley quotes from a sermon by Dr. Tooke Horne in his *Defences of Unitarianism, For the Year 1786* (Birmingham, 1787), Letter IV, "It was the Holy Spirit

who came forth from the Father and the Son, through the preaching of the word, and the administration of the sacraments, by his enlightening, healing, and comforting grace, to apply to the hearts of men" (*Works*, XVIII: 341). The final lines should be read to harken back to the opening proem and the Spirit that "Dove-like satst brooding on the vast Abyss/And mad'st it pregnant." The metaphoric double meanings (paronomasia if not quite derogated punning) and the personifications of Providence and Spirit suggest at least an allegoric tinge: none of this is strictly probable but it is greeted as encompassing truth by the believer. Following the guide Providence will lead Adam and Eve and their progeny (humankind) to a place of rest (ultimately the Heavenly Seat), but wandering steps may not always follow their guide. *De doctrina christiana* talks of God's Providence broadly as "His Universal Government of Things," which "is either General or Special" (I: viii). Following chapters look at providence before and after the Fall, and in chapter xiv specifically at humankind's restoration through Jesus Christ. The Holy Spirit is "both of the Father and of the Son" (I: vi); "he is a minister of God...created, that is, produced, from the substance of God, not by natural necessity, but by the free will of the agent." See *Complete Prose Works of John Milton* (New Haven: Yale University Press, 1973), VI, ed. Maurice Kelley, "De doctrina christiana," trans. John Carey; 326 ff., 281, 298.

14. See Michael Lieb, *The Sinews of Ulysses: Form and Convention in Milton's Works* (Pittsburgh: Duquesne University Press, 1989), ch. 6, "The Dialogic Imagination," 76–97.

15. One way of thinking about James Joyce's *Finnegans Wake* is the typological, for parallels in different wide-diverging periods of history are set up for the reader to conceive all at once, in a single instant. The "message" establishes the similarities among people and events in history which repeat endlessly through time (including Viconian perspectives), but there is no allegory and no didacticism in that paralleling.

16. The rather obtuse Barthesian notion that the author is dead once the literary work is born points to the equally obtuse critical view that a piece of literature is important only in what we learn of the author's being, biographical or psychological, ignoring the intrinsic literary production. For further remarks on what I call authorial presence, see "The Poet in the Poem: John Milton's Presence in *Paradise Lost*," *The CEA Critic* 48/49 (1986): 32–55. The so-called "new historicism" falls between these two extremes, downplaying both the work as work and the author as writer, looking rather at the work as document in its contemporary world and the author as "political" being. The linkage of Marxian critical stances emphasizes what can be learned politically and socially about the past and the use of such knowledge in today's world. Milton's presence is therefore a sign of the political world of his poem and of the political theory or attitudes the poem sustains. For me, that is only one of Milton's presences within the epic, albeit an important presence.

17. A paper by Kevin L. Cope delivered at the 1989 convention of the American Society for Eighteenth-Century Studies, entitled, "A 'Roman Commonwealth' of Knowledge: Fragments of Belief and the Disbelieving Power of Didactic," later published under the same title in *Studies in Eighteenth-Century Culture* 20 (1990): 3-25, discusses these matters thoroughly, and I am indebted to his perceptions in this paragraph.

18. In a forthcoming book, "Allegorical Poetics and the Epic: The Renaissance Tradition and Paradise Lost," Mindele Treip argues persuasively for the central place

Allegory, Typology, and Didacticism 71

of allegory and allegorical artistry in *Paradise Lost*, and consequently for a more limited view of typological imagery than has been common in the reading of the epic.

19. Compare Michael Murrin's views in *The Allegoric Epic: Essays in Its Rise and Decline* (Chicago: University of Chicago Press, 1980), especially "The Language of Milton's Heaven," 153–71. Murrin begins this chapter by writing, "Milton did not allegorize the war of the angels in *Paradise Lost*, and this choice signals the end of a tradition" (153), although as I note below it can be seen as allegoric, not only when we combine Hughes's and Clarke's ideas (and compare Leslie's). Toward the end of his study, finding "allegory, a method rarely used in *Paradise Lost*," Murrin cites only "brief personification allegories with Sin and Death, the visit to Limbo, allegorical passages...confined to the world of fallen experience and...associated with Satan" (169). Milton was cut off from the traditional language of analogy, he maintains, and his scriptural literalism denied a system of correspondences. We should remark the difference of opinion about the Paradise of Fools (very frequently alluded to in eighteenth-century writings) between Voltaire (n25) and Murrin (and most others). An instructive reading of this allegory is that of Robert A. Kantra in *All Things Vain: Religious Satirists and Their Art* (University Park: Pennsylvania State University Press, 1984). We should also remark that the critics have ignored the Chaos and Old Night section, which is hardly a mimetic narrative and could not possibly have a typological reading.

20. John Hughes, *The Works of Spenser. In Six Volumes* (London, 1715), "An Essay on Allegorical Poetry. With Remarks on the Writings of Spenser," I: [xix]–xli (see xxi).

21. Charles Leslie, *The History of Sin and Heresy Attempted* (London, 1698), Preface, A2^v.

22. John Clarke, *An Essay Upon Study* (London, 1731), ch. 2, §2, 202–14.

23. I might note incidentally that the term "Arian" was associated with Milton earlier than 1824 when *De doctrina christiana* was rediscovered, on the basis of the interpretation of his remarks therein. Zacharias Conrad von Uffenbach wondered about the whereabouts of "ein Systema Theologie von Milton" that a bookseller had and that evidenced "Arianismus"; see *Merkwürdige Reisen durch niedersachsen Holland und Engelland. Dritter Theil* (Ulm, 1754), 585.

24. Letter, *Gentleman's Magazine* 8 (March 1738): 124–125; letter, 8 (April 1738): 201–202. A further letter, quoting one in the *Daily Gazetteer*, 7 August 1738, declares Theophilus' aim to be "to deter well-meaning People from reading a Poem wherein the Idolatry and Superstition of the *Heathens* and *Papists* are exposed with all possible Strength and Beauty, by brandishing the Author with the odious Mark of a *Heretick*"; see *GM* 8 (August 1738): 417.

25. Voltaire, *An Essay Upon the Civil Wars of France...And also Upon the Epick Poetry of the European Nations From Homer to Milton* (London: 1727), "Milton," 102–21 (*passim*). Voltaire finds the Paradise of Fools (which he does not recognize as allegorical) laughable, expressed only by "low, comical Imaginations, which belong by Right to *Ariosto*." The bugbear of "romance" has again entered to deflate Milton as it has so often Spenser.

26. The status of Sin and Death is reexamined by Philip J. Gallagher who concludes that they are "consistently real (i. e., physical and historical)...their allegorical onomastics notwithstanding." See "'Real or Allegoric': The Ontology of Sin and Death in *Paradise Lost*," *English Literary Renaissance* 6 (1976): 317–25. Knapp (135) has cogent objections to this position. What Gallagher presents, I think, is simply that they consistently represent what could basically be "real" actions and "real" psychology; but surely Sin's generation is not, the hell hounds gnawing at her womb are not, the building of the bridge to Earth is not. As I remarked before allegory may be built on narratives which provide semblances of a realistic action by persons who appear to be "real." But such signs mean more than just the signified, uniting the "real" and the allegoric. Gallagher was, of course, trying to confute certain objections to the figures in the poem, but like the objectors he moves to an either/or position, a position that has obscured the allegoric nature of the only "two natural Persons" in the poem, among other things.

27. *An Essay on the Different Styles of Poetry* (London: 1713), [iv]; reversed italics.

28. See Duff's remarks in n6. Charles Batteux similarly describes this symbolic mode: "Il y a deux sortes d'Allégorie: l'une qu'on peut appeller Morale, & l'autre Oratoire. La premiere, cache une vérité, une maxime: tels sont les Apologues: c'est un corps qui revêt une ame: L'autre est un masque qui couvre un corps; elle n'est point destinée à envelopper une maxime; mais seulement une chose qu'on ne veut montrer qu'à demi, ou au travers d'une gaze. Les Orateurs & les Poétes se servent de celle-ci quand ils veulent louer ou blâmer avec finesse. Ils changent les noms des choses, des lieux, les personnes, & laissent au Lecteur intelligent à lever l'enveloppe, & à s'instruire lui-même. La premiere espèce d'allégorie peut être mise en usage dans l'Epopée; mais elle est, comme nous l'avons dit, peu vraisemblable & peu conforme à la nature de l'esprit humain. La seconde espèce entre avec beaucoup de grace dans un Poëme; mais elle n'est point de son essence...Il en est de même de l'allégorie de plus, mais elle n'en fait point l'essentiel. L'epopée n'est essentiellement, que le récit d'une grande action & de ses causes" (*Les Beaux Arts reduits à un même principe* [Paris: 1746], 202–3, note).

29. Thomas Green, *Extracts from The Diary of a Lover of Literature* (Ipswich: 1810), under date of 2 February 1800, 192. See Edmund Burke, *A Philosophical Enquiry into the Origin of Our Ideas of the Sublime and Beautiful* (London, 1757), 48–49. Compare William Smith's "Notes and Observations," 87–88, in his translation of Longinus (*An Essay on the Sublime: Translated from the Greek of Dionysius Longinus; with Notes and Observations* [London: 1756]).

30. Richard Hurd, *Letters on Chivalry and Romance* (London: 1762), 118.

31. Kenneth J. Knoespel, "The Limits of Allegory: Textual Expansion of Narcissus in *Paradise Lost*," *Milton Studies* 22 (1986): 79–99.

32. Regina Schwartz, *Remembering and Repeating: Biblical Creation in Paradise Lost* (Cambridge: Cambridge University Press, 1988).

33. See Sigmund Freud, "The Uncanny," *The Standard Edition of the Complete Psychological Works of Sigmund Freud* (London: Hogarth Press, 1955), XVII: 219–52, and Otto Rank, *The Double: A Psychoanalytic Study*, trans. Harry Tucker, Jr. (Chapel Hill: University of North Carolina Press, 1971).

34. A misdirection that some feminist criticism of the poem and Milton has taken lies in the simplistic equating of Eve and Sin. The parallel, as Schwartz demonstrates, is between Eve and Satan, but further such criticism has not acknowledged the parallel between Adam and Satan and the male-oriented omission of recognizing that it is Adam who wilfully disobeys, not Eve, who disobeys only through fraud. It is Adam's act that "completes the mortal Sin Original." That word "mortal" puns on its being human and bringing death (*mors*), but it also contrasts with the nonhuman Sin Original of Satan, which brings forth Death. The analogy of Eve and Adam's actions and Satan's allegoric ones drives home the allegoric nature of Eve and Adam's actions. Eve and Sin do not equate; that both are female allows the sexual and generational content of the Falls and their aftermaths to be expressed. (In the background of influence is also St. Augustine's assignment of sexual intercourse as defining original sin.) The allegories in both Falls play upon the precept that disobedience begets disobedience and other negative concepts which in turn beget more, as well as the importance of the Other, not only Eve's view of the Other and Self, but Adam's and Satan's. God the Father begets the Son and they, the Holy Spirit; Satan, envious, "begets" Sin and they, Death; Adam miraculously "begets" Eve, and they, death The analogies are there even if they invoke Godhead metaphorically. (Compare remarks from Leslie and others cited before.)

35. The word is associated with Satan six other times, two most appropriately in the same way within Eve's dream: the "gentle voice" (and contrast the warning voice of the pool scene) reports the stars of heaven "with ravishment/Attracted by thy beauty still to gaze" (V: 46–47), and his gaze on the Forbidden Tree (V: 57). Four other uses of the word (IV: 351; V: 272; VIII: 258; XI: 845) involve Sun/Heaven/water reflection. Its use in the "Nativity Ode" where "The Stars with deep amaze/Stand fixt in stedfast gaze" upon the Christ child indicates to a student of Milton's works the resonances of Satan's appropriation reported in the dream as well as in the temptation scene. Like most images that Milton uses "gaze" can be both positive and negative, the negative often appropriating a positive context to insinuate itself.

36. Julia Kristeva's discussion of the "gaze" as involving the Other, with its sexual content, is certainly significant to Satan's appropriation of the word and idea, and delineates the sexual content of Eve's experience. The narcissism in "gaze" melds the viewer with the object, the self with the Other. In the creation scene she looks at the seeming Other who looks back with sympathy and love; on it her eyes could have been "fixt" and "pin'd with vain desire." The potential of the gaze is there only. Later, seduced by the phallic serpent, her gaze is "Fixt on the Fruit," a womb symbol and thus a repetition of the narcissistic in sexual terms. The gaze in Kristeva's Lacanian interpretation indicates both the fascination with what one is not sexually and with one's own sexuality. Although the word is not associated with Adam, his fascination with Eve, which he recounts to Raphael (VIII: 521–59), emphasizes "Beauties powerful glance" and the "outward shew/Elaborate." See Kristeva, "Stendhal and the Politics of the Gaze: An Egotist's Love," *Tales of Love* (New York: Columbia University Press, 1987), 341–64.

37. The "this" that Adam is "taught" is "that suffering for Truths sake/Is fortitude to highest victorie,/And to the faithful Death the Gate of Life." Note, too, "Upon the Circumcision" (15–16): "O more exceeding love or law more just?/Just law indeed, but more exceeding love!"

38. Dennis Danielson, "Through the Telescope of Typology: What Adam Should Have Done," *Milton Quarterly* 23 (1989): 121–27.

39. Such as the miracle which saves the Son on the pinnacle in *Paradise Regain'd* and such as the miracle which saves the Israelites in Milton's earliest complete poem, "A Paraphrase on Psalm 114."

40. Talking of the heroic poem, he says that "Milton, if the devil had not been his hero, instead of Adam," would have provided "a better plea" for the poem's status—"Dedication of the Aeneis," *The Works of Virgil* (London: 1697); *Works*, ed. George Saintsbury, XIV: 144.

THE ALLEGORY OF ALLEGORY
Unlockeing Blake's "Crystal Cabinet"

Thomas A. Vogler

While there is a debased allegory against which there is a reasonable and well-founded prejudice, there is also a genuine allegory without which no art can be fully understood. It is of course confusing that the same word is used in both senses.
   (Northrop Frye)

Allegories are the natural mirrors of ideology.
   (Angus Fletcher)

By the end of the eighteenth-century "allegory" had become one of the most important words in the European aesthetic vocabulary. It had also become almost meaningless, remaining in the critical vocabulary primarily as a marker in a system of structured oppositions that privileged "symbol" as the glamour term of Romanticism. Only in the twentieth century has allegory been recuperated as a theoretical concept with interpretive potential related to a respectable literary practice. Blake's "Crystal Cabinet," composed around 1800, comes at a significant turning point for the study of allegory, with its declining status as a critical term and as a literary and artistic practice.[1] Even as Blake was working on his poem, the Romantics were being led into battle by Coleridge, with his borrowed formulae for the opposition between allegory and symbol. Soon allegory would have such a bad name that Melville could parody the anti-allegorists by having Ishmael inscribe an "affidavit" of facticity, so that no one would mistake his tale for "a monstrous fable, or still worse and more detestable, a hideous and intolerable allegory."[2] In spite of critical interdictions that found it to be prolix, mechanical and uncouth, authors like Melville continued to find in allegory their most productive mode of expression. Perhaps no one distrusted or disliked allegory more than writers like Coleridge, Melville, Hawthorne or Arnold, who could write nothing else, but felt they should write something else. "Realistic" writers like Stendhal, George Eliot or Frank Norris could not avoid allegory in spite of their lack of respect for the mode. In a "Preface" to the first edition of his *Poems* (1853), Matthew Arnold condemned the "false aims" of that "false practice" for which the "the highest thing that one can attempt in the way of poetry" was "an allegory of the state of one's own mind," and sacrificed his own "Empedocles on Etna" to the cause.[3] Yet in his self-conscious attempts to produce the proper "art which imitates actions" he gave us "Sohrab and Rustum," surely one of the most morbidly painful allegories of the poet's own mind ever written.

Starting with Walter Benjamin, the gradual recuperation of allegory as a productive critical term has been a notable feature of twentieth-century theory and critical practice that can enable us to approach eighteenth-century literature without some of the handicaps of Romantic mystification. Benjamin's *Ursprung des deutschen Trauerspiels*, a study of allegory in the German baroque drama, can now be seen as a challenge to German Romantic criticism in particular, and in a wider context to the ideological formulation that idealized the symbolic at the expense of allegory. "What else is his entire book," writes Terry Eagleton, "but an effort to salvage allegory from the 'enormous condescension' of history, as allegory's whole striving is itself for the painful salvaging of truth."[4] Even more suggestive is his linking of the pre-Romantic with the modern, both being in their essence allegorical, and his exemplification of the ways in which the thought process of the theorist of allegory is itself already allegorical.[5]

A sure indication that key rhetorical terms are undergoing significant changes and are at the center of important tensions is a radical equivocality in their use. In 1712 Joseph Addison claimed that "Allegories, when well chosen, are...like so many tracks of light in a discourse that makes everything about them clear and beautiful."[6] Later in the century (1753) William Hogarth thought that "allegories and riddles, trifling as they are," deserve to be tolerated because "it is a pleasing labour of the mind" to solve them and they "afford the mind amusement."[7] Two years later, in contrast to this patronizing attitude, Winckelman was adding the concluding comments on allegory to his *Reflections on the Imitation of Greek Works in Painting and Sculpture* (1755), providing a high point in the eighteenth-century valorization of a combined aesthetic of allegory and imitation:

> An artist of thoughtful mind...wants to show his poetic ability and paint figures by means of significant images, that is, paint allegorically...by images signifying general ideas. Any painter who thinks beyond his palette wants to have readily available a learned store of meaningful and clear images for abstract ideas A more thorough study of allegory could purify...taste and provide it with reality and common sense (*Wahrheit und Verstand*) [provided the artist] has learned to use allegory not to conceal his ideas but to clothe them.[8]

As the most prominent painter of the late eighteenth century in England, Reynolds stretched the dignity of allegory to its limits, producing a gallery of learned charades in the many "allegorical" portraits he painted of aristocratic women, personified in the guise of classical deities and personages. Blake's use and evaluation of the term provides an even greater range, from the completely negative ("fable or allegory are a totally distinct & inferior kind of poetry") through the dismissing adjectival ("allegoric pomp" "allegoric delusion & woe") to a suggestive ideological analysis ("allegory of idolatry or politics"; "For God is only an allegory of kings and nothing else amen"). Yet he could boast on completing his Milton that he had produced "a Sublime Allegory, which is now perfectly completed into a Grand Poem...I consider it as the Grandest Poem that this World Contains. Allegory address'd to the Intellectual powers, while it is altogether hidden from the Corporeal Understanding, is my Definition of the Most Sublime Poetry."[9] Michael Murrin has pointed out that when Blake distinguishes "Vision" from "allegory" his sense of "Vision" is "what Spenser would call allegory, and when the nature of the "symbol" came to be defined, it often sounded like the elevated definitions of "allegory" from a century before.[10] Even Coleridge, as Paul de Man has pointed out, pushed the spiritualization of the symbol "so far that the moment of material existence by which it was originally defined has now become altogether unimportant; symbol and allegory alike now have a common origin beyond the world of matter. The reference, in both cases, to a transcendental source, is now more important than the kind of relationship that exists between the reflection and its source."[11] The same point can be made by comparing Coleridge's famous definition in *The Statesman's Manual* ("a symbol...is characterized by a translucence of the special in the individual or of the general in the especial or of the universal in the general.")[12] with the formulation of John Hughes, in the "Essay on Allegorical Poetry" he wrote to introduce his edition of *The Works of Mr. Edmund Spenser* (1715), where he claims that for allegory "the wholle literal Sense...is a kind of Vision, or a Scene of Imagination, and is everywhere transparent, to show the moral Sense which is under it."[13]

Similar examples of conflicting usage and valuation could be multiplied indefinitely to little effect, so I propose instead to look at Blake's "The Crystal Cabinet," a poem that presents itself as conspicuously allegorical, showing a poetic surface that provokes the reader to look elsewhere in order to find "other" (the *allos* in allegory) words to explain what it represents. By focusing my attention in what follows on an "allegorical" interpretation of a poem that turns out to be an allegory of allegory, I hope to avoid the kind of tempting but fruitless commentary that would aspire to an inductive formulation of the late eighteenth-century meaning of the term. I am more interested in exploring a systematic practice that can be understood from our late twentieth-century perspective as profoundly allegorical, than I am in trying to define the eighteenth century's explicit theory of allegory or William Blake's "private" one. This will be a double journey—first, to locate the poem in its eighteenth-century context, showing how it can be followed through a number of re-turns, beginning with the eye as organ of visual perception. Here I use "re-turns" rather than the more common "levels" to emphasize an important feature of Blake's allegorical machine: once inside it, there is no exit; its end returns us to its beginning, but with a difference. In this it is a miniaturized model of allegorical form, driven by the allegorical desire that always seeks an end but never finds it, so that it must keep repeating itself until it finally breaks off.[14]

The Allegory of Allegory

My second goal will be to make use of certain features of the twentieth-century rediscovery of allegory as a system (or *the* system) of signification, to show that Blake's poem can be read as a poem about allegory as a structural enterprise where the mind, trying to tell its story as the story of a "self," exemplifies the inevitable dynamics of that enterprise. As a text of its time, it is a condensation of over a century's epistemological theorizing and allegorical practice; as an anatomy of allegorical structure it is a poem fully relevant to twentieth-century theoretical concerns.

II: The Lockd Eye

If Perceptive Organs vary: Objects of Perception seem to vary...
The Eye of Man a little narrow orb closd up & dark...
All who see, become what they behold...
For the Eye altering alters all...
(William Blake)

The Crystal Cabinet

The Maiden caught me in the Wild
Where I was dancing merrily
She put me into her Cabinet
And Lockd me up with a golden Key

Another Maiden like herself
Translucent lovely shining clear
Threefold each in the other closd
O what a pleasant trembling fear

This Cabinet is formd of Gold
And Pearl & Crystal shining bright
And within it opens into a World
And a little lovely Moony Night

O what a smile a threefold Smile
Filld me that like a flame I burnd
I bent to kiss the lovely Maid
And found a Threefold Kiss returnd

Another England there I saw
Another London with its Tower
Another Thames & other Hills
And another pleasant Surrey Bower

I strove to sieze the inmost form
With ardor fierce & hands of flame
But burst the Crystal Cabinet
And like a Weeping Babe became

A weeping Babe upon the wild
And Weeping Woman pale reclind
And in the outward air again
I filld with woes the passing Wind.

This poem has received remarkably little critical attention, and most of what it has received typifies several interpretive tendencies I will try to avoid here.[15] All these critics see the poem as an allegory of sex that turns out to be an allegory for something else; they are all simplistically and reductively "allegorical." They discourse on Vision without considering vision, ignoring the poem's rhyme scheme, ballad form, and polysemy. If this is really the way Blake's art works, why should anyone bother? What is interesting about these readings is the way they all parallel the dynamic process related in the poem. While criticizing the "youth" (Harold Bloom) for committing a "possessive act" (John Beer) in an "attempt to grasp" (Kathleen Raine) some form of merely sexual understanding, they all bring to the poem their own forms of sexual reduction in an attempt to possess its meaning. "Like Prometheus, he wants the final secret," writes Beer;[16] and like the speaker of Blake's poem, the critics too strive "to seize the inmost form," *reflecting* in their allegoresis the mirror poem that traps them at the very moment they presume to have unlocked it with their "keys." As I will show, the only "sex" in this poem is in the eye of the beholder. Even though it is very much concerned with how things fit together and are contained in each other, the focus is on how meanings are produced and received; it is both "about" allegory and an example of allegory. These readers want to read it as Blake's allegory about some *other* allegory—to superimpose a "correct" allegory on it, and to judge the speaker of the poem from a perspective outside his and outside the poem itself in a vantage point of Truth. That the speaker does not judge himself (he doesn't "understand" his experience) is a deficiency, a lack of meaning that must therefore be supplied by the allegorical exegete. Even more significant is the failure of these readers to recognize the most conspicuous starting-point for entering the poem: the fact that it begins as an extremely precise allegory of the eighteenth-century model for optical perception, as formulated by John Locke in his *Essay Concerning Human Understanding* and repeated endlessly throughout the century in every conceivable form of embodiment.

Our first and most conspicuous clue for an allegorical reading is the verb "Lockd," emphatically capitalized in contrast with all the other lower-case verbs in the otherwise generously capitalized text. We know that Blake read Locke early, with his usual active critical attentiveness, from his annotations to Reynolds: "Burke's Treatise on the Sublime & Beautiful is founded on the Opinions of Newton & Locke on this Treatise Reynolds has grounded many of his assertions...I read Burkes Treatise when very Young at the same time I read Locke on Human Understanding & Bacons Advancement of Learning on Every one of these Books I wrote my

Opinions...I felt the Same Contempt & Abhorrence then; that I do now. They mock Inspiration & Vision" (E 660) His poetic engagement with Locke is visible from the very beginning of his career, as this moment from *An Island in the Moon* (1784) suggests:

> Then Scopprell & Miss Gittipin, coming in Sopprell took up a book & read the following passage
> An Easy of Huming Understanding by John Lookye Gent. John Locke said Obtuse Angle, O ay Lock said Scopprell. (f4ᵛ)[17]

The word-play in this comic interlude signals the primary focus of "The Crystal Cabinet," as well as anticipating that poem's punning modus operandi. The "easy" prosaic style of Locke's work is captured by the transformation of "Human" into "Huming," which also gestures towards the influence of Locke on David Hume and the many other commentators on the nature of human understanding who flourished in the eighteenth century.[18] The transformation of Locke's name into "Lookye," together with the other vision puns (*Scop*prell, "O *ay*") reflects the visual-perceptual emphasis of Locke's whole system.

Blake was not alone in finding the model of visual perception to be the key to Lockean epistemology. The fascination with optics inaugurated by Kepler's discovery that the eye works like a *camera obscura*, in which the lens causes the image of an external object to be focused on the retina—a discovery elaborated on by Descartes and further augmented and systematized by Locke and Newton—had led to a widespread infatuation with the many applications that could be spun out of a knowledge of the mechanics of the eye and optical perception.[19] In the aptly named *Spectator* (1711–1712) Addison made a condensed version of Locke's system widely available, claiming that "our sight is the most perfect and most delightful of all our senses....We cannot indeed have a single image in the fancy that did not make its first entrance through the sight...[so that] by the pleasures of the imagination I mean only such pleasures as arise originally from sight" (138–9).[20] Other poetic versions and endorsements of Locke burgeoned in works like Akenside's *Pleasures of the Imagination* (1744), Blackmore's *Creation* (1712) and Thomson's *Seasons* (1726–1748). Artists looked at the world through Claude glasses and many, including Sir Joshua Reynolds, enjoyed their own *cameræ obscuræ*. In *An Island in the Moon* Blake satirized these optical pursuits: "Thus these happy Islanders spent their time...with glasses, & brass tubes, & magic pictures" (E 462).[21] "No said Inflammable Gass. I have got a camera obscura at home what was it you was talking about" (E 452).

Children could read in widely available works like *Tom Telescope* (1761)[22] a condensed version of the mainstream philosophy of man—the senses, the nature of understanding, and the origin of ideas, with a great deal more on optics and the prism.[23] By 1780 there were specialized toy shops throughout London where one could buy educational "scientific" toys like cheap camera obscurae made especially for children.[24] Altick has charted the passion for "shows" that prompted profitable inventions like the Panorama, the Diorama and the Eidophusikon.[25] In 1791 Erasmus Darwin modelled his *Botanic Garden* after the *camera obscura*,[26] and William Paley, in what proved to be one of the most popular "science" books ever written, chose the eye as the instrument most clearly showing the necessity of God's existence.[27] Jeremy Bentham's Panopticon project (1791) was the architectural realization of a century's dream come true.[28] Equally serviceable in his mind's eye for prisons, schools and factories, it was a physical structure inside of which all life's stages and functions could be carried on. The unseen warder in the center of this eye-shaped translucent building was the new word made flesh, a living embodiment of Adam Smith's psychological metaphor of the "Impartial Spectator."[29]

This brief overview of the domination of the eye in the optical epistemology of the eighteenth century can help provide a context that makes it unnecessary to turn to Blake's private "system" to trace the allegorical implications of his poem. Locke's favorite image for the human mind was the "cabinet of perception," imagined as a *camera obscura* or "little Sensorium" (Newton's term) where little pictures of the external world were projected on the retinal "wall." This cabinet is described from inside in the poem, according to Locke's two-stage theory of the progress of human understanding. The first stage begins with the passive reception of sensory stimuli as they are constituted on the level of primary ideas, followed by the exercise of the faculty of "reflection" which actively operates on the passively-received sensory input. Locke provides an active, dynamic model in his system, a "progress" in the full eighteenth-century sense of that term, motivated by serial stages of self-reflection and recognition. In its initial state the mind can be described as "white Paper, void of all Characters, without any *Ideas.*" What Locke calls "*Perceptions* of things" are the effects of objects on this white paper, through the operations of what he calls "SENSATION."

According to Locke, there are two "Fountains of Knowledge, whence all the Ideas we have, or can naturally have, do spring." The first fountain is the action of "*external, sensible Objects*" on the white paper; the second fountain is "*the internal Operations of our Minds, perceived and reflected on by our selves.*" It is this second "fountain" that provides the allegorical key for the first phase of Blake's poem. For Locke the ideas man gets by "REFLECTION" are

> such only, as the Mind gets by reflecting on its own Operations within it self. By REFLECTION then...I would be understood to mean, that notice which the Mind takes of its own Operations...Men then come to be furnished with fewer or more simple *Ideas* from without, according as they more or less *reflect* on them...And hence we see the Reason, why 'tis pretty late, before most Children get *Ideas* of the Operations of their own Minds...till the Understanding turns inward upon it self, *reflects* on its own *Operations*, and makes them the Object of its own Contemplation.[30]

First we see the little images on the retina, then we see ourselves seeing them ("Another England there I saw") in the second stage of reflection. In stanzas two through five the speaker of the poem describes his experiences in this second stage after his mind has been stored by sensation with primary ideas. There, perhaps with the help of Tom Telescope and the *Spectator*, or even John Lookye himself, he *reflects* on the operations of his own mind as a sophisticated observer who understands his transition from the "Wild" of unorganized sensory perception to the reflective organization within the cabinet of the mind. It is in this second stage that the discovery of the lack of correspondence between the mental representations "inside" the cabinet and their material causes "outside" can be made as the result of the futile attempt to "seize the inmost form" of images that are phantoms. The bursting of the cabinet can be seen as a second transition, in which the epistemological cabinet of perception becomes a metaphysical prison. The attempt to "seize the inmost Form" reveals that there is nothing "there" (inside) and that the "primary qualities" that are "outside" and that cause the "secondary qualities" or affective sensations in our "little lovely Moony" sensorium have no resemblance to those effects: *"Ideas, produced* in us by...*Secondary Qualities,* have no resemblance of them at all. There is nothing like our *Ideas,* existing in the Bodies themselves." In his *Opticks* Newton found the century's most vivid example of this argument in his experiments with the refraction of light:

> And if at any time I speak of Light and Rays as coloured or endued with Colours, I would be understood to speak not philosophically and properly, but grossly, and accordingly to such Conceptions as vulgar People ...would be apt to frame. For the Rays to speak properly are not coloured. In them there is nothing else than a certain Power and Disposition to stir up a Sensation of this or that Colour. For as Sound in a Bell or...other sounding Body, is nothing but a trembling Motion, and in the Air nothing but that Motion propagated from the Object.[31]

Blake condenses the conclusion of this discursive description into his image of the "passing Wind," a perfect image for Newton and Locke's ultimate physical reality, where everything we can perceive is nothing but a bare effect of Power. This is why Mont Blanc represented the epiphanic sublime for the eighteenth-century quester; there was nothing there that could be perceived.[32] Blake's "Crystal Cabinet" is an allegoric version of Shelley's "Mont Blanc," its ballad-like simplicity a parody of the matter-of-fact acceptance of the Lockean system in eighteenth century thought that kept finding allegorical variations for the same inevitable conclusion:

> In short, our souls are at present delightfully lost and bewildered in a pleasing delusion, and we walk about like the enchanted hero of a romance, who sees beautiful castles, woods, and meadows; and at the same time hears the warbling of birds and the purling of streams; but upon the finishing of some secret spell, the fantastic scene breaks up, and the disconsolate knight finds himself on a barren heath, or in a solitary desert. It is not improbable that something like this may be the state of the soul after its first separation, in respect of the images it will receive from matter. (Addison, 148)

I clasp'd the phantoms, and I found them air,
O had I weigh'd it ere my fond embrace!³³

With this general sense of the progress of the poem and the poem as cyclical "progress" from "Wild" to "wild", we can re-turn our attention to some of its key words and their allegorical significance.

"*Lockd*" is the word that first begins to unlock the allegory. Punning, as Quilligan has demonstrated, is not an arbitrary but rather an essential component of the doubling that characterizes the allegorical mode. The pun on Locke's name can be seen as motivated since his system itself is "locked," in that it denies the mind access to anything outside itself.

> The simple ideas we receive from sensation and reflection are the boundaries of our thoughts; beyond which the mind, whatever efforts it would make, is not able to advance one jot; nor can it make any discoveries when it would pry into the nature and hidden causes of those ideas...whensoever we would proceed beyond these simple ideas we have from sensation and reflection, and dive further into the nature of things, we fall presently into darkness and obscurity...what a darkness we are involved in, how little it is of Being and the things that are, that we are capable to know." (II.xxiii.29; II.xxiii.32; IV.iii.29)

This pun is not "made" but is "found" in the structure of the English language and its relevance to Locke's system. The same point can be made without directly punning, as when Isaac Watts exclaims: "I hate these Shackles of the Mind/Forg'd by the haughty Wise; Souls were not born to be confin'd,/And led like Samson Bound and Blind";³⁴ or when Condillac—*perhaps* the eighteenth century's most persistent expounder of Locke—notes that impressions must be *renfermés* ("locked up," an anticipation of Freud's emphasis on the machinery of "cathexis") before they can be considered by the mind.³⁵ Gombrich can refer casually to the "locks of our senses" that artists open with their artificial "keys,"³⁶ and William James could assert that "Every living creature is in fact a sort of lock, whose wards and springs presuppose special forms of keys."³⁷ There is an extra effect, however, in linking the concept with its originator, the "LOCKE I Who made the whole internal World his own,"³⁸ that leads Joseph de Maistre, writing in

French, to pun in English on Locke's name—"Locked in"[39]—and has been exploited by poets from Pope (*The Rape of the Lock*) to John Berryman.[40]

The "golden **key**" is a pun too, because keys can both lock and unlock. In this case the golden key with the bright promise of knowledge that will unlock the mysteries of how the human mind works, is instead an "epistemological key" that locks us into a way of perceiving and understanding the world. The **me** who is locked in is at the initial phase a bundle of sensory perceptions caught by the mechanism of the eye in its little dark room, or *camera obscura*. Locke's metaphor for the mind as cabinet constantly plays on the punning isomorphism between the two containers, so that Blake's crystal cabinet links the **crystal** of the eye[41] with the implicit mirrors in the mind seen as a **cabinet** of perception, the "little sensorium." Knowledge of the optic nerves as part of the mechanism for "catching" the sensory impression and turning it into an image add cabi***net*** to the repertoire of puns at work in this stanza: "The forms caught in this net are brought to sight/And to his eye are lively pourtrayed."[42] The **wild** is in its first instance the incoherence of the sensory manifold before it is brought into the form of images through the operation of the optic lens. Like the key, this image works both ways, producing equivocal affect. Its negative sense is caught in Fielding's *Jonathan Wild*, structured around a moral opposition between characters named Wild and Heartfree. Wild, who is presented as an intuitive Hobbesian, is "wild" even when he is in prison (and a "slave" to his material desires whether in or out of prison, hence always imprisoned *in* his wildness). Heartfree carries his freedom with him even into prison. "Wild" can also have positive connotations, even when it must give way to controls, as when Dorothy's "wild eyes" in "Tintern Abbey" remind Wordsworth of his own before] he had "learned to look on Nature."

The **Maiden** and her cabinet make it hard to resist a "sexual" reading for most critics, even though the active nature of this maiden gives the male what might be considered an unusual passivity for copulatory action.[43] Part of the equivocation here is that "sex" (as gendered active/passive, male/female) is an allegory for something else—the play of relations between man/nature, mind/nature, direct/reflected light (as when, in *Paradise Lost*, Raphael explains "Male and Female Light,/Which two great Sexes animate the World"[44]). This allegorical gender is not an essence, or an anatomical characteristic, but a structural (relational) phenomenon.⁴⁵ The same entity ("man") can be "female" in one relationship (vis-à-vis God) and "male" in another (vis-à-vis woman). Being locked is not a result of gender, but a gender-producing transition involving perception, especially liminal perception of the difference between "inside" and "outside." This phase of the poem is analogous to the traditional allegory of the male-gendered soul being made flesh in the female womb; but here (at the initial stage of optical allegory) the allegory is of a ray of light, being caught and turned into an image that is perceived as the passive result of an external cause. For Locke, in his favorite analogy, "the understanding [is] like the eye" (8). To be caught by a Maiden is thus in this sexist epistemology to be feminized or made "female" as a trope of passivity—the "act" of becoming passive.⁴⁶ In his dedicatory letter to Pembroke, Locke personifies knowledge of Nature, or "truth," as female, to be pursued ("hawking and hunting" (7) is another favorite trope) for the sake of an "intimate acquaintance with her, in her more retired recesses" (3–4). The allegorical implications of Blake's poem focus on this equivocal moment, in which the acts of catching and of being caught are one (the acts of climbing and creeping, as Milton and Swift pointed out, are performed in the same posture). To accept the Lockean Truth is to presume to unlock the mystery of the mind and to be "lockd" into a mode of mastery, to catch and to be caught.

The mind, pursued to its more retired recesses in the crystal cabinet, and its reflective rather than generative operations, turns out to be figurable as "feminine" in Locke's system:

The Mind proceeds, and to Reflection goes,
Perceives she does Perceive, and knows **she** Knows⁴⁷

With inward View
Thence on th' ideal Kingdom swift **she** turns
Her Eye; and instant, at her powerful Glance,
Th' obedient Phantoms vanish or appear;
Compound, divide, and into Order shift,
Each to **his** Rank, from plain Perception up
To the fair Forms of Fancy's fleeting Train;
To Reason then, deducing Truth from Truth,
And Notion quite abstract.
(Thomson, "Summer" 1788–1796)

The interior of the cabinet is described as **Night**, as is fitting for the darkened chamber of the *camera obscura*. The inner world, "opened" as the outer world is closed off, is little at this stage because the images formed on the retina of the eye are, quite literally, little.[48] Its illumination is **Moony** because its source of light is always elsewhere, like the earth itself according to God's optical expert, Uriel: "that Globe whose hither side/With light from hence, though but reflected, shines" (82). The images in the inner world are **Another** version of the external world. According to Locke the mind's "simple ideas are not fictions of our fancies, but the natural and regular productions of things without us." The ontological status of the pictures in the eye and in the "mind's eye" is a crucial part of Locke's system, and a basis for much of the eighteenth-century's discussion about the status of artistic representation as modelled on Lockean epistemology. In his *Lectures on Light* (1705) Robert Hooke takes pains to explain how the eye is a "Microcosm, or a little World" that forms a perfect double for the external world, having within itself "a distinct Point...for every distinct Point without it self in the Universe; and when a Hemisphere of the Heavens is open to its view, it has a Hemisphere within it self."[49] As I will show later, this "duplicate world" relationship makes frustrated allegory the inevitable mode of knowing that "other" (*allos*) world of what Locke calls "things without us," that produce in us—"by the Wisdom and Will of our Maker"—an "other" world of perception that has "all the real conformity it can or ought to have, with things without us." God, in Locke's system, is the original allegorist.

The **Threefold** enclosure of the Maiden is one of the most over-determined passages in the poem, and its suggestion of reflective mirror-multiplication could well make the allegorical exegete wish for an ideal case of insomnia.[50] From Plato on, triplication has figured the uncanny way mirrors can multiply images as semblance rather than substance.[51] Horace calls the Moon a "triform goddess" (suggesting both the three visible phases and the three lunar divinities: Luna, Diana, Hecate) and Milton's Raphael explains to Adam how "the neighboring Moon" reveals "With borrow'd light her countenance triform" (III: 730). When Satan reaches the bound of Hell he finds "thrice threefold the Gates; three folds were Brass,/Three Iron, three of Adamantine Rock." Locke was very fond of triplication in his exposition. "We have the ideas but of three sorts of substances: 1. *God*. 2. *Finite intelligences*. 3. *Bodies*" (II.xxvii.1). He devotes a whole chapter to "Our Threefold Knowledge of Existence" (intuition, demonstration, sensation) and distinguishes "Perception, which we make the act of the Understanding" into "three sorts," the "perception of ideas in our minds," of the "significance of signs," and of the "connexion or repugnancy, agreement or disagreement, that there is between any of our ideas" (IV.ix). My point here is not that these are the source analogues for Blake's "Threefold" emphasis, but rather that "threefoldness" itself can be seen here as the threefold invocation of threefold form as a conspicuous allegorical gesture. Whatever it signifies, it signifies itself as a sign that must stand for something beyond itself, demanding a translation into "other" terms. It can also function as an allegorical signifier of replication and deferred meaning. Thus Benjamin, in his discussion of the fallen nature of the allegorical desire for absolute knowledge, finds "three original satanic promises": the illusion of freedom, the illusion of independence, and the illusion of infinity—the threefold allegorical promise of an inmost form or totalizing meaning for the endlessly replicated images after the fall.[52]

The passing **Wind** is a perfect image for the modes of invisible and incomprehensible Power that dominated eighteenth-century science, producing effects that reveal and hide the power at the same time.[53] Newton's Gravity, or his pure unrefracted white light, or Adam Smith's "invisible hand" are other names for this invisible efficacy which the Romantics would try to make the "symbol" that would answer their allegorical desire, in the hope that "Visionary power/Attends upon the motions of the winds."[54] At the same allegorical "moment" that the speaker of Blake's poem, expelled from his crystal cabinet, is filling with woes the passing wind, Wordsworth presents himself "coming from a house/Of bondage" to find "blessing in this gentle breeze" and awakens "within/A corresponding mild creative breeze" with "vernal promises" (*Prelude* I: 1–50). Coleridge was wondering "what if all of animated nature/Be but organic Harps diversely fram'd,/That tremble into thought, as o'er them sweeps/Plastic and vast, one intellectual breeze,/At once the Soul of each, and God of all?" ("The Eolian Harp"). And Shelley was invoking the West Wind as "unseen presence" through the "incantation" of his verse for another turn of the seasons, a re-turn and a re-birth of poetry: "O Wind,/If Winter comes, can Spring be far behind?" ("Ode to the West Wind"). But the only promise of Blake's "Crystal Cabinet" is a return to the Wild of the poem's beginning and a re-turn of the same allegorical machinery. That is the route I shall now take in my allegorical tour of the poem, knowing that the anti-allegorical Romantic moment will be waiting—as always—at each new turn of the allegorical machinery.

III. The Lockd "I"

> What *indeed* does *man know about himself? Oh! that he could but once see himself complete, placed as it were in an illuminated glass case! Does not nature keep secret from him most things, even about his body...? Nature threw away the key; and woe to the fateful curiosity which might be able for a moment to look out and down through a crevice in the chamber of consciousness.* (Friedrich Nietzsche, Truth and Falsehood in an Extra-Moral Sense*)*

> *Whenever I think I must think myself—I think I do—In the first place. (Aradobo,* An Island in the Moon*)*

The first time through the poem I concentrated on its "subject" at the optical level. We can compare this inaugural focus on the eye in Locke's system and Blake's allegory with the way Freudian analysis organizes developmental progression of the infantile drama around bodily zones (mouth, anus, genitalia) as organic models for self-identification and relationships (swallowing, enclosing, retaining, spitting, expelling) and with the analogous conception of feelings, events, ideas, words as food, urine, feces, semen, babies, etc. In Locke's system we get a comparable model of the organization of the inaugural formation of the "self, "with its potential functions and relations organized around the accepted model of the eye and its mode of functioning. Now I propose to look more closely at the psychological implications of the allegory as they follow from making the model of mind isomorphic with the model of the eye, and from founding epistemological certainty on the model of "reflection" as a metaphor for that mode of thinking that has itself for its own object. Here we shall see that the isomorphism brings over to the production of the subject the same representational mediation encountered in the model of the eye, where the world is not perceived directly, but rather through "pictures" imprinted on the retinal surface. Since those pictures are in the eye, there must be another eye, a "mind's eye" capable of perceiving them.

If we ask who is this implicit "I" who is telling his own story as a "me," we find that it is the Lockean "self," telling the story of how it came to be a self, in a system of identity formation that made him a prisoner of his own self-representation. The story is an allegory of the production of the subject, in which the process cannot be imagined as a gradual progression in which "Shades of the prison-house begin to close/Upon the growing Boy (Wordsworth, "Ode: Intimations of Immortality"). It is rather a *moment* of recognition that can only be known in the past tense. Having accepted Locke's invitation to "turn his thoughts inwards upon what passes in his mind" (II.xxi.119) the speaker must find his starting point in a "turning-point," the moment in the chronology of a self that is also the origin of self, the moment in which his being became constituted as a "self" and the "eye" of his passive perception advanced to a mental "I" of self-conscious reflection. The moment is like a second birth, the first having been into Nature or the body, the second into self-consciousness and temporality. This is clearly an ancient psychological fable of individual development that must be retold in any new system. It is most familiar to us in its Freudian form where the "Wild" is "a condition of frightened and irrational helplessness, lack of self-definition, and domination by fluid or mobile instinctive drives." If healthy development occurs, one moves from this "Wild" state to "a condition of stability, mastery, adaptability, self-definition, rationality, and security."[55] Although the wild stage is imagined as coming before the cabinet stage, there is an inevitable sense in which as representation it can only be produced retroactively from inside the cabinet, as its temporal "outside" or preconscious past, a diachronic boundary of self: "And as far as this consciousness can be extended backwards to any past action or thought, so far reaches the identity of that person; it is the same self now it was then; and it is by the same self with this present one that now reflects on it, that that action was done" (II.xxvii.11). The same emphasis on self-representation can be seen in the emergence of Narcissism in Freud's theory, where the primordial, polymorphously autoerotic state that precedes the ego gives way to a mode of self-love based on an image of self, the Narcissism or self-love mediated by the mirror that Lacan describes as "the mirror stage," in a formulation almost perfectly congruent with the allegory of the Crystal Cabinet.[56] I invoke Lacan here because he has provided a well known and succinct model for the process of identity formation in its specular stage. He is doing what Blake is doing in terms of model-building, and his model is similar to Blake's allegorical model in several significant ways.

Lacan's focus in this classic statement is on *"the function of méconnaissance* that characterizes the ego in all its structures."[57] The mirror "stage" is imagined as effected in a single moment that is a turning point, when the infant's fragmented body (*le corps morcelé*) is "caught" by the mirror reflection that will be the basis for an alienated self-identity that has no "inmost form." Henceforth the subject's relation to itself will always be subject to representation in the form of a mediating image that has come from outside. It is the moment in which the self becomes aware of its "self" as a self-presence with a past. Thus the self paradoxically comes into being as a turning point in the history or chronology of a self, but it is also the origin of a self that did not exist before. In Lacan's formulation, "it is this moment that decisively tips the whole of human knowledge into mediatization through the desire of the other,"[58] but it is also a moment that tends to elude our conceptual grasp. As Sterne and others noted, Locke's system, like Lacan's, involved a narrativized genealogy of the individual:

> Pray, Sir, in all the reading which you have ever read, did you ever read such a book as Locke's Essay upon the Human Understanding?—I will tell you in three words what the book is—It is a history—A history! of who? what? where? when? Don't hurry yourself—It is a history-book, Sir, (which may possibly recommend it to the world) of what passes in a man's own mind.[59]

I emphasize the diachronic difficulty found in the mirror phase because the easy, matter-of-fact tone and ballad form of Blake's poem seem to belie the narrative complexity of the story it is telling. It is a story in which the subject becomes a subject *for* narrative at the moment it is constituted as a sub*ject by* narrative; the moment in time that recognizes the self in time—the moment it acquires a "past." Telling his own story then is a form of self-representation by the speaker of the poem quite comparable to the "project" undertaken by Sterne in *Tristram Shandy* and by Wordsworth in the poem on the growth of his own mind. For both the self is understood as a narrative project and a narrative product.[60] Bender argues that "accounts of the self are the self" for the eighteenth century.[61] Schafer's insistence that "the self is a telling" and that "we narrate ourselves" shows the tenacity of the narrative circle in which events can only be constituted as events by being brought under a system of representation. For Lacan the mirror stage is only the beginning of a process of alienated self-identification that makes the subject the effect of the signifier, and the unconscious an allegorical "discourse of the Other." The next crucial turn for Lacan will be the further loss of being as a consequence of the entry into language, causing the split in the subject that gives rise to the science of psychoanalysis. This division of the subject "is what makes the psyche a critical allegory of itself and is what justifies psychoanalysis as the allegory of that allegory."[62]

The emphasis on visual representation in "The Crystal Cabinet" brings us to the "spatial" equivalent of the narrative problem I have been discussing. For Lacan "the mirror stage is a drama whose internal impetus lunges forward...and which, for *the subject captivated by the lure of spatial identification*, machinates the succession of fantasies which go from an image of the body in bits and pieces (the "Wild") to a form which we will call orthopedic of its totality."[63] How can the self "see" itself if, as Hume (following Locke) insists, "we never really advance a step beyond ourselves, nor can conceive any kind of existence but those perceptions which have appear'd in that narrow compass. This is the universe of the imagination, nor have we any idea but what is there produc'd" (II.ii.6). The self is emphatically a mode and moment of self-presence; but how can it find a vantage point to see itself without breaching self-presence by some form of representational mediation? Bentham emphasizes the spatial aspect of the problem: "Of nothing that has place, or passes, in our minds can we give any account, any otherwise than by speaking of it as if it were a portion of space, with portions of matter...Of nothing, therefore, that has place, or passes in our mind, can we speak, or so much as think, otherwise than in the way of Fiction."[64] Freud provides a useful example of this fiction-making, along with some optical echoes of "The Crystal Cabinet": "we should picture the instrument which carries out our mental functions as resembling a compound microscope or a photographic apparatus, or something of the kind. On that basis, psychical locality will correspond to a point inside the apparatus at which one of the preliminary stages of an image comes into being" (SE V: 536). But where are we located when we "picture" our own "psychical locality" as a point "inside" some mental apparatus, and what mental apparatus do we use to make the picture? This is a point where Locke's picture-making emphasis and his homey figures of speech consistently obscure a problem inherent in his representational strategy. Fredric Jameson provides a perfect example of the same process at work in our own time.

> In matters of art, and particularly of artistic perception...it is wrong to want to decide, to want to resolve a difficulty. What is wanted is a kind of mental procedure that suddenly shifts gears, that throws everything in an inextricable tangle one floor higher and turns the very problem itself...into its own solution...by widening its frame in such a way that it now takes in its own mental processes as well as the object of those processes. In the earlier, naive state, we struggle with the object in question; in this heightened and self-conscious one, we observe our own struggles and patiently set about characterizing them.[65]

In this matter-of-fact description of what he calls "metacommentary," Jameson shows what is *wanted* (and wanting) in the Lockean system of self-reflection. The approach to the "turn" of self-recognition in the dynamic structure of Lockean psychology does indeed try to turn the problem of self-representation into its own solution. Just widen the frame to include yourself observing yourself! "That the absurdity does not so immediately strike us, that it does not seem equally unimaginative, is owing to a surreptitious act of the imagination."[66] "The Crystal Cabinet" allegory pushes this tropical strategy to the limits, anticipating the outcome of a system of self-identification that indefinitely defers the desired realization.

The self produced by the Lockean system is based on the premise that it is "impossible for any one to perceive without perceiving that he does perceive...Thus it is always as to our present sensations and perceptions: and by this every one is to himself that which he calls Self" (II.xxvii.11). The self constituted as such in the moment of self-recognition is by the mechanism of Lockean self-perception split or doubled and hence no longer—or not yet—whole. Morris Golden has observed that "wherever we look in the period, we are reminded that its guiding epistemological concept is Locke's divided mind, one part operating on signals from without and one observing these operations."[67] This is what Wordsworth describes as a problem "That almost seems inherent in the creature, Sensuous and intellectual as he is,/A twofold frame of body and of mind" (*Prelude* XI: 167–169) and causes him to feel, reflecting on his earlier spontaneous sensuous self, that he is "Two consciousnesses—conscious of myself,/And of some other being" (*Prelude* II: 32–33). But this is only one phase of the division; in order to complete the Lockean curriculum, we must observe ourselves observing, see ourselves seeing; that is the unavoidable *division* in the Lockean model of the mind that makes his "*principium individuationis*" inevitably a principle of allegorical otherness (II.xxvii.2). The "Crystal Cabinet" is a poem where we see the I of the poem seeing seeing—not the real *act* of seeing, we might say, only a reflection of it; but yes really, because seeing is already only a reflection, in the Lockean see-me-optics that works like a Peircian semiotics of infinite regress.[68] When I say I *see* myself *seeing* myself, I am caught in a play of mirrors that defers to infinity the immediately present subject and subverts the notion of an original "I."

The implications of this potentially infinite regressive series were already familiar to the late eighteenth-century philosophical discourse as part of the frustrating inheritance that led Coleridge ("Great indeed are the obstacles which an English metaphysician has to encounter" [*Biographia* 1.290]) to his self-appointed task as executor of the Lockean discourse, hoping that the German transcendentalists would provide the cure for his existential Ängst. His own experience led him to conclude that our inner flow of perceptions (no matter how much we reflect on them) could not guarantee self-unity, and made Kant's differentiation between this empirical consciousness and a "transcendental" consciousness (holding out the promise of a base on which to connect our thoughts and experience as *ours*.) seem like a salvation. Coleridge's eighteenth-century problem has continued into modern phenomenological epistemology, where we can find Derrida's critique of Husserl's "now" as a myth based on spatial and mechanical metaphors.[69] If consciousness of self is defined in terms of knowledge of things, whereby I am a unique kind of thing since, when I hold myself up to my own "introspection" in an act of self-presentation, I am present to myself as no other object could be, then the *presentness* of the self's presentation can never be guaranteed (as the model assumes) because reflection and representation introduce difference. Such a model leads only to an infinite regress.

> Representation mingles with what it represents, to the point where one speaks as one writes, one thinks as if the represented were nothing more than the shadow or

reflection of the represented. A dangerous promiscuity and a nefarious complicity between the reflection and the reflected which lets itself be seduced narcicissistically. In this play of representation, the point of origin becomes ungraspable. There are things like reflecting pools, and images, an infinite reference from one to the other, but no longer a source, a spring.[70]

Coleridge was helped to an awareness of this inevitability by his reading of transcendental philosophy, and especially by Kant's formulations calling for a "principle of self-consciousness," without which "we must be driven back from ground to ground, each of which would cease to be a ground the moment we pressed on it. We must be whirl'd down the gulf of an infinite series" (*Biographia* I: 285). He therefore takes his stand with the transcendental philosophy to affirm "that the act of self consciousness is for us the source and principle of all our possible knowledge" (I: 284), with the transcendental emphasis on an originary act of self-presence as a way to get out of the otherwise engulfing endless series of self-representations.

The emphasis on act is an important feature in Kant, for whom there must be an "I think" that accompanies all mental representations (*Vorstellungen*) because without it something could be represented in consciousness "that could not be thought at all."[71] This "I think" is transcendental because (*contra* Locke) it cannot be derived from the ideas and experience that it unites in the unity of the subject. It is a "representation which can be given prior to all thought" and "this representation is an act of spontaneity [*ein Aktus der Spontaneität*]" (16, B132). By differentiating between a transcendental and an empirical consciousness Kant is able to recognize both that our real inner flow of perceptions (no matter how much we reflect on them) guarantees no self-unity and that we must nonetheless attribute to something (the "I think") the ability to connect our thoughts *as ours*.

The problems inherent in Kant's formulation arise from the fact that Kant gives this "act of spontaneity" the form of a *representation* ("a representation which must be capable of accompanying all other representations"). Thus at the critical moment he introjects the status of empirical psychological representation into the transcendental act that would necessarily enable the unity of representation, risking the fall into an infinite regress of transcending (or grounding) subjects that we saw associated with the Lockean model

The Allegory of Allegory

of representation it is designed to transcend. If the transcendental "act" guaranteeing unity is conceived of in terms of representation and reflection, then calling it an "act" cannot preclude the fact that we would have to look for yet another existing representation "accompanying" and guaranteeing the unity of the guarantor, *ad infinitum.*

In my reading of "The Crystal Cabinet" the attempt to "sieze the inmost form" that bursts the Cabinet is an allegory of the attempted shift from reflection (or representation) to "act" as a way out of this chain of endless mediation. But to invoke a rhetoric of action over against a model of reflection and representation is not automatically to accomplish that act, as Coleridge discovered along with Goethe's *Faust* and other Romantic *hors de combat.* The turn to an act that shatters the allegorical machine of the cabinet will prove to be a reflex produced by the machine as its own destructive fulfillment.

IV: The Allegorical Machine

Distanced at the beginning from its source, allegory will set out on an increasingly futile search for a signifier with which to recuperate the fracture of and at its source, and with each successive signifier the fracture and the search begin again: a structuring of continual yearning, the insatiable desire of allegory. (Joel Fineman, "The Structure of Allegorical Desire")

Representation in the abyss of presence is not an accident of presence; the desire of presence is, on the contrary, born from the abyss (the indefinite multiplication) of representation, from the representation of representation, etc. (Jacques Derrida, Grammatology*)*

So far I have pursued the isomorphic trail of the Lockean model from the eye to the I. Now I will follow it one more step, from these models of structure to what I will call the "allegorical machine," emphasizing the ways in which "The Crystal Cabinet" identifies the allegorical aspects of Lockean epistemology and psychology by functioning as an allegory of allegory, so that the poem can be read as an anatomy of allegory in its basic structural form. One of the most common complaints against allegory is that it is mechanical, implying that its results are not produced by "human" activity (spontaneous, imaginative, creative) but by a machine that can operate automatically, without "human" intervention: "the allegory disallows true organic form."[72] I hope to show that this complaint is the result of an intuitively accurate perception of an allegorical machine that produces a form of constructed experience based on a narration *of* (simultaneously from and about) something called mind. There is no autonomous essence or identity in the cabinet of allegory that can be "freed" from its confines to a realm of pure self-presence. The "I" that exists in the structure as its product is informed by an allegorical desire that is also the product of the machine—a consequence of its structuring principles of mind as "container" of experience, with mental eyes (the "mind's eye") located somehow outside the container so they can look in to see what is (was) going on. This mode of introspective narrative is marked from the beginning by a mode of passivity that hides its active, self-constituting aspect in which the observer does not construct or create a life but rather watches it. The passivity vis-à-vis the external world seems equally true of the internal world of reflection where, as Blake writes, "All who see. become what they behold" (E 218).

The etymology of "allegory" calls attention to its other key structural features—the existence of duplicate realms and a mode of relationship between them which is simultaneously discontinuous (allegory requires a "meaning" that cannot be inside it, but must be elsewhere, detachable) and connected by a perfect congruence and closeness. We have an allegorical structure when a text signals that it exists in corresponding relation to some other structure(s) of experience; hence it is something considered to be "outside the text" that gives the text its interest and importance. But that outside can never be brought inside the allegorical text, which can only exist in relation to it as its "Other." Allegory is thus in its simplest form a structural relationship of otherness. Samuel Johnson defines the "allegorical" as the "not real; not literal" and in this basic sense all literature, all language, is pointing to something existing independently outside itself that gives it meaning and justification. Swift illustrates this most basic point negatively in *A Tale of A Tub*, first by having his allegory be about an allegory that is about "nothing," then by having the *Tale* itself gradually disappear, leaving only peripheral commentary or allegoresis, without even a *Tale* about nothing to explicate. Swift's tale is a parody of allegory gone mad, like the porridge pot that won't stop in the fairy tale; it is an illustration of what Fineman has called "allegorical desire, a desire for allegory, that is implicit in the idea of structure itself and explicit in criticism that directs itself towards the structurality of literature."[73] In this and several other important features we can identify a structural system for a general "mode" of allegory that transcends the limitations of period: seen this way allegory is more like a complex rhetorical figure than a literary "genre."

Although I disagree with Maureen Quilligan's insistence on seeing allegory as a distinct genre, I find her emphasis on the importance for allegory of a "shared fact—the generation of narrative structures out of wordplay" a crucial insight into the mechanism of allegory. Conspicuous exhibition of its "otherness" in the exploitation of the punning duplicity of language is an inevitable feature of allegory:

> The "other" named by the term *allos* in the word "allegory" is not some other hovering above the words of the text, but the possibility of an otherness, a polysemy, inherent in the very words on the page....A sensitivity to the polysemy in words is the basic component of the genre of allegory. This sensitivity is structural, for out of a focus on the word as word, allegory generates narrative action.[74]

This point too had already been made negatively by Swift in the *Tale*, where the "otherness" of language reflects the internal division in an autonomous allegorical activity that does not relate to anything outside of itself. Milton had made the point even more emphatically in *Paradise Lost*, by identifying an internally divided Satan with polysemy and allegory. In particular, the exaggerated allegorical presentation of Sin and Death can be seen as originating within (and as a result of) Satan's internally divided consciousness, so that the "meaning" of the allegory is that it *is* allegory, in contrast with the inspired unified vision of the narrator. As Ferry has shown, Milton uses allegory as an example of fallen modes of language, so that "by the equation of allegory with fallen vision in *Paradise Lost*, the episode of Sin and Death then becomes a kind of serious parody of what is presented as a false literary style" (139).[75] After Sin identifies herself to Satan as "Likest to thee in shape and count'nance bright" (II: 753) she goes on to describe her birth out of Satan's head and to make the point with a self-exemplary pun:

> Then shining heav'nly fair, a Goddess arm'd
> Out of thy head I sprung: amazement seiz'd
> All th' Host of Heav'n; back they recoil'd afraid
> At first, and call'd me Sin, and for a Sign
> Portentous held me. (II: 754–61)

The sign of the sin and the sin of the sign are both born at once, and in their sinister shining semblance are examples of the sibilant "shape" in the language of Satan, the "dismall universal hiss...hiss for hiss return'd with forked tongue/To forked tongue" (X: 508, 518–19). The "bliss" of univocal utterance and meaning is endlessly deferred in the hell of allegory. Allegory forces us to recognize its occupation of the position of the sign, and thus becomes the name for a mechanism that not only precludes recuperation of the linguistic Eden with its "language of Adam," but insists, through its repetition, that we recognize it as a symptom of that inaugural world's original dispersal. The originary meaning has always gone somewhere else, leaving behind only fragments and signs in need of decipherment.

Fletcher has an interesting meditation on the way allegory seems by its very nature to be incomplete, never fulfilling its grand designs.[76] Like Satan, who "hies" and "lights" it can ascend to a trans-allegorical state only in "semblance," not in "substance." In *The Tractate on Education*, Milton writes that "The end then of learning is to repair the ruins of our first parents by regaining to know God aright."[77] The pun on "ruins" (act of falling; result of falling) here confirms the location of allegorical word-play in a merging of history and textuality in a world of ruins, much like that invoked by Benjamin:[78]

> The allegorical physiognomy of the nature-history, which is put on stage in the *Trauerspiel*, is present in reality as a ruin. In the ruin, history has physically merged into the setting. And in this form history does not strike one as the process of eternal life so much as the advance of unending decay. Allegory thereby confesses itself to be beyond beauty. Allegories are in the realm of thoughts what ruins are in the realm of things.[79]

In this fallen world, as Fletcher suggests, "it is logically quite natural for the extension [of allegory] to be infinite, since by definition there is no such thing as the whole of any analogy; all analogies are incomplete, and incompletable, and allegory simply records this analogical relation in a dramatic or narrative form." Seen in a slightly different way, allegory does not "record" a previously existing incompletion, but reveals in itself "a tendency towards infinite extension." This is another reason why, as structure, allegory can go on forever. "The typical allegory threatens never to end...it has no inherent limit."[80] But this also means that allegory can stop at any point, for as a structure of endlessly extendable analogical relation, it is always already "complete" in its structural form. Thus for Benjamin allegorical structures confirm themselves *as ruin*, their allegorical edification confirming their status as works of art in a fallen world.[81] Allegories may be "monuments to our ideals," as Fletcher contends, but they are monuments that are already ruins.

Blake's poem ends with a return to the "wild," which we can now see as the inaugural field of its operation in yet another sense. The "Wild" is a world without a coherence or meaning unified in the self-consciousness of a subject. Thus it is a ruined world of fragments, needing a "key" that will facilitate their (re)union in a cabinet of allegorical perception. But that unity will prove to be "only" allegorical, failing to satisfy the allegorical desire that shatters its structure to re-turn to a "wild" that now includes among its ruins the fragments of the cabinet. The destruction of the allegorical machine comes from within, is already part of the machinery, a function of its operation. The desire that initiates the allegory is the desire that destroys it only to commence anew in its ruins. Thus Fletcher can make the interesting formal comparison between allegory and Freud's compulsive syndrome, because the two share "a form which for our purposes exists as a thing in itself."[82]

Quilligan criticizes Nabokov's *Pale Fire* as improper allegory because it "does not lead beyond itself into the Other, but seduces us deeper and deeper within wonderful labyrinths of its own verbal complexities." Here as elsewhere she is invoking a criterion for allegory that defines it as fiction that is "aimed at leading the reader out of the fiction, to a place where he can view himself in relation to his world, seen again in its eternal dimensions; only there, outside himself, in touch with the Other, is man happy."[83] What this means is that allegory wants to stop being allegory, to get outside its structural limits as a discourse of the other. But the quotation from Quilligan shows that you can only get out of allegory allegorically— rather, that the "allegorical desire" can only be stated in an allegorical formulation. In practice allegory does not lead to Quilligan's apocalyptic "Other," but only to an other, and another, and another, and another. As "The Crystal Cabinet" shows, the door leading "outside" is a revolving door that is part of the same machinery that produces the desire. Allegorical desire is not the essential attribute of a subject, nor is it initiated or stimulated by proximity to a desirable object; it must be understood in terms of a structural system that produces it as an effect of structure. The more constrictive the confinement within the allegorical cabinet, the more intense the desire of allegory will be to get out, to end the allegorical modality. The structural economy of allegorical desire is that of a simultaneously self-destructive and self-replicating machine. It is in this sense that the allegorical machine is homologous with the mechanism of the "repetition compulsion" (*Wiederholungzwang*) that intrigued Freud for most of his career—that ungovernable process originating in the unconscious that causes the reproduction (usually in a disguised, "allegorical" way) of the elements of a past unresolved conflict. Thus we can see the allegorical desire as a heroic attempt to bring the (allegorical) world to an end by interpreting it conclusively, to reach the end of its abyssal structure by achieving the closure of totalized meaning. Since this can only be accomplished allegorically, the allegorical machine must continue to produce more and more allegory, expanding its reflections and refractions in its counterproductive attempt to achieve finality. And theorists too, whose "thought process...is already allegorical *avant la lettre*," can endlessly rediscover that the meaning of allegory is—more allegory.[84]

V: The answer, my friend, is blowin' in the wind.

Blow, ye winds! lift me with you!
I come to the wild
Fold closely, O Nature!
Thine arms round they child.
(Arnold, "Switzerland")

To be imprison'd in the viewless winds,
And blown with restless violence
round about

The pendent world
(Shakespeare, Measure for Measure*)*

...his floating hair!
(Coleridge, "Kubla Khan")

In this final section I return again to the crucial moment of re-turn in "The Crystal Cabinet." I take it to be premonitory of the crisis of the Romantic *afflatus*, with its subject lutes that become defrauded harps, only to prompt still more strenuous efforts to make "the dull/Sirocco air of...degeneracy/Turn as thou mov'st into a healthful breeze/To cherish and invigorate thy frame" (*Prelude* X: 974–977). Like a child with a toy windmill, the Romantic poet must keep running into the wind to make it whirl ever faster, to achieve the effect of visionary power that "attends upon the blowing of the winds."[85] The Romantic attempt to free Nature from allegory, to find in the natural sign a symbol rather than what Coleridge scorned as the mechanical "phantom proxy," is continually reclaimed by allegory as its own creature:

'The horse is taught his manage, and the wind
Of heaven wheels round and treads in his own steps,
Year follows year, the tide returns again,
Day follows day, all things have second birth.

...when the sun
That rose in splendour, was alive, and moved
In exultation among living clouds
Hath put his function and his glory off,
And, turned into a gewgaw, a machine,
Sets like an opera phantom. (*Prelude* X: 70–73; 936–941)

Shelley's fragment of a pre-ruined poem, *The Triumph of Life*, is so perfect an epitome of the allegorical structure that it might well be called *The Triumph of Allegory* and read as the epitaph for the Romantic trope: "And for the morn of truth they feigned, deep night/Caught them ere evening" (214–215). With its Dantesque machinery and *terza-rima* scheme, its abyssal structure (dream within dream within dream, shadows of shadows of phantoms), and its fragmentary form, it would be an easy exercise to trace the mechanism at work in its lines. I prefer to look in closing at a more challenging specimen, written by the theorist of the "symbol" who hoped to end the reign of allegory. If Coleridge's "Kubla Khan" fits the paradigm of "The Crystal Cabinet," my argument will have been confirmed.

Nothing could be more indicative of the dominant power of allegory than the anti-allegorical impulse that marks the rhetoric of Romanticism. Coleridge was one of the most creative inventors and practitioners of rhetorical strategies designed to redefine the semiotic game by finding ways in which the effect of an unmediated relationship or bond could be established between subject and object: the first-person utterance with its seeming guarantee of presence, poems as representations of voice (the poet "as a man speaking to men" in Wordsworth's formulation), the privileging of metonymies (or synecdoches) over metaphor, of "symbol" over "allegory," and the discovery of the "creative imagination" (vs. "fancy") which made the author the origin of his own utterance.[86] These strategies would not have been so crucial if there had not been a pervasive awareness of the fact that in reading texts one is always deceived by illusion, and that representation is made possible only by an order of linguistic difference. Romanticism can be seen as the attempt to establish a new myth of origin, or a myth of renewed origin, that must hide and mystify the nature of its own linguistic procedures and practices—the myth of a recovered linguistic Eden, where all signs are motivated and where words and things are inseparably bonded. The desire for a fully unified subject evokes the notion of poetic "symbol" as "the unit of language in which the subject-object synthesis can take place"[87] in opposition to the internally divided subject of "allegory" with its inevitable distance in relation to its own origin.

"Kubla Khan" ends with the image of a poet in an etymologically literal state of ecstasy (*ex*, "out" + *histanai* "to stand"), leaving the rest of us on the other side of a thrice-woven barrier of absolute difference. But is that the end of the "text" Coleridge presents under the title "Kubla Khan?" One of the problems with the complete text as published by Coleridge is that it is a chiasmic structure (prose—poem : poem—prose) that leads us in a circle, with the prose preface introducing the poem and the poem leading us back to the preface for its commentary. For a variety of reasons readers are tempted to take the "poetic" utterance as primary in this structure. Brisman, for example, contrasting "Porlock...conceived as a person...*the person*, as opposed to *the poet* in the poet," claims that Porlock is "unwilling to recognize his subordinate status of interpreter to a more original text."[88] "Coleridge the poet is already there, preceding and preparing the way for his interrupter and belated successor." But the chronology of the prose starts before the poem and ends after the interruption; we could just as easily say that the dream and its poem interrupt the mundane world of "business" from which the poet had retired, the world that the man from Porlock reasserts. Even though he is "belated" for Brisman, "Porlock habitually comes too soon," suggesting that he always gets "there" before the endlessly deferred climax of the dream/poem.[89]

But in fact neither of these positions does justice to the model structure Coleridge has produced, a structure of difference in which each pole needs the other as that which it is not, its claim for self-identity presupposing difference from something else. Both are part of a structure of other-relations in an endless chain of differentiation in which alterity itself is radical, so that the series can never be closed by a final stopping-point that is also an absolute origin. Frye, while pointing out that "all commentary is allegorical," suggested that "the relation of such commentary to poetry itself is the source of the contrast which was developed by several critics of the Romantic period between 'symbolism' and 'allegory.'"[90] This is indeed the effect that Coleridge's staged contrast is designed to produce, leading us to forget that one of the terms ("allegory") is also a name for the kind of structured differentiation that permeates the text of "Kubla Khan" and the numerous other parodies of edited texts that he left behind. The structure of prose/poem is paralleled by the opposition between the writing practice of normal consciousness and the effortless production of a dream state, "if that indeed can be called composition in which all the images rose up before him as things...without any sensation or consciousness of effort." But this too is another of Coleridge's ways of articulating the distinction between allegory and symbol. Allegory "cannot be other than spoken consciously; whereas in the former (the symbol) it is very possible that the general truth represented may be working unconsciously in the writer's mind during the construction of the symbol....The advantage of symbolic writing over allegory is, that *it presumes no disjunction of faculties, but simple predominance.*"[91] Presumably this means that the disjunction of allegorical consciousness will disappear in the dominating presence of the unitary truth; the symbol, although it comes later, will turn out to have been first.[92] We are thus witnesses to what de Man calls a "fallacious retotalization" in the "ambiguous valorization" of terms:

The deconstruction of a system of relationships always reveals a more fragmented stage that can be called natural with regard to the system that is being undone. Because it also functions as the negative truth of the deconstructive process, the "natural" pattern authoritatively substitutes its relational system for the one it helped dissolve. In doing so it conceals the fact that it is itself one system of relations among others, and it presents itself as the sole and true order of things, as nature and not as structure.[93]

This basic fact, that symbol can only be defined as *not* allegory, poetry as *not* prose, the unconscious as *not* conscious, is the structural model for the entire text of "Kubla Khan". It is present even within the poem as the opposition between the model of the first pleasure dome (the Khan's) and the second (the poet's). Within the pleasure dome of the Khan, it is intertextually present in allusions to the Miltonic introduction of the "real" paradise: "*Not* that fair field/Of *Enna*...*nor* that *Nyseian* Isle...*Nor* where *Abassin* Kings their issue Guard,/Mount *Amara*, though this by some suppos'd/True Paradise" (IV: 268–82). But even before that, it is enacted *within* the prose preface, by the introduction of imagery and a quotation from Coleridge's poem "The Picture" (1802). The first 117 lines of this conspicuously allegorical "dream vision" are devoted to what the poem is not. In the most extreme instance, we are told that no pool in the dreamscape's stream "did e'er reflect the stately virgin's robe" (72–74), then we are given at some length a visual picture of a maiden who was not there, who was (or was not?) worshipped by a "poor youth" as a "watery idol" or "phantom-world" in the form of her reflection, which she then (in the lines quoted in "Kubla Khan") destroyed. After this the pool becomes a mirror again, but this time without the reflection—leaving the youth in "mad love-yearning by the vacant brook," contemplating her now internalized image in his "sickly thoughts...her shadow still abiding there,/The Naiad of the mirror!" (109–111). Thus we have a poetic representation of the pursuit of a mental *image*, based on a reflected mirror image, of a maiden who was not thereto illustrate what this poem is *not* going to be ("Not to thee, O wild and desert stream! belongs this tale"). I take this to be a rather elaborate way of saying that what's left of this poem is not going to be about an allegorical "phantom proxy," but rather about something real. Therefore we shift to a first-person narration in which the speaker wanders on until he sees a cottage:

> But what is this?
> That cottage, with its slanting chimney-smoke,
> And close beside its porch a sleeping child,
> His dear head pillowed on a sleeping dog—
> One arm between its fore-legs, and the hand
> Holds loosely its small handful of wild-flowers,
> Unfilletted, and of unequal lengths. (152–8)

We are deliberately tricked by the conspicuous precision of this description, for the cottage scene turns out to be "A curious picture, with a master's haste/Sketched" leaving traces that enable the poet to imagine its authorship:

> Divinest maid!
> Yon bark her canvas, and those purple berries
> Her pencil! See, the juice is scarcely dried
> On the fine skin! She has been newly here;
> And lo! yon patch of heath has been her couch—
> The pressure still remains! (161–6)

The trick is justified by the fact that this "picture" is every bit as "realistic" as the fictive reality level in the poem; both are representations, the poem at this point presenting itself as a (word) picture *of* a picture. The verbal description of the pictorial content is organized along the syntagmatic axis, each element touching the next in the metonymic relationship that Jakobson associated with the "realistic" tendency in literature as opposed to the merely formal trope of metaphor.[94] The scene of representation is marked by a cluster of images of "indexical" signs as defined by Peirce, where the hole in the door is a non-arbitrary material sign of the actual presence (at some point in time) of its originating cause in the form of a bullet.

I deal with "The Picture" at such length to show that the thematics of "Kubla Khan" are opened up already within its prose commentary, revealing a potential abyss of mediated representation unless the poet can trace the picture (which is only a "trace") to its source. Otherwise, "'twill but idly feed/The passion that consumes me" (182–3). The pun here on "idle" and "idol" (from *eidolon*, "image" or "phantom") reinscribes the difference between the "picture" as reflection and its source. No matter how good the picture is, even if it's painted with berry-juice, and written with metonymies, the poet can't eat it, for it hasn't achieved the status of symbol as presented in the climax of the *Statesman's Manual* definition:

> The other [allegories] are but empty echoes which the fancy arbitrarily associates with apparitions of matter, less beautiful but not less shadowy than the sloping orchard or hillside pasture-field seen in the transparent lake below. Alas! for the flocks that are to be led forth to such pastures! 'It shall even be as when the hungry dreameth, and behold he eateth; but he waketh and his soul is empty: or as when the thirsty dreameth, and behold he drinketh; but he awaketh and is faint!' (Isaiah xxix: 8).

The illusion of material substantiality rhetorically produced by picture of a picture, like the sensory pictures painted on the retina and their reflected forms in the mind's eye, dissolves, revealing itself as mere reflection of an originating unity that shows itself in the material world only in mediated form. Can "Kubla Khan" do anything, as poem, to advance us beyond this dilemma already inscribed it its preface before it starts?

The first part of the poem can be read as an exhibit of the now familiar cabinet of perception, with its enclosed "dome" establishing the necessary inside-outside distinction and relationships. The Khan's creation by decree suggests the kind of ordering done on the second level of reflection, where the hordes of images have become hoards for reflection, augmented in Coleridge's case by the "reservoir" of "images which had flashed on the inner eye from the pages of innumerable books [that]...flock up, with their potential associations, from the deeps."[95] Although he doesn't acknowledge it, and in fact mystifies it at times by his over-excited rhetoric, Lowes's *Road to Xanadu* provides an exemplary model of Lockean reading in which the activities of the Khan and of the poet mirror each other perfectly. Into the poet's mind and poem "poured...a throng of mingling reminiscences....The images which streamed together...out of the kaleidoscopic play of images..."

> —out of this segment of chaos, there was framed a shape of balanced symmetry, a lucid equipoise of part with part which as a form foreseen had been imposed upon the flux

of interpenetrating images of memory. And then, thus perfected in its own inner harmony, this complex structure, deliberately built out of the stream, was *locked*, in all its radiant succinctness, into the crescent arch of the design...*every crystal-clear picture* there, is an integral part of a preconceived and consciously elaborated whole.[96]

The couplets and doublings in the poem (twice five miles; tumult-tumult; Kubla-Khan; damsel-dulcimer, etc.) and the reflected image of the dome all provide strong mirroring effects, and gradually qualify what at first seems to be a totally desirable terrestrial paradise. As the written representation of a representation in a dream, prompted by reading a representation in a book based on other books and reports, of a pleasure dome that is itself based on a model of reflection, the status of the poem is as thoroughly mediated or distanced from the Khan's "original" dome as that dome is distanced from the original Paradise in Eden. The Khan's decree and resulting dome are a *not it*, and the past-tense of the poem reminds us that the future-tense prophecy ("Ancestral voices prophesying war!") has long since come true. Like all things created in time, the pleasure dome was destined to become a lost ruin that can now only be rebuilt as a textual ruin; the transitoriness of these material embodiments simply doubles that of the earthly globe itself, which the "ancestral voice" of God has pronounced transient.[97] Milton indulges himself in a pun to make the point as clear as possible; the real paradise will not be in (punning) language, it will be a *not*-this, but a *not* that is *not* the *knot* of art ("Flow'rs worthy of Paradise which not nice Art/In Beds and curious Knots, but Nature boon" (IV: 241–2).

The transitory fragility and representational limits of the dome are also shown to be the limits of language and textuality. Whatever its "source," the poet's dome/poem is built in language; and within it we see reflected the Khan's linguistic utterance or "decree" that gives rise to his dome as an effect of language. Among all the other rivers that have influenced Coleridge's Alph, the closest is perhaps the classical Alpheus, and its momentary invocation in "Lycidas": "Return Alpheus, the dread voice is past,/That shrank thy stream" (132–133). But that dread voice (in contrast with the Khan's voice and the poet's voice which it is *not*) is in abeyance only for a moment, "For so to interpose a little ease,/Let our frail thoughts dally with surmise" (152–153). The "space" of the Khan's pleasure dome is thus the transitory space of language. It begins with the classical river associated with the origin of poetry, Alpheus, reduced to "Alph." Like the alphabet, this language river flows between its Alpha and Omega in the Khan's linguistic pleasure dome, towards its end in the "lifeless Ocean."[98] As we should expect in an allegorical text, the combinations of these letters reveal the pervasive otherness of the word as word—the polysemic field of language with its punning play of mirrors.

If Coleridge actually fell asleep reading *Purchase his Pilgrimage*, his text would have given him a "Cublai Can" in "Xaindu" (first and second editions) or in "Xamdu" (third and fourth editions).[99] Word-play with the name alone can generate the problematic issues of the poem. Transporting the language into English illustrates the same ambiguity of the vowel in the Khan's title that has allowed the two verbs "can" and "con" to develop from the same Old English root, *cunnan*, meaning to know how, to be able (see the German *können, kann*). Three of the eight syllables of the poem's first line give us forms of the same verb: do-did-can, emphasizing present and past indicative in contrast with the lingering subjunctive of the second part: "*Could* I revive..." The poet tells us that what the Khan *can do* he *did do*, in Xanadu; then he tells us what he would do if he *could* (a month before leaving for Germany to study I. Kant). The puns on verb forms are only part of the word-play in this Coleridgean textual maze. There are four puns on "Khan" in the preface alone, where we are told that the poet had retired to the Exmoor *con*fines of Somerset and Devonshire; the poem is a *con*sequence of taking an anodyne, after which the author *con*tinued his three hour sleep during which he has the most vivid *con*fidence—he had already "composed" the poem. These "con" words are all Khan words in a double sense, not only as homophonic echoes but also as key elements of the thematic focus of the poem and its prose commentary. The Khan has the Khanfidence that the poet lacks, to erect the Khanfines of his garden (a container of contents including canals) that will Khantinue until it reaches its temporal limit or Khanfine in the Khanflict prophesized by the ancestral voices; thus it is not the true (Biblical) land of promise, Canaan. Like Milton's Satan, it is "far beneath/His confidence to equal God in power" (VI: 342–3). The poet's activity parallels the Khan's, as he presumes on our confidence to play his con-game, confiding in us his canard about the man from Porlock.

The Allegory of Allegory

The sense of enclosed space, a dome with walls, contributes to the emphasis on containment that both defines the Khan's power (to measure and make limits) and that power's limitations. As container the pleasure dome is isomorphic with Locke's mind, a cabinet that gets filled up with contents—man's little sensorium ("twice five miles") as an inside divided from the "wild" ("measureless to man") outside. This is the opposite of a view of the mind as a fountain or source rather than receptacle, a difference crucial to the Romantic Imagination, as Blake's Devil's proverb suggests: 'The cistern contains: the fountain overflows" (E 36). No one has employed this conflicting imagery (or provoked it in his critics) so much as Coleridge, with his "life of allegory" suggesting the polar images of creative genius and cunning plagiarist. "For there is amongst us a set of critics, who seem to hold, that every possible thought and image is traditional; who have no notion that there are such things as fountains in the world, small as well as great; and who would therefore charitably derive every rill ["gardens bright with sinuous (sin-you-us) rills"] they behold flowing, from a perforation made in some other man's tank. I am *con*fident, however." This quotation is from the prose preface to "Christabel," defending Coleridge's claim to "originality" in its composition. "The dates are mentioned for the exclusive purpose of precluding charges of plagiarism or servile imitation from myself." Like the "Kubla Khan" preface, it was written for publication in 1816, commenting on a text claimed to have been written in 1797. It too includes a poem (borrowed and translated) within the prose, making the comic plea that if something belongs equally to several (Coleridge, Scott and Byron), Coleridge should have the credit, "for I/Am the poorer of the two" (213–215). In this hydraulic combat Coleridge is claiming the **power** to be the **pourer**. If the poet can be imaged as a "tank," then with equal aptness he can be a "can," and the word-play continues with the issue of what *kind* of can is the Khan? Do his rills have real water, or merely allegorical water? Even Milton could not avoid the possibilities in this context, as the punning redundancy in Adam's acknowledgement of his limited capacities illustrates: "my fill/Of knowledge, what this vessel can contain" (XII: 558–9). When Dorothy writes in her journal, "I breakfasted and carried Kubla to a fountain in the neighbouring market-place, where I drank some excellent water," did she have a manuscript of the poem—or a "can" jokingly named the "Kubla can" by Coleridge?[100]

All claims for the status of originality, or "origin" outside of language for the Khan's pleasure dome, are further contaminated by its exaggerated inter-textual status. As Lowes shows, the poem is an echo-chamber of allusions to all the textual false paradises that Coleridge had read about, and the many mythic versions of the quest for the true "source" of the Nile. The Khan's originating "decree" was no doubt an attempt to copy a garden he had read about, the garden whose original version is always "wide remote" (in Milton's phrase) from its phantom proxies, somewhere outside the textual wake evoked by Barthes:

> They [the coded elements] are so many fragments of something that has always been already read, seen, done, experienced; the code is the wake of that already. Referring to what has been written, i. e. to the Book (of culture, of life, of life as culture), it makes the text into a prospectus of the Book.[101]

Coleridge's immersion in this wake was not the esoteric specialty that it is sometimes made out to be; the same "elements" can be found in some of the most popular and available texts of the eighteenth century. Thomson could present the whole package ("the secret Bounds Of jealous Abyssinia") in a fifty-line set piece of clichés ("Summer," 751–802), and Johnson turned to the Abyssinian to write his allegorical autobiography, *Rasselas*, in the popular genre of the oriental tale. Thus the "location" of the Khan's pleasure-dome was not "wide remote" in time and place; it was the most familiar place in the eighteenth century—the human mind itself, charted and chartered by Locke. All versions of the false paradise emphasize its confined nature; many (Johnson, Thomson, Milton, Purchase and others) literalize this confinement by putting locks on its gates, or by having a locked enclosure within for the Khan's children. Thus Rasselas/Johnson begins his life, like the speaker of Blake's "The Crystal Cabinet," by being Lockd up; and after breaking out he completes the circle by choosing to return at the end, sadder but wiser; a knowing—if not altogether willing—prisoner of the (merely) earthly paradise, the best that the Can-Man/Con-Man can do. In other words, Rasselas/Johnson has written the history of how one becomes an allegorist—someone who has the knowledge, as Benjamin emphasizes, to gaze out from his prison in melancholy contemplation of the ruins and fragments of a world seen as script-image (*Schriftbild*) of the already-written.

Coleridge too knew what it was like to live and write in this prison:

> What are Words but air? & impulses of air? O who has deeply felt, deeply, deeply! & not fretted & grown impatient at the inadequacy <of Words to Feeling,> of the symbol to the Being?—Words—what are they but a subtle matter?...O what then are Words, but articulated Sighs of a Prisoner heard from his Dungeon! powerful only as they express their utter impotence! Life may be *inferred*, even as intelligence is from black marks on white paper—but the black marks themselves are truly "the dead letter."[102]

To return to this prison of language, in language, is to return to the scene that prompts the revived desire for escape from allegory. As the echo of Paul anticipates, this escape from the dead letter can only be made in the "spirit" of allegory.

The second part of Coleridge's poem condenses into eighteen lines the Romantic promise of freedom and its simultaneous conflation with Benjamin's threefold "Satanic promise" of allegory. It also invokes Michael's promise to Adam at the end of *Paradise Lost*: "then wilt thou not be loath/To leave this Paradise, but shalt possess/A paradise within thee, happier far" (XII: 585–7). As we leave this paradise of the Khan, to consider a poetic revival *within*, we make the same shift Michael makes in Book XII, from an emphasis on the visual to an oral presentation of vision. This shift from the "ineluctable modality of the visible"[103] to the ear, with its greater claims on presence, is a pervasive Romantic strategy that we can see enacted here in its purest form.[104] As a rhetorical strategy, the æolian harp image could collapse the inside/outside distinction by being located precisely on the threshold of perception, giving the sense of a pure interiority of consciousness that is somehow also always and already "outside" as an other. The "symphony" of the damsel with a dulcimer suggests this "sounding together" (sun = together, phone = voice/sound) in the achievement of "one Life within us and abroad, as well as the passive, open, receptive posture in which the desired experience of sensory plenitude in a present moment can be experienced.

But at the crucial poetic moment the poet must become active in order to revive the symphony and song; the self-presence of consciousness can only be produced poetically as an effect, constructed—as the Khan's dome was—with certain linguistic rules and procedures that govern its construction. Thus the poet is introduced into the poem (or the "frame" is expanded to include an image of the poet) as a poetic "I" that brings with it the self-distancing effects of commentary and the abyssal structure of representation. The three lines that evoke the unity of re-vivication also enact the self-division of replication:

> Could I revive within me
> Her symphony and song,
> To such a deep delight 'twould win me,
> That...

The intensification of doubling effects here combines with the only pure-repetition rhyme in the whole poem, where the poet contemplates himself as interiority at the distance of the second person: "in me." The exact rhyme could be said to produce the effect of the desired revival "within" the poet; but it also intensifies the doubling of the poet in a mirror repetition. The ambiguous scansion here, with either a weakly forced spondee or the only feminine endings in the poem, catches the effect of the subjunctive verb tense to further qualify the force of the lines. Like the infant before the Lacanian mirror, the poet who sought escape from self-reflection into the transcendental I AM is trapped within the structure of infinite regression. He risks the "constant danger of sliding back again into the chaos from which he started; it hangs over the abyss of a dizzy Ascent in which one can perhaps see the very essence of Anxiety."[105] He is unable to "see himself" or to represent himself to the reader without specular mediation, and "what can look at itself is not one; and the law of the addition of the origin to its representation, of the thing to its image, is that one plus one makes at least three."[106]

The poem's "Abyssinian maid" suggests another knowing Coleridgean wager with Milton's text, striving for an authentic homology and homophony between his "***Abyssinian maid***" and Milton's muse, who "Dove-like satst brooding on the vast ***Abyss/And mad'st*** it pregnant" (I: 21–22). Coleridge's maid, like Milton's muse, must be symphony *and song*; she must communicate in words that are not God, not the timeless now of divine interiority: "Immediate are the Acts of God, more swift/Than time or motion, but to human ears/Cannot without process of speech be told" (VII: 176–178). The Abyssinian maid must be represented in language, limiting the fulfillment of the poet's desire to language with its abyssal structure of endless mediation. The vision is Abyssinian-made, made with an abyss in it; or rather, it is in Derrida's formulation born from "the structural necessity of the abyss....Representation in the abyss of presence is not an accident of presence; the desire of presence is, on the contrary, born from the abyss (the indefinite multiplication) of representation, from the representation of representation."[107]

As Lowes has shown, one of Coleridge's favorite books was James Bruce's *Travels to Discover the Source of the Nile*, an account of the attempt to solve a mystery that "had baffled the genius, industry, and inquiry of both ancients and moderns, for the course of near three thousand years."[108] Abyssinia, as the fabled source of the Nile, offered itself as an image of the human mind containing somewhere within it the Romantic Imagination: "That awful Power rose from the mind's abyss/Like an unfathered vapour (*Prelude* VI: 595–6)

> ...like the mighty flood of Nile
> Poured from his fount of Abyssinian clouds
> To fertilize the whole Egyptian plain.
>   (1850 *Prelude* VI: 614–16)

This image of the human mind as a prolific source-abyss (rather than a "devouring" abyss) is as far from the true scene of creation as the fabled Abyssinian paradise from the true one, or James Bruce's discovery that there was no single source for the Nile. The actual Nile was divided at its origin, like the human mind divided at its very source. The poem's "Mount Abora," which Brisman has hailed as "the *aboriginal* word" (26) has inscribed within itself this plurality of the source rather than the expected unity (*ab* = from; *ora* = plural of *os*, mouth).

There is another divided source, or source of division, that is approached in the poem at this point—one that has been explicated at length by Joel Fineman, in his reading of the opening of *The Canterbury Tales* as an enactment of the structurality of the primal scene of allegorical desire. Fineman reads the figurative piercing of March by April in Chaucer as a parallel between the poem as textual structure and the beginning of the year as sequence requiring binary opposition (rainy April vs. dry March, etc.). He then proceeds to use Jakobsonian structural linguistics to explore the significance of the phonemic patterning in Chaucer's opening opposition between *ap* and *ma* in "Aprill with his shoures soote" and "The droghte of *March*." Jakobson applied structuralist methodology to determine that the maximum binary opposition that could be formed in the human mouth was /pa/, with its vocalic /a/ and the voiceless labial stop /p/.[109] Thus as a representation of absolute phonological difference in the mouth, /pa/ can be plausibly claimed to be conceptually the first syllable. Jakobson went on from this theoretical notion to studies in language acquisition and aphasia that showed /p/ to be the first utterance children learn and the last aphasics lose. The opposition holds true with either order (/pa/ or /ap/) and with /b/ as well, since at this stage the distinction between voiced and voiceless has not been made.[110]

Jakobson's further researches provided cross-cultural support for the first-syllable status of /pa/, and established that /ma/ (and reversals like ema, ama) fulfilled the need for a second binary opposition, structurally opposable to the first. Once /m/ is articulated as a distinctive linguistic feature the possibility of establishing a structure of phonological sound in a paradigmatic code is established, since /p/ and /m/ are both opposed to /a/ and opposed to each other. Here too we can see Coleridge (in 1794) intrigued by the same kind of linguistic topic: "Smile from subrisus. B and M both labials/hence Infants first utter a, Ba, pa, a, milk."[111]

Before the introduction of /ma/ the status of the utterance /pa/ would be pre-linguistic, the sheer diacriticality of contrast (silence/sound; consonant/vowel). But after the introduction of the second opposition each term in the series will be significant only with respect to its opposition to the other term in the structure; the "originality" of the differential determination /pa/ will be totally sublated or "retroactively effaced" so that "the origin will be structurally determined as a ghost, a palpably absent origin, by virtue of the very structurality it fathers."[112]

Fineman brings these structural principles to bear on the piercing of March by April in Chaucer's opening, in order to show that

> the allegorical structure thus enunciated has already lost its center and thereby discovered a project: to re-cover the loss dis-covered by the structure of language and of literature...this journey back to a foreclosed origin writes itself out as a pilgrimage to the sacred founding...In terms of literary response, the structurality of the text holds out the promise of a meaning that it will also perpetually

defer...This is the formal destiny of every allegory insofar as allegory is definable as continued metaphor. (44–45)

I bring in Fineman here because of the uncanny aptness of his observations for the critical moment in "Kubla Khan" where, at the very moment of finding the "aboriginal word," like the fabled source of the Nile, the linguistic pa-radise is lost through the diacriticality of language: "It was an *Ab*yssinian *ma*id." Coleridge's formulation here echoes the key phonemic feature of Milton's inaugural moment where "from the first" his muse "Dove-like satst brooding on the vast *Ab*yss/And *ma*d'st it pregnant," and chimes with Wordsworth's epiphanic image of the "I*ma*gination—here the Power so called/Through sad incompetence of human speech,/That awful Power rose from the mind's *ab*yss." Wordsworth's formulation makes explicit what is implicit in the other formulations: that the poem inscribes not the primal word, but the primal difference of language and human speech.

As Mileur has pointed out, Coleridge's poem is presented as having been interrupted precisely at the critical moment when its figuration and allegorization become dangerous, "at precisely the point at which it pretends to complete itself and become more than figurative."[113] The danger is that the gap between the infinite allegorical aspiration and the mediated limits of its vehicle will force the recognition that we are trapped within allegory, that our knowledge can never be other than allegorical, and that to write is to allegorize the already allegorical. The poem is thus both an interrupted fragment, and complete in its embodiment of the structural features of the allegorical machine. Coleridge backs off at this point from an attempt to represent the "esemplastic act" of union, as if he anticipated the inevitable failure of any attempt to guarantee the unity of the act in terms of representation and reflection (*not* act), which would require yet another representation to guarantee the unity of the first, and another for that one, in the infinite series that results from the attempt to ground the transcendental in representation.[114] The failure of this act, as shown in the allegory of "The Crystal Cabinet," would reduce the machine to ruins. So, in order to avoid that result Coleridge has left us a pre-ruined structure, like the unwritten thirteenth chapter of the *Biographia*. There the fictional Friend breaks in, like the prose commentator on the Kubla Khan poem or the Porlockian visitor on its author, to point out that no matter how long the (unwritten) manuscript of the chapter might be, its author would "have been obliged to omit so many links, from the necessity of compression, that what remains, looks...like the fragments of the winding steps of an old ruined tower (302–303). No matter how long it is, allegorical extension can never traverse the links of an infinite extension; its author will inevitably be "whirled down the gulph of an infinite series" (285).

Thus the moment of self-presence that would constitute the escape from the allegorical cabinet can only be infinitely deferred. The man from Porlock is a representative of poor Locke, a Porlockian or pour-Lockean, for whom the sensory plenitude and riches of man's *can*, the little sensorium or paradise within, is *only* within. The interruption from poor Locke reestablishes the duplicate world structure with its thrice-woven barrier between inside and outside, forever part of the same structure of difference. Coleridge had the saving sense of humor of the true melancholy allegorist; a few years after *Kubla Khan* he attempted to use it to exorcise the demon in "Dejection: An Ode," hoping that the storm of the "Mad Lutanist" in the "Wind that rav'st without," and his own storm within, might prove to "be but a mountain-birth." The allusion is to Horace: "*parturient montes, nascetur ridiculus mus*" ["the mountains labor only to give birth to a ridiculous mouse"].[115] The frenzied vision of the poet in "Kubla Khan," with his flashing eyes and floating hair, might have proved to be a dulcimer-induced Mount-Abora-birth, had the man from Porlock not interrupted to preserve it as the allegorical ruin of a symbolic "inmost Form."

NOTES

1. One of the "Pickering Manuscript" poems, probably composed by Blake between 1800–1804 and written out in fair copy after 1805.

2. Herman Melville, *Moby-Dick*, ed. Harrison Hayford and Hershel Parker (New York: W. W. Norton & Co., 1967), 177. Subsequent references are incorporated in the text.

3. Matthew Arnold, *Poetry and Criticism of Matthew Arnold*, ed. A. Dwight Culler (Boston: Houghton Mifflin, 1961), 208–209. Subsequent references are incorporated in the text.

4. Terry Eagleton, *Walter Benjamin: Or Towards a Revolutionary Criticism* (London: Verso, 1981), 6.

5. Northrop Frye's *Anatomy of Criticism* (Princeton: Princeton University Press, 1957) was originally planned as an introduction to the theory of allegory. Since his discussion of allegory centered on Benjamin and Bloch (in *Marxism and Form* [Princeton: Princeton University Press, 1971]), Fredric Jameson has been pursuing his own hermeneutic model combining a Marxist critical stance with the invocation of allegorical structure in the relationship between History and Text(s). Paul de Man, especially in "The Rhetoric of Temporality," in *Blindness and Insight: Essays in the Rhetoric of Contemporary Criticism*, 2nd ed. (Minneapolis: University of Minnesota Press, 1983), 187–228), and in *Allegories of Reading* (New Haven: Yale University Press, 1979) has made notable theoretical and interpretive advances, as have Joel Fineman ("The Structure of Allegorical Desire," in *Allegory and Representation*, ed. Stephen J. Greenblatt [Baltimore: The Johns Hopkins University Press, 1981], 26–60) and Charles Bernheimer (*Flaubert and Kafka: Studies in Psychopoetic Structure* (New Haven: Yale University Press, 1982)). Edwin Honig (*Dark Conceit: The Making of Allegory* [New York: Oxford University Press, 1966]), Angus Fletcher (*Allegory: The Theory of a Symbolic Mode* [Ithaca: Cornell University Press, 1964]) and Maureen Quilligan (*The Language of Allegory: Defining the Genre* [Ithaca: Cornell University Press, 1979]) have contributed to an understanding of allegory as a generic mode.

6. Joseph Addison, *Essays in Criticism and Literary Theory*, ed. John Loftis (Northbrook: AHM Publishing, 1975), 177. Subsequent references are incorporated in the text.

7. William Hogarth, *The Analysis of Beauty* (London: 1753), 42.

8. Johann Joachim Winckelmann, *Reflections on the Imitation of Greek Works in Painting and Sculpture*, text of *Gedancken über die Nachahmung der Griechischen Werke in der Mahleren und Bildhauer-Kunst*, tr. Elfriede Heyer and Roger C. Norton (La Salle: Open Court, 1987), 61–69.

9. David V. Erdman, ed., *The Complete Poetry and Prose of William Blake* (Berkeley: University of California Press, 1982), 554, 248, 249, 687, 669, 730). Unless otherwise indicated all quotations of Blake will be from this edition, identified as "E."

10. Michael Murrin, *Veil of Allegory* (Chicago: University of Chicago Press, 1969), 198.

11. "Rhetoric of Temporality," 192.

12. Samuel Taylor Coleridge, *The Statesman's Manual*, ed. W. G. T. Shedd (New York: Harper and Brothers, 1875), 438.

13. John Hughes, ed., *The Works of Mr. Edmund Spenser* (London: Jacob Tonson, 1715), xxxix.

14. Maureen Quilligan rightly criticizes "our ordinary way of talking about different 'levels' of meaning" (27) and claims that "it would be more precise to say...that allegory works horizontally, rather than vertically, so that meaning accretes serially" (28). This formulation needs to be expanded to include the possibility for fusion of seriality and cyclicality frequently found in allegory.

15. For the most part the poem has been simply snatched up as an illustration of the critic's explication of Blake's system, its most conspicuous features translated into some form of Blakese. For Frye (*Fearful Symmetry* [Princeton: Princeton University Press, 1947], 234), the poem illustrates a "highly technical but crucial point in Blake's argument." Kathleen Raine (*Blake and Tradition* (Princeton: Princeton University Press, 1968) sees in it yet another descent of intellect (or light) into matter (or darkness) finding in it "recondite alchemical symbolism which Blake may have found in Vaughan's Aula Lucis" (I: 274), suggesting that we read it as "a paraphrase of Vaughan's allegory" (I: 275), ignoring the significant fact that both Blake and Vaughan take their models from optics. The poem's "triplicity is an alchemical theme" (I: 276). Leopold Damrosch (*Symbol and Truth in Blake's Method* [Princeton: Princeton University Press, 1980], 200) simply summarizes and combines Frye and Raine in a one-sentence explication. John Beer, in *Blake's Humanism* (New York: Barnes & Noble, 1968), 89, claimed that "Blake presents the height of Vision as it is given to man in his sexual relationships—a delight to be enjoyed, but also to be recognized for what it is, a passing revelation, and relinquished without regret." A year later he borrowed the Vaughan quotation from Raine to use as an epigraph for *Blake's Visionary Universe* (New York: Barnes & Noble, 1969), ix. Bloom observes that "To be put into her Cabinet, and locked up with a golden key, is a fairly unequivocal statement of sexual intercourse...The youth [is] baffled in his ambition to find an apocalypse in sexual satisfaction" (*Apocalypse* [Garden City: Doubleday, 1963], 300).

16. *Blake's Humanism*, 89.

17. The autograph manuscript is in the Fitzwilliam Museum, Cambridge. Michael Phillips has produced an excellent facsimile version for those unable to consult the original (Cambridge: Cambridge University Press, 1986). In it the "an" in "Human" has been overwritten by "ing" to produce "Huming." "Gent" has overwritten the first part of a longer word (words?) ending in "man." I agree with Keynes (*The Complete Writings of William Blake* [London: Oxford University Press, 1966], 52) that the base word was "Pantryman," because the downstrokes on the "P" and "y" are clearly visible. I am also influenced by the satirical relevance to Locke's constant emphasis on the mind's "store of ideas" and their proper inventory and disposition. G. E. Bentley (*William Blake's Writings* [Oxford: Clarendon Press, 1978], 886) finds the base word illegible. Erdman (849) and Phillips (43) both read "Gentleman."

18. By the time Hume wrote his *Treatise of Human Nature* (1734–1737) during a stay in France, he could confidently assert as commonplaces the basic assumptions of Locke's epistemology: "We may observe, that 'tis universally allow'd by philosophers, and is besides pretty obvious of itself, that nothing is every really present with the mind but its perceptions" (L. A. Selby-Bigge, ed., *A Treatise of Human Nature*, rpt. of [1739] ed. [Oxford: Clarendon Press, 1968], 67).

19. Svetlana Alpers, in *The Art of Describing: Dutch Art in the Seventeenth Century* (Chicago: University of Chicago Press, 1983), has a useful condensed history of optical discoveries and their implications for northern art. In his *Philosophy and the Mirror of Nature* (Princeton: Princeton University Press, 1979), Richard Rorty explores the topic of optical epistemology, arguing that the mainstream of modern Western philosophy began at the moment the paradigm for knowing and the central problem for philosophical thought fused in a focus on the model of a knowing subject as the container [the internal "space" of the mind] of representational contents endowed with consciousness. He locates the historical origin of that focus in the rise of epistemology as the study of mental representations in the seventeenth century, and the identification of "knowledge" with mental representations based on the model of optics. A number of studies have explored the importance for eighteenth-century English literature of this optical epistemology; there are too many to list here, but among those I've found useful is A. D. Nuttall's *A Common Sky: Philosophy and the Literary Imagination* (Berkeley: University of California Press, 1974). In *Confinement and Flight: An Essay on English Literature of the Eighteenth Century* (Berkeley: University of California Press, 1977), W. B. Carnochan traces the theme of "epistemological prisons" in its relationship with Locke's "version of mind as screened off from reality" (7), emphasizing Johnson's notion that "the mind is locked in and that being locked in is what inspires the poet to airy flights and panoramic views" (162). In *Imagining the Penitentiary: Fiction and the Architecture of Mind in Eighteenth-Century England* (Chicago: University of Chicago Press, 1987), John Bender's focus is on "philosophy as exemplified by Locke and Hume, the realist novel, and the penitentiary as envisioned by Bentham" (36).

20. Addison concludes the first of his "pleasures of the imagination" series with this note: "I have here supposed that my reader is acquainted with that great modern discovery which is at present universally acknowledged by all the enquirers into natural philosophy: namely, that light and colors, as apprehended by the imagination, are only ideas in the mind and not qualities that have any existence in matter. As this is a truth that has been proved incontestably by many modern philosophers...[and] in the eighth chapter of the second book of Mr. Locke's essay on human understanding" (148).

21. Blake makes the identity of this allegorical eye-land even more clear at the beginning: "In the Moon, is a certain Island near by a mighty continent, which small island seems to have some affinity to England. & what is more extraordinary the people are so much alike & their language so much the same that you would think you was among your friends" (E 449).

22. *The Newtonian System of Philosophy...by Tom Telescope, A. M.* (London: J. Newbery, 1761).

23. "All our ideas, therefore," says Tom, "are obtained either by *sensation* or *reflection*, that is to say, by means of our five senses...or by the *operations of the mind* [upon them]." This little illustrated book, "Adapted to the Capacities of young GENTLEMEN and LADIES, and familiarized and made entertaining by Objects with which they are intimately acquainted," tried to do for children what Locke had done for their parents.

It was one of John Newbery's great successes, going through ten editions between its initial publication (1761) and the turn of the century, and it was far from unique. J. H. Plumb, "The First Flourishing of Children's Books," in *Early Children's Book and Their Illustration* (New York: The Pierpont Morgan Library, 1975), discusses *A Museum* (fifteen editions between 1750–1800) and other examples of the genre.

24. Plumb, xxix.

25. See Richard D. Altick, *The Shows of London* (Cambridge: Harvard University Press, 1978).

26. "GENTLE READER! LO, here a CAMERA OBSCURA is presented to thy view, in which are lights and shades dancing on a whited canvas, and magnified into apparent life! thou art perfectly at leisure for such trivial amusement, walk in, and view the wonders of my ENCHANTED GARDEN" Erasmus Darwin, *The Botanic Garden; A Poem in Two Parts* (Dublin: J. Moore, 1793), xv.

27. William Paley, *Natural Theology* (London, 1822), 12–33.

28. *Panopticon: or, the Inspection-House* (Dublin and London: T. Payne, 1791).

29. See Adam Smith, *The Theory of Moral Sentiments* (Indianapolis: Liberty Classics, 1976).

30. John Locke, *An Essay Concerning Human Understanding*, ed. Alexander Campbell Fraser (New York: Dover Publications, Inc., 1959), II.i.*passim*. Subsequent citations are incorporated in the text.

31. Isaac Newton, *Opticks* (New York: Dover, 1952), 124. Subsequent citations are incorporated in the text.

32. "Remote, serene, and inaccessible...the power is there" (Shelley, "Mont Blanc" 97, 127, in *The Complete Poetical Works of Percy Bysshe Shelley*, ed. Thomas Hutchinson [London: Oxford University Press, 1960]). I explore some of the rhetorical implications of this theory in my "The Tropology of Silence in Eighteenth-Century English Blank Verse," *The Eighteenth Century: Theory and Interpretation* 26 (1985), 211–238.

33. Edward Young, *The Poetical Works of Edward Young* (Westport: Greenwood Press, 1970), 1, 7).

34. Isaac Watts, "Free Philosophy,", in *Horæ Lyricæ*, 1706.

35. Etienne Condillac, *Essai sur l'origine des connaissances humaines*, ed. Charles Porset (Paris, 1973).

36. Ernst Gombrich, "Illusion and Art," in *Illusion in Nature and Art*. Ed. R. L. Gregory and Ernst Gombrich (New York, 1973), 201.

37. William James, "What is an Emotion?" *Mind* 9 (1884).

38. James Thomson, *The Seasons*, ed. James Sambrook (Oxford: Clarendon Press, 1981), 130. Subsequent citations are incorporated in the text.

39. Joseph de Maistre, *Soirées de Saint-Petersbourg*, in *Oeuvres complétes* (Lyon, 1884), vol. 4, 364.

40. See John Berryman, *Berryman's Sonnets* (New York: Farrar, Strauss and Giroux, 1967), 25.

41. "Crystal" is part of the traditional poetic description or figuration of the eye as glass: "His eyes are crystall windows, cleare and bright." See Francis Quarles, "Mans Bodie's like a house," commmendatory poem for Fletcher's *The Purple Island* (1663), in Giles and Phineas Fletcher, *Poetical Works*, ed. F. S. Boas (Cambridge: Cambridge University Press, 1908-1909), vol. 2, 11. In *Edge Hill*, Richard Jago goes on at great length and in great detail about the workings of the eye (in *The Works of the English Poets*, vol. 17, ed. Alexander Chalmers [London: J. Johnson, 1810], 298):

> These metaphysic subtleties, and mark
> The curious structure of these visual orbs,
> The windows of the mind; substances how clear,
> Aqueous or crystalline! through which the soul
> As through a glass, all outward things surveys. (298)

42. Phineas Fletcher, *The Purple Island*, in F. S. Boas, ed., *Giles and Phineas Fletcher: Poetical Works* (Cambridge: Cambridge University Press, 1909), vol. II, 60.

43. We are perhaps over-conditioned by Freudian allegory, where the male is armed with "the key that opens...a decidedly male symbol." "'Where is the key?' seems to me to be the masculine counterpart to the question 'Where is the box?' They are therefore questions referring to the genitals." The equation is one of the most frequently noted by Freud: "Boxes, cases, chests, cupboards and ovens represent the uterus, and also hollow objects, ships, and vessels of all kinds. Rooms in dreams are usually women ['*Frauenzimmer*']. "The female genitals...[represented] by receptacles, boxes, trunks, cases, chests, pockets, and so." See Sigmund Freud, *The Standard Edition of the Complete Psychological Words of Sigmund Freud* (henceforward abbreviated "SE," trans. James Strachey (London: The Hogarth Press, 1986), XV: 158, VII: 97, V: 354, XV: 156 (subsequent citations incorporated in the text).

44. John Milton, *Paradise Lost*, ed. Merrit Y. Hughes (New York: The Odyssey Press, 1962), II: 645-6. Subsequent citations are incorporated in the text.

45. Those who know Blake's work will think of other examples, as when the discursive voice in Milton pronounces: "The nature of a Female Space is this: it shrinks the Organs/Of Life till they become Finite & Itself seems Infinite" (E 104).

46. William Walker ("Locke Minding Women: Literary History, Gender, and the Essay," *Eighteenth-Century Studies* 23 [1990], 245-268) takes advantage of some close reading of Locke's text to explore "the complexities of Locke's designation of mind as a space of socio-erotic activity" (247). Epstein and Greenberg study a number of eighteenth-century examples of the "male mind" and "female nature" figured in terms of sexual intimacy between an aggressive male mind (Newton's) and a passive female

Nature "open" to the penetrating male gaze. Julia L. Epstein and Mark Greenberg, "Decomposing Newton's Rainbow," *Journal of the History of Ideas* 45 (1984), 115–40.

47. Richard Blackmore, *Creation: A Philosophical Poem Demonstrating the Existence and Providence of a God* (London: 1718), VII: 253–254.

48. "In considering vision as achieved by the means of an image formed at the bottom of the eye, we can never reflect without wonder upon the smallness, yet correctness, of the picture, the subtilty of the touch, the fineness of the lines. A landscape of five or six square leagues is bought into a space of half an inch in diameter...The prospect from Hampstead-hill is compressed into the compass of a sixpence" (Paley, *Natural Theology*, 21–22).

49. Robert Hooke, "Lectures on Light," in *The Posthumous Works of Robert Hooke* (London: 1705), 121. "Another" is the word used by philosophers to describe the relationship, as when Hobbes writes, "the object is one thing, the image or fancy is **another**" (3) or Hume: "I observe first the universe of objects or of body: the sun, moon and stars; the earth, seas, plants, animals, men, ships, houses, and other productions either of art or nature...After this I consider the other system of beings, viz. the universe of thought, or my impressions and ideas. There I observe **another** sun, moon, and stars...and in short, everything I can discover or conceive in the first system" (242).

50. Unfortunately the world has lost Swift's Tale-Teller's *A Panegyrical Essay upon the Number* THREE, written "in imitation of that prudent Method observed by many other Philosophers and great Clerks, whose chief Art in Division has been, to grow fond of some proper mystical Number, which their Imaginations have rendered Sacred, to a Degree, that they force common Reason to find room for it in every part of Nature...Now among all the rest, the profound Number THREE is that which hath most employ'd my sublimest Speculations, nor ever without wonderful Delight...I have by most convincing Proofs, not only reduced the *Senses* and the *Elements* under its Banner, but brought over several Deserters from its two great Rivals SEVEN and NINE" (*A Tale of a Tub*, ed. A. C. Guthkelch and David Nichol Smith, 2nd ed. [Oxford: Clarendon Press, 1981], II: 57–58).

51. In Plato's critique of art as a form of mirror production he argues that artists' imitations are "three removes from nature...three removes from reality, and easy to produce without knowledge of the truth. For it is phantoms, not realities, that they produce" (Plato, *The Republic*, trans. Paul Shorey, in *The Collected Dialogues of Plato* [Princeton: Princeton University Press, 1969], 822–4).

52. Walter Benjamin, *The Origin of German Tragic Drama*, tr. John Osborne (London: New Left Books, 1977), 211 ff.

53. "The Learned Æolists, maintain the Original Cause of all Things to be Wind, from which Principle this whole Universe was at first produced, and into which it must at last be resolved" (Swift, *Tale*, 150).

54. William Wordsworth, *The Prelude: 1799, 1805, 1850*, ed. Jonathan Wordsworth, M. H. Abrams, and Stephen Gill (New York: W. W. Norton, 1979), V: 619–620). Quotations are from the 1805 version and are henceforward incorporated in the text.

55. Roy Schafer, "Narration in the Psychoanalytic Dialogue," *Critical Inquiry* 7 (1980), 29–53.

56. "We have only to understand the mirror stage as an identification, in the full sense that analysis gives to the term: namely, the transformation that takes place in the subject when he assumes an image...This jubilant assumption of his specular image by the child at the *infans* stage...would seem to exhibit in an exemplary situation the symbolic matrix in which the I is precipitated in a primordial form" (Jacques Lacan, *Écrits: A Selection*, trans. Alan Sheridan [New York: Norton, 1977], 2). Jane Gallop (*Reading Lacan* [Ithaca: Cornell University Press, 1985], ch. 3,) has a very useful discussion of Lacan's theory and its formulation.

57. Lacan, *A Selection*, 6.

58. Lacan, *A Selection*, 5.

59. Laurence Sterne, *The Life and Opinions of Tristram Shandy, Gentleman*, ed. Melvyn New and Joan New (Tallahassee: The University Presses of Florida, 1978), 98.

60. Donald Ault, in *Narrative Unbound: Re-Visioning William Blake's The Four Zoas* (Berrytown, New York: Station Hill Press, 1987), has explored the possibility of finding in Blake's *Four Zoas* a narrative strategy that subverts the narrativizing structures of consciousness. A preliminary version of this challenging work can be found in his "Re-Visioning The Four Zoas," in Nelson Hilton and Thomas Vogler, eds., *Unnam'd Forms: Blake and Textuality* (Berkeley: University of California Press, 1986).

61. Bender, *Imagining the Penitentiary*, 53.

62. Fineman, "The Structure of Allegorical Desire," 47.

63. Lacan, *A Selection*, 4. Italics added.

64. Jeremy Bentham, *Works* (New York: Russel & Russel, 1962), VIII: 199.

65. Fredric Jameson, *The Ideologies of Theory: Essays 1971–1986* (Minneapolis: University of Minnesota Press, 1988), I: 4.

66. Samuel Taylor Coleridge, *Biographia Literaria*, ed. James Engell and W. Jackson Bate (Princeton: Princeton University Press, 1983), I: 267. Subsequent citations are incorporated in the text.

67. Morris Golden, *The Self Observed: Swift, Johnson, Wordsworth* (Baltimore: Johns Hopkins Press, 1972), 10.

68. Peirce's argument is that a third element or "interpretant" will necessarily be involved in the relationship between a sign and its object, so that "the meaning of a representation can be nothing but a representation...Lo, another infinite series" (C. S. Peirce, *Collected Papers* [Cambridge: Belknap Press, 1965], I: 171).

69. See Jacques Derrida, *Speech and Phenomena*, tr. David B. Allison (Evanston: Northwestern University Press, 1973), *passim*, especially ch. 5, "Signs and the Blink of an Eye."

70. Jacques Derrida, *Of Grammatology*, tr. Gayatri Chakravorty Spivak (Baltimore and London: The Johns Hopkins University Press, 1976), 36.

71. Immanuel Kant, *Critique of Pure Reason*, tr. Norman Kemp Smith (London: MacMillan, 1953), 16; B132. Subsequent quotations from this edition are incorporated in the text.

72. Fletcher, *Allegory*, 368.

73. Fineman, "Structure of Allegorical Desire," 26.

74. Quilligan, *Language of Allegory*, 26–33.

75. Anne Davidson Ferry, *Milton's Epic Voice: The Narrator in Paradise Lost* (Cambridge: Harvard University Press, 1967), 139. Both Milton and Swift use grotesquely exaggerated allegory as a parody not only of literary style but of Catholicism, which is characterized as an "allegorical" religion. Quilligan summarizes Ferry's main points (180–182) and both draw on Christopher Ricks's discussion in *Milton's Grand Style*. The three should be supplemented with Edward Le Comte's *Dictionary of Puns in Milton's English Poetry* (New York: Columbia University Press, 1981).

76. Fletcher, *Theory of a Symbolic Mode*, 174–80.

77. John Milton, *The Tractate on Education*, ed. Thomas R. Hartmann, in *The Prose of John Milton*, ed. J. Max Patrick (Garden City, New York: Doubleday, 1967), 230.

78. See Le Comte (x) for a discussion of this pun here and elsewhere in Milton. I discuss *Finnegans Wake* as a "ruined form" in Benjamin's sense in "Wonder did He Wrote It Himself: Meditations on Editing *Finnegans Wake* in the 'Gabler Era'" *Studies in the Novel* 22 (1990) 192–215.

79. Benjamin, *Origin*, 354.

80. Fletcher, *Theory of a Symbolic Mode*, 177, 367.

81. Shelley's "Ozymandias" is a beautifully condensed example of an allegory that confirms itself as a ruin commemorating a ruin "Round the decay/Of that colossal Wreck, boundless and bare." The same name, "Ozymandias," governs the poem—as ruin of a poem of a ruin—and its historical pretext.

82. Fletcher, *Theory of a Symbolic Mode*, 286.

83. Quilligan, *Language of Allegory*, 153–4.

84. Jameson, *Marxism and Form*, 60.

The Allegory of Allegory 127

85. Wordsworth uses the windmill symbol himself. See *Prelude* X: 341 ff.

86. See my "Rhetoric and Imagination" (*Stanford Literature Review* [Spring 1989], 73–94) and my "Coleridge's Book of Moonlight" (in *Coleridge's Biographia Literaria: Text and Meaning*, ed. Frederick Burwick [Columbus: Ohio State University Press, 1989]) for more extended discussion of some of these strategies.

87. De Man, "Rhetoric of Temporality," 199.

88. Leslie Brisman, *Romantic Origins* (Ithaca: Cornell University Press, 1978), 32.

89. Brisman, *Romantic Origins*, 46.

90. Frye, *Anatomy*, 89.

91. Coleridge, *Miscellaneous Criticism*, ed. E. T. M. Raysor (London: Constable, 1936), 99. Italics added.

92. The prose preface to "The Wanderings of Cain," another "fragment" written contemporaneously with "Kubla Khan, gives us an interesting pun on this "truth." After declining to record the "set of petty mishaps and annoyances" that caused the work to remain incomplete, he concludes: "I must be content therefore with assuring the friendly Reader, that the less he attributes its appearance to the Author's will, choice, or judgment, the nearer to the truth he will be" (*The Complete Poetical Works* (Oxford: Clarendon Press, 1957), 287 [subsequent references to this edition are incorporated in the text]).

93. De Man, *Allegories of Reading*, 249. Tzvetan Todorov lists what he calls "the full panoply" of distinctions accredited to the symbol/allegory distinction by the Romantics: The symbol is "productive, intransitive, motivated; it achieves the fusion of contraries; it is and it signifies at the same time...In contrast, allegory, obviously, is already made, transitive, arbitrary, pure signification, and expression of reason" (*Theories of the Symbol*, trans. Catherine Porter [Ithaca: Cornell University Press, 1982], 206–7).

94. Coleridge anticipates the distinction by directly equating the trope with the symbolic: "The symbolical cannot perhaps be better defined in distinction from the Allegorical, than that it is always itself a part of that, of the whole of which it is representative.—'Here comes a sail,'—(that is, a ship) is a symbolical expression" (*Miscellaneous Criticism*, 29).

95. Jonathan Livingston Lowes, *The Road to Xanadu: A Study in the Ways of the Imagination* (Boston and New York: Houghton Mifflin, 1927), 345.

96. Lowes, *Xanadu*, 412.

97. See my "Tropology of Silence" for more examples and discussion of this theme of transitoriness in the eighteenth century.

98. In *Coleridge the Visionary* (New York: Collier Books, 1962), 218–20, Beer discusses the Alph as "alpha" in the context of Coleridge's interest in language. The omega is at both "ends" of Alph's course through the dome ("But Oh!...").

99. See Beer's *Coleridge The Visionary*, 347–8. The spelling "Khan" appears in Purchas's other work, *The Pilgrims* (with its fools' paradise, discussed at length by Lowes).

100. I agree with Griggs and Margoliouth that this must have been a communal joke in the Wordsworth household. See Beer *Coleridge the Visionary*, 347–8, for details. See also Dorothy Wordsworth, *Journals*, ed. Ernest de Selincourt (London: Macmillan, 1941).

101. Roland Barthes, *S/Z*, tr. Richard Miller (New York: Hill and Wang, 1974), 20–21.

102. *The Notebook of Samuel Taylor Coleridge*, ed. Kathleen Coburn (Princeton: Princeton University Press, 1957, 1961), 2998.

103. James Joyce, *Ulysses* (New York: Random House, 1962), 37.

104. Wordsworth's "Intimations Ode" provides a classic case, when the failing eye prompts the unsuccessful shift: "Shout round me, let me hear thy shouts" (35) "I hear, I hear, with joy I hear!/—But" (50–51). His "On the Power of Sound" assumes the "Here I am" (21) of vocal presence, and the imagines the apocalypse as a vocal act: "A Voice shall finish doubt and dim foreseeing, I And sweep away life's visionary stir" (211–212). Nietzsche, under the early influence of Wagner in *The Birth of Tragedy*, claims that music can do things that word and image alone cannot accomplish: "And above all, it is through music that the tragic spectator is overcome by an assured premonition of a highest pleasure...so he feels as if the innermost abyss of things spoke to him perceptibly" ("So dass er zu hören meint, als ob der innerste Abgrund der Dinge zu ihm vernehmlich spräche") Friedrich Nietzsche, *The Birth of Tragedy* trans. Walter Kaufmann (New York: Random House, 1967), 126). See also Thomas A. Vogler, "The Desire of Discourse and the Discourse of Desire," in *English and German Romanticism: Cross-Currents and Controversies*, ed. James W. Pipkin (Heidelberg: Karl Winter Universitatsverlag, 1984), 111–43.

105. Jacques Lacan, "Some Reflections on the Ego," *International Journal of Psychoanalysis* 34 (1953): 11–17.

106. Jacques Derrida, *Grammatology*, 36.

107. Derrida, *Grammatology*, 163.

108. Quoted in Lowes, *Xanadu*, 371.

109. See Roman Jakobson, "Phonemic Patterning," in Jacobson and Halle, eds., *Fundamentals of Language* (The Hague: Mouton, 1971).

110. Coleridge's language studies led him to a similar point, according to Carlyon's account of Coleridge's conversation in Germany: "In order to illustrate, as was supposed, the inscrutable nature of the Deity, His name "Abba" was bandied through all its changes, as, for instance, AB—BA————AB—BA—backwards and forwards—forwards and backwards AB—BA." This would have been shortly after the writing of "Kubla Khan" in 1798 (C. Carlyon: Early Years and Late Reflections, quoted in Beer, *Coleridge the Visionary*, 220).

111. Coleridge, *Notebooks* 1.41.5. For Jakobson, see "Why 'Mama' and 'Papa'" in *Selected Writings* (The Hague: Mouton, 1962).

112. Fineman, "Structure of Allegorical Desire," 44.

113. Jean-Pierre Mileur, *Vision and Revision: Coleridge's Art of Immanence* (Berkeley: University of California Press, 1982), 19.

114. Merleau-Ponty has given an apt phenomenological account of the problem. "We cannot subject our perception of the world to philosophical scrutiny without ceasing to be identified with that act of positing the world, with that interest in it which delimits us, without drawing back from our commitment which is itself thus made to appear as a spectacle, without passing from the fact of our existence to its nature, from the *Dasein* to the *Wesen*" (M. Merleau-Ponty, *Phenomenology of Perception* trans. Colin Smith (London: Routledge & Kegan Paul, 1962), xiv)).

115. Horace, Horace on Poetry: The "Ars Poetica," ed. C. O. Brink (Cambridge: Cambridge University Press, 1971), 139.

THE ALLEGORY IN REALISM

Grant Holly

I: Representation and the Real

Binx Bolling, the hero of Walker Percy's novel, *The Moviegoer*, cannot believe in the reality of his environment until he sees something that resembles it in a movie. Neither can we. Indeed, what I wish to investigate here is the way that there emerges from modernity's continuing quest for the real a subjectivity that is the product of the dominant technologies of representation. What is striking about Percy's novel is not only that it presents a powerful and, one wants to say, original emblem of the alienation of the modern subject, but also the way it manages to repress—under the guise of its very originality and the apparent peculiarity of the protagonist's neuroses—the awareness that being held hostage to representation is a familiar condition of a modernity that reaches back to the Renaissance. In recent literature, that repressed awareness is a constitutive characteristic of the anti-hero: characters, who, like Binx Bolling, seek to secure their own reality by refusing to play what they perceive to be the constructed, and, therefore, fictional role of the hero, but end, either in their stunned passivity or their quixotic rebellions, by becoming emblems of their and our involvement in fictions that seem to grow out of and emplot the attempt to avoid fictions. This is not only a recent phenomenon, however. The irony of *Don Quixote* is not that the Knight is a fool for taking texts for reality, but that readers could draw such a conclusion from a work that in its introduction of surrogate authors, missing pages, lying translators, and a second half populated by characters that have read the first half of the novel, utterly problematizes the distinction between the world and the text.

This irony is implicit in the progress of modernism, for what defines modernism in its progressive mode is the repression of the way the techno-methodological procedures it has developed for determining the nature of reality become, themselves, the territory they explore. From the Renaissance forward, we see in the rapid development of the culture of representation, or to put it more directly, culture as representation, a condition in which both subjects and objects gain their reality as they are placed in alignment with various representational grids.

Recently there has been an attempt to isolate the emergence of a "scientific aesthetic" during the eighteenth century, an aesthetic which turned away from the sensibility of the Grand Tour and the picturesque in landscape painting and gardening. According to this view, this "scientific aesthetic," which appears both in literature and the graphic arts, is based on a new respect for the facts of the world which it represents straightforwardly and without bias in an unmediated vision. While these standards of objectivity are applied to and become crucial in the creation of works of art, this argument goes, they are derived from the demands of the "real world" of scientific world exploration and the need for objective accounts, both verbal and graphic, which these voyages of discovery produced.[1] The aesthetic of the Grand Tour, on the other hand, was corrupted by a variety of psychological and ideological concerns. The grand tourists were not so much interested in the world as they were in themselves—the world being useful to them only insofar as it titillated their own sensibilities, and when it ceased to do that, the world was summarily remade to be more inspirational.

There are fundamental problems with this view. First, it is hardly new. There is a long tradition in eighteenth-century studies of emphasizing the preeminence of the empirical. Second, it ignores what we have come to think about the way science is developed. From Karl Popper to Thomas Kuhn and Paul Feyerabend, an argument has been put forward, which though it contains a number of contradictions, is consistent in its insistence that science is not the product of an unmediated vision, the mere releasing of the gaze from the prison of superstition and ideology to expatiate freely and without bias over the facts of the world. On the contrary, these writers have opened the way to our seeing that science is driven by hypotheses, models, paradigms, fictions, all of which are, or have, a fundamental relationship to narrative.

Significantly this view has evolved, not from the philosophy of science, that is, the search for the absolute and unchanging principles of "scientific method," but from the history of science, that is, the growing conviction that even epistemological questions must be considered in the framework of historical contexts. It is this conviction which joins the sciences and the human sciences in the way that, for example, the work of Gaston Bachelard looks both towards the sciences and towards the work of the *Annales* historians and Foucault.

What I want to do in this essay is to explore, not only the contexts of this developing "realism," but also the dynamics and the significance of the contextual per se. I see this study as preliminary to an examination of the scientific voyage in the eighteenth century and its relation to the history of world exploration and western colonialism. Here, however, I will only be able to touch on that subject because I need first to place the development of realism in what seems to me to be the relevant cultural contexts. I am interested, in other words, in the way the modern subject is constructed and the consequences to living and thinking when increasingly the real environment has always already been transformed into a representational account. In brief, my argument will be that what counts as realism on a cognitive level is perception within the framework of representational practices, practices which, though they direct perception, remain concealed from it—except, as we shall see, insofar as perceptions within such a context, in their attempt to represent the world, always also represent, however indirectly (or, as I will put it, allegorically), the very perceptual framework that enables them.

II: The Rhetoric of the Real

When Barbara Stafford writes in *Voyage into Substance* that:

> During the eighteenth century an admirable campaign was waged to get at the truth of the phenomenal world without imprisoning it in self-revelatory idiosyncrasy. The nominalistic impulse will be seen to be most precisely located in the historical context of a modern secularizing movement directed against the falsehoods of ancient imaginings of reality.[2]

is she not paying attention to historical contexts? My argument here is that in important ways she is not. That there was a "secularizing movement" in the eighteenth century is true and important, but how is it possible not to consider the impulse towards secularization (or any impulse, for that matter) as not "self-revelatory?" We might try to pursue the shadowy distinction between self-revelation and self-concealment. We know that they produce and are signs of one another. What is an impulse if not a revelation of the self, on the level of the drive, on the level of unconscious motivation, which is to say on the level of deep "imaginings," ancient or modern? And how could an attempt to understand historical contexts succeed that did not take the relationship between self-revelation and self-concealment into consideration, that did not see the impulse as precisely that which does not speak for itself, but needs to be interpreted?

When Stafford tells us that "the illustrated factual travel account presents an almost pure instance of the possibilities thought inherent in this mode of vision for getting to the bottom of things," because it stays "aloof from any generally available convention of signification," she does not reflect on the way that "getting to the bottom of things" is an archetype of the journey, not to mention a primal scene, or that there is no signification without convention. When she goes on to distinguish "the explorers' implementation of a method of discovery based on a willed nonmetaphoric scrutiny of the particulars of this world," she raises the question of whether a "willed nonmetaphoric scrutiny," an imposed and therefore in an important way an artificial nonmetaphoric scrutiny, does not simply mean, or cannot escape from meaning, a "metaphoric scrutiny"? Similarly, while it is fascinating to point out the "the traveler in search of fact relied on an exploratory method consonant with that of empirical science as it was defined in the seventeenth century," it does not quite make sense to say that this is done by "resisting allegorical or any other nonoptical transformational modes," first because the argument would seem to be in part that the journey is in some way an allegory for science, or at least that there has been a nonoptical transformation, that is, a transformation or a translation in principle of the techniques of scientific analysis, which is primarily an analysis of the cabinet or the laboratory, to the new arena of the world; and second because, as I began by saying, science itself is a relation of procedures or praxis to premises. Whether we call these premises hypotheses, paradigms, or fictions, their relation to the praxes they produce consists in a difference and is, therefore, allegorical. It requires, either implicitly or explicitly, a sustaining explanatory and interpretive narrative.

It is not that I disagree that there developed in the eighteenth century an "arduous aesthetic" of fact that "preferred plain transcription of material things to their facile amplification," so long as we are talking on the level of preference, which is to say on the level of the unacknowledged or unconscious dependencies and assumptions which constitutes precisely what needs to be interpreted. Given that caveat, it becomes necessary to say that it is impossible to imagine "plain transcription" except as an oxymoron: that is to say that given the meaning of transcription, a "copying" from one writing system to another (where the possible differences in the systems already problematize the idea of the copy), and the situation of the traveler's attempting to record the material world on the page according to the regulations and limitations of narrative or graphic depiction, there can be nothing "plain" in the process. As Roland Barthes has put it:

> Thus, realism (badly named, at any rate often badly interpreted) consists not in copying the real but in copying a (depicted) copy of the real: this famous *reality*, as though suffering from a fearfulness which keeps it from being touched directly, is *set farther away*, postponed, or at least captured through the pictorial matrix in which it has been steeped before being put into words: code upon code, known as realism. This is why realism cannot be designated a "copier" but rather a "pasticheur" (through secondary mimesis, it copies what is already a copy).[3]

Facts, we say today, are theory laden, and we find that worth saying because it appears to be counterintuitive: facts, we thought, were those things which had no ulterior motives. Ironically, when we consider the word etymologically, we see that the theoretical nature of the fact has always been there. Fact comes from *facio*, to make. The past participle, *factus*, neuter form *factum*, a thing made or a thing done, does give the sense of completion necessary to our sense of the straightforwardness of the fact—it is important that the processes have ended and that boundaries be established in order for there to be taxonomy, analysis, that is, the procedures necessary to scholarship, science, and the law. But that it is made, a product of manufacture (which in an archaic form is merely "facture") begins to rob the fact of its authenticity. We somehow expect that the fact should be autochthonous, that it should be born of the nature of things without artifice or instrumentality. That a fact is made, manufactured, closes the gap between fact and artifact. Factitious is not, then, counterfactual, but expressive of the productive nature of the fact. Fact, which is related to fetish, comes from the same complex of signification as does its supposed opposite, fiction.[4]

If, then, we are to try to understand the literature of fact, it is necessary to confront the literature of fiction, or what is perhaps more important, to see the preeminence of literature as a concept in the development of factual discourse. Here it is worth noting that *facio* gives us not only fact, but face. A face, in other words, is not simply a "fact," nor can it be taken at face value. It is rather, a thing made, and as such implies a history and a strategy. It is a palimpsest or an allegory, and this is true for what we might call the narratives of the face that develop during the eighteenth century, the narratives of character: the novel, biography, and autobiography. These are also, of course, narratives of fact. Consider for example this factual account given us by Moll Flanders:

> What the Bundle was made up for, or on what Occasion laid where I found it, I knew not, but when I came to open it, I found there was a Suit of Child-bed Linnen in it, very good and almost new, the Lace very fine; there was a Silver Porringer of a Pint, a small Silver Mug and Six Spoons, some other Linnen, a good Smock, and Three Silk Handkerchiefs, and in the Mug wrap'd up in a Paper Eighteen Shillings and Six-pence Money.[5]

On the one hand the passage seems cautious and objective. What can only be speculated upon ("What the Bundle was made up for, or on what Occasion laid where I found it") appears to be ignored. Only that which can be corroborated by empirical observation ("when I came to open it, I found" etc.) is mentioned. And this scientific, factual discourse, by abstaining from the speculative, remarkably earns our trust: remarkably because we seem to dwell upon the value of the items for their own sake, to treat them as some kind of bargain, and to take pleasure in the orderly way they are recounted, forgetting that they are in fact the booty of a thief (rather like the way, I think, the expeditions of the eighteenth and nineteenth centuries managed to bring the treasures of the near east to the museums of Europe under the aegis of the developing taxonomies of archaeology and anthropology and with the imprimatur of the new understanding of culture).

On the other hand, however, what seemed objective in Moll's language can also seem coy. What the bundle was made up for, and how it came to fall within Moll's grasp, are questions we cannot help but speculate on in this narrative. In the content of the bundle—the child-bed linnen (almost new), the silver porringer, the small mug—and the way it is left for Moll to find, the careless mother and the abandoned child, elements which combine to form a continuing motif in the novel, are over determined.

The precision of the language and the attempt to establish the identity of language and fact, that is, language as fact, overdetermines language itself. Language which is meant to refer to fact refers to language, to another story. In this example, a perfect example of the double coding of allegory, Moll's list, supposedly sufficient in itself, begins to refer to Moll's life. What obtains here in the discourse of fact, obtains as well in the description of Moll's face. Moll is a paradigm for prosopopoeia, the giving of a face to the absent, the dead, the inanimate. In absolute control of the language of the text she becomes language; perpetually masked, both physically and emotionally, she becomes a sign (even as her name makes her a double entendre in a text worked, or laced, with double entendres). Her face is identical to the narrative that produces it, changing according to the needs of that narrative—being made beautiful or old or beautiful again, masculine or feminine, as the narrative demands, and instantaneously, in the fiat of utterance.

The situation is similar to what J. Hillis Miller has recently described as the relationship between narrative and ethics:

> One glimpses here a curious relation between the necessity of narrative in any discourse about ethics and the necessity of using analogies or figures of speech in place of an unavailable literal or conceptual language. Narrative, like analogy, is inserted into that blank place where the presumed purely conceptual language of philosophy fails or is missing.[6]

We, of course, would substitute for ethics, the fact, or truth, or reality, terms from the philosophical discourse of epistemology—or the face, which raises epistemological questions but might bring in the discourse of aesthetics. The point remains the same. As we approach the fact or the face, we find analogy and more narrative. This is not a curiosity of Defoe's text, but a condition of the representation of fact. To get a true likeness, of Moll to be sure, but this is a general point, one that Reynolds, for example, plays with in his portraiture, to get a true likeness, there must be an insertion of the other, the allegorical; for likeness to be true to itself must, like Zeno's paradox, keep its distance from identity, remain perpetually a similitude. What is perhaps most powerful about likeness is not the establishment of identity, but the *possibility* of identity, which is to say, since possibility is a condition which preserves the option of non-occurrence, the immanence of difference. The likeness, not only portrays the subject—the image of the coherent being—but also the other: the possibility of incoherence, nonbeing, death.

III: The Veil of Allegory

Calling this veiled representational process "allegorical" is both in keeping with and varying from the traditional definition of allegory. The "other speaking" of allegory is, of course, always a veiled discourse, but in the classic allegories of the Middle Ages and the Renaissance, both visual and verbal, the veil is the precise location of the art of allegory: the skill and mastery by means of which the artist is able to embed meaning in the work, the evidence of the artist's control over the work, and, by analogy, the sense that the world itself is ordered in a similar way. The root of allegory, *allos + agoreuein*, in suggesting a discourse other than the open, public speech of the marketplace, implies a private understanding and perhaps a circle of cognoscenti who share in that understanding.[7] Here we see the origins of the public suspicion of politics, both deserved and paranoid. Indeed, the difficulty in making the distinction between justified suspicion and paranoia is part of the problematic dynamic of allegory, for the successful conspiracy is that which makes the evidence of its existence appear to be evidence of its nonexistence. If we follow the logic of this deceptive form through its tangled web, we see that it leads to the perplexing conclusion that the proof of the existence of the ultimate allegory is the absolute lack of evidence for its existence. Veiled discourse, then, is what allows us to see the classic allegory as an intentional structure and as the reflection of the intentional structure of the world. It is also that that problematizes all interpretation, for it brings to our awareness a condition in which, as Benjamin says,

The Allegory in Realism

"any person, any object, any relationship, can mean absolutely anything else."[8]

Of course, it is this intentionality that the modern sensibility will first find limiting in allegory and then try to problematize, even in classic allegories, on the grounds that the human psyche and or systems of representation per se are based on fundamental ambiguities that make the attribution of intention problematic. In a move that parallels on the plane of representation the great voyages of discovery, allegory will be replaced by the symbol—in Coleridge, for example, as a way of replacing the recurrence to a foregone conclusion with the rich possibility of the discovery of the new. Based on the symbol, both the psyche and systems of representation become *terra incognita*, rich repositories of unexplored potential. While we might locate the modern preference for the symbol over allegory in Coleridge, the larger version of the process I describe here goes back to the humanism of the Renaissance and its expansive vision of human potential.

The modern attempt to save allegory is to claim for it the imaginative richness and authenticity that Coleridge attributed to the symbol. My argument here, however, reverses that position. It is, to paraphrase Paul Ricour, that the symbol gives rise to allegory, that the apparently new turns out to be, disconcertingly, a version of the old. Just as we might name the expansive vision of Renaissance humanism, "imperialism and colonialism," and show the voyage into the new as the subjugation of the other through the reestablishment of the familiar, so too we can see the symbolic voyage as a veiled account, as an allegory of the impossibility of embarking.

Such a perception emerges from the modern dissatisfaction with the intentionality of classic allegory, to be sure, but it is also suspicious of the alleged authenticity of the symbol. As a result intentionality returns, but it is what we can only call an unintended or an unconscious intentionality. Allegory is still a driven form from this point of view, but it is driven by a relentless semiosis of which it has only partial control. An autobiographical narrative, for example, or a narrative of a journey or a voyage, narratives that offer themselves as progressive movements through time and space, can be seen as obsessive returns to issues that are unacknowledged in these narratives, or acknowledged only in a secondary way. In this regard, we can think about the way the narrative progress of Fielding's *Tom Jones* can be seen as an obsession with a series of primal scenes that dominate the structure of the novel to the point where we might say that the novel's discursive development is a contrivance to allow them to recur, and about the way *Gulliver's Travels*, tied by similitude to the limits of the familiar, can be read as an allegory of its own indecipherable textuality.[9]

IV: The Rhetoric of Culture

It is not necessary, however, to exemplify this veiled allegory with fictive works alone. In fact the significance of this form is that it eliminates the boundary between the fictive and the factual account. The particular sublime of veiled allegory is not that numerous meanings have been artfully embedded in a narrative, but that what one has done straightforwardly and without guile suddenly appears to have an unexpected but systematic significance—that what one thought was real, in other words, turns out to have been allegorical. The separation between subject and object, so important to classic allegory, breaks down. The viewer sees the world as a picture in which he or she is figured, the reader finds him or herself textualized. Identity, the self, becomes mere personification, a representation in the context of representations. Freud will dramatize this scenario through the agency of the unconscious in a format that is not without its ironies. Allegory is a word that Freud rarely uses, and when he does, it is with a dismissive tone. In keeping with his modernist, medical ambitions, it is the symbol that dominates Freud's analysis. Here Freud, and we can take as a specific example his discussion of religion, is in the direct line of the realist analysis of the Enlightenment from Bayle to Voltaire and Diderot. And yet it is precisely the extent to which Freud's discourse is allegorical, that it seems continually to unfold in the direction of a reading other than the immediate one, and thereby to bring into being a revolution that undermines its own revolutionary interpretation, that engages the potential of the concept of the unconscious and has led to Freud's contemporary importance. In this (perpetual) secondary interpretation, we can see the deep connection of the Freudian narrative and the narrative of the novel. As in the particular case of *Moll Flanders*, the novel as a genre begins by paying homage to the world in a way that makes its development one of the most important and one of the most characteristic occurrences in the realist, empiricist, scientific, tradition. But as we have seen, the realist reading can be undermined by an allegorical one. In this light we can see Freud's work (and indeed we can make the same claim for those thinkers who contribute to the radical revision of the understanding of culture, from Nietzsche to Foucault and Derrida), coming historically at the point where the novel is firmly established as an artistic and cultural form, as a continuation and a vindication of the novel. Freud reverses the expectation that the novel is like the world by showing that the world, as it is perceived by human consciousness, is like the novel. Consciousness can perceive that what it took to be the random or rationally related events of its life can be read as (allegorically) indicating another narrative emplotting the life of consciousness in a way of which it had been unaware.

My argument is not to claim for Freud some pure scientific insight. Rather I want to suggest that the Freudian hermeneutic is the logical outcome of the culture of representation. The Freudian vindication of the novel is made possible because in important ways the novel invents Freud. Certainly those most characteristic aspects of the psychoanalytic session—the silent analyst listening to the discourse of the other—and the dynamics of the transference (although according to this scheme, the counter transference precedes and provides a model for transference) have been practiced for two hundred years before Freud by readers reading novels and identifying with characters. The objection, raised by Freud himself and others, that the examination of texts is fundamentally different from the discourse between analyst and analysand, represses the fact that, in analysis, speech is virtually never regarded existentially. It is, rather, regarded textually, as a representation of an otherness to which the analyst again responds as if it were a text. The goal or game of analysis can then be described as the analysand's coming to believe that he or she is a character in the same "novel" that the analyst imagines him or her to be in. One way of understanding Freud's treatment of Dora is to see it as the superimposition on Dora's life of plots of virtually all the novels about women up to that time. Dora, in the suspicion she arouses in her reader (Freud) that she is more sexually involved than she admits, is Pamela, who has aroused the same suspicions in her readers; in her terminating the analysis abruptly, but in a way that allows the male narrator to preside over the remainder of the narrative, she is Clarissa, et al.

This critique of Freud is less of an attempt to undermine his insight than it is to reposition that insight in the context of representational culture which it reflects (as opposed to analyses) brilliantly. Part of my point is that representational culture is constantly producing, under the guise of realism, what it calls analyses but what can be seen as allegories of its own ideology. A powerful account of this state of affairs has been given by Louis Althusser in his "Ideology and Ideological State Apparatuses." In his discussion of social formation, Althusser follows Marx in saying that "the ultimate condition of production is the reproduction of the conditions of production."[10] In the "capitalist regime," as he puts it, "unlike social formations characterized by slavery or serfdom...this reproduction of the skills of labor power tends...decreasingly to be provided for 'on the spot' (apprenticeship within production itself), but is achieved more and more outside production: by the capitalist education system, and by other instances and institutions."[11] The most important product of a productive system, in other words, is the labor force that can continue to operate the system; which is to say that human subjectivity is a product of the very economic system of which that subjectivity thinks it is in charge. The means by which social formations "interpolate subjects," "hail" them, or call them into being is ideology, which Althusser defines as *"a 'Representation' of the Imaginary Relationship of Individuals to their Real Conditions of Existence."*[12] Individuals, in other words, exist in society like characters in an allegory, fictions created and emplotted by a cultural rhetoric that alludes to the real conditions of their existence, but in an illusory way.

The conditions that lead to the perception that culture and consciousness are being produced by representational processes of which they are only dimly aware and not in control precede the nineteenth and twentieth centuries. Vico, in a discussion that anticipates important elements in more recent thinkers (including Lacan's "mirror stage," so important to Althusser's thought) had already begun to thematize this process in his *New Science* which had reached its full development by 1744.[13] According to Vico's analysis, it is the evolution of language and institutions rather than human volition that determines the course of human history. History is nothing other than the history of language and institutions, and it is this that speaks humanity (Vico actually sees the evolution of rhetorical forms as one of the forces that governs the development of culture) and carries humanity along in its wake. The significance of history is only available to human consciousness as what I have called a veiled allegory, for although what takes place is a consequence of human behavior, it is not a consequence of human intention. Humanity is an invention of its own inventions (language and institutions) and lives to serve them.

Indeed, culture reveals itself as an artifact, as allegorical, and as historical, in Vico's sense, precisely as it veers away from human intention. Being characters in history is like being characters in a text. We have the same problems in reading our fate as do characters in a novel. Having created techniques of representation, and the artificial environment of culture, humanity is reproduced as a representation by its own forms of representation, an artifact of its own artifacts.

Vico's radical understanding of this process would not be explicitly engaged by thinkers until the nineteenth century, but there was nothing premature in his formulation. There are many examples of the predominance of representation in the eighteenth century, an important one of which is Diderot's *Encyclopédie*. The illustrations to this work are especially evocative of a humanity caught in the grip of productive forces which it understands dimly, if at all. One sees here the image and perhaps the origin of Foucault's emphasis on discursive formations, the archive, the medicalized body, on cultural practices, on the gaze, etc. Consider the dull yet dangerous presence of the surgeon with his drill, and the way the inset of the patient reduces his being to a representational trick, putting him on the same level as mere instruments. The human in these plates is graphically portrayed as a discursive or rhetorical practice. It is in short a figure of speech—a synecdoche like the drilled head, or the staring eyes, the hands that operate on them [*Figs. 1, 2*] or the feet, the feet of the dead, perhaps, that pose and pirouette in the shoes of antiquity [*Fig. 3*]. Or it is a metonymy, like the wigs (that in Hogarth's version will also become synecdoches), or the coats and pants of various professions [*Figs. 4, 5*].[14] Because mere artifacts are as animated as the depiction of humans [*Fig. 6*] we are made to feel that the human is always already a personification, the production of a representational process. This is the truth about humans that we learn from the *Encyclopédie*. It is the graphic version of the world of Pope's "The Rape of the Lock," "Where Wigs with Wigs, with Sword-knots Sword-knots strive," "And Garters, Stars, and Coronets appear," "And Maids turn'd Bottles, call aloud for Corks."[15] It is also the graphic version of Nietzsche's celebrated definition of truth as "a mobile army of metaphors, metonymies, and anthropomorphisms."[16] In the *Encyclopédie*, we see the expansion of the plane of representational culture, the culture of the substitute and the simulacrum where representations point to one another from Pope, to Nietzsche, to Foucault and Baudrillard.

144   ENLIGHTENING ALLEGORY

Figure 1: Denis Diderot, *Encyclopédie (Planches)*, 3.
Courtesy Hobart and William Smith College Library and Grant Holly

The Allegory in Realism 145

Errata

The 15 illustrations in this essay were erroneously transposed for the 15 illustrations in Kevin L. Cope's essay beginning on page 183. The captions in both essays are correct as printed.

ENLIGHTENING ALLEGORY

VELUTI in SPECULUM
*Wisdom in artful Fables lies,
And Charms us in her gay Disguise.*

Figure 3: Denis Diderot, *Encyclopédie (Planches)*, 11.
Courtesy Hobart and William Smith College Library and Grant Holly.

The Allegory in Realism 147

Figure 4: Denis Diderot, *Encyclopédie (Planches)*, 8.
Courtesy Hobart and William Smith College Library and Grant Holly.

148 ENLIGHTENING ALLEGORY

Figure 5: Denis Diderot, *Encyclopédie (Planches)*, 9.
Courtesy Hobart and William Smith College Library and Grant Holly.

The Allegory in Realism 149

Figure 6: Denis Diderot, *Encyclopédie (Planches)*
Courtesy Hobart and William Smith College Library and Grant Holly.

As an intellectual enterprise, of course, the *Encyclopédie* seems on the face of it to represent the cause of enlightenment and modernity. It stands for the victory of the real over myth, ignorance, and superstition. It is a demonstration of rationality and order. The world, it tells us, can be mapped, its dark places illuminated, its mysteries dispelled, its species discovered, their habits described, their forms depicted. All is exposed. No secrets remain. Nothing is so simple that it avoids being cross listed on complex grids of overlapping taxonomies, or so complex that its intricacies cannot be clearly diagramed.

It is an irony of the growing possibility of privacy that develops at the same time as the *Encyclopédie*, that the *Encyclopédie* leaves nothing private. Surfaces are automatically laid bare, interiors opened, secrets revealed. In this massive census of all that is, nothing escapes notice, nothing remains hidden. The exotic is made familiar, the remote is made available. Of course the explanation of this irony would seem to be that it is the private agency of the reader that is being respected. Here is a premonition of revolution: an end to aristocracy and privilege. Through literacy, information and the power attendant on it becomes accessible to all.

The effect is not so simple, however. A sublime sense of alienation rises from the *Encyclopédie*. Its very inclusiveness becomes a threat, for it implies that the representational world of the text sets the standard for the real. Taxonomy governs everything. Everything is part of an order. Everything can be typed, classified, enumerated, and reproduced through representation. It is this reproduction through representation that is crucial, that contributes most strongly to the mysterious textuality of the *Encyclopédie* and the sublime sense of alienation it produces, for it gives the sense that representation, the textual manifestation, creates both the object and the subject. Since everything, including human beings, is best understood as part of a taxonomic system, it follows that things are best seen as representations of those systems that explain them. The system is not merely descriptive, it is formative. In this light, the illustrative depiction takes on an uncanny power. Its significance lies not in the way it captures an appearance, indeed the cut away and cross sectional views of the *Encyclopédie* undermine our faith in appearances, but in the way its being a product of a rigorous technological order—of engraving, mechanical reproduction, book production—makes it the embodiment of the real. The real, in other words, is defined as a function of representation.

Surely, one of the most important things to be said about representations is that they can be bought and sold. Indeed, one of the key developments in the spread of what I have called the culture of representation, was the institution of paper money by John Law in France during the second decade of the eighteenth century.[17] It would appear that Law's argument for paper money was an attempt to find a currency stable enough to retain its face value, but his attack on the inherent valuableness of specie, and his development of the position that all currency is merely a representation, can be seen as part of trend that privileges the representation over any particular thing to be represented. The simultaneous development of the Linnaean taxonomy should be seen as a parallel occurrence. Though it is clear that Linnaeus believed in an essentialism—believed that he was naming the separate and unique identity of each species—he continually modified that essentialism throughout his work, and his decision to include "man" in his taxonomy, a decision he found troubling, dealt that essentialism a severe blow.[18] It was a step in the direction of seeing the human as just one species among others. Law's devaluation of specie, therefore, can be seen as an early step taken in the journey towards "the origin of species," a journey that will eventually characterize the human as an artifact of an ahuman (genetic) representational system over which it has no control.

It is in this context that we ought to consider the emphasis on technology and industrial production in the *Encyclopédie* [*Figs. 6, 7*]. It is as if the illustrations make the argument that there are only a few fundamental systems and these are shared by industrial and organic processes, thus eliminating, or at least blurring the distinction between the inorganic and the organic, between the human and the non human. In the context of the illustrations, the cut away view of the intestines is doubly subversive. First it subverts the trust in physical appearances and the simple desire to see the naked body. Here is a level of nakedness that is an antidote to lust, if not to curiosity. The second subversion is more serious. The juxtaposition of illustrations suggests the interior of the body is, in this case, analogous to the interior of a mine, or in the case of the circulatory system [*Fig. 8*], that the body is very like a tree. In either case, the human is explained in terms of the inhuman. This is a curiously alienating form of explanation, because it mystifies even as it reveals. If our understanding is human, but what we are to understand is ahuman, we are left with a perpetual incomprehensibility at the heart of understanding.

Similarly, the human inhabitants of the world of manufacture seem themselves to be products of manufacture. The depiction of the case makers workshop, for example, raises a number of conceptual questions which, I think, are common to many of the illustrations [*Fig. 9*]. How, psychologically, are we to regard such a scene? Is it a scene, or is it a series of stages in a manufacturing process? Is this an existential moment, captured photographically, as it were, or is it a schematization, a diagram, a kind of map in which objects are arrayed as part of a catalogue? The depiction of the production of playing cards [*Fig. 10*] raises the same questions in a dense little conceit, for the figures in the factory have as much personality or as little as face cards. It is in the gulf opened by these questions that we can look to find one of the sources of modern existentialism. Typically, some of the figures are more life-like than others. In the case maker's shop, the depiction of the central figure, both in its appearance and its psychological absorption suggests that lifelikeness, but the discrepancy between this figure and the cut outs or automata that surround it seem to stand for the alienation of the subject and the absurdity of existence. This same problematic reaches out to the reader, for this figure which we have taken to be a depiction of the real is merely "fig. 5," the implication being that we too are similarly figurative.

This effect is underscored by the depiction of the instruments which subtends the scene of the work place. These instruments, we realize, are the true subjects of the illustration. The human forms are only indices, themselves produced by the instrumentality of one technology (mechanical reproduction) to serve as illustrations for another. The instruments possess a reality that is archetypal or ideal in a virtually Platonic sense. These are true forms. Their essential nature is proved by the precise specifications necessary to establish their identity. The human forms, on the other hand, are mere ciphers or signs. The marks of their personality and individuality, marks we inevitably look for, are like the figures of allegory, disquietingly arbitrary. There is no motivation that makes a particular identity, a particular countenance, hair style, or body type more essential to the representation than any other. In the cycle of production and reproduction that constitutes the engine of capitalism, we can see here that among the reasons for the mysterious power of the commodity fetish is the identification of the subject with the commodity. To be a subject under capitalism is to be a commodity, to be the product of a reproductive process that takes its value from an economic system. One of the reasons for the rise of the novel is the conjunction of the novel as a mass produced commodity with the mass production of subjectivity in representational culture. We identify with characters in novels not because the novel tells the story of the developing sense of individual identity and freedom, for that freedom has been inculcated by a precession of represented models, like the figures in the *Encyclopédie*, that coerces subjectivity into being. We identify with characters in novels because of their artificiality. In that artificiality is the dawning of our coming into being in the mirror of productive and ideological forces.[19] Like the novelistic character who walks among (accounts of) statues, paintings, theatrical performances, in an apparent assertion of his or her own greater reality, we are figures of speech, mere personifications vainly trying to distinguish ourselves from the personifications that surround us.

The theme of the figurativeness of the human is one that frequently emerges form the illustrations in the *Encyclopédie*. Consider, for example, the depictions of Anatomy, Surgery, and Design [*Figs. 11, 12, 13*]. The appearance of the figures is more than similar, as if we were encountering the same figure in different guises as we make our way through the volumes. In this context, the appearance of the illustration of Design turns knowledge into vaudeville, or, given the characteristic grotesqueness of the subject, Grand Guignol. What we see here is like the revelation of the magician's trick. We have, in effect, walked into the actor's dressing room between scenes. Science and medicine are revealed to be modes of representation. Even more serious, however, is the implication produced, by the incised and flayed appearance of what appears to be the same character, that being and identity are merely figurations, forms of depiction.

It is the *Encyclopédie* itself, I would argue, that is quintessential example of the ahuman origins of the human. In a way that prefigures science fiction, there is something parental about this work that seems able to answer all our questions, and whose ultimate answer seems to be that what is comes to be through the same kind of representational reproductive process which brings it into being [*Fig. 14*]. One sees here the concept of "man" joined to mannequin and manufacture. Such a conjunction is responsible for the uncanny way the robot, from the automata of the eighteenth century, to Hoffman's Olympia, to the (obsession with) robots in

Figure 7: Denis Diderot, *Encyclopédie* (Planches), 1.
Courtesy Hobart and William Smith College Library and Grant Holly.

The Allegory in Realism 155

Figure 8: Denis Diderot, *Encyclopédie* (Planches), 1.
Courtesy Hobart and William Smith College Library and Grant Holly.

Figure 9: Denis Diderot, *Encyclopédie* (Planches), 4.
Courtesy Hobart and William Smith College Library and Grant Holly.

The Allegory in Realism

Figure 10: Denis Diderot, *Encyclopédie* (Planches), 2.
Courtesy Hobart and William Smith College Library and Grant Holly.

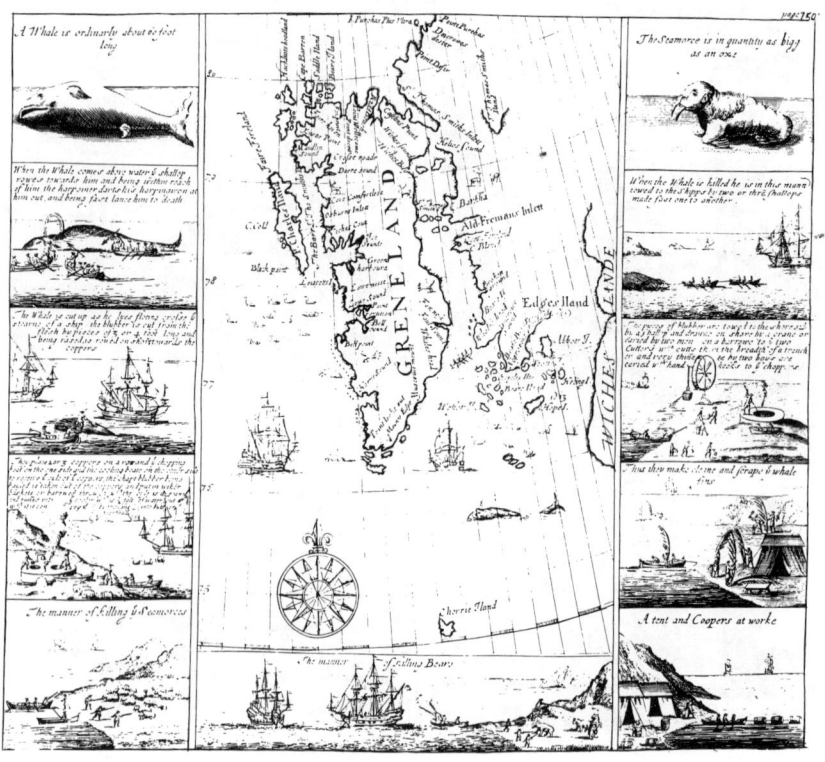

Figure 11: Denis Diderot, *Encyclopédie* (Planches), 3.
Courtesy Hobart and William Smith College Library and Grant Holly.

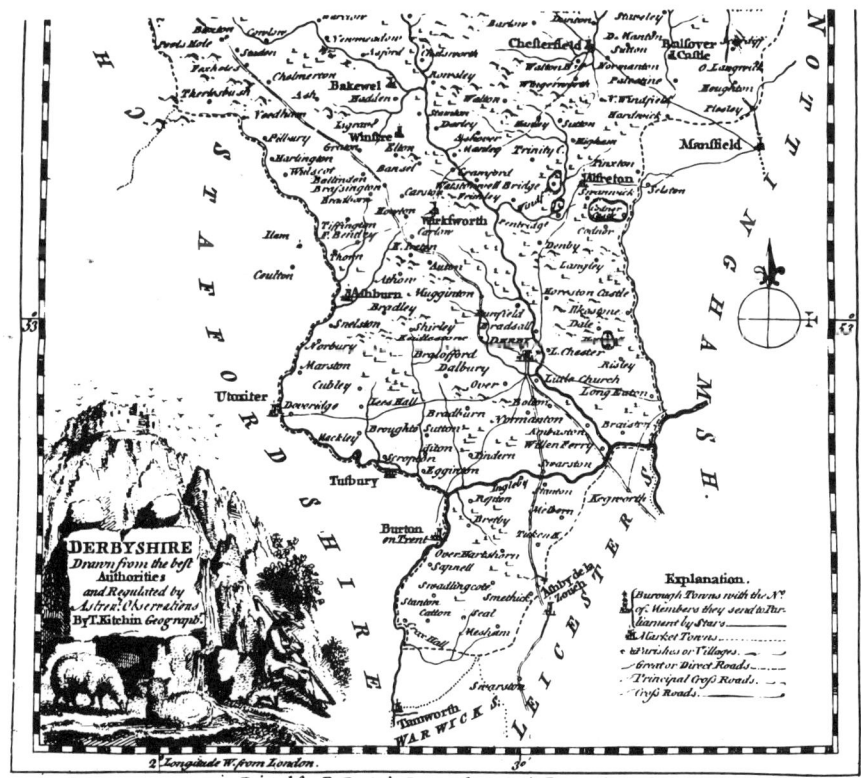

Figure 12: Denis Diderot, *Encyclopédie* (Planches), 3.
Courtesy Hobart and William Smith College Library and Grant Holly.

160 ENLIGHTENING ALLEGORY

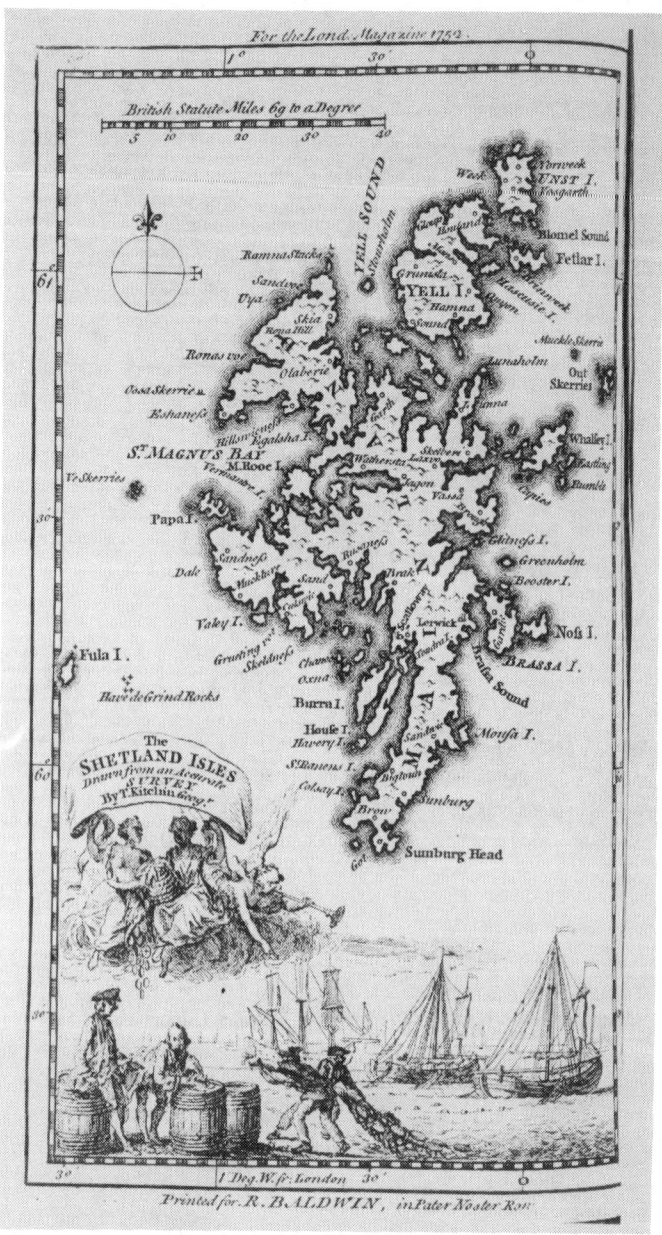

Figure 13: Denis Diderot, *Encyclopédie* (Planches), 1.
Courtesy Hobart and William Smith College Library and Grant Holly.

The Allegory in Realism 161

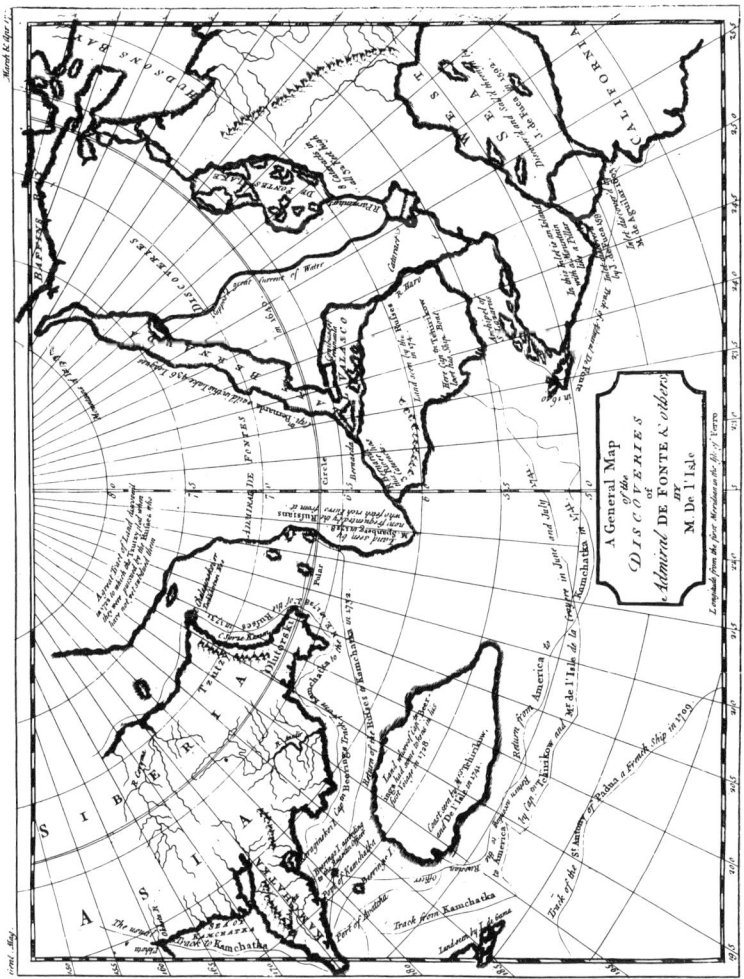

Figure 14: Denis Diderot, *Encyclopédie* (Planches), 3.
Courtesy Hobart and William Smith College Library and Grant Holly.

contemporary films such as *Terminator*, *Short Circuit*, and *Edward Scissorhands*, to name but a few, becomes the site of a certain humanity. In fact, whether it be the indefatigable protestant work ethic of Arnold Schwarzenegger's terminator, or the belief that Number 5 is alive, or the Greuze-like sentimentality emanating from the sad eyes of Edward Scissorhands, the paradox of representational culture is that the quintessential expression of humanity, indeed of "life" itself, is the robot. The effect of the *Encyclopédie* is to reduce all to the same level of production and commodification. But that is to be expected, for the *Encyclopédie* was itself a commodity, pursued and produced very much as a business venture, and establishing in the process a pattern for commodification in which representations, from information to art, have been bound up from that time to this.[20]

V: The Voyage into Representation

Explorers and those who follow them do not set out without expectation of what they will find. They have usually clear and frequently highly developed ideas about their destination. There is, in other words, no such thing as "the unknown."[21]

The major conceptual framework within which the scientific voyages of the eighteenth century took place was mapping. The mapping of lands, oceans, winds, and currents that had begun with the first voyages and continues today, provided information crucial to navigation. In addition, the scientific voyages of the eighteenth century were involved in a cataloguing of biological species, races, types, minerals, climates, geography, which is no less correctly described as a mapping. While I would not deny that the methods of these undertakings are scientific and empirical, and that the motives are utilitarian, I want to problematize these concepts. Maps, in other words, are always, in addition to their grasp of reality, metaphorical. From the very beginning, the map has proved to be a particularly evocative document, communicating far more than the technical information that apparently constitutes its reason for being. Not that this should come to us as any surprise. Even in the age of the microchip, the miniaturization engaged by the map must still be considered as ambitious. Indeed, the technology of mapping, an intricate combination of mathematical and graphic representation, must be considered among the most significant of inventions. The application of a powerful technology would seem to increase knowledge through instrumentality by separating the viewer from the material to be observed (observer from object, subject from object). Indeed such technologies seem to give rise to the modern subject, and the paradoxes accompanying them are also the paradoxes of subjectivity. The more successful, definitive, powerful the *techne*, for example, the more it undermines the knowledge conditions it seemed designed to promote, because the technology, if it is so powerful, can also map, or imply the potential mapping of the mapper. Thus absorbed, the subject becomes objectified; the self is in rapid succession, reinforced (as practitioner of the instrumentality) and alienated (as the other upon which such practices are committed).

I want to address the issue of maps by bringing together two works, one on maps and the other on techniques for producing landscape drawings. In 1774 J. H. (probably Dr. Hawkesworth) published *A New Introduction to the Knowledge of Maps* which included *Remarks on Dr. Solander (sic) and Mr. Bank's Voyage to the Southern Hemisphere and also some Late Discoveries Near the North Pole with Observations Astronomical, Philosophical, and Geographical.*[22] Hawkesworth, of course, was criticized as a popularizer of the scientific voyage, but that is part of my point. Maps and accounts of voyages were immensely popular and profitable objects of publication:

> Near the end of the seventeenth century, a Frenchman claimed that in his country "voyagers have come to credit and now hold first place" with the reading public, having supplanted the popular romances. By the third quarter of the eighteenth century, dozens of great collections of voyages had been published in all the countries of western Europe...For editing one such collection, John Hawkesworth received six times the sum paid Henry Fielding for what is perhaps the best novel of the century...After analyzing the publishing trends of the period, Edward Arber has concluded that for at least the early eighteenth century the most widely read books were travels, collections of voyages, and geographical compilations.[23]

While this little book is ostensibly a primer on how to read maps, we quickly see that the function of maps is to allow their readers to fantasize about the world and its inhabitants. The book itself becomes the site of discovery. The references made early in the work to the obscurity which cloaks the southern hemisphere are picked up later, when the technical description of the reading of maps is illustrated through the fold out maps in the book, by accounts of Banks's voyage. Looking at the map we are asked to imagine the lively and varying scenes of the voyage, as if we were exploring the territory ourselves. The map ceases to be a way of controlling information, and becomes instead prosopopoeia, or prosopographia, stories and pictures of absent people and places. The tropics are discovered to be a trope.

In his afterword to Dampier's *Discourse of Winds, Breezes, Storms, Tides and Currents*, A. Colquhoun Bell emphasizes the importance of Dampier's work as a handbook for seamen.[24] True as that is, it does not explain the success of such works on the popular market or its presence in the homes of those who would never go to sea. What we have in such works is a premonition of the Weather Channel: a technology that produces the phantasy medium which establishes the specifications according to which the inhabitants of representational culture can imagine they know the world. Between Dampier's narratives of his travels and the Weather Channel we have Hegel's *The Philosophy of History*, where the map becomes a landscape allegory of the course of human history. For example, there are, for Hegel, three principle types of terrains:

(1) The arid elevated lands with its extensive steppes and plains.
(2) The valley plains—the land of Transition permeated and watered by the great Streams.
(3) The coast region in immediate connection with the sea.[25]

These terrains produce characteristic peoples who have in turn characteristic histories. This view produced a series of phantasy map/landscapes in the nineteenth century [*Fig. 15*]. The map has become the territory.

In 1785, Alexander Cozens published *A New Method of Assisting the Invention in Drawing Original Compositions of Landscape*. Though this is ostensibly a very different kind of book than T. H.'s (as different, for example as we generally take maps to be from paintings), both are, I think, joined in the way they reverse what are typically understood to be the polarities of the

The Allegory in Realism

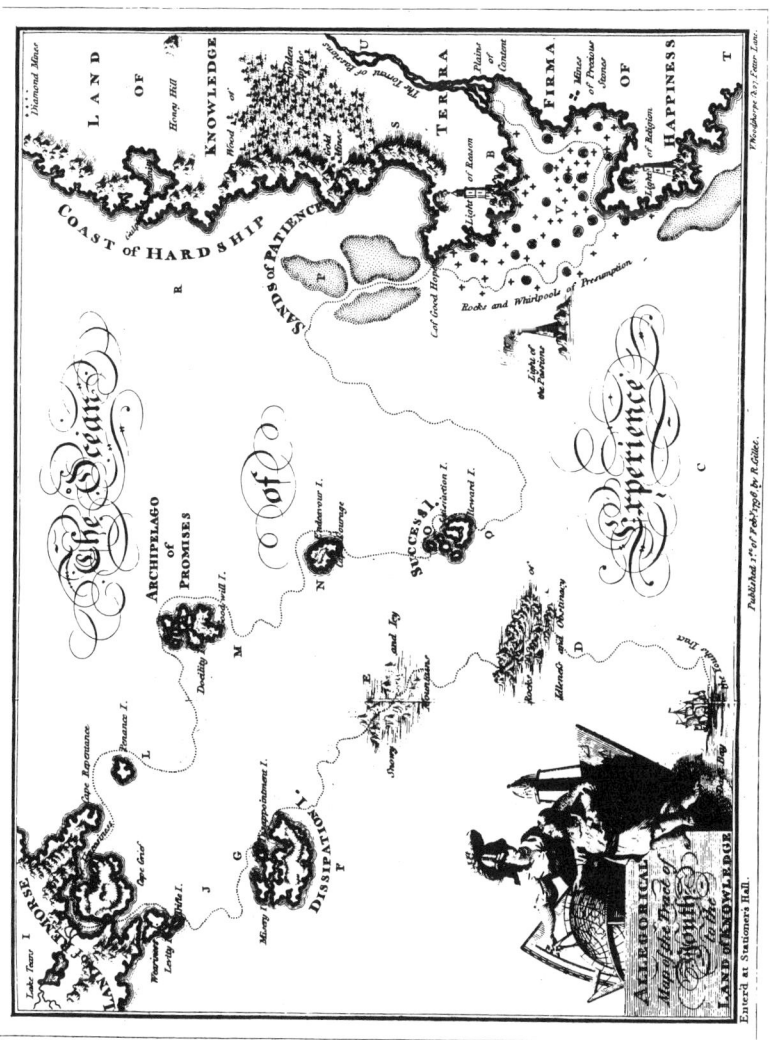

Figure 15: Exemplary Imaginary Map.
From the private collection of Grant Holly.

representational situation. Instead of subordinating the representation to the "facts" of the world, whether those facts be construed empirically or, as will be the case towards the end of the nineteenth century, psychologically, that is, accounting for the way the world appears to the perceptual apparatus of the viewer, these works make the reality of the world a function of the techniques of representation. Briefly, just as a careful reading of the work on maps reveals that the techniques of cartography are chiefly valuable because they provide a rationale for a virtually limitless series of narrative landscapes, scenarios, both macrocosmic and microcosmic, about the world and its inhabitants, so Cozens's work takes Leonardo's famous observation that ideas for paintings can exist in patterns on stones, etc. a step farther. In arguing that arbitrary blots on paper can represent the world more powerfully than carefully planned paintings, Cozens has naturalized the representational process and made the world its artifact.

From Dampier forward, it is clear that part of the art of the factual travel narrative was to produce what we might call "the factual effect," realizing that this modifies the notion of the fact considerably. The fact, we can say, is the representation of the idea of the real. Its importance lies at least partly in its evocative power. In the factual travel account, then, the fact itself is problematic, for the fact is not observed and recorded in a disinterested way. The fact is part of a predetermined harmony into which it must fit and according to which it is selected and described. Behind the fact and before it is the Linnaean taxonomy and its reification, the museum. In his dedication, Dampier avers that he has not the "vanity" that "this plain piece of mine, deserves a place among your more Curious Collections," but offers, nevertheless, "to bring my Gleanings here and there in Remote Regions, to that Great Magazine of the Knowledge of Foreign Parts, which the Royal Society thought you most worthy the custody of."[26] Banks wants to catch a fish that appears in Sloane's collection or fill in the blanks in the taxonomic structure which justifies his research.[27]

The significance of this belief in the museum has been eloquently described by Eugenio Donato:

> The set of objects that the museum displays is sustained only by the fiction that they somehow constitute a coherent representational universe. The fiction is that a repeated metonymic displacement of fragment for totality, object to label, series of object to series of labels, can still

produce a representation which is somehow adequate to a nonlinguistic universe. Such a fiction is the result of an uncritical belief in the notion that ordering and classifying...can produce a representational understanding of the world. Should the fiction disappear, there is nothing left of the *Museum* but "bric-a-brac," a heap of meaningless and valueless fragments of objects which are incapable of substituting themselves either metonymically for the original objects or metaphorically for their representations.[28]

The most important of the factual travel accounts was, of course, the voyage of the Beagle. Darwin's articulation of the principle of natural selection, with its uncanny wedding of chance and necessity, robs the voyage of its direction, and destroys the illusion of the fixed world of the Linnaean taxonomy. Nietzsche was quick to realize this and, partially under Darwin's influence, produced an analysis that turned the stable elements of the Western system of values into bric-a-brac, which is to say the arbitrary elements of allegory.

NOTES

1. Of particular importance in the distinguishing of the scientific aesthetic and its relationship to the development of romanticism are Barbara Maria Stafford, *Voyage into Substance: Art, Science and Nature, and the Illustrated Travel Account, 1760–1840*, (Cambridge: The MIT Press, 1984), and Bernard Smith, *European Vision and the South Pacific 1768–1850: A Study in the History of Art and Ideas* (Oxford: Clarendon, 1960). For a different points of view somewhat more similar to my own see Lennard Davis, *Factual Fictions*, and Robert Lawson-Peebles, *Landscape and Written Expression in Revolutionary America* (Cambridge: Cambridge University Press, 1988).

2. Stafford, 1.

3. Roland Barthes, *S/Z*, tr. Richard Miller (New York: Hill and Wang, 1974), 55.

4. See *The Oxford English Dictionary*, 2nd ed., prepared by J. A. Simpson and E. S. C. Weiner (New York: Oxford University Press, 1989); and Eric Partridge, *Origins, a Short Etymological Dictionary of Modern English* (New York: MacMillan, 1958).

5. Daniel Defoe, *Moll Flanders*, ed. Edward Kelly (New York: W. W. Norton Company, 1973), 150.

6. J. Hillis Miller, *The Ethics of Reading: Kant, de Man, Eliot, Trollope, James, and Benjamin* (New York: Columbia University Press, 1987), 25.

7. Angus Fletcher, *Allegory, the Theory of a Symbolic Mode* (Ithaca: Cornell University Press, 1964), 7, n1.

8. Walter Benjamin, *The Origin of the German Tragic Drama*, tr. John Osborne (London: NLB, 1977), 175.

9. Of course, the major contribution to our understanding of this kind of reading has been provided by Paul de Man in *Allegories of Reading: Figural Language in Rousseau, Neitzsche, Rilke, and Proust* (New Haven: Yale University Press, 1979). For the specific example of *Gulliver's Travels*, see Grant Holly, "Travel and Translation: Textuality in *Gulliver's Travels*," *Criticism* 21 (1979): 134–52; rpt. *Modern Critical Interpretations: Jonathan Swift's Gulliver's Travels* (New York: Chelsea House, 1986), 147–62.

10. Louis Althusser, "Ideology and Ideological State Apparatuses," in *Lenin and Philosophy and Other Essays*, tr. Ben Brewster (New York: Monthly Review Press, 1971), 127.

11. Althusser, 131–2.

12. Althusser, 162.

13. Giambattista Vico, *The New Science*, 3rd ed. (1744), tr. Thomas Goddard Bergin and Max Harold Fisch (Ithaca: Cornell University Press, 1984).

14. Figures 1 through 14 are from Denis Diderot, *Encyclopédie ou Dictionnaire Raisonné Des Sciences, Des Arts et Des Métiers*, 35 vols. (Paris: Braisson, David, Le Breton, Durand, 1751–1780); *Recueil Des Planches sur Les Sciences, et Les Arts Méchaniques, Avec Leur Explanation*. Photographs courtesy of the library and audio visual department of Hobart and William Smith Colleges. Figure 15 is from a private collection and is reproduced with permission of the owner.

15. Alexander Pope, "The Rape of the Lock," in *Poetry and Prose of Alexander Pope*, edited by Aubrey Williams (Boston: Houghton Mifflin Company, 1969), I: 101; I: 85; IV: 54.

16. Friedrich Nietzsche, "On Truth and Lie in the Extra Moral Sense, " in *The Portable Nietzsche*, edited by Walter Kaufman (New York: Viking Press, 1968), 46.

17. See John Law, *the Present State of French Revenues and Trade* (London: 1720).

18. For a discussion of the philosophical backgrounds of Linnaeus's thought, see Knut Hagberg, *Carl Linnaeus*, translated by Alan Blair (London: Jonathan Cape, 1952); and Gunnar Broberg, "*Homo Sapiens*: Linnaeus's Classification of Man," in *Linnaeus: The Man and his Work*, ed. Tore Frangsmyr (Berkeley: University of California Press, 1983), 156–94.

19. For a discussion of the relationship between the forces of production and the development of subjectivity under capitalism see Jean Baudrillard, *The Mirror of Production*, tr. Mark Poster (St. Louis: Telos Press, 1975).

20. See Robert Darnton, *The Business of the Enlightenment: The Publishing History of the Encyclopedie 1775–1800* (Cambridge: Harvard University Press, 1979).

21. Robert Lawson-Peebles, *Landscape and Written Expression in Revolutionary America* (Cambridge: Cambridge University Press, 1988), 9.

22. J. H., *A New Introduction to the Knowledge of Maps* (London: 1774).

23. Percy G. Adams, in William Dampier, *A New Voyage Round the World* Percy G. Adams (New York: Dover, 1968), xi.

24. William Dampier, *Voyages and Discourses*, ed. Clenell Wilinson (London: Argonaut Press, 1931), 221.

25. Hegel, *The Philosophy of History*, tr. J. Sibree (New York: Dover, 1956), 88.

26. William Dampier, *A New Voyage Round the World*, 1.

27. Joseph Banks, *The Endeavour Journal of Joseph Banks: 1768–1771*, ed. J. C. Beaglehole (Sydney: Angus & Robertson, 1962), I: 166.

28. Eugenio Donato, "The Museum's Furnace," in *Textual Strategies: Perspectives in Post-structuralist Criticism*, edited with an introduction by Josue V. Harari (Ithaca: Cornell University Press, 1979), 223; quoted by Douglas Crimp in "The Museum's Ruins," in the *Anti-Aesthetic: Essays on Postmodern Culture*, edited by Hal Foster (Port Townsend, Washington: Bay Press, 1983), 49.

DIRECTIONS TO SIGNIFY
Exploring the Emblems of Enlightenment Allegory

Kevin L. Cope

What also remains is the mystery, which may be the best we can hope for with Reagan. He readily ascribes several of his successes—even his survival—either to luck or to some higher being. Nancy, in her book, My Turn, *recalls the shaft of sunlight that broke down upon him as he began his first Inaugural Address in 1981. In an uncannily similar episode, when Air Force One came to a stop on the tarmac at Shannon airport in Ireland in 1984, not only did the sun come out, but a rainbow on a hill on the far side of Shannon Bay framed the President and his plane for the waiting TV cameras. (Barrett Seaman,* Time, *November 5, 1990)*

The heroes of a Spenser or a Chrétien caper over countryside or hoof across foreign fields, but the denizens of Enlightenment allegory explore a smaller semiotic space. Great gulfs divide the City of Destruction from the New Jerusalem, yet John Bunyan's hero-pilgrim carries out his quest within the small space of the episode, that narrative counterpart of the Puritan congregation. Global his policies may be, but that master of modern allegory, Ronald Reagan, encircles his world-stage with a 6,800–foot rainbow.[1] Even in pre-modern allegories, wide-ranging, peregrine programs of high adventure remain the prerogative of the best people. Only Lancelots and Britomarts, not porters in cramped doorways or trolls under bridges (those original new-historicist oppressees), get to do the travelling.

In the enclosure-obsessed eighteenth century, the collapsing space of allegory shrinkwraps the heroes and heroines of high tales as well as those stuck in the "Field of Folk." Chaucer's open road to Canterbury retracts to Blake's 500 visionary acres; Blake's homestead seems like the open air of Arizona when compared to Clarissa's bed. The twentieth-century preoccupation with the *text* of allegory, often at the expense of attention to illustrations, statues, or other spatially extended materials, slims down allegory to one-dimensional lines or to the infinitesimal point of consciousness. The prestige of sculptural tropes like personification decreases as conceptualized narratives displace muscular, voluminous narratees.[2]

The depreciative neglect of later seventeenth- and eighteenth-century allegories stems from a bivalent tendency, especially among pan-historic or theorizing critics, to prize semiotic distance while devaluing physical space and place. By emphasizing the reference-less "*allos*," the far-away "other," in "allegory," Jon Whitman downplays the nearby "*agoreuein*," the locating of this elusive "other" in the local marketplace. His pursuit of the mystical, skeptical, and elusive leads him right past the earthy storytelling going on in small shops in the confined but public *agora*. Jumping over the Reagan-Shannon rainbow, this de Manian critic exults in the divergence of meaning from appearance.[3] Maureen Quilligan picks up on (and distorts) C. S. Lewis's neo-Hermetic notion that allegory counterpoints sacramentalism, that we down here on parochial earth imperfectly allegorize a divine idea.[4] Quilliganesque allegories "signal their membership in a class" so as to "guide the reader's response." Alerted by Quilligan's semaphoric texts, responsive readers scan for meanings that recede into a Derridean world beyond their symbols.[5] Quilligan forgets that, in most modern allegories, it is not the reader who chases after the meaning, but the meaning that pursues the reader. William Cowper was hounded into the madhouse by his fear that newspapers were thrusting allegorical representations of his misdeeds right under his doorstep. Shafts of light struck Ronald Reagan, but Ronald Reagan never beamed up the heavenly ray.

All this is not to say that understanding seventeenth- and eighteenth-century allegory requires only common sense. Rather, it is to draw attention to the turbulent complexity of this canon of work. It is to affirm that this most local, multiplicative, and diversely-contextualized of forms encourages a more extensive criticism than that available in theoretically-intense formulations like those of the popular deconstructive critics (curiously, allegory seems to have resisted the forays of neo-Marxist writers, if only because it must first be demoted to "narrative" before facing down their ordnance).[6] Angus Fletcher, for one, drew attention to the "segmented" life of allegorical characters, noting that their adventures and personalities are always varied.[7] Carolyn Van Dyke and Clifford Gay celebrate the "radically complex" character of a form that they define as the "focus of multiple interpretations."[8] Quilligan and Whitman grudgingly allow that allegory is plagued by an internal impetus toward brevity and fragmentation.[9] Like it or not, allegory is most allegorical when it makes short, understandable points.

In this paper I shall encourage the advent of lighter and breezier allegorisms. I shall try to open windows into some popular traditions around, within, and behind the grand allegories that my colleagues have so ably explicated. The hermeneutical richness of allegory—its restless susceptibility to interpretation—abides not in its deep mysteriousness. Rather, it shimmers on its surface, from its superficiality, its repetitiveness, and its locality. While enjoying the diffusion of this allegorical glow over emblems, maxims, and maps, I shall look at a group of traditions concerned with the representation of localities and particularities—traditions in which, Althusser et al. aside, repetition and reproduction not only promote, but *are*, knowledge. Rebutting both Marxist and deconstructive critics, I shall evaluate the compression of other meanings, other places, and generic otherness into the immediately viewed but implicitly expansive plane of allegorical representation. Observing the mutation of maxims and anecdotes into enlarged cartographic or emblematic fields, I shall venture to describe a natural history of allegory, detailing its growth from bits and pieces of meaningful lore into a complex but familiar field of narrative knowledge.

II: Natural Metaphor: Maxim and Emblem

Emblem books were pricey undertakings. Few required less than 25 engravings, most had at least 50, and lavish productions offered hundreds. Even considering the often spectacular recycling of used emblems into new collections, the total cultural investment in emblem books would stagger scholars and publishers of the 1990s.

Peter Daly estimates that, between the first English-language emblem book (1586) and the end of the eighteenth century, 600 authors produced 2,000 titles. Some books ran through as many as 170 editions. Not all of these books were in English, but most enjoyed a wide circulation among British readers.[10]

So persistently voluminous a tradition argues against too restricted an audience. Not even the wealthiest collectors could soak up the flood of emblemata without help from the less affluent. The enormous popularity of emblem literature also erodes confidence in overly abstruse approaches to its interpretation. Baptized in the individual-empowering hermeneutics of Protestantism (a tradition of personal interpretation that even Catholic productions, like Hugo's *Pia Desidera*, were wont to invoke), emblem books evidence a readiness for, rather than a recalcitrance to, explication.[11] Rosemary Freeman, for one, posits a superfluity of meaning in emblemata. "All objects" and "patterns" in emblems have "allegorical significance," the stress here falling strongly on "all."[12] The first English-language emblem book, emblematically enough, depicts Drake's Golden Hind resting atop a globe. Framing both world and voyage, this most cybernetic of pages tells us that the forthcoming flood of emblematically miniaturized allegories would encapsulate a whole world of meanings.

Popular, repetitive, and pointed, free-ranging but fragmentary, emblems and emblem books coincide, formally and historically, with the great age of aphoristic and anecdotal literature. An emblem, after all, is a three-part production, a motto or maxim followed by a visual and textual explication.[13] Both emblem and maxim books are recyclable, mass-media forms in which decontextualized quotations invoke a range of meanings, applications, and authorities.[14] Both genres demonstrate Whitmanian "divergence," in which brief texts represent vast compendia of secret meanings.[15] A glance at maxim and aphorism collections can thus reveal a great deal about the foundations of their more complex, allegorizing counterparts.[16]

Metaphor, all critics agree, is the principle trope of both allegory and emblem. Maxim books show that writers of earlier periods hesitated to accord to metaphor the semi-mystical powers that Coleridge and his successors bestowed upon it.[17] Counterpointing the artificial, esoteric, and strained metaphors of a Spenser or a Donne, aphorists deal in what might I shall call "natural metaphors." Rather than following the lead of a Herbert or a Marvell by enlarging the distance between idea and image as far as language will allow, aphorists minimize this semiotic space. They undo metaphysical trickery by devising metaphors featuring as little internal contrast as possible. Condensing rather than expanding catachresis, they aspire to achieve witty effects with a minimal expenditure of energy. Emergent metaphors just barely stretch out of unmetaphorical prose; clever sayings seem to flip out of the down-home saucepan. The author of *Rules and Maxims for the Conduct of Life*, for example, announces that "Money like Dung does no good, 'til tis spread" and that "Curiosity" is "the Itch of the Ear that breaks out at the Tongue."[18] Using a single homely verb equally applicable to cash and crap, this author compresses a polysemous idea into a single verbal action, thereby avoiding the opening up of a "metaphysical" or deconstructive gap between sign and signified. A personification, "Curiosity," prescinds from metaphor to medicine, acting like, even possessing, the reader's body. Devising a plausibly witty otolaryngology, this author recapitulates the natural history of a metaphor.

"Natural metaphors," in which tenor and vehicle are conceptually distinct but tangibly joined, undermine post-structuralist assumptions about allegories establishing artificial codes. One possible meaning of "allegory" is "speaking one thing but meaning another," an interpretation from which many critics conclude that the link between allegorical token and implied meaning is at best a manufactured one. Whatever their political or religious allegiances, most expositors of the seventeenth and eighteenth centuries regard the sign-signified relation as somewhat more than arbitrary. The writings of Emanuel Swedenborg, for one, sanctify the sensual encounter with meaning. Swedenborg's heaven and hell are married; his allegory is a form of "conjugial" [sic] affection. It has been all too easy to miss this conjunctive force in the disjunctive Smaragdine formula, "as above, so below." A spectrum of factions, from Rosicrucian neo-Hermeticists to melancholy graveyardists like Blair, Young, and even Thomson insist that "nature's transcript" both allegorizes and directly discloses the mind of God, much as an alphabet both signifies and triggers mentalized sounds during the act of reading.[19]

Interpretation thus proves as inescapable as the human body. Charles Bradbury stocks his *Cabinet of Jewels* (1785) with creatures who naturally, physiologically, signify their aspiration for celestial lodgings.

> A philosopher observeth, that all bipedes, creatures with two feet, are still looking upward. Birds and fowls seldom stay long upon the earth...Beasts, though they cannot mount upward, and are made so they look downward, yet they are often seen to lift their heads toward heaven, especially in the time of extremity...They tell us of a fish which hath but one eye, which is seated like a vertical point upon the top of its head, always looking toward heaven...Some affirm, that the sap in trees precisely follows the motion of the sun...Naturalists speak of several stones, in which there is some representation of the heavenly bodies.[20]

Further examples abound. A maxim collection in the process of turning into a narrative allegory, Bradbury's book collates evocative quotations into connected series of sentences. His self-contained paragraphs yield textual emblems of the questions they examine. Conventional wisdom holds that allegory proceeds from defined, individual signs to mists of meanings, but Bradbury accumulates caches of signs into a single treasury. He refuses to disconnect his emblematic aphorisms from their meaning. Volant birds are winging toward heaven, in fact as well as in interpretation. The heaven-beholding fish is in the process of swimming upstream along the rivers of paradise. These creatures are what they are, but they are also their meaning—as well as the interpretive process by which observers link images to interpretations. The eye *is* part of the fish, *is* the beholding of heaven, and *is* enacting the process by which the fish in the flood becomes the piscine symbol plastered on Christian bumper-stickers. Bradbury need not even see an emblematic object if he can imagine the interpretative process that that object embodies. Like George Berkeley's tar-water, Bradbury's "sap" oozes inside a tree. The mere mention of the process by which invisible sap affirms its visualized meaning, the mere thought of its heavenward movement, draws this otherwise elusive fluid into the emblematic field.

The process of joining emblematic animals to philosophical implications also unites complexity with simplicity and artifice with nature. The editor of *Choice Emblems* suggests that "many of the brute creatures seem so formed by instinct, as to make up an universal satire on mankind—For where is the Undutiful Child but must be ashamed to see himself outdone by the Stork in filial Duty and affection?"[21] One of the most complex of literary modes, satire requires sophisticated comparisons between ideal and real, high literature and muckraking. Nevertheless, a genuine birdbrain can both portray and perform satiric acts, especially at the behest of simple instinct. The exploration of the gradual, incorporative progress by which emblems *become* rather than simply signify meanings allows for the discovery of allegorical meanings in artificial objects, whether telescopes, microscopes, compasses, or ships. Mechanical objects whose meaning is less discovered than installed—for example, calipers, daggers, and the whole machinery of heraldry—belong to a world somewhere between Bradbury's earthbound stone and the heaven of knowledge that it refracts.[22] Incorporating use and meaning (what else can a dagger mean besides "the power to stab"?), these emblems of artifice can be interpreted as both satiric and sacramental.

Schoolbooks like *Choice Emblems* appealed to an educated middle class. Exploring the middle-earth between physical signs and empyrean wisdom, they appealed to persons in middling social stations. Benjamin Cole, an engraver who sold to the school market, had a knack for landing flatfooted between visual presentation and moral application. In his *Tales and Fables* (1756), animals look like people while people look like animals.[23] Monkey and man—or, for the gender-conscious, monkeyette and woman[24]—converge on each other, much as low satire and authoritative instruction coincide in the accompanying fables [*Fig. 1*]. Gesture matters as much as appearance, as evinced by the cocktail-party manner of the elephant visiting Cole's bookshop [*Fig. 2*] Cole's eco-analogy of man and beast demonstrates that, among allegorists, similarity overwhelms difference. The point of the fable is lost if the reader fails to notice the correspondence of elephant to man or to acknowledge the naturalness of the metaphor. No less than John Evelyn, after all, endorsed "this *Theriologic Physiognomy*, and resemblance of *Brutes*, to the Heads and Faces of *Men*, as a secondary part of that...Doctrine of Signatures."[25]

Similarity is a form of repetition. Echoing their antecedents, Cole's images establish a continuum of meaning. For Cole and many others, allegory could be described as a form of data compression. In order to make a startling statement, a large continuum of similarities is compressed into an efficient and brief communication, whether picture, poem or prose. Emblems specialize in shocking comparisons and contrasts, yet even the starkest differences stand against and are somewhat dispersed by an implied background of mediating similarities. Cole's fables repeat the stories of that favorite eighteenth-century fabulist, Aesop, yet they place Aesop in so starkly modern a context that readers easily forget—although they feel—the derivative, historically extensive nature of Cole's enterprise. The entropic, similarity-seeking Cole attaches an easy, de-mystified moral "Application" to each evocative, critically-demanding fable. These modern morals alternate between verse and prose, gravitating toward a mid-point between imitation and originality, classic heroism and modern business. All the while, they repeat commonplaces in new interpretive contexts. It is natural that Cole should attach to his fables a collection of shopworn "Prudential Maxims," including some comic lines from Pope and Dryden that have been re-contextualized into serious lessons for children. Background repetition of familiar data underlies his project, literally and figuratively.

III: Digesting Reference

The emblems of the Enlightenment contain rather than exalt paradox. Positing correspondences between words, images, and meanings, they absorb the resulting divergences into a limited, defined, and manageable spaces. Emblems and emblem books are digestive. They ingest all possible interpretations of an image into accompanying lists, poems, or, in the case of Bradbury's sappy tree, into the allegorical object itself. The repetition of images across emblem books—who could estimate how many storks and pelicans appears in Daly's 2,000 titles?—is also a process of absorbing and animating diverging interpretations. The *corpus* of all emblem books eventually consumes all possible presentations and exegeses of a given image. As emblems migrate from book to book, pelicans, storks, alligators, and the whole meaningful menagerie come to life. Fixed signs cinematically metamorphose into exegetical acts. Such a metamorphosis is condensed in the frontispiece to Cole's *Tales and Fables* [*Fig. 3*], where "Fables" turns to join her sister, "Wisdom," to join the uphill stroll to knowledge. Intertwined, plural Fables and singular Wisdom not only resemble one another but also, despite their intended journey, remain fixed within their frame. Proximately allegorical, different but adjacent, both wear wings; ready to fly into otherness, both effuse hermeneutical potential. The expected enlightening sun is blocked by a looming tree, which also wraps the characters into the middle of the page. This eclipse matters little, for Wisdom, her solar badge tells us, has already incorporated the *corpus* of meanings.

Cole's French counterpart, Jean Perrin, venerates not the mystical meaning of fables, but the fabulist's own *je ne sais quoi*: "ce qui y plaît aux personnes de bon goû...c'est une certaine gaieté, un charme particulier, un je ne sais quel enjouement qui est plus facile à concevoir qu' à expliquer, & dont LA FONTAINE est le meilleur modèle."[26] For Perrin, whose fables provided translation exercises for English ladies, the direct experience of a story leads more quickly to this mysterious excellence than does the technical explication of its details. So Cole's "Wisdom" and "Fable" play out the whole story of extra-textual interpretation without leaving the narrative apartment of the emblem or without risking surgery on Wisdom's translucent body.

Personifications like "Wisdom" and "Fables" enjoy a putative life. They may not attain full development as psychologically complex characters, but their pictorial presentation as persons rather than as entexted ideas endows them with a Perrinian vitality. An abstraction may not be a character, but a personification gives character to an abstraction. In borderline maxim-emblem projects like Bradbury's *Cabinet of Jewels*, the ascription of personalities to concepts duplicates the attribution of aphoristic utterances to notable spokespersons.[27] Whether by personifying ideas or by quoting lawgivers, Bradbury and others try to enter the mind of a personification. There, like Perrin, they can live through the experience of styling oneself into a symbol, of setting oneself up as an authority, of speaking a law, and of hearing and interpreting one's edicts. Bradbury tells a story concerning Socrates. When examined by one of those chiropractors of popular allegory, a physiognomist, this famous sage was diagnosed as a great criminal. Socrates's students chided the charlatan, but Socrates confirmed the diagnosis, reporting that only harsh spiritual exercises had kept his criminal impulses under control.[28] Half personality, half personification, Bradbury's Socrates affirms his standing as a living emblem, a physiognomically allegorical text. He demonstrates the process by which interpretations, in this case a deviously satirical one, are generated and appropriated. He acts out the answer to the age-old question, "What is it like to be Dame Philosophy?"

Authoritative personalities, like emblems, travel in flocks. John Evelyn, another enthusiast for physiognomy, recommends making an allegorical-aphoristical collection of heads. He argues that, while man *in general* may indeed microcosmize creation, physiognomists would still benefit from a more voluminous study of the assorted editions of the human encyclopedia.[29] Flipping through Evelyn's pages of busts and medals is like flipping through an emblem book in which a single idea assumes dozens of forms. Evelyn charts a course for allegory in the Enlightenment, for he moves toward an increased condensation of meaning. Rather than individual, Castiglionian jacks-of-all-trades who can interpret a thousand different emblems, Evelyn's individual writers are themselves physiognomical signatures of a thousand interpretive possibilities. If nothing else, Evelyn's list of faces makes for a more compact hermeneutical joust than do the full-body portraits or topographical subjects shown in most emblems.

Maxim and emblem collections are essentially lists. As early as 1631, John Done created the textual equivalent of an emblem by listing the numerous analogies between man and the *polis*, the political field, in which man's meaning is played out.

> *Man is like a Citie.*
> His skin the walls
> His eyes and eares the Factors and Merchants
> His hands the trades men
> His legs the porters

and so on.[30] Done's serial affirmations sequentially depict a city, culminating in a polysemous picture of a good government. Done's aphoristic image is both constructed of and contained in its explicated parts. A century later, Andrew Wilson, a pre-Shandeian and mystical onomastician, would argue that the "genius of the language" creates history out of "prophetical" names through a similar accumulative process. History, a closed system, is produced, interpreted, and contained by a series of nouns.[31] Even more spectacularly, Jean Theophile Desaguliers, a principal of Britain's Masonic lodge, listed correspondences between the surrounding solar system and the surrounded Hanoverian court. Desaguliers, alas, could never enjoy his fame as an allegorist. His enthusiasm turned to disappointment after he unsuccessfully opposed the revision of the calendar, out of fear that too sudden a gerrymandering of time would throw the Queen's birthday out of kilter with the cosmos, right in the middle of the first year of her reign—a bad move, allegorically speaking.[32]

The serializing tendencies of allegory lend legitimacy to the dubious habit among commercial booksellers of recycling used engravings. George Wither's emblems offer a spectacular example. Wither's work could be characterized as a "pure" collection, a gathering of materials lacking any original, uncollected version. As if they had a life of their own, "Wither's" engravings commenced congregating long before Wither took up the pen. They had been first amalgamated for Gabriel Rollenhagen's *Nucleus emblematum selectissimorum* (1611), another work whose "original" form was as a collection. Wither gathered and completely re-interpreted these emblems for his collection of 1635.[33] Versions of Wither's newly secondary collection appeared anonymously in 1684 and 1732, under variations of the title *Delights for the Ingenious*. Peddled by Nathaniel Crouch, the *Delights* was a cut-down collection, paring Wither's 200 to "R. B.'s" 50 emblems.[34]

As Wither had gingerly edited and re-interpreted Rollenhagen's emblems, so Crouch (and his heirs) re-arranged Wither's proto-cavalier collection to suit the tastes of their millennium-preoccupied, aphorism-loving audience. One-quarter the size of Wither's volume, Crouch's easy-read moral Baedeker exploits the ideological potential of form. It edits out Wither's elaborately conservative "century" scheme while moving emblems of instability, ephemerality, apocalypse, and especially emblems of exploded sovereignty to climactic or other prominent positions [*Fig. 4*]. Over the course of 121 years, Rollenhagen's persistent emblems thus repeat and re-repeat themselves. Always finding new interpreters and editors, they gradually incorporate even that great jumble of meaningful newness, the apocalypse, into a their final, retrospectively inclusive panel.

"Wither's" emblems retained their popularity for so long partly owing to their appetite for their own meanings. In the well know pelican feeding scene [*Fig. 5*], the nest diorama and the crucifixion scene copy and consume one another, down to the spurts of blood and the circle of hungry disciples. Sandwiched between repetitive icons, Christ's cross is topped by an attention-stealing, reiterative model of the pelican vignette! The feeding pelican, not Christ, dominates the picture. "For this our *Hieroglyphick* would express/That *Pelican*, which in the *Wilderness*/Of the vast *World*, was left (as all alone)/Our miserable *nature* to bemone." Placed at approximately the same level in the picture-plane as the crucifixion, the pelican family seems to reject and displace the implied hierarchy of meanings. The shaft of explicative light entering from above the scene is outshone by a brilliant blaze behind Christ's head. Epideictic rhetoric—"Look!" "See!"—punctuates the accompanying verse, leaving viewers in no doubt that the pointed, fragmentary picture of a moving event outperforms the comprehensive, rational narrative of God's superintending plan for mankind.

Emblems portray functions and processes. They always do more than illustrate ideas; they are never mere snapshots of mindless objects. Allegorical, they lead from (and show the procession of) image to meaning and from representation to idea. One of Wither's explicative poems argues that stars, shown in the distant background of the emblem, govern human life. At the end of the poem, Wither reverses himself, arguing that wisdom can counteract astrology. The emblem echoes this change of heart, showing both the heavenly stars and the proximate star in the wise ruler's breast. This monarch's unstable posture atop a globe of the heavens [*Fig. 6*] echoes both the poet's turning of opinion and the turning of fate. Rolling forward toward the audience, the emblem enacts the gradual motion from providential stellar guidance into the personal experience of the morally responsible reader. Like Cole in his frontispiece, this emblematist plucks the heavenly eyes from the firmament, transplanting them into the good man's cheerful chest.

The Rollenhagen/Crouch/Wither emblems were more popular in the Restoration and eighteenth century than at the time of their engraving. Their habit of realizing function, of connecting abstract, open-ended, and interpretative processes to palpable experience, could only increase their popularity with an empiricizing audience. When Wither's God sends out helping hands, those hands link up with and even look likes Moses's. When winged wit shoots heavenward, it physically sprouts from the drossy, physical arms of poverty [*Figs. 7, 8*]. When Crouch re-edits Wither's 200 emblems, he comes up with an octavo of 50 ready to drop into Everyman's hands.

IV: Joining in the Fun

The emblematic literalizing of interpretative processes points up the easy availability of allegorical experience during the English Enlightenment. Anyone could figure out the meaning of God's funky helping hands or expect to meet with them in daily life. The dwindling of allegorical texts in the later seventeenth and eighteenth century is partly attributable to the fact that so much of allegory took place in life rather than books. Methodism, Rosicrucianism, and other alternative lifestyles promoted the living as well as the reading of allegory, as did writers like Bunyan, Winstanley, Wharton, and Blake. Experiential allegory, alas, vanishes along with its experiencers.

Directions to Signify

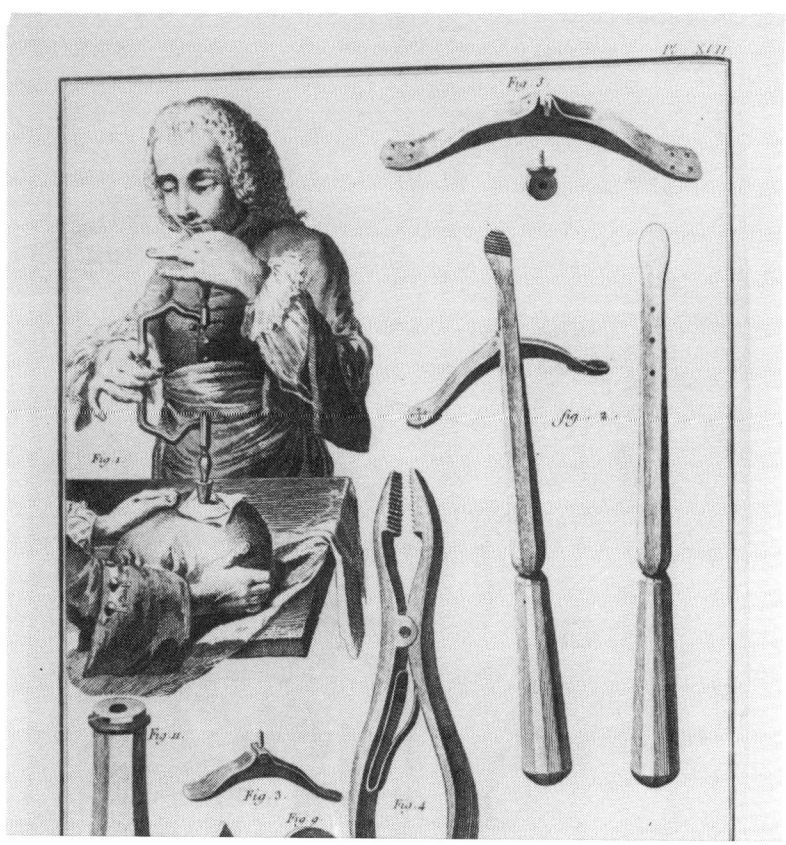

Errata

The 15 illustrations in this essay were erroneously transposed for the 15 illustrations in Grant Holly's essay beginning on page 144. The captions in both essays are correct as printed.

Figure 2: From Benjamin Cole, *Select Tales and Fables*.
Courtesy Division of Archives and Research Collections, McMaster University Library.

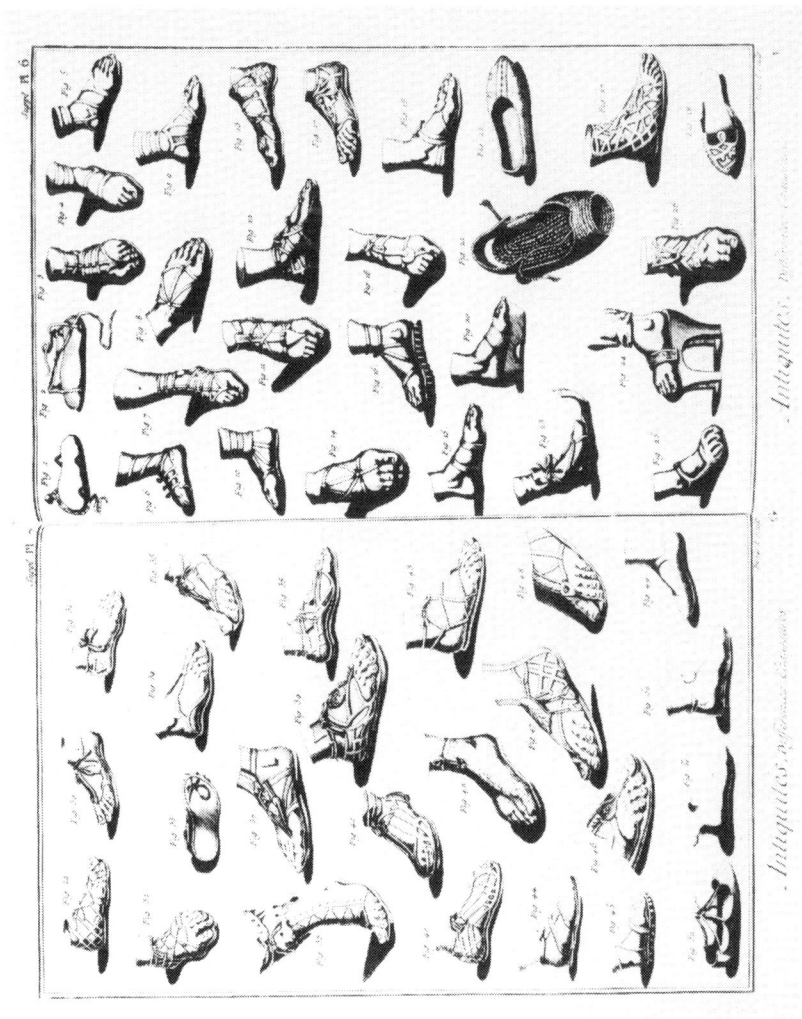

Figure 3: From Benjamin Cole, *Select Tales and Fables*.
Courtesy Division of Archives and Research Collections, McMaster University Library.

186 ENLIGHTENING ALLEGORY

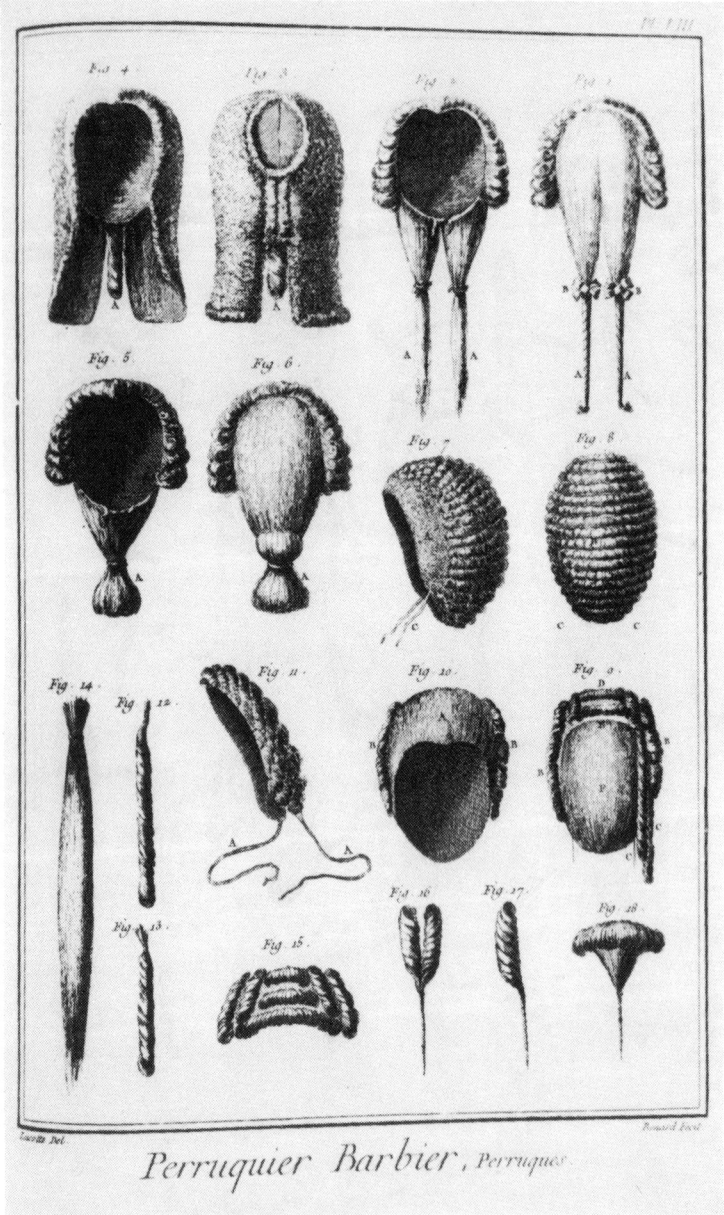

Figure 4: From Nathaniel Crouch, *Delights for the Ingenious.*
By permission of the Newberry Library, Chicago.

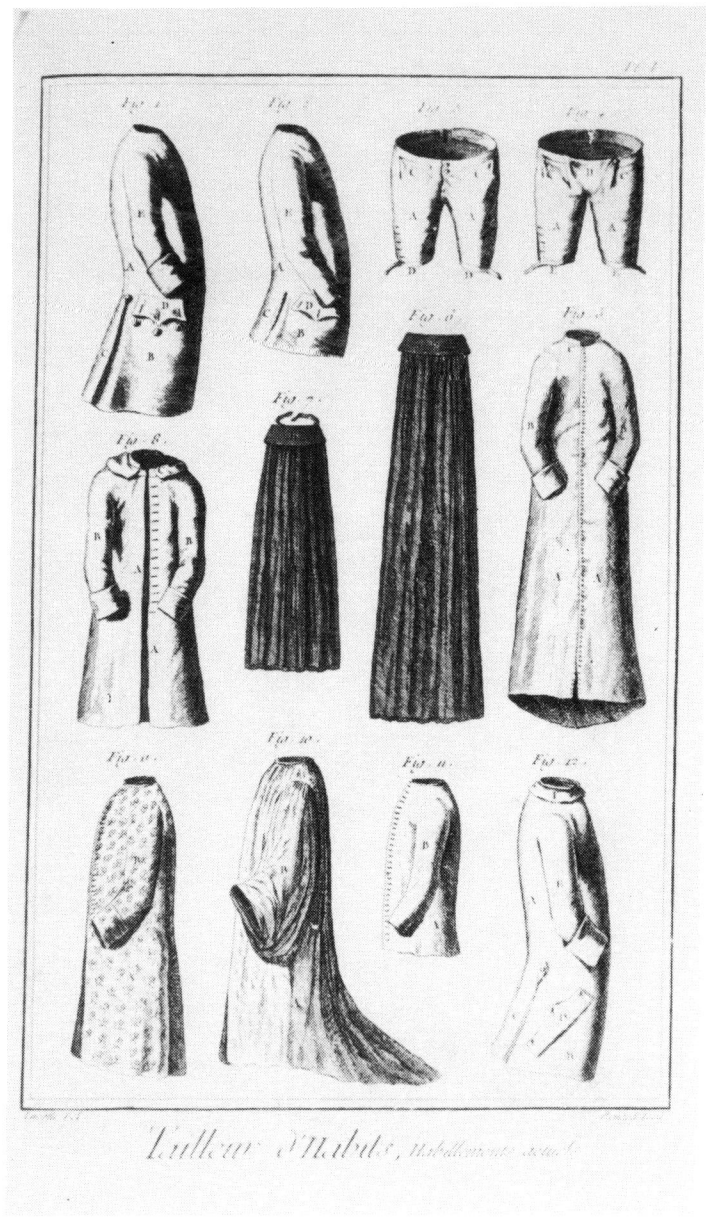

Figure 5: From Nathaniel Crouch, *Delights for the Ingenious*. By permission of the Newberry Library, Chicago.

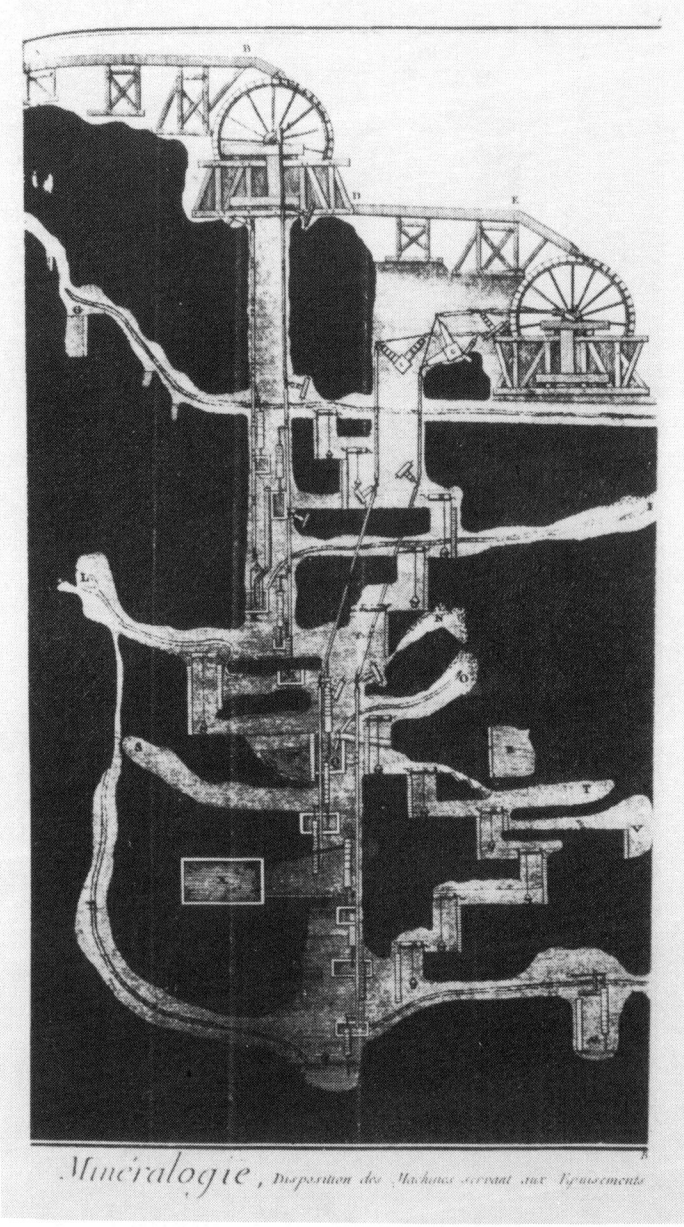

Figure 6: From Nathaniel Crouch, *Delights for the Ingenious*.
By permission of the Newberry Library, Chicago.

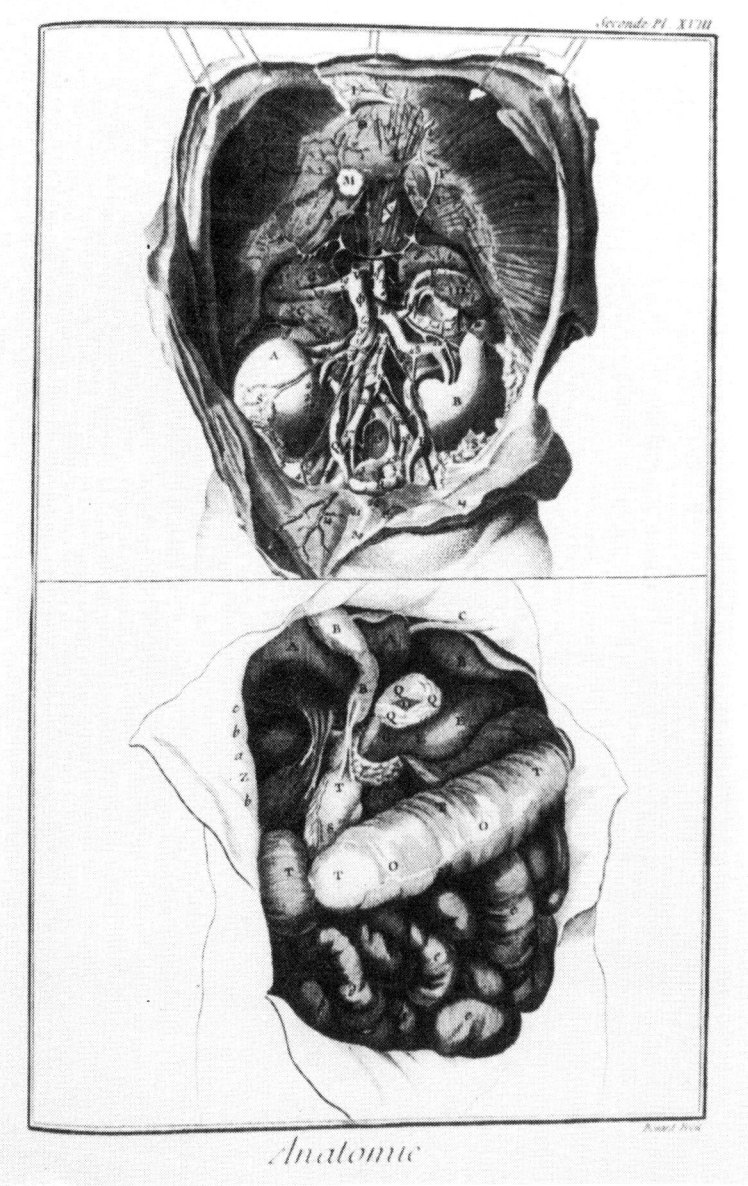

Figure 7: From Nathaniel Crouch, *Delights for the Ingenious*.
By permission of the Newberry Library, Chicago.

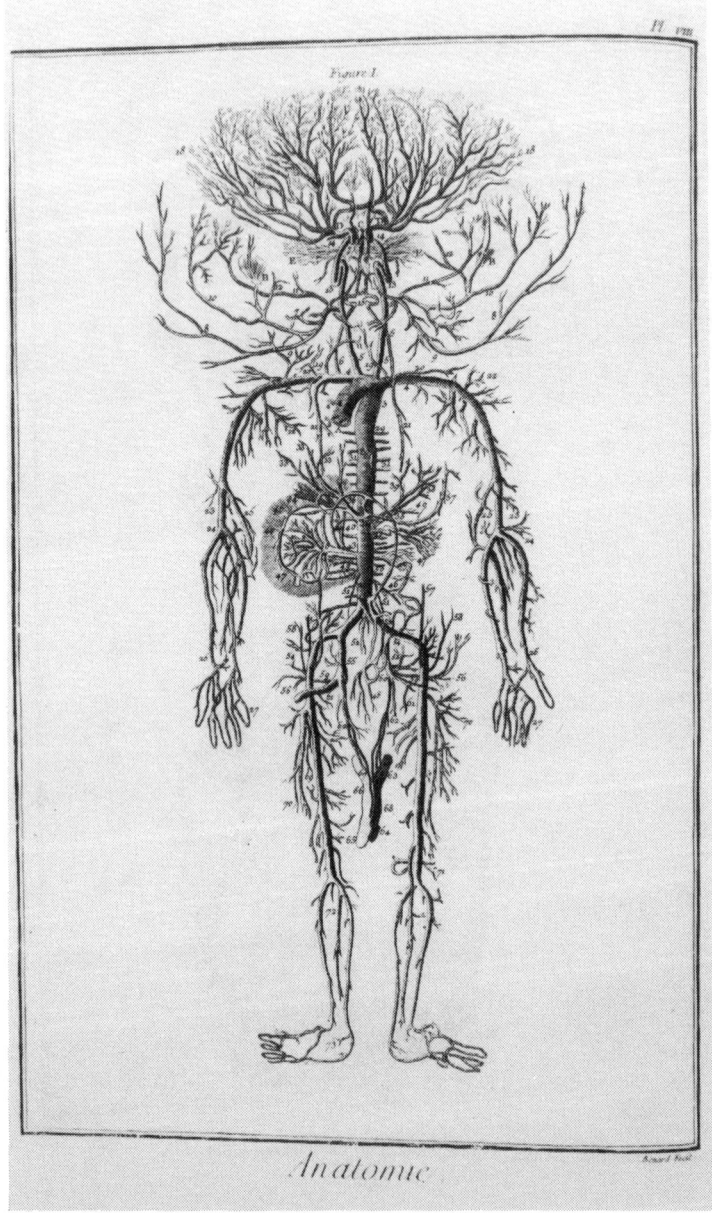

Figure 8: From Nathaniel Crouch, *Delights for the Ingenious*. By permission of the Newberry Library, Chicago.

The vitality of Enlightenment allegory calls into question the detached, spectatorial approach of a Whitman or de Man or Quilligan, but it supports a participatory theory like Nuttall's.[35] Exegetes like Lancelot Andrewes or Benjamin Keach may have adopted disinterested, scholastical approaches to interpretation, but Wither, Dryden, Watts, and Berkeley drank, as well as interpreted, their allegorical tar-water.

Popular allegorical texts abound with complex, allegorical figures who participate in as well as represent ideas, issues, and stories. Allen Ramsay celebrates this empowerment of the personification in his allegorical-didactical poem, *Health*. "Health," Ramsay's leading lady, is a state of (medical) affairs, a process, a (healthy) person, and a personification. Poems on this lucky lady populate the period, not the least ingenious being a snippet from Susannah Watts's *Chinese Maxims* (1784), a versification of Dodsley's *The Oeconomy of Human Life*. Watts's "Health" swaggers with the arrant vigor of a Leona Helmsley and the sartorial splendor of a Barbara Cartland:

> But who is she with steps of winning grace,
> And lively air that trips the verdant trace?
> Her blushing cheeks confess the blooming rose,
> And from her lips the morning sweetness flows?...
> Her name is Health, that fair and blooming child,
> Of mod'rate exercise, and temprance mild.
> [Her] sons inhabit where north breezes flow,
> And hills extend o'er San-Ton-Hoe.
> Valour, activity, and mirth they bear,
> And all the virtues of their sister share.
> Vigour their nerves, and strength their bones employ,
> Successive labour's all the day their joy.[36]

The consummate experiential allegorist, Watts wanders into sentimentality yet always pays scrupulous attention to anatomical details, genealogical affiliations, and topographical contexts. However stylized, Health could pass as a real person with vigorous offspring. She recalls the Queen's golden head on Britain's 1990 Christmas stamp, which floats, as both a stylized and a familiar presence, directly in the line of sight of real, fun-loving, winter-sledding children. The minimally idealized "Health" household is no more or less realistic than the households in the "realistic" novels of Fielding or the autobiographies of Wordsworth. Watts's contemporary, Dorothy Kilmer, extends this brand of experiential allegory to the animal kingdom. She serves up a hybrid allegory-dialogue in which emblematic animals converse with one another, albeit in a language that no human can understand.[37]

Kilmer's bizarre dialogue calls attention to the fact that most emblems portray living creatures. Unlike their counterparts in medieval bestiary lore, emblematic fauna derive first from the observation of nature and only secondarily from authority, tradition, or myth. Their job, exemplifying ideas, is actively dramatic as well as pictorially hieroglyphic. Collectively, they define a "participation" allegory in which real animals, like John Wayne's Green Berets, mean exactly what they do and say. Their actions implement their meanings, whereas, in bestiaries, meanings force half-imaginary animals into proverbial roles. John Brathwait's mixed-media maxim-emblem-courtesy book, *The Ladies Love-Lectvre* (1641), bristles with business-like beasts.

> It is reported of the Camell, that they usually hood-winke him, when at any time they bring his mother unto him: which act (observe this incestuous hate) he no sooner knowes, than he tramples her under his feete, and kickes her to death with his heeles. So egregiously hatefull is incest, even to brute Beasts, whose native instinct abhorres such obscene commixtures.[38]

Observation, instinct, passion, indignation, and a host of processes propel this picture out of the interpretative museum and into life. There is little comment here (or in any of Brathwait's other stories) about the shape, the size, or the other habits of the camel. What we see and what we interpret are actions. Were roosters to evidence the same behavior, then Chanticleer would replace the camel in the picture. Brathwait's righteous camel not only teaches by acting but knows and feels what he means. Conversely, but to the same effect, Fulke Greville (not the Renaissance poet, but "the other" Fulke Greville) asks readers to step into the picture, there to convert inert substances into a signifying icons. "What an amazing quality has turpentine! stir and agitate its particles, you give it prodigious force, leave it to itself it has none at all: emblem of the faculties of man!"[39] Physical intervention elicits an emblematic application of this solution to the interpreting mind. Interpretation, emblems, and intervening readers disclose rather than deconstructively obfuscate one another. John Aubrey's collection of ominous prodigies repeatedly demonstrates that emblematic omen and precocious reader make and interpret one another. "A little before the Death of *Oliver* Protector, a *Whale* came into the River *Thames* and was taken at *Greenwich*,...[ellipses are part of text] foot long. 'Tis said, *Oliver* was troubled at it."[40] Oliver, part of the scene and story, is the first to make something of the prodigy. Aubrey, inserting ellipses into the narrative, imitates the cognitive process by which Oliver, both topic and reader of the omen, transforms a whale into a warning.

V. Matrix, Margin, Map

Seventeenth- and eighteenth-century allegory may no longer belong to Aaron Copeland's "common man." Oliver Cromwell is no average Joe on 34th Street. Yet Enlightenment allegory is more the province of technologists or handypersons than of scholarly recluses. Poly-political but fundamentally neo-Puritan, it is a didactical mode, one associated with lawgivers and mechanics who want meaningful suggestions when difficult problems require practical solutions. Anecdotal, emblematic, the allegory of this era specializes in the moderately general. Seldom stooping to teach nail-driving, never rising to pontification, it explains how to think about the turning of screws, the organizing of cities, or the solving of crises. It copes with particulars by explaining procedures. The practicality and thinkability of allegory accounts for both its tendency to invade a variety of genres and for its immense popularity.

One practical, popular, and personable genre in which allegory plays a leading role is cartography. Nowadays few people think of a technology like surveying as an idiosyncratic, literary, or allegorical enterprise. Yet a glimpse of any eighteenth-century map will expose immense imaginative, didactical, and expressive capacities. Maps from the period, rich in anecdote and ornament, show far more than the shape of a coast line or the height of a mountain. To borrow a term from that traveller and allegorist of turpentine, George Berkeley, these maps offer "compendious," coded and allegorical, interpretations of everything from wind direction to native customs.[41] They show how to get to and what to think about a place as well as where to find its roads and rivers. Using familiar images and conventions, these maps reveal to a public, practical-minded audience what few viewers—and perhaps few cartographers, as Swift quips[42]—can hope to observe.

Even without the benefit of the great explorations, even had if it had looked no further than the neighboring countryside, cartography would have developed allegorical inclinations. Maps encode a landscape into a form that everyone recognizes but that no one, save for a few astronauts, has ever seen. They speak a kind of marketplace-talk about an unusually familiar "other." Allegory, conversely, is always cartographical. Because allegory makes everything significant, it draws attention to and charts the purlieus of its settings. No one could be more of an allegorist than that self-appointed "Secretary of Nature," the Rosicrucian virtuoso John Heydon. Heydon opens his dream vision, *The Harmony of the World*, in a placeless "irrepressible obscurity." Working with assorted topographical and other navigational clues, he pries open the windows of his apartment in obscurity, quickly concluding that he has landed "upon the south-side [of] *Hewill* upon *Hazle-hill* in *Warwick shire*."[43] Sextant in hand, he fixes himself on the allegorically significant sunny south side of his windy hill. This cartographical impulse is not unique to Enlightenment allegory. Allegories from every point of the literary compass, from *The Pearl* to *Utopia* and onto *Ulysses*, stress locality and narrative mapping. Cartographers and critics alike can revel in the knowledge that most early maps were published not as independent sheets, but as part of travel narratives, literary magazines, emblem books, geographies, encyclopedias, and book-like atlases.[44]

Many of these early maps deploy a mixture of anecdote and allegory resembling that found in emblem books. When looking on an unknown and only partially charted land, the first cartographers frame the vast territory of all possible geographical knowledge within confidently drawn meridian and parallel lines. Included within this mostly empty grid are hedging comments about the uncertainty of surveys, the deplorable lack of exploration, and the range rather than the accuracy of data. Comments about the odd or unknown ways of the inhabitants of distant lands punctuate these apologies. In one map in the *London Magazine* of 1753, the clearly defined curve of the Mississippi River wends through a few settlements and around a whole lot of uncharted space. Cartographers abhor vacuums, and this surveyor of the Mississippi is no exception. The blank, uncartographical space on the map is filled in with vague, anecdotal narratives about what certain French travellers claimed might be happening in this and that place. The text alongside the map recruits the viewer into the open-ended application of similarly unspecific ideas. It describes English-

Cherokee border issues, then suggests that the reader should speculate, in a general way, on the future importance of a military alliance with so populous an Indian nation.[45] Hermann Möll, a scoundrel who produced maps in droves whether or not he had reliable information, could likewise construct an entire map by superimposing anecdotes on vaguely defined regions. Open spaces marked with legends like "part of Asia" or "parts unknown" offer an unhelpful grab-bag of allegedly practical miscellanea (what solace would a wastrel lost in the desert find in the comment, "thought to be about 3160 miles"?).[46]

In this imaginative school of cartography, the unknown is imported into knowable cartographic frames. Reassured by firm grids and state-of-the-art projections, viewers, readers, journalists, and mapmakers conspire to convert open area into interpretative narrative. They outline and domesticate histories of the unknown. An oddly public secrecy, after all, was an integral part of cartography. Cartographers, hired by military men, concealed by revealing.[47] They kept strict silence about routes important to military or trade objectives, releasing only enough information to create the illusion of disclosure. This art of involuting instruction was perfected by the German cartographer Gottfried Hensel, whose glossographical maps of Europe, Africa, and assorted "parts unknown" offer only bare outlines of continents but spangle every region with teasingly brief anecdotes, all written in the languages spoken in the indicated places. Teaching geography and linguistics without really saying anything that anyone can understand, Hensel implies that those wealthy, polylingual illuminati who have the wherewithal to travel to these alien lands will find, as did Aphra Behn, many novels to be written.[48] Stay-at-homes can gape dumbly at his tablets of Babel.

Hensel's and others's strange, thematic maps of far-away places shed light on another familiar but depreciated eighteenth-century form, the city guidebook. Gostling's *A Walk in and about the City of Canterbury* is a representative case.[49] Gostling opens up his volume with a simple outline map of his town, to which he appends a collection of quips and insiders' jokes about assorted locations. Gobbled up by a people curious about the unknown in their own backyard, these anecdote-enriched but often inaccurate navigational aids were denigrated by the cognoscenti but relished by gossipy countrymen.[50]

The cartographic enclosure of inscrutability, especially the distribution of the unknown into anecdotal narratives, attains its apogee in those showpieces of unhelpful practical information, cosmological maps.[51] There could be no better example than one well-known candidate for deconstruction, Halley's map of the path of an eclipse.[52] Halley pictorially narrates the journey of a shadow of an other-worldly event that holds more scientific and superstitious interest than practical significance. With unmatched precision, it tells the whole story of the shade of an event. Equally penumbral productions pervade periodicals and ephemera. Two Dodsley productions, *The Preceptor* (1748) and *The London Magazine* (1752), offer maps of the orbits of noteworthy comets.[53] In both maps, the orbits appear as shallow parabolas intruding on the chart from parts unknown. They complicate the otherwise neatly concentric solar system. The tracks of the orbits underline anecdotal reports of each comet's first sighting, return date (or the unknowability of that date), and closest approach to the sun. In a long explanatory passage accompanying both charts, the author laments our ignorance of the celestial sphere, calls for better charts, proceeds blindly with his survey, and suggests that, eventually, one of these comets may collide with the earth, thus putting a period to journalism, cartography, humpty-dumpty, and all. This last melancholy observation extends the cartographic pursuit of the unknown to the verge of its own extinction. Dodsley's cosmological map simultaneously allegorizes the universal breadth of the explanatory process and the invincibility of ignorance, for it presents a comprehensive (and emblematic) chart of the ultimate, consumptive fate of knowledge.

The cartographical impulse suffuses those quasi-emblematical texts, acrostics, texts, or pictures that feature the unknown as their subject. The non-juring Rev. John Mason opens his authoritatively oracular Christian maxims with a textual matrix that functions as a map of interpretations of deep mysteries:

Christ's blood }		{ ransom.
Christ's Spirit }		{ comforter.
Christ's word }	is the soul's	{ food.
Christ's supper }		{ feast.
The Lord's Day }		{ market day.[54]

Opposing phrases are paired with one another, but the congregation of all the phrases into a two-dimensional array within a single set of brackets converts a mere five propositions into a complex network of propositions. One could draw navigational lines from any one phrase to any other, marking out a textually emblematic map of the many avenues to salvation. This frontispiece to Wither's and Crouch's perpetually redacting emblem collection, a sort of optimistic pre-last judgment scene, can also be read as a map of the thousand paths to salvation. The irregular composition reminds modern viewers of the game *Chutes and Ladders*, with several entry and exit points replacing the one straight and narrow road to Jerusalem. Crouch and Wither sandwich their entire emblem book between two maps, the Bunyanesque frontispiece and an immense lottery wheel stamped in the endpapers. The latter is designed to guide—that is, seduce—the more sinful members of the readership through the complex labyrinth of withering moral instruction. Readers can enter the book directly, from the front, or crazily, from the back, or even intravenously, through the enclosed emblems themselves, for many of the panels allude to these supervening illustrations. Emblems, frontispiece, and wheel multilaterally engross an array of paths, just as any good map might show several possible routes to any one destination.

By far the most spectacular interdisciplinary forays by allegorizing cartographers decorate the frontispieces of popular geographical texts. In these extraordinary engravings, complication, expansion, repetition, and compression of unfamiliar ideas compose busy, bizarre scenes, scenes often explicitly identified as "emblematical" or "allegorical." In the frontispiece to Millar's *System of Geography* [*Fig. 9*],[55] personifications of the four continents are shown in the act of importing barrels full of local produce into the small universe of the frame. Falling into the picture, they clearly belong to a super-prosperous, supply-side world far beyond the margins of the engraving. Yet their headlong, bushel-basket plunge into the scene removes any mystery concerning foreign resources or the mercantile motivations of Britannia. Even the route to the unrepresented other world is fully and familiarly illustrated in the hackneyed, eminently repeatable image of Poseidon. The process of travelling across the ocean, to "the other," rears up on a small scale, as kitsch clip-art of a primeval Billy Barty. Lest the turbulence of the image unsettle our wits, Mercury flies in with a big, silly banner proclaiming "New Discoveries, and Valuable Improvements." Fruits, trees, and maps repeat the theme of superabundance (and geographical ignorance). The allegorical referent, things foreign and the enthusiasm for them, is, despite its inherent elusiveness, successfully represented by means of repetition, by naming it over and over again through a series of visual anecdotes. Inverting the 1586 image of Drake's ship atop the world, a newly marginalized globe now tops this pictorially local but ideologically international scene. As if to anticipate deconstructive criticism, a ship drifts off toward the horizon, on its way not to obfuscate but to import still more information, still more allegorical significance, into the picture. Working to bring the distant near to hand, the ship accelerates the process of interpretation. It compresses the time and distance between the image and the object. To top—or bottom—it all off, the allegory gets a detailed, narrative explication immediately beneath the frame.

Millar's frontispiece is no isolated oddity. Geographies of the period abound in lavishly allegorical illustrations. A similar array of emblemata—a referent-retrieving ship, a professor shown in the allegorizing process of turning geographical data into maps and globes, a book of proto-novelistic travel narratives expressly labelled "Voyages perform'd by British Seamen," and no less allegorical a visitor than a neo-Miltonic "Urania"—fronts Frederic Watson's *Geographical Dictionary*. [*Fig. 10*][56] There are, indeed, as many or more such illustrations as there are geographies.

Geographical illustration was far from a marginalized form. Indeed, the frontispiece, the edge of the book, vaunted to contain—cartographically, emblematically, and allegorically—the whole book. In the same way, a little-evaluated form, the side-strip illustrations for maps of remote lands, helps to fill in the semiotic spectrum from anecdotal report to the abstract map. One aggressively inaccurate outline map of Greenland deploys a series of didactical and anthropological side-strip cameos. Some of these illustrations depict the work (fishing, hunting) done in that chilly land, others show scenes from native life [*Fig. 11*].[57] Rather than jumping from detailed print report to cartographical representation, rather than losing enriching, interpretable detail, viewers of this map make a gradual transition from life to illustration and finally to chart.

These side-strip illustrations suggest that allegory, knowledge, detail, and repetition go hand-in-hand. Once one has seen one map of Greenland, once one has seen one emblem of a pelican, one has seen them all. Yet the repetition of these images in book after book, a repetition driven by a lust for new interpretations of relentlessly alluring, unfamiliar places, encouraged the production of more and more marginal illustrations. The traditions of distortion built up by these comic-book images often found their way into the maps themselves and thence into the canon of interpretations.

Those who wonder why formulaic romances or videotapes of old television shows endlessly fascinate their avid purchasers need only review a few illustrated maps to recognize that, structuralism aside, it is the slightly varying details, not the repeating storyboard, that generate variant interpretations and implement the allegorical process.

The enamourment with marginal illustration was a long-lived one, as best evidenced by a strip map of the Rhine valley (1838). This mammoth, 1 x 25' production shows the Rhine running down the center of the page. The river abuts larger, more interesting renderings of the tourist sights beside the river, which carry anecdotal stories about their subject.[58] As early as 1675, John Ogilby published series of strip maps that show roads as straight lines, with the locations of inns and other landmarks being indicated alongside.[59] Throughout the seventeenth century, writers (or printers for writers) like Brathwait and Hobbes outlined their frontispieces with emblematic caricatures of the varieties of human character. It was only a matter of time before strip-map and strip-illustration converged to yield cartographical strip illustrations. Other nations were speedier in uniting margin with map. Jan van Doeticum's 1598 map of Belgium presents his country in the form of a semi-emblematic, semi-natural lion.[60] Ackermann's popular London guidebook co-annihilates the central image and map, emblematizing the disclosure of London by placing a veiled sphere in the center of a frontispiece, then projecting St. Paul's and the heart of London around the edge.[61] This image would give new meaning to the street address of America's MCI Telecommunications Corporation, a company located at the world's most deconstructible site, "Perimeter Terrace Center."

Ackermann's emblematic re-centering of cartographic and allegorical mystery makes for a good comparison to the cartouche for the introductory map in John Nieuhoff's *Travels*. In the Nieuhoff ornament, a blanket atop a sphere is being unfurled by a cherub eager to peek into a partially disclosed world.[62] Far from discouraged by the cartographical uncertainty implied by this sheathed globe, the cherub assumes that everyone will eventually see what he sees. So side-strip illustrators assume that everyone will eventually be able to learn about Greenland or other exotic places.

Corner cartouches became the rule of the day in eighteenth-century cartography. Few struck so heroic a pitch as that in Nieuhoff's book, but all served an important, popularizing, didacticizing, and allegorizing function. Placed within the map but near the margin, they could moderate between the common experience of the reader and the stylized, emblematic universe of the chart. Cartouches could repeat and re-repeat familiar images, beginning and then smoothing the process of didactical distortion that led from unorganized anecdotes to informative map. Constructive, cartouches could teach readers to reconstruct familiar stories into useful, accurate surveys. Conversely, they could give maps new meaning and force by implying that, were one to take an extremely close look at the map, one might see the life of that places. Cartouches, in other words, were anecdotal maps on a magnified, detailed scale. They offered emblematic representations of the social, political, economic, and moral structure of a place. Put a telescope up to a map and you might see a cartouche; put a telescope up to a cartouche, and you might see someone you know—or might be able to gather the materials for a novel about ordinary life.

The allegorical, narrative power of the cartouche was explored most extensively by Emanuel Bowen, Thomas Kitchin, and Thomas Condor, all well-known cartographers for assorted periodicals (Kitchin and Bowen enjoyed stints as royal cartographers and royal hydrographers).[63] Most of their maps illustrate either a shire in England or a region in the British Isles. All of their maps carry cartouches bearing the name of and often some text about the area mapped. Surrounding this colophonic placard are images of activities endemic to the area. These quaint cuts impart a certain life to the map. In *London Magazine* (1752) maps of Derby and Shetland, for example, shepherds lazily tend rams and tarpaulins work nets and ropes [*Figs. 12, 13*]. To ease another transition from text to map via cartouche, Kitchin labels some nondescript barrels "mustard seed," jokingly assuring his audience that the cartouche really does represent mustard-producing Durham. In works like Cheevers's *Mappa Britanniae Septentrionalis*, cartouche-allegorization takes on a historical dimension. Roman fasces and other antique apparatus surround the title emblem.[64] Maps like Cheevers's argue that the hermeneutical process, from image to meaning and back again, can be extended and clarified narratively. Like archaeologists digging up remains, decorative cartographers, those masters of lovely land masses, bring treasuries full of hidden meanings into the technically precise world of cartographical illumination.

The elaboration of the cartouche coincides with the profusion of geographical illustration. Like cartographers, publishers and

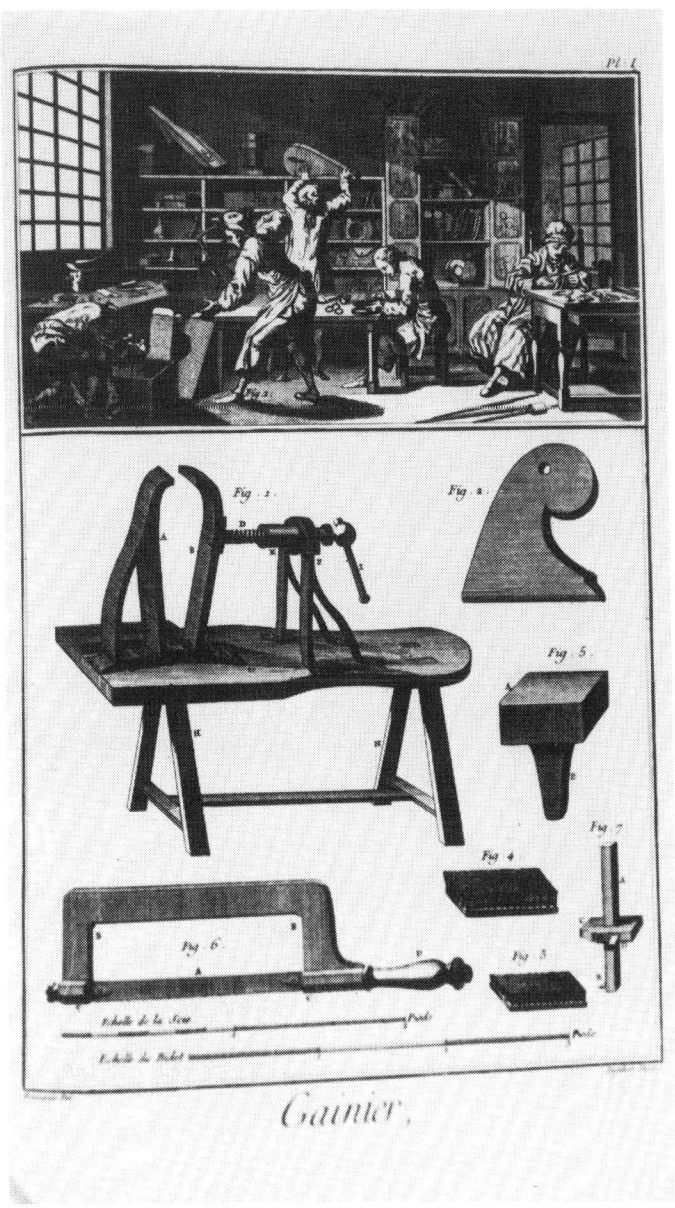

Figure 9: Frontispiece, George Henry Millar's *New and Universal System of Geography*. Courtesy Division of Archives and Research Collections, McMaster University Library.

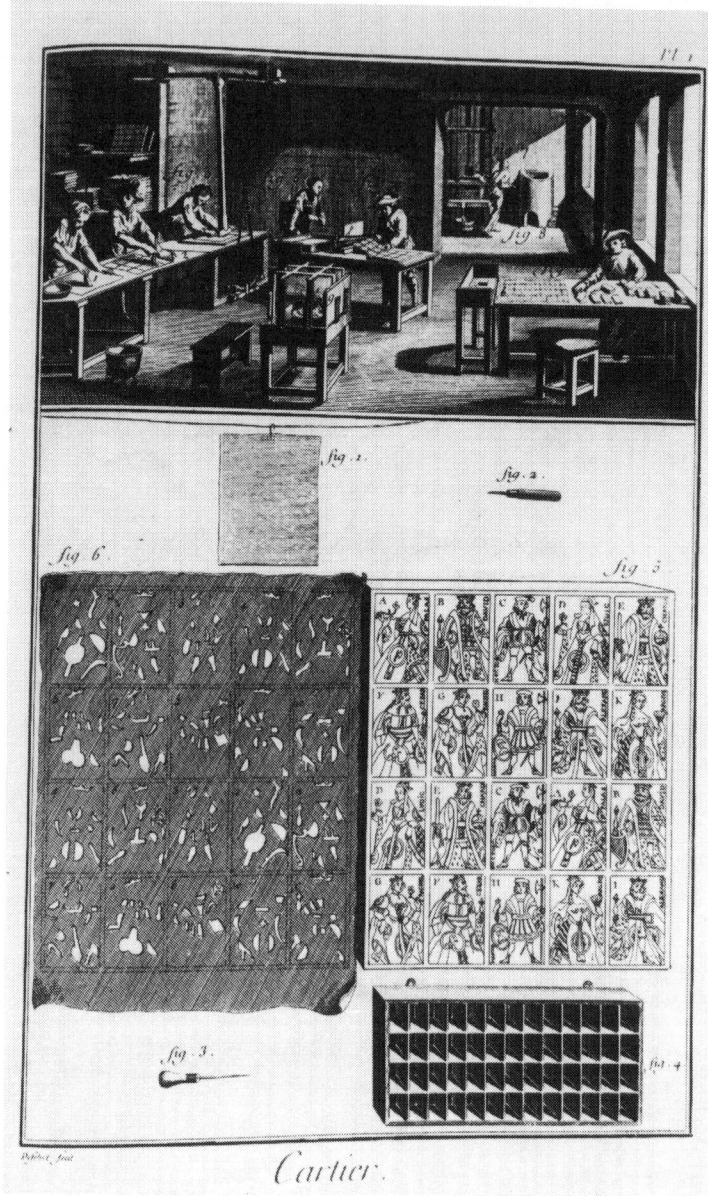

Figure 10: Frontispiece, Frederic Watson's *New and Complete Geographical Dictionary*. Courtesy Division of Archives and Research Collections, McMaster University Library.

Directions to Signify 203

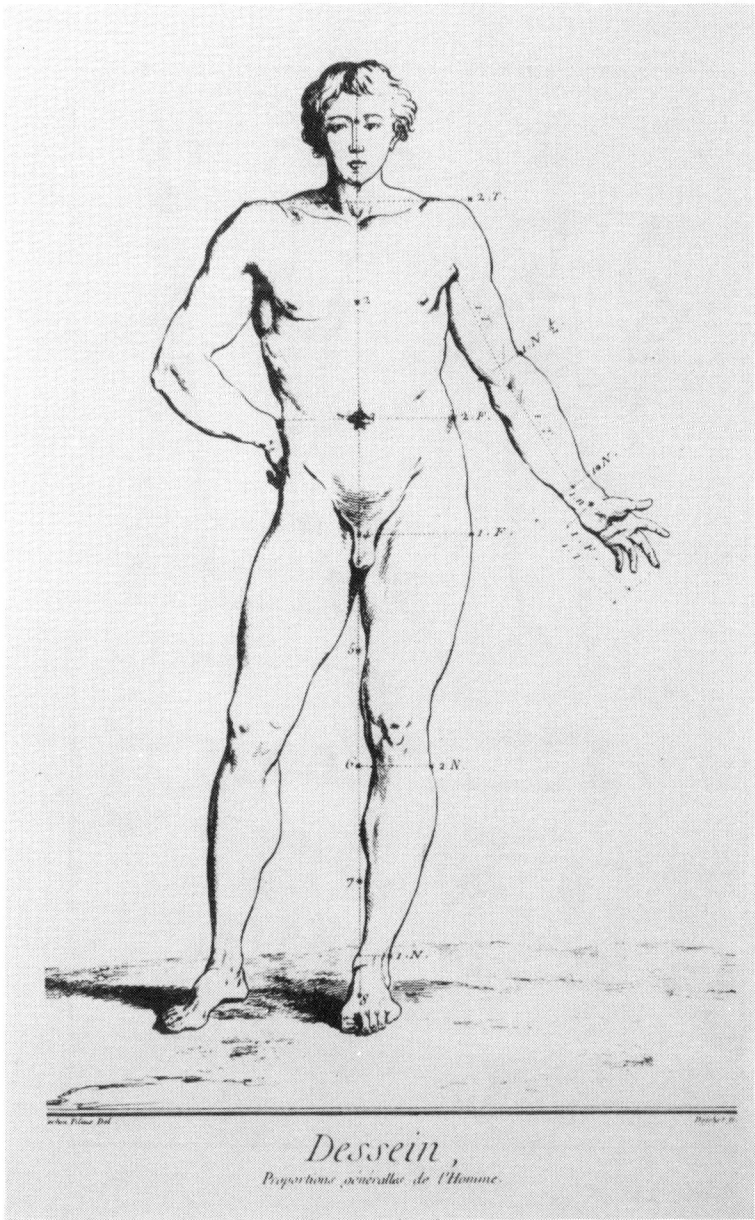

Figure 11: Map of Greenland, Edward Pellham's *God's Power and Providence*.
Courtesy Division of Archives and Research Collections, McMaster University Library.

204 ENLIGHTENING ALLEGORY

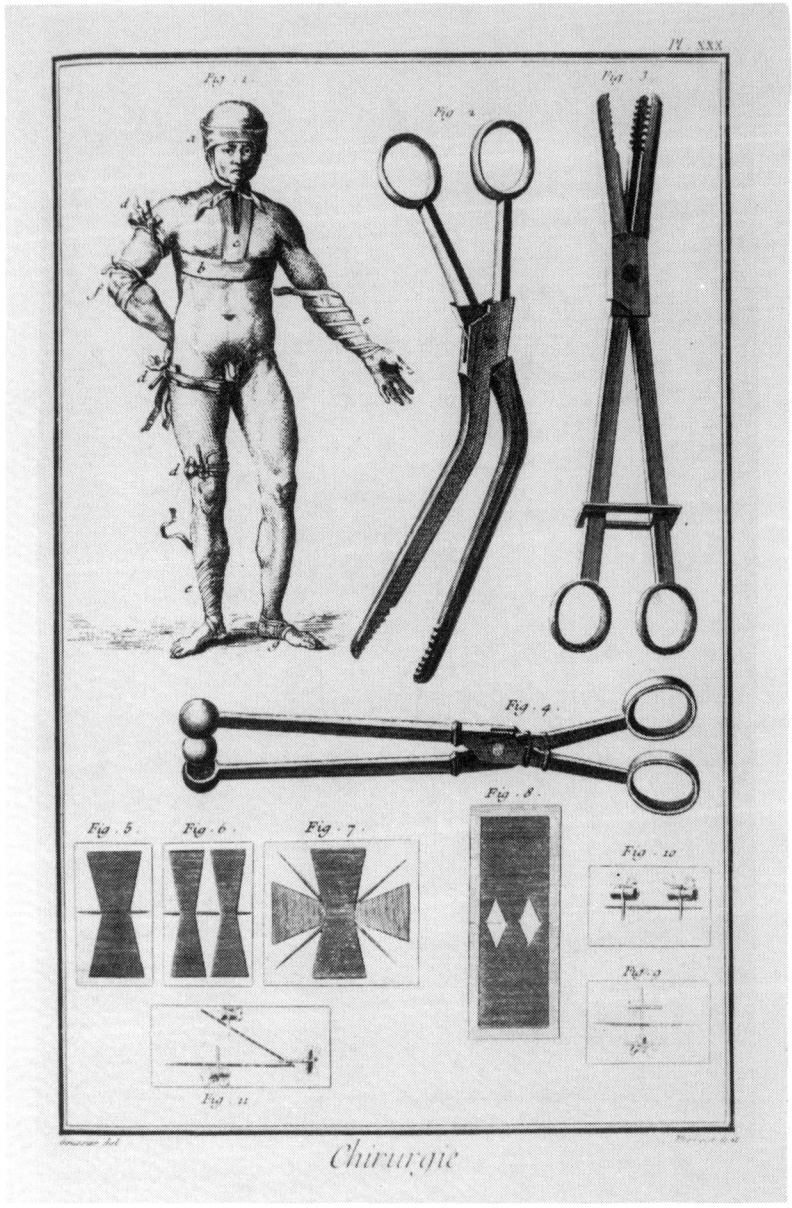

Figure 12: Map of Derby, from *London Magazine* (1752).
Courtesy Division of Archives and Research Collections, McMaster University Library.

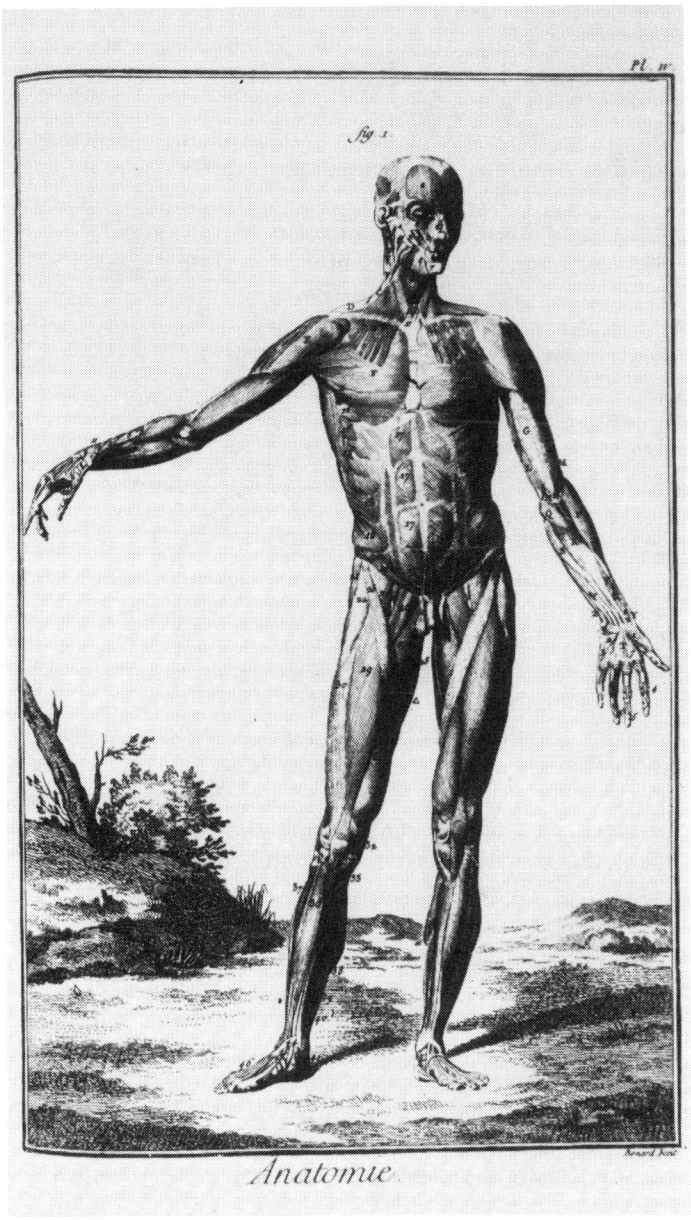

Figure 13: Map of Shetland, from *London Magazine* (1752).
Courtesy Division of Archives and Research Collections, McMaster University Library

hack engravers saw both semiotic and fiscal potential in expensive graphics. The engravings in the geographies were more than supernumerary or discretionary elements. Not only did the public expect them, but publishers bragged more about them than they bragged about their texts. The professionally immodest George Henry Millar headlines every illustration for his *New and Universal System of Geography* with banners proclaiming the originality, perspicuity, and outright magnificence of the attendant engraving. One should not mistake these illustrations for simple pictures of familiar places. They evidence the same anecdotal, semi-fictional quality as do anecdotal remarks on the undefined regions of explorers' maps. In his chapter on France, for example, Millar provides a large engraving of that semi-legendary occasion on which Sterne-*cum*-Yorick confronted the beggars of Montreuil. Like Sterne (and like allegorical cartouches), Millar's engraver explores the complex, multidimensional boundary between verisimilitude, didactic, and fabrication—between precise presentation of the historical landscape, engagement of morally appetitive readers in the scenes before them, and production of a good, if fictional, story.

Although it provides few graphics, the anonymous *Compendious Geographical Dictionary* takes a textual approach to this same matter of anecdotal illustration. This dense reference work intersperses an alphabetically arranged series of technically precise entries with anecdotes, legends, short narratives, and aphorisms. Repetition through diversification provides the key to knowledge. With all too many entries we learn (for the umpteenth time) that "the natives are Pagans, worshipping the sun, moon, and stars," then learn the specific latitude at which these diabolical rites are (once again) practiced.[65] By treating his dictionary as a repetitive series of illustrative quotations linked by a network of navigational positions, this geographer presents the map of the world as a field of telling occasions, a surface speckled with sites capable of underwriting a narrative. The cartographic field replaces Ariosto's list or the Sir Orfeo's countryside as the foundation for the allegorical enlargement of appearances. Our old friend and carefree re-publisher of emblems, Nathaniel Crouch, thus found himself at home in the gazetteer business. Playing up to its somewhat superstitious Restoration audience, Crouch's *Admirable Curiosities* begins its entries with details (crops, rainfall, latitude), then proceeds to wondrous stories, whether debunked (like the groaning tree of Lincolnshire) or still mysterious. Crouch achieves the same mixture of data and legend, survey and allegory, that would flourish in the later geographies.

This interaction of allegorical otherness with technical precision—this eruption of illustrations, details, and stories from mere points on a plane—percolates into the peculiar genre of fantasy maps.[66] Most scholars know that spurious maps introduce each book in Swift's *Gulliver's Travels*. Many other imaginary maps appeared throughout the period. Some pretended to truth, others embraced absurdity, but most hovered in that allegory-enriched area between fact and fiction. In 1708, the *Monthly Miscellany, or Memoirs for the Curious* fabricated a story about one "Admiral De Fonte," whose name may derive from the seventeenth-century explorer Bartelme de Fuentes or from a bawdy pun on Latin *"fundus."*[67] This imaginary voyager allegedly stumbled upon the Northwest Passage in 1642. The legend of this doughty admiral persisted at least until 1768, when it was still being invoked to encourage exploratory expeditions. Its tenacity accounts for the posting of a £20,000.00 bounty for the discovery of a northern waterway. Around 1754, someone assuming the semi-allegorical name of one of De Fonte's co-discoverers, "M. De L'Isle," published a map of the adventuring admiral's supposititious route(s) [*Fig. 14*].[68] Although apparently intended to increase the credibility of the map, the anecdotes cited on this mostly blank chart are themselves legendary, imaginary, or, as Hollywood producers say, "based on facts." In the Arctic Sea, where no land ever rose, floated, or sank, an entry reports "A great Tract of Land discover'd in 1722 to which the *Tzutzy* fled when they were pursued by the *Russes* who have not yet subdued them." Every supposed continent is sharply framed in parallels and meridians, but only the coast of Siberia resembles the world as it was known in the eighteenth (or any) century. It is almost as though the outrageous unlikelihood, the imaginative cheekiness of this map contributes to its believability.

The De Fonte map redeems blankness and ignorance. The specious land-masses and their superimposed anecdotes drift out like primeval continents to the edges of the map, opening up unexplored blank space for De Fonte's imaginary routes. The resulting network of imaginative peregrinations links together, in quasi-narrative form, the numerous continents about which we (still) know nothing. The projection of the world-landscape becomes an aggressive representation—and affirmation—of possibility. It proclaims the availability of *some* space for *any* story or interpretation. Rambunctious, it affirms the chartability of that space, the possibility of finding a route from any place to any anecdote and onto any meaning. The probability that this map is a satire need not lessen its role as a redeemer (and resettler) of fiction. Through its comical claims of veracity, it assimilates raillery and sobriety into a single, comprehending series of literary voyages. A serialization of the cartographical imagination, the map records a progression from one place, meaning, theory, and anecdote to another, hooking together stories in historical, not rational order.

Seldom does literary history provide a single all-encompassing instance of a thesis. If there is a consummate example of my argument, it is certainly the bilingual *The Pleasures of Reason*—a work which, happily enough for a writer in search of a climax, dates from the end of the eighteenth century.[69] A condensed galaxy of forms—maxim collections, conduct manuals, women's fictions, educative tracts, century cycles (the work contains 100 "Thoughts"), rhapsodies, miscellanies, and maps, the book proposes a set of helpful hints, in English and French, by way of teaching moralized French to young women. It concludes with an "Allegorical Map of the Tract of Youth to the Land of Knowledge," replete with an allegorical cartouche and a referent-importing index, the latter to be used in explicating the sundry sites visited on the voyage [*Fig. 15*]. The map portrays an imaginary world that may bear some resemblance to the Pacific rim, as newly charted by Captain Cook. A familiarly unfamiliar universe, it emblematizes a life that everyone has lived but that no one has lived in quite this way. The lands along the way—"Success Island," "Sands of Patience," and many others—combine personification with allegory in "participatory" interpretation. Real but representative people really go to these quasi-real-life places. The text preceding the map, a series of maxims, specializes not in coded talk about stick figures, but in full, psychologically complex characters. Like the great humanist conduct books, this compendium collection aims to produce a well-rounded, upper-middle class personality.

Within these aphorisms, multiple, complex, and repetitive allegories abound. Allegorical characters can put on or take off other allegorical guises, as though they themselves were real, complicated persons playing sundry roles. "The *Genii* of Idleness under the form of winged boys, vainly endeavouring to seduce her from her duty," reads the caption to the frontispiece, as though Idleness were a real person and winged boys a mere allegorizing disguise, rather than vice-versa or neither one. Acquiring a life of

Directions to Signify 209

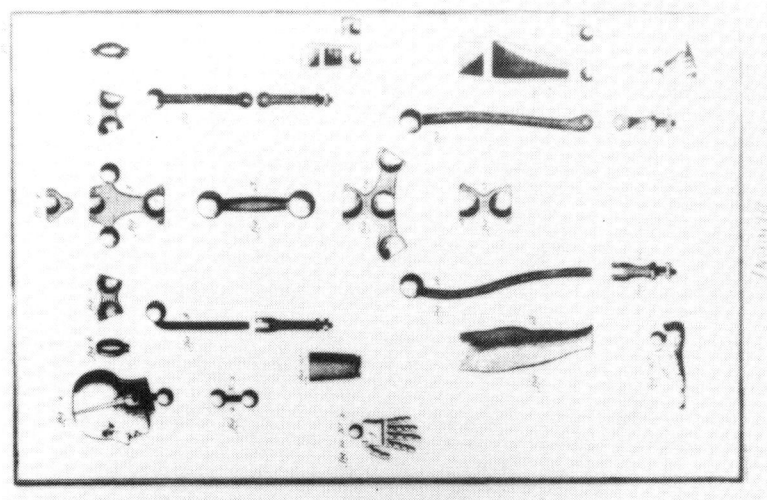
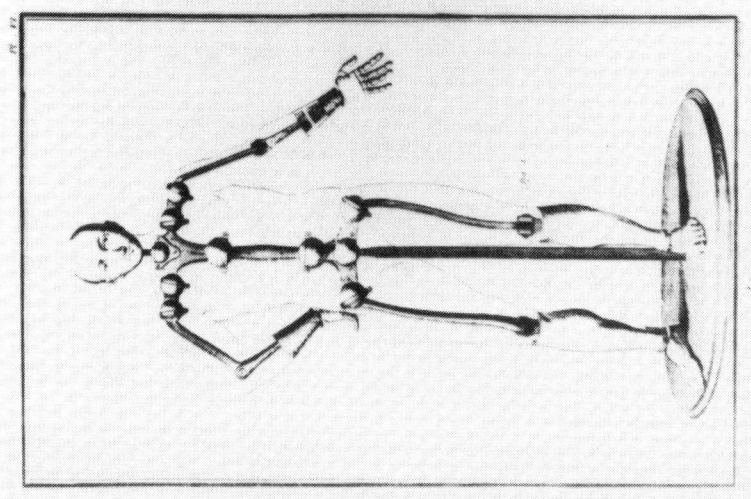

Figure 14: Anonymous, *A General Map of the Discoveries of Admiral De Fonte*. Courtesy Division of Archives and Research Collections, McMaster University Library.

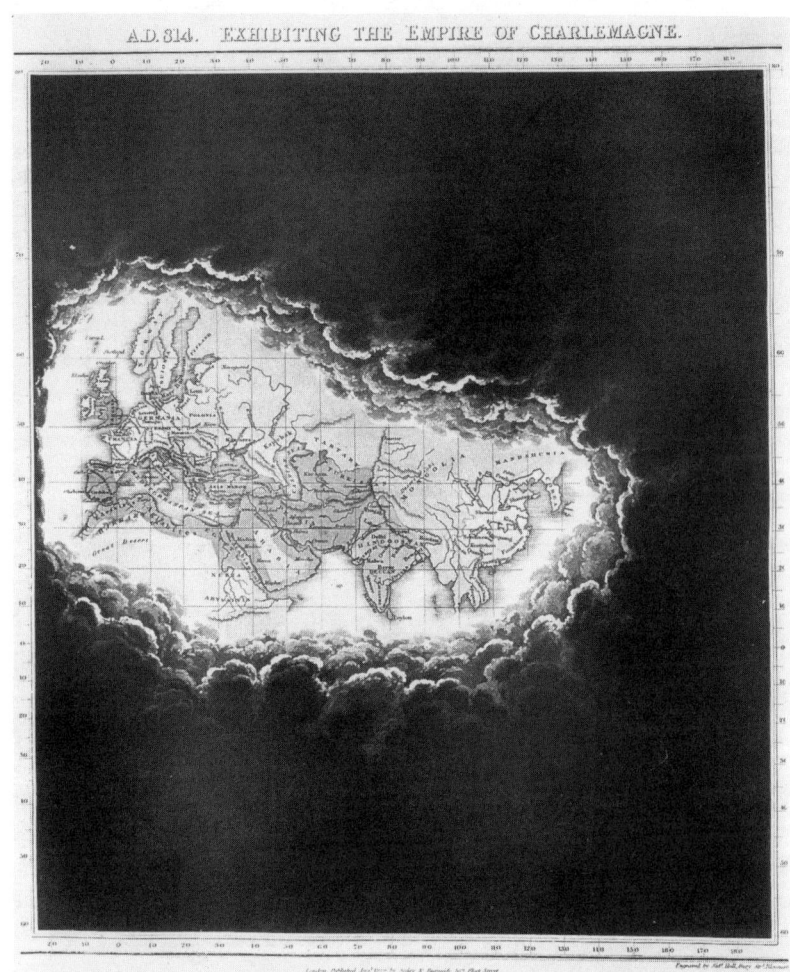

Figure 15: From Robert Gillet, *The Pleasures of Reason*.
Courtesy Division of Archvies and Research Collections, McMaster University.

its own, the referent of the emblem, Idleness, inhabits a naturalized, almost domestic setting. She appears at home with her family. There Idleness acts out the allegorizing process, soliciting an easy, direct explication from the viewer.

As did the "Admiral De Fonte" map, the chart in *The Pleasures of Reason* abounds with open space. The undifferentiated Ocean of Experience appears as a repetitive, entropic invitation to interpretation, a field of time-consuming possibility rather than an instantly encountered veil of obscurity. The repetition and monotony of voyaging, voyaging, and voyaging again gives way to detail and variety. The trip from one land to another wiggles across curves, coasts, and even straightforward open ocean. Allegory comes to life as subject, sign, referent, and field of interpretation are compressed into lively experience. Would-be mariners follow the "Light of the Passions" into a more comprehensive understanding of allegory, an understanding open to the spray of experience as well as to dry exegesis, and an understanding able to make camp in the well-charted "Land of Knowledge" and "Terra Firma of Happiness."

Allegory is a complex subject. No one map, whether navigational, allegorical, fantastical, or critical, can contain it, if only because containment is the task of allegory itself. Far from a mystifying code designed to befuddle the *hoi polloi* or indict the hegemonical habits of imperialist discourse, allegory accommodates truth. Whether easing communication among initiates of a cult or feeding mental manna to ignorami craving instruction, allegory renders knowledge convenient, compressed, and compact. Semioticians, authors, and engravers from across the ideological spectrum made a consistent effort to import the most elusive meanings, whether the mystery of the trinity or the whereabouts of the elusive Northwest Passage, into a manageable picture frame. As technology permitted, maps marked out more and more of meaning's mansions, providing travellers with guides to physical shelter and critics with seamarks for navigating between meanings, words, and works. Allegory in the Enlightenment became an emblem of itself, an eternal process of repetition and expansion contained in the open, lively space between the querying viewer and the cooperating—if confined—page.

NOTES

1. The rainbow is only apparent, not objective. Nevertheless, the height at which it is refracted, relative to the viewer, may be determined. Nimbostratus clouds, the principle producers of rain, rise from a base of 7,000'. The rainbow is apprehended at an angle incident to the viewer of 42°. The maximum apparent height of the rainbow, therefore, is approximately 3,400' above the viewer. Its apparent diameter at its base is about 6,800 feet. For this information I am indebted to the state climatologist of Louisiana, Dr. Paul Müller, of Louisiana State University.

2. This process of contraction is played out in Steven Knapp's excellent bibliography of studies on personification. The later the critical essay, the less the attention to or respect for this trope. See *Personification and the Sublime: Milton to Coleridge* (Cambridge: Harvard University Press, 1985), 160. The most balanced approach to the problem of personification remains that of Chester Chapin, in his *Personification in Eighteenth-Century English Poetry* (New York: King's Crown Press of Columbia University, 1955), especially 16–17, 76.

3. Jon Whitman, *Allegory: The Dynamics of an Ancient and Medieval Technique* (Cambridge: Harvard University Press, 1987), 2, 263.

4. C. S. Lewis, *The Allegory of Love* (Oxford: Oxford University Press, 1936), 45–47.

5. Maureen Quilligan, *The Language of Allegory: Defining the Genre* (Ithaca: Cornell University Press, 1979), 20–21.

6. A case in point is that of Steven Knapp's abortive attempt to link allegory with sublimity. Crucial passages in Burke's *Philosophical Inquiry into the Origin of our Ideas of the Sublime and Beautiful*, Knapp warns, introduce words like "consider." Such words purportedly show that "the sublime itself depends on an act of reference" involving "the interference of intellect in a process whose unreflective immediacy Burke above all wants to establish" (72–73). Knapp has assumed a post-Kantian understanding of "intellect" as a single faculty at a distance from its object. He neglects the possibility that, for the rhetorically flamboyant Burke, words like "consider" may denote a complex, integrated process involving several faculties, faculties that are conditioned by a physiological response to the sublime environment and are thus not truly at odds with experience.

7. Angus Fletcher, *Allegory: The Theory of a Symbolic Mode* (Ithaca: Cornell University Press, 1990), 35.

8. Carolyn Van Dyke, *The Fiction of Truth: Structures of meaning in Narrative and Dramatic Allegory* (Ithaca: Cornell University Press, 1985), 165; Clifford Gay, *The Transformations of Allegory* (London: Routledge and Kegan Paul, 1974), 53.

9. Quilligan, 130; Whitman, 7.

10. Peter M. Daly, *Emblem Theory: Recent German Contributions to the Characterization of the Emblem Genre* (Liechtenstein: KTO Press, 1979), 11.

11. For a theoretical attack on the notion that emblems advance enigmas or other inscrutabilities, see Daly, 21.

12. Rosemary Freeman, *English Emblem Books* (London: Chatto and Windus, 1948),

13. Daly, *Emblem Theory*, 21.

14. See Kevin L. Cope, "Instant Processing of the Modern State," in press, and *Criteria of Certainty* (Lexington: University Press of Kentucky, 1990), ch. 2.

15. Whitman, 2; see also Stephen A. Barney, *Allegories of History, Allegories of Love* (Hamden: Archon, 1979), 23.

16. See Peter M. Daly, "The Cultural Context of English Emblem Books," in Peter M. Daly, ed., *The English Emblem and the Continental Tradition* (New York: AMS Press, 1988), 51—60. Daly attacks Rosemary Freeman and Mario Praz for restricting emblem lore to emblem books. He argues persuasively that emblems and emblematic materials appear in many media, from tapestries to conduct and maxim books.

17. For an exposition and a discussion of the background of the Renaissance definition of allegory as an extended metaphor, see Rosemond Tuve, *Elizabethan and Metaphysical Imagery* (Chicago: University of Chicago Press, 1947), and *Allegorical Imagery* (Princeton: Princeton University Press, 1966).

18. Anonymous, *Rules and Maxims, For the Conduct of Human Life* (London: 1745), 8, 12.

19. For information on the Hermetic cult of the alphabet I am indebted to Nicholas Hudson of the University of British Columbia.

20. Charles Bradbury, Minister of the Gospel, *A Cabinet of Jewels Opened to the Curious, By A Key of Real Knowledge. Containing, a Great Number of Sayings and Sentences, Collected from Heathen Authors and others, Applied and Adapted to the Various States of Mankind* (Berwick: 1785), 17–20.

21. Anonymous, *Choice Emblems, Natural, Historical, Fabulous, Moral, and Divine; For the Improvement and Pastime of Youth: Displaying the Beauties and Morals of the Ancient Fabulists; The Whole Calculated to Convey the Golden Lessons of Instruction Under a New and More Delightful Dress. For the Use of Schools* (London: 1784 [5th edition]), xiv.

22. See, for examples, *Choice Emblems*, 13, and Jane Gomeldon, *Maxims Composed by J. Gomeldon* (Newcastle: 1779).

23. Benjamin Cole, *Select Tales and Fables, with Prudential Maxims, and other Little Lessons of Morality, in Prose and Verse, Equally Instructive and Entertaining. For the Use of Both Sexes. Wherein their Foibles, as well as Beauties, are Presented to their View in the Fairest and most Inoffensive Point of Light. The Whole embellished with Sixty Original Designs, Expressive of each Subject, Neatly Engraved on Copper Plates* (Dublin: 1756).

24. Like so man ambitious collectors and engravers of his time, Cole is careful to direct his production to "BOTH SEXES" (see title page).

25. John Evelyn, *Numismata: A Discourse of Medals, Antient and Modern. Together with some Accounts of Heads and Effigies of Illustrious, and Famous Persons, Sculps, and Taille-Douce, Of Whom we have no Medals Extant; And of the Use to be Derived from them. To which is Added a Digression Concerning Physiognomy* (London: 1697), 295.

26. Jean-Baptiste Perrin, *Fables Amusantes: Avec Une Table Générale & Particulière Des Mots, Et de leur Signification en Anglais. Selon l'Ordre des Fables, Pour en Rendre la Traduction Plus Facile à l'Ecolier* (London: 1771), vi.

27. On the close relations between anecdotes, allegories, and personifications, see Freeman, *Emblem Books*, 22.

28. Bradbury, *Cabinet of Jewels*, 55.

29. Evelyn, *Numismata*, 292–4.

30. John Done, *Polydoron: or A Miscellanea of Morall, Philosophicall, and Theologicall Sentences* (London: 1631), 1–2.

31. Andrew Wilson, *The Creation the Ground-Work of Revelation, And Revelation the Langauge of Nature. Or, a Brief Attempt to Demonstrate, that the Hebrew Language is Founded upon Natural Ideas, And, that the Hebrew Writings Transfer them to Spiritual Objects* (Edinburgh: 1750), 31.

32. Jean Theophile Desaguliers, J. T., LL. D. FRS. *The Newtonian System of the World, The Best Model of Government: an Allegorical Poem. With a Plain and Intelligible Account of the System of the World, by Way of Annotations: with Copper Plates: to which is Added, Cambria's Complaint Against the Intercalary Day in the Leap-Year.* (Westminster: 1728), 30–34 and *passim*. For the identification of Desaguliers I am indebted to Linda Troost, Margaret Hunt, and Jan Snoek, who provided me with information concerning Desaguliers via the C18–L electronic discussion network.

33. Rosemary Freeman, ed., *A Collection of Emblemes Ancient and Modern*, by George Wither (Columbus: University of South Carolina Press, 1975), vii, xvii–xviii.

34. R. B. [Nathaniel Crouch, after George Wither], *Delights for the Ingenious, in above Fifty Select and Choice Emblems, Divine and Moral, Ancient and Modern. Curiously Ingraven upon Copper Plates. With Fifty Delightful Poems and Lots for the more Lively Illustration of each Emblem, whereby Instruction and Good Counsell may be Promoted and Furthered by an Honest and Pleasant Recreation. To which is Prefixed an Incomparable Poem, Intituled Majesty in Misery or an Imploration to the King of Kings* (London: 1684).

35. See A. D. Nuttall, *Two Concepts of Allegory* (London: Routledge and Kegan Paul, 1967), 48.

36. Susannah Watts, *Chinese Maxims. Translated from the Oeconomy of Human Life. Into Heroic Verse. In Seven Parts* (Leicester: 1784), 18.

37. M[ary] P[elham], [pseud. for Dorothy Kilmer], *The Rational Brutes; Or, Talking Animals* (London: 1799).

38. Richard Brathwait, *A Ladies Love-Lecture: Composed, and from the Choicest Flowers of Divinitie and Humanitie Culled, and Compiled: as it hath beene by sundry Personages of Eminent Qualitie, Upon Sight of some Copies Dispersed, Modestly Importuned; for Whose Sweet Sakes he Originally Addressed this Labour* (London: 1641), pp 430–31.

39. [Fulke Greville], *Maxims, Characters, And Reflections, Critical, Satyrical, and Moral* (London: 1756), 66–67.

40. John Aubrey, *Miscellanies, Viz. I. Day-Fatality. II. Local-Fatality. III. Ostenta. IV. Omens. V. Dreams. VI. Apparitions. VII. Voices. VIII. Impulses. IX. Knockings. X. Blows Invisible. XI. Prophesies. XII. Marvels. XIII. Magick. XIV. Transportation in the Air. XV. Visions in a Beril, or Glas. XVI. Converse with Angels and Spirits. XVII. Corps Candles in Wales. XVIII. Oracles. XIX. Extasie. XX. Glances of {Love {Envy. XXI. Second-Sighted Persons* (London: 1696), 37.

41. On the popularity of map collecting, see Sarah Tyacke, "Samuel Pepys as Map Collector," *passim*, in Robin Myers and Michael Harris, *Maps and Prints: Aspects of the English Booktrade* (Oxford: Oxford Polytechnic Press, 1984), 1–29; Helen M. Wallis, "Geographie is Better than Divinitie: Maps, Globes, and Geography in the Days of Samuel Pepys," 36–37, in Norman J. W. Thrower, ed., *The Compleat Plattmaker: Essays on Chart, Map, and Globe Making in England in the Seventeenth and Eighteenth Centuries* (Berkeley and Los Angeles: University of California Press, 1978), 1–43; Sir Herbert George Fordham, *Some Notable Surveyors and Map-Makers of the Sixteenth, Seventeenth, and Eighteenth Centuries and their Work* (Cambridge: Cambridge University Press, 1929), *passim* and 75, who notes that John Cary alone produced over 1,000 maps, books, and other publications; Margarita Bowen, *Empiricism and Geographical Thought from Francis Bacon to Alexander von Humboldt* (Cambridge: Cambridge University Press, 1981), 110, 116, 148, who records John Locke's keen interest in geography and describes, in a fine portrait of John Ray, the myth of the "natural desire in man to study strange creatures"; and J. B. Harley and David Woodward, *The History of Cartography*, vol. I (Chicago: University of Chicago, 1987), 506, who make a case for the widest possible interpretation—"cultural, economic, intellectual, political, ideological, technological, ethical, and aesthetic"—of the cartographic phenomenon.

42. "So Geographers in *Afric*-maps
With Savage-Pictures fill their Gaps,
And o'er unhabitable Down
Place Elephants for want of towns"

(Jonathan Swift, *On Poetry, A Rhapsody* (1733), cited in Wallis, 37).

43. John Heydon, Gent., Philonouos, a Servant of God, and Secretary of Nature, *The Harmony of the World, being a Discourse of God, Heaven, Angels, Stars, Planets, Earth; the Miraculous Descentions and Ascentions of Spirits, with the Nature and Harmony of Mans Body; the Art of Preparing Rosie Crucian Medicines to Cure all Diseases. Their Rules to Raise Bodies Decayed, which are Verified by a Practical Examination of Principles in the Great World* (London: 1662), "Preface."

44. See David A. Woodward, "English Cartography, 1650–1750: A Summary," 189–190 and *passim* in Thrower, *Compleat Plattmaker*, 159–193. Of particular interest are Hermann Möll's illustrations for Salmon's *New Geographical and Historical Grammar* (1749), Kitchin's lengthy series of maps for the *London Magazine* (1748–1760), and Thomas Jefferys's contributions to *Gentlemen's Magazine*, beginning in 1736.

45. *The London Magazine*, 1753, 96 and facing page.

46. Mr. Salmon and Hermann Möll, *Modern History: Or, the Present State of all Nations. Describing their Respective Situations, Persons, Habits, and Buildings; Manners, Laws and Customs, Religion, and Policy; Arts and Sciences, Trades, Manufactures and Husbandry; Plants, Animals, and Minerals. By Mr Salmon. Illustrated with Cuts and Maps, Accurately Drawn According to the Geographical Part of this Work, By Hermann Moll* (London: 1744 [3rd ed.]), facing 400.

47. See Norman J. W. Thrower, *Maps and Man: An Examination of Cartography in Relation to Culture and Civilization* (Englewood Cliffs: Prentice Hall, 1972), 70.

48. Shown in Arthur Robinson, *Early Thematic Mapping in the History of Cartography* (Chicago: University of Chicago Press, 1982), 54.

49. William Gostling, M. A. *A Walk in and about the City of Canterbury, with many Observations not to be Found in any Descriptions hitherto Published* (Canterbury: 1784).

50. Michael Harris, "London Guidebooks before 1800," 43, in Myers and Harris, *Maps and Prints*, 31–66.

51. Harley and Woodward, 507, argue convincingly that maps of the cosmos had assorted practical applications—or intentions—ranging from navigation to confirmation of the legitimacy of political systems. As Swift's writings show, however, the utility of specialized branches of the discipline was lost on the layman.

52. Illustrated and explained in Arthur Robinson, *Early Thematic Mapping*, 50.

53. *London Magazine, 1752*, 564–6; Anonymous [with parts by Samuel Johnson and published by Robert Dodsley], *The Preceptor: Containing a General Course of Education. Wherein the First Principles of Polite Learning are Laid down in a Way most Suitable for Trying the Genius, and Advancing the Instruction of Youth. In Twelve Parts. Viz. I. On Reading, Speaking, and Writing Letters. II. On Geometry. III. On Geography and Astronomy. IV. On Chronology and History. V. On Rhetoric and Poetry. VI. On Drawing. VII. On Logic. VIII. On Natural History. IX. On Ethics, or Morality. X. On Trade and Commerce. XI. On Laws and Government. XII. On Human Life and Manners. Illustrated with Maps and Useful Cuts* (London: 1748), vol. 1, 227.

54. Reverend John Mason, M. A., *Select Remains of the Reverend John Mason, M. A., Late Rector of Water-Stratford, in Buckinghamshire, Author of the Songs of Praise to Almighty God; Containing a Variety of Devout and Useful Sayings, on Divers Subjects, Digested under Proper Heads; Religious Observations; Serious Advice to Youth; Occasional Reflections, & c. and Christian Letters* (London: 1812 [new edition]), 11.

Directions to Signify

55. George Henry Millar, Esq; Assisted by several Gentlemen. *The New and Universal System of Geography: Being a Complete Modern History and Description of the Whole World*...[Millar's complete title is over 1,000 words long]. (London: 1750).

56. Frederic Watson, M. A., Vicar of Sutton, and several other gentlemen. *A New and Complete Geographical Dictionary. Containing a Full and Accurate Description of the several Parts of the Known World, as Divided into Continents, Islands, Oceans, Seas, Rivers, Lakes, & c. The Situation, Extent, and Boundaries, of all the Empires, Kingdoms, Provinces, States, & c. in Europe, Asia, Africa, and America. Their Climates, Zones, Constitutions, Revenues, Forces, Produce, Languages, Manufactures, Trade, Commerce, Cities, Chief Towns, Universities, Curious Pictures, Antiquities, Mines, Vegetables, Minerals, Mountains, Desarts, Forts, Castles, Harbours, Natural and Artificial Curiosities. Together with the Religion, Learning, Policy, Manners, Customs, Stature, Shape, Colour, And Length of Lives of the Inhabitants; their Virtues and Vices; their Ceremonies at Births, Marriages, and Funerals; their Political and Church Government, & c.* (London: 1773).

57. Edward Pellham, *God's Power and Providence, Shewed in the Miraculous Preservation and Deliverance Of Eight English-Men, Left by Mischance in Greenland, Anno 1630. Nine Months and Twelve Days. With a True Relation of all their Miseries, the Shifts and Hardships they were Put to, their Food, & c. Such as neither Heathen nor Christian ever before Endured. With a Description of the Chief Places and Rarities of that Barren and Cold Country. Faithfully Reported by Edward Pellham, One of the Eight Men aforesaid. As also with a Map of Greenland*, 780, in Anonymous ["printed by assignment from Messrs. Churchill"], *A Collection Of Voyages and Travels, Some now first Printed from Original Manuscripts, others now first Publish'd in English*, vol. IV (London: 1732).

58. F. W. Delkeskamp, *Neueus Panorama des Rheins von Mainz bis Cöln* (Frankfurt: 1837).

59. See G. P. Crone, *Maps and their Makers: An Introduction to the History of Cartography*, vol. 1 (Chicago: University of Chicago Press, 1987), p. 100.

60. Illustrated in Tony Campbell, *Early Maps* (New York: Abbeville Press, 1981), 94. For an extended study of animals, illustrations, and maps, see Wilma George, *Animals and Maps* (Berkeley and Los Angeles: University of California Press, 1969).

61. Shown in John Ford, "Ackermann Imprints and Publications," 114, in Myers and Harris, *Maps and Prints*, 109–124.

62. [Henry Nieuhoff], *Mr. John Nieuhoff's Remarkable Voyages and Travels to Brasil*, in [Awnsham and John Churchill, compilers], *A Collection of Voyages and Travels, some now first Printed from Original Manuscripts, others now first Published in English. In Six Volumes. With a General Preface, Giving an Account of the Progress of Navigation, from its first Beginning. Illustrated with a great Number of Useful Maps and Cuts, Curiously Engraven*, vol. II (London: 1732).

63. On the narrative potential of the cartouche, see John Booth, *Looking at Old Maps* (Westbury, Wiltshire: Cambridge House Books, 1979), 94, and R. V. Tooley, *Maps and Map-Makers* (1949; rpt. New York: Bonanza, 1971), 5, 71, 96–98. Tooley has some interesting comments on the technological changes in the engraving and printing industry

that made possible the elaboration of the cartouche. Cartouche illustrations before the Restoration were generally panegyrical and attributive, either to author or patron, or genealogical, showing the ancestry of the patron of the realm charted. Seldom were they primarily informational or allegorical. For a fine example of the transition between the two modes, see the map shown in Sarah Tyacke, "Samuel Pepys as Map Collector," 10–11, which offers two huge illuminations overlaid on one map: one showing a genealogy, the other a scene from the British shipping industry. For a specialized survey of maps in periodicals, see David Jolly, *Maps of America in Periodicals before 1800* (Brookline: David Jolly, 1989).

64. J. Cheevers, *Mappa Britanniae Septentrionalis Faciei Romanae Secundum Fidem Monumentorum Per Viteram Depicta Ex Ricardo Corinense, Monarcho Westmonasterii Emendata* [c. 1790].

65. Anonymous, *A Compendious Geographical Dictionary, Containing, a Concise Description of the most Remarkable Places, Ancient and Modern, in Europe, Asia, Africa, & America, Interspersed with Historical Anecdotes. To which are Added, a Chronological Table from the Creation to the Present Time; a Monthly List of all the Fixed Fairs in England and Wales; and, a Table of the Coins of the Various Nations, and their Values in English Money. To the Whole is Prefixed, an Introduction, Exhibiting a View of the Newtonian System of the Planets, & c. Embellished with Maps* (London: 1795 [2nd ed.]), *passim*.

66. On the comparatively recent development of the fantasy cartographic genre, see Thrower, *Maps and Man*, 15–16.

67. An account of the Admiral De Fonte story can be found in R. A. Skelton, *Explorers' Maps: Chapters in the Cartographic Record of Geographical Discovery* (New York: Praeger, 1958), 130. For the material on De Fuentes and *"fundus,"* I am indebted to Karl van Ausdal and Kevin Berland, who communicated their information to me via the C18–L electronic discussion list.

68. Anonymous (McMaster University Archives Accession # 102945), *A General Map of the Discoveries of Admiral De Fonte & Others. By M. De l' Isle*. c. 1754.

69. Robert Gillet, *The Pleasures of Reason: Or, The Hundred Thoughts of a Sensible Young Lady. In English and French* (London: 1796). I am indebted to Margaret Foley of the Division of Archives and Research Collections of the Mills Memorial Library of McMaster University for generously bringing this work to my attention.

Part II

PRESENCES

Acts, Events

THE LANGUAGE OF REVOLUTION
Allegory in Volney's *Les Ruines*

Nanette Le Coat

One of the more provocative efforts of late to describe the modalities of that elusive literary form, the allegory, is Maureen Quilligan's.[1] Identifying "sensitivity to the polysemy in words" (33) as allegory's fundamental component, Quilligan argues that the genre lost favor during the eighteenth century because neoclassical decorum "decreed a ban on wordplay" (157), and language ceased to be viewed as a "numinous object in its own right" (281). Though she relies on a French theorist—Michel Foucault—to buttress the historical claims of her argument, her examples are drawn primarily from English literature. One way of evaluating her generalizations, therefore, would be to investigate the fate of allegory in a different national context.

In what follows I consider an example drawn from French literature: C. F. Volney's allegory, *Les Ruines, ou Méditation sur les Révolutions des Empires* (1791).[2] This text, drawn from the Revolutionary period when allegory enjoyed immense prestige, provides an interesting test of Quilligan's thesis. If she is right, it should not have been written. Volney and his fellow 'Idéologues' (Destutt de Tracy, Cabanis, DeGérando and others) possessed an attitude toward language that was anything but "suprarealist." They dreamed of an analytical, well-ordered language that would permit the precise classification of all things. Their ideal language, far from being imbued with the "magic phenomenality" that Quilligan claims is the necessary condition for allegory, would be algebraic in its rigor.

Les Ruines thus elicits the question: How could an allegorical work have been produced by one whose attitude toward language was seemingly so incompatible with the genre? To answer this question it is necessary to have some sense of how allegory was generally understood in late eighteenth-century France, how it was deployed, and what appeal it held for revolutionaries. Allegory, I shall argue, was especially valued as a propagandistic device; as a preceptive tool, however, it was not always as efficacious as hoped. I shall discuss the use of allegory in the revolutionary festival and point to some of allegory's inherent limitations that are revealed in that context—limitations with which Volney was forced to come to terms in his narrative, *Les Ruines*.

II

While twentieth-century critics may question the existence of a true allegorical genre in eighteenth-century literature, there can be no doubt that aesthetic theorists of the period considered allegory a powerful literary and artistic device. The terms in which allegory was discussed attest to the ubiquity of a linguistic model for all the arts of representation. It was customary to speak of "the language of the passions," "the language of architecture," etc. The German theorist, Winckelmann, whose celebrated treatise on the subject had an enormous influence in France, declared that, "La nature elle-même enseigna l'allégorie, et ce langage paroît lui être beaucoup plus propre que les signes arbitraires des pensées inventées postérieurement par les hommes" (25).[3] [Nature itself teaches allegory, and this language appears much more apt than the arbitrary signs of thoughts invented subsequently by men.] But Winckelmann's definition of allegory was vague, and he seems to make little distinction between the ways literary and visual allegories convey meaning. "La signification propre du mot allégorie veut dire quelque chose qui diffère de ce que l'on veut indiquer" (21). [Allegory proper...means something differing from what one is indicating.] Though his treatise is addressed to writers and artists alike, it is clear that he conceives of allegory primarily in visual terms. Allegory is "l'expression des idées par le moyen des images" (21) [the expression of ideas by means of images]. This definitional vagueness was not unique to Winckelmann: it derived in part from the doctrine of *ut pictura* poesis, which held that the visual and narrative arts could be equally effective in telling a story or relating a coherent message. Allegory was an integral part of that doctrine.

Not all theorists, however, were so vague. One of Winckelmann's commentators faults him for not discriminating more finely between figural and narrative allegory.[4] Winckelmann's treatise, he points out, is really a study of emblematics. The critic invokes the conventional definition of poetic allegory—the transition from the literal to the figurative, or extended metaphor—citing as exemplary the Horatian ode in which civil war is depicted as a ship of state awash on a stormy sea. He mentions Jean de Meung's *Le Roman de la Rose*, Voltaire's *Henriade*, and Boileau's *Le Lutrin* as more or less successful exemplifications of the genre in the French tradition. The article "Allégorie" in the *Encyclopédie* likewise focusses on literary allegory, and curiously cites the same definition and example from Horace.[5]

Quatremère de Quincy, who along with David was one of the pageant masters of the Revolutionary festivals (and thus a kind of cultural czar), declared, rather grandiosely, that allegory was the very language of Revolution. He understood allegory as "[une] imitation jusqu'à un certain point inimitative" [an imitation that is to a certain extent nonimitative].[6] Like the grammarian De Beauzée, whose ideas he applied to architecture, Quatremère believed that allegory was useful as a didactic tool because it permitted "the presentation of a thought under the image of another thought in such a way as to render it more perceptible and striking than if it had been presented directly without any kind of veil."[7] These two features of allegory—its didactic potential and its veiled quality or indirection—were frequently to prove incompatible, revealing a problem that constantly dogged allegory: the problem of intelligibility. The presentation of abstract notions in fancy dress did not always facilitate greater understanding. Veiled thoughts could be variously interpreted since the referent was not always clear. The latitude for interpretation that allegory permitted clearly undermined its didactic efficacy. The question thus remains: Why did theoreticians like Quatremère de Quincy value allegory as a pedagogic and propagandistic tool? Why was indirection deemed necessary? Could a representational device that was essentially learned function as a vehicle of popular expression? How well did old forms and images serve a new social order? How appropriate, in short, was allegory as the language of Revolution?

Nowhere was more liberal use of allegory made than in the countless festivals celebrating the Revolution's milestones and commemorating its heroes and martyrs: the Bastille Day Festival, the Festival in honor of national guardsmen who died in service to their country, the Festival of Republican Reunion, the Pantheonization of Marat, and the Festival of Gratitude and of Victories. Fairly typical of such events was the festival organized in June, 1792 to honor Simonneau, a provincial mayor killed two years earlier by rioting mobs. For upholding a government directive on the rationing of food, this hapless official was championed as a defender of Law. A contemporary journal, *Révolutions de Paris*, described the fête's ceremonies:

> Sur une chaise curule dorée, surmontée d'une petite sainte Minerve, s'offrait à tous les regards le livre figuré de la loi, tout ouvert. Un groupe de femmes suivait, présidé par la dame de Gouges...La statue colossale de la loi fermait la marche; elle était représentée par une femme assise et appuyée sur les tables des droits de l'homme, qu'elle semblait vouloir recouvrir sous son manteau. On lui donna pour attribut un sceptre...On nous ménera loin avec l' inscription placée sur le socle de cette figure: les hommes vraiment libres sont esclaves de la loi.[8]

> [On a gilt curule chair, surmounted by a small silver statue of Saint Minerva, was offered to all eyes a representation of the book of the law, open...A group of women followed, presided over by the Dame de Gouges...The colossal statue of the law brought up the rear; it was represented by a seated woman, leaning on the tablets of the rights of man, which she seemed to be trying to cover under her cloak. She was given a scepter as attribute...Much might be said of the inscription placed under the pedestal of this figure: "Truly free men are the slaves of the law."]

The Festival of the Constitution, celebrated August 10, 1793 on the Place de la Bastille, featured a monumental Egyptianate statue of Nature from whose gushing breasts water flowed. This statue of Regeneration bore the inscription: "We are all her children" and the various commissioners of the primary assemblies went forth to fill their goblets at this source. One of the most famous festivals of all—the Festival of Reason—was celebrated in Paris by a "performance" in Notre-Dame, now dubbed the Temple of Reason. Musicians of the National Guard joined with those of the Opera to play patriotic anthems. Celebrations of the festival in other cities featured variants on the same theme: a huge cardboard throne decorated with the various attributes of the Ancien Régime would be set afire, and as the symbol of the monarchy went up in flames, the altar of the fatherland, on which was placed the statue of Liberty, would emerge triumphant.

As these examples evidence, the allegory that was incorporated into the festival was primarily visual and the allegorical figures predominantly female. Feminine allegories of the Republic, or abstract civic values such as Liberty, Equality, Nature, Reason, and Victory, were not limited to festivals; they also appeared on engravings and medallions. According to Lynn Hunt, the emergence of these figures signalled a major change in political attitude. Prior to 1792, prints frequently depicted scenes of the French people claiming their liberty en masse. After the Republic was established in September, 1792, allegorical representations began to replace crowd scenes. "The collective violence of seizing liberty and overthrowing the monarchy were effaced behind the tranquil visage and statuesque pose of an aloof goddess."[9]

Maurice Agulhon has suggested in his study of "feminine civic allegory" some of the many probable reasons governing the choice of female figures.[10] The sexual imagery of a goddess was diametrically opposed to the representation of power in the Ancien Régime. Whereas the King was a living, flesh and blood person who might wield power in an arbitrary manner, a goddess was a beneficent figure who exercised power only in the imagination. She had the maternal connotation of a nurturing, life-giving force. Her serene countenance was a reassuring presence which seemed to rise above the violence and brutality of everyday political struggles. Lynn Hunt sees still other symbolic advantages motivating this predilection for female allegories. The Marianne figure, for example, is linked to the tradition of the Virgin Mary. And the goddess of Liberty evoked on the Republic's seal was like a Counter-Reformation saint "she represented the virtues so desired by the new order: the transcendence of localism, superstition, and particularity in the name of a more disciplined and universalistic worship. Liberty was an abstract quality based on reason. She belonged to no group, to no particular place."[11] It was her very remoteness from real life that constituted her appeal.

More than one critic has noted the contradictions inherent in this use of female figures. Joan Landes observes: "Liberty herself is a profoundly ironic symbol, a public representation of a polity that sanctioned a limited domestic role for women"[12] Marina Warner has also emphasized this split between sign and signified, noting that "Justice is not spoken of as a woman because women were thought to be just, any more than they were considered capable of dispensing justice...Often the recognition of a difference between the symbolic order, inhabited by ideal, allegorical figures, and the actual order of judges, statesmen, soldiers, philosophers, inventors, depends on the unlikelihood of women practising the concepts they represent."[13] Not only did these female allegories bear little relation to real life, they were so stylized as to be virtually indistinguishable, and it was not always obvious which civic value was being allegorized. The journalist who described the Festival in honor of the murdered mayor Simonneau observed that while the statue of the Law was given a scepter, more appropriately a brake, the conventional attribute of law among the ancients, might have been given; there was the danger that with the scepter the people might confuse the Law with the Monarch.

The ambiguity of the goddess' significance was intensified b y artifice that was frequently used to underscore her power—her appearance and disappearance. Concealed in a throne she would emerge as flames devoured the symbol of monarchy. Or, swathed in veils in the beginning of the ceremony, she would gradually be unveiled by its end. The connotations of these rituals seem obvious enough: purification, controlled destruction, the darkness of the Ancien Régime banished by an enlightened Republic. But this ritual could be subject to misinterpretation, as a debate in the people's club of Saint-Omer attests. Some citizens argued that the veil that had covered Reason, and was removed during the ceremony, must ultimately be replaced to signal the end of the ceremony. Other citizens argued that once Reason had emerged she should never again disappear, for if the appearance of the goddess in the course of the ceremony signalled the triumph of Reason over the darkness of the Ancien Régime, her subsequent disappearance might be read as the eclipse of Reason and a return to the old order.

Ambiguity was not, of course, the exclusive property of feminine allegories. The vagueness of other types of allegorical representation sometimes suggested ludicrous interpretive possibilities, as the ironic comments of a contemporary journalist reveal:

> Le plus curieux de toute la procession était une espèce de requin porté en haut d'une pique qui le transperce; l'animal marin ouvre la gueule et montre les dents; sur son corps est écrit, respect à la Loi. On dit que la pique est la loi; le peuple est le requin. Nous croyons au contraire que la pique est le peuple, le requin sera tout ce qu'on voudra, ou le despotisme, ou l'aristocratie, ou le fanatisme religieux. Le département auroit bien dû dans son programme prévenir les incertitudes du spectateur à cet égard. Ce trait de finesse nous échappe. Le roi des Chinois, il est vrai, a pour armes un poisson; mais nous ne sommes pas à Pekin. M. Quatremer nous doit deux mots d'explication; c'est lui qui était le maître de cérémonie. Des gardes nationales en grand nombre semblaient escorter le monstre marin, qui n'effraya personne, et qui fit rire tout le monde.[14]

> [The most curious item in the procession as a whole was a kind of shark raised aloft on the end of a pikestaff; the sea animal had its mouth open and was showing its teeth; on its body was written, "Respect for the law." It is said that the pikestaff represented the law and the shark the people. It is our opinion, on the contrary, that the pikestaff is the people and the shark what you will—despotism, aristocracy, or religious fanaticism. The departement should have taken care in its program to forestall the spectator's uncertainty in this respect. We missed any such indication. The king of the Chinese, it is true, has a fish as his arms; but we are not in Peking. M. Quatremer owes us a few words of explanation, for he was the master of ceremonies. Large numbers of national guardsmen seemed to support the marine monster, who frightened nobody, but made everybody laugh.]

A device had to be found, therefore, to circumvent allegory's ambiguity; such a device was the inscription. As Mona Ozouf has remarked, the slogan of Revolutionary aesthetics might have been: "rien ne va sans dire" (253) [nothing goes without saying]. Even if inscriptions proved as inadequate as they did in the case of the unfortunate shark, rare was the bust, image or statue that did not have its verbal supplement. An extreme case is the project for a gigantic statue that the artist David proposed to the Convention.[15] The statue was to be built on the remains of statues from Notre-Dame. It was to represent the people. On its forehead would be inscribed the words "Light," on it chest the words "Nature," on its arms "Strength," and on its hands the words "Work." These inscriptions were analogous to the endless speeches and recitations around which the festivals were organized. Judith Schlanger, who has written brilliantly about the relationship between Revolutionary theater and the festival, refers to the verbosity of the Revolutionary festival as "un didactisme du plein" [fulsome didacticism].[16] Through constant repetition correct ideas would be engraved in the spectator's mind. Inscriptions would modulate and orient the spectator's response. This rhetorical overkill, a redundancy of word and image, was intended as a kind of outpouring of Revolutionary enthusiasm that would edify and bring about group cohesion and consensus.

Yet this verbal overdetermination revealed a certain insecurity. The perceived need for verbal explanation betrayed a distrust of the image and, by extension, a lack of confidence in the educative power of visual allegory, as if mere images were potentially so ambiguous they must be reinforced by commentary. An alternative interpretation of the festival's reliance on the word is suggested by the German critic Hans Ulrich Gumbrecht in his study of epideictic discourse.[17] Oratory, and particularly epideictic oratory, was an integral part of the ceremonial of the festival. Taking issue with what he terms Schlanger and Ozouf's functionalist hypothesis, Gumbrecht argues that the doubling of verbal with extra-verbal forms was necessary, not redundant, and can be explained by the nature of social relationships. The speeches praising Marat and denouncing his enemies were read first at the festivals and then at the Convention. Prelude to the Terror, they testified to the growing gap between the sans-culottes and the bourgeois delegates to the Convention. Sans-culottes orators praised Marat, condemned the enemies of the Republic responsible for his death, exhorted the members of the Convention to establish a holiday in his honor, urged the punishment of Marat's assassins, and hinted darkly at reprisals if these actions were not carried out. They also called for ceremonies to institute the cult of Marat and outlined the specifics of the rituals. The Société populaire de Langres, for instance, was to carry a pyramid ornamented with crepe and an urn supposedly containing the ashes of their dead hero. The pyramid would bear three inscriptions: "Aux mânes de Marat, le véritable ami du peuple," "Citoyennes, vous avez l'honneur de votre sexe et de la République à venger," "Laissez-les faire, ils porteront leur tête sur l'échafaud."[18] [To the shades of Marat, the true friend of the people, Citoyennes, you must avenge the honor of your sex and the Republic, and Let them do as the will, they will carry their heads to the scaffolding.] Group cohesion was thus achieved through shared ritual and through the identification of a common enemy, in this case, the Girondins. The overstatement and categorical affirmations of this epideictic discourse, and the redundancy of image and text that they called for, expressed not so much enthusiasm as a deep-seated fear that the Republic was menaced by internal and external enemies, and a suspicion on the part of the sans-culottes that the bourgeois revolutionaries did not wholeheartedly share their aims.

Ozouf's and Schlanger's remarks about the doubling of the allegorical image and Gumbrecht's explanation for the vehemence of Revolutionary discourse remind us of the primacy of the word even in an age that accorded great prestige to the visual. Since no interpretation could be left to chance, words were made to control the proliferation of meanings. But, if clarity was paramount, why was allegory used at all? Gumbrecht's hypothesis about the divergence of class interests may provide some clues. Sans-culottes, speaking on their own behalf, did so directly. Epideictic discourse allowed for the vigorous expression of feelings: admiration, enthusiasm, disapproval, fear. The bourgeois organizers of the festivals, on the other hand, sought to create a forum for the outpouring of popular feeling, but only if that feeling could be controlled. Official festivals were in fact conceived as alternatives to the more spontaneous but often riotous popular ceremonies such as the planting of maypoles or "liberty trees." Though many of the events commemorated by official festivals were themselves violent affairs—the storming of the Bastille, or the martyrdoms of Simonneau, Marat, Bara, and Viala—organizers sought in the festivals to downplay this violence and to emphasize instead joyful unanimity. The bloodiness and brutality of real life events were draped over with a decorous veil and ennobled with the emblems of classical antiquity. Theatrical representations, however, were for the most part eschewed because it was felt that the artifice associated with spectacle—masks, makeup, machinery—was essentially dishonest. Simulacrums or reenactments risked blurring the line between reality and representation, and degenerating into mimetic violence. What more appropriate way, then, to allude to important events without reviving their destructive energies than an "imitation that is to a certain extent nonimitative," that is, allegory? The graceful, conventionalized forms of allegory distilled abstract meaning from untidy events. They allowed French revolutionaries to idealize and utopianize their political goals while distancing themselves from the violence of the everyday life and death struggle. Allegorical representations, they hoped, would stir imaginations while at the same time assuring that popular energy could be domesticated, contained, and directed. While monumental statues, mountains, and sacred altars conferred dignity on a festival, it was not certain that all the occasion's participants would draw the correct inferences. Speeches and inscriptions were thus the essential complements to abstract visual representation compensating with their directness for the indirection of allegory. In this way French revolutionaries sought to resolve the contradiction between allegory's didactic purpose and its intrinsic remoteness and ambiguity.

III

One way that was found to diminish the ambiguity of visual allegories like festival props, engravings, statues and medallions was to supply an accompanying textual explanation. But this use of graphic supplements testifies to a general devaluation of the image. While it was axiomatic in aesthetic theory since the Renaissance that the pictorial arts, though mute, were as eloquent as poetry, mere figural representation came to be seen as inadequate to the task of conveying the lessons of the Revolution. François Furet, Marie-Hélène Huet, Joan Landes, and other students of French revolutionary culture have called attention to a progressive displacement of image by sign that occurred in the eighteenth century.[19] This shift, writes Landes, "from the motivated iconic imagery of the father-king toward an abstract system of representation in which the impersonal order of law, writing, speech, and its proclamation prevailed," was responsible for bringing about a new symbolic politics (41).

Another way that was found to exploit allegory's suggestive power while assuring that the intended message was conveyed, was to resort to narrative allegory, and this, I would argue, is the solution of the writer Volney in his 1791 piece *Les Ruines, ou Méditation sur les Révolutions des Empires*. Significantly, Volney's work recombines in a literary medium many aspects of the Revolutionary fête: it commemorates a significant event, its tone is respectively elegiac and celebratory, and its narrative progression is punctuated by long speeches. And *Les Ruines* goes one step further—it stages a Revolutionary festival within its narrative.

Volney imagines a traveler who comes upon the ghostly ruins of Palmyra while crossing the Syrian desert. This spectacle of desolation inspires a melancholy reverie on the causes of the decline of great empires. If nothing remains of Palmyra and other once great cities of antiquity but broken pillars and crumbling walls, the traveler muses, might not the same fate befall European civilization? While he is immersed in these thoughts a "Genie" appears and scolds him for attributing man's fate to divine retribution rather than to human failings. This tutelary spirit then explains the causes of prosperity and decline of ancient states in terms of Natural Law philosophy. To illustrate this lesson, he sweeps the traveler up into the stratosphere to give him a panoptic view of world. From this vantage point the traveler is able to observe two conflicts: a battle in the Crimea between the Russians and the Turks, and, presented as a future event, a struggle in some unspecified country between the People and the Privileged.

The focus then shifts from the Genie and the Traveler to these latter antagonists. The People triumph over their oppressors but soon find their new-found freedom threatened by anarchy. In order to counter these threats, they decide to draft a social contract and delegate representatives to the task. The Legislator emerges as a leader of these representatives and he convokes a World General Assembly in which all the peoples of the world are gathered together under colorful emblematic banners. Feuds erupt between the various religious groups and soon make it apparent that the principal obstacle to world harmony is religious superstition. With the Legislator still presiding over the assembly, a figure comes on the floor and requests to speak. The Orator attempts to demystify religion by delivering a lengthy discourse on the relation of natural signs to notions of the divine and on the correlation between the world's major cults and astrological symbolism. This demystification allows the Legislator to make a powerful appeal to Reason, and, at scene's end, he persuades the world's People that their new government should be founded on a secular and not a religious basis.

Les Ruines possesses many of the conventional characteristics of allegory inventoried by Angus Fletcher in his magisterial

Allegory: The Theory of a Symbolic Mode. The work's title signals that "doubleness of intention" which Fletcher, borrowing from Coleridge's famous definition, sees as allegory's most fundamental characteristic. The disjunction between literal surface and moral referent are conveyed by the meanings of the word "revolution." In its first, cosmological meaning the word "revolution" evokes the inexorable, circular movement of heavenly bodies; in a second, metaphorical meaning, it figures the prosperity and decline of states as following this same regular rotation. The second meaning alludes, in turn, to a third understanding of "revolution" as momentous social upheaval. The ultimate referent, of course, is *the* Revolution of 1789. By inscribing the Revolution in this cosmological framework, Volney both magnifies it and suggests its precariousness. The "paysage moralisé" of the opening scene establishes ruins as the originating image that generates the work. Palmyra's shattered monuments function not only as metaphor—a sensible image of moral decay and a haunting foreshadowing of one possible outcome of the Revolution—but as synecdoche. The ruined city stands as a fragment of the ancient world and a reminder of the very fragility of order itself.

There are, to be sure, many other ways in which *Les Ruines* conforms to traditional definitions of allegory. Its "plot" is organized around a quest and enacts a series of debates. Its agents are abstract types: the Traveler is a sort of Everyman, the Genie an embodiment of Reason, and the Legislator, an exponent of the Law. Its effects are magical: characters appear and disappear instantaneously, time is telescoped, physical perspective is elastic. The work also suffers from several of allegory's notorious defects such as the tendency towards artificiality, abstractness, and didacticism. Because its agents personify faculties of mind or philosophical notions rather than complex human beings, the direction of the narrative grows out of the logic of disputation rather than the engagement of personalities. This leads to an engulfing of the action by long, expository digressions, and the "plot" functions as little more than a vehicle for introducing a new articulation in the argument. The speeches of the Genie, the Legislator, and the Orator are in essence variations on the same theme: the cause of the decline of empires is moral decay, which itself arises out of an order governed not by Reason and Natural Law, but by religious superstition. Volney's allegory is thus overdetermined from the philosophical standpoint, and this "teleological control of intention," as Fletcher has called it, tends to suppress any ambivalence, irony, or dialectical subtlety.

In his effort to redefine allegory as a "protean mode" Angus Fletcher has done much to demonstrate its "omnipresence in Western literature," but his discussion of the form is lacking in historical specificity, and his work tells us little about how allegory was understood in particular cultural contexts. While her strictures about allegory's self-reflexive use of language are perhaps too exclusive, Maureen Quilligan comes closer, I think, to appreciating those contexts when she observes that "all true narrative allegory has its source in a culture's attitude toward language" (15).

In this respect too, allegory's fortunes can be seen to be affected by a shift, not so much in the privileging of sign over image, but in the very concept of the sign itself. The attitude toward language that prevailed in late eighteenth-century France was contradictory. On the one hand, words were no longer seen to evoke magical correspondences between things; meaning was not something to be uncovered or divined but to be constituted through signs; analysis came to replace interpretation. Michel Foucault, who has described, better perhaps than any other historian, this conceptual shift, insists on the arbitrariness of the sign system that was to link all knowledge to language and eventually even "replace all languages with a system of artificial symbols and operations of a logical nature."[20] The ideal language of the new *episteme* was abstract, arbitrary, and universal, and the Logos that was valued was not the Word made incarnate but the Logos of Reason. Chiefly responsible for promoting this 'scientific' view of language were Condillac and his philosophical heirs, the 'Idéologues,' among whom Volney ranked prominently.

On the other hand, there has never been a period in which greater power and passion were invested in words than the years of the French Revolution. Streets, towns, and whole provinces were renamed; terms associated with the Ancien Régime became taboo; styles of address were democratized; loyalty oaths were endowed with ritualistic significance; to use the wrong word could have fatal consequences. Certain key words acquired an incantatory power—Nation, Virtue, the Law. Significantly, these words were abstractions and yet while they provided no key to the world's secret resemblances, they unquestionably had a performative power, for language had become the foremost instrument of political authority. A contemporary observer of the French Revolution, the playwright and critic, Jean-François de La Harpe, deplored the sacred aura with which revolutionary language had become endowed and railed against it in a pamphlet entitled *Du Fanatisme dans la langue révolutionnaire.*[21]

Allegory brought to the fore these contradictions inherent in the late eighteenth-century's attitude toward language. Quilligan writes: "allegory always presupposes at least a potential sacralizing power in language and it is possible to write and to read allegory intelligently only in those cultural contexts which grant to language a significance beyond that belonging to a merely arbitrary system of signs" (156). Revolutionary language was at once resolutely abstract and arbitrary and yet imbued with a sacred authority, and it is this dichotomy that Volney's *Les Ruines* embodies. Like the Festival in honor of Mayor Simonneau, Volney's allegory celebrates an abstract concept—the Law; its climactic event is the foundation of the state under the aegis of reason, and its prime figure is the Legislator. Yet it also demonstrates the magical power of language. *Les Ruines*' various agents—the Genie, the Orator, the Legislator—preach rationalism in the language of religious mysticism. The Legislator, like the Genie, has almost supernatural powers: through his words he is able to unify the people and bring the nation into being. And the gathering of the peoples of the world is represented as a mystic union, as a festival cementing the social bond. Volney's theme instantiates Mona Ozouf's observation that "the festival was an indispensable complement to the legislative system, for although the legislator makes the laws for the people, festivals make the people for the laws" (9). Speechmaking, it must be emphasized, was an integral part of the festival serving both to glorify the Law and to create a new social order.

The Legislator's crucial discursive role in forming the citizen and the state was underscored by a contemporary, L'Abbé Grégoire, himself an active legislator responsible for drafting a significant portion of legislation relating to cultural matters.

> When one reconstructs a government anew, it is necessary to republicanize everything. The legislator who ignores the importance of signs will fail at his mission; he should not let escape any occasion for grabbing hold of the senses, for awakening republican ideas. Soon the soul is penetrated by the objects reproduced constantly in front of its eyes; and this combination, this collection of principles, of facts, of emblems which retraces without cease for the citizen his rights and his duties, this collection

forms, in a manner of speaking, the republican mold which gives him a national character and the demeanor of a free man.[22]

Grégoire's astute observation may provide a key to the puzzle of why a rationalist like Volney should have chosen allegory as a vehicle for communicating his vision of the new republic, or why he should have cast his demystification of religious superstition and his call for an order based on Reason and Natural Law in the form of a new cosmology. It also calls attention to the self-reflexive nature of Volney's representation. Ever attentive to signs, the sometime legislator, Volney, imagines an allegorical narrative designed to grab hold of the senses and awaken republican ideas. In that narrative the Orator's role is to be the debunker of the old religion, but the Legislator's role is to be the high priest of the new. The Legislator's superior position in the social hierarchy is conveyed by a gesture of the People, who, Volney wrote, "éleva un trône immense en forme de pyramide; et y faisant asseoir les hommes qu'il avait choisi, il leur dit: 'nous vous élevons aujourd'hui au-dessus de nous afin que vous découvriez mieux l'ensemble de nos rapports, et que vous soyez hors de l'atteinte de nos passions'" (101–2). [[The people] raised an immense throne in the form of a pyramid where they seated their chosen representatives saying to them: "We place you above us today so that you can better understand the nature of our relationships and so that you will not be affected by our passions."] Here, the Legislator and his cohorts are glorified and mythologized as wise and omniscient but also remote leaders. The figure of the Legislator thus provides insight as to how bourgeois lawmakers, like Volney, imagined their own position vis-à-vis the sans-culottes citizens they felt called upon to instruct. The Legislator is above the compromises, the foul play, the "passions" of quotidian politics. Allegory's idealized types were well-suited for characterizing the lofty role Volney and his colleagues aspired to play in the Revolution. The form's inherent tendency towards excessive didacticism and longwinded exposition were seen by Volney, not as an aesthetic defect but as an advantage, for it allowed him to incorporate the long sermons that were to be an essential part of his fellow citizen's political reeducation.

Yet the Legislator's philosophical remove also inadvertently reveals the distance bourgeois revolutionaries felt from the struggle's more plebian combatants. Though the Legislator disparages the social relations induced by formal religion—that is, a passive, superstitious congregation led (duped) by more highly educated (crafty) priests—his own position vis-à-vis the People actually reproduces that relationship. It is one of the ironies of the Revolution's efforts at dechristianization that the major strategy deployed for eradicating the old religious cult was the institution of a new one. Mona Ozouf has aptly termed this endeavor, with its symbols, rituals, and priests, a "un transfert de sacralité" (317) [a transfer of sacrality]. Allegory was an essential tool for appropriating religious symbols. Doubtless, this appropriation was not entirely cynical. Volney and the pageant masters of revolutionary fêtes were sincere in their desire to vivify the abstract principles inspiring the Revolution and to honor its accomplishments by instituting dignified rituals, but they ran the risk that their new cult would degenerate into another kind of mystification.

There was, as Lynn Hunt has shown, a tension between the belief of Robespierre and his fellow revolutionaries in the possibility of transparency and the need for didacticism.[23] They dreamed of an ideal republic in which virtue would reign supreme and government would be the spontaneous and unmediated expression of the popular will, yet these same revolutionaries formulated thoroughgoing pedagogical programs to reshape society and to school the popular will. Allegory was an important element of these mediations. The conflicting demands of transparency and didacticism can be read as one manifestation of the degree to which political authority had become alienated from its true popular source, the nearly opposing tension between the desire to instruct and the need for a certain opacity as another. Allegory was used as much to cover over problems as to enlighten the populace and consequently its own didactic function was undermined. In elaborating symbols of power that would represent the Revolution, revolutionaries found allegory's abstractness and indirectness of greater use than more spontaneous but less manageable popular inventions. The discreet veil which draped allegorical representations could be used to conceal as well as reveal. What bourgeois revolutionaries sought to conceal—from themselves as much as from anyone else—was how fragile the social consensus really was.

Volney's *Les Ruines* manages to convey simultaneously the exhilaration of "un siècle nouveau" [a new century] and a deep anxiety about the future of the nation. It fully embodies the tension between didacticism and a certain deliberate opacity. On the one hand, the speeches of its various agents are the functional equivalent of the inscriptions accompanying figural representations: their purpose was to convey an unequivocal lesson. On the other, the generating metaphor of the ruin casts an enigmatic veil over the whole piece. *Les Ruines* is polysemous, but only at a supralinguistic level; it would not, therefore, meet Quilligan's requirement for true allegory. Quilligan may be right in identifying the eighteenth century as the moment when allegory had outlived its usefulness. As a vehicle for expressing or even influencing popular will, allegory proved to be fairly ineffectual. And the literary posterity of *Les Ruines* would seem to confirm her thesis, for although the work's influence was far-reaching, writers were inspired more by its private, melancholic reflection than by its public and didactic allegory. Yet, in an ironic sense, allegory might have functioned quite appropriately as "the language of the Revolution," mirroring the Revolution's many contradictions and reflecting in its generic hesitancy the instability of an era in which all the old certainties were open to question.

NOTES

1. Maureen Quilligan, *The Language of Allegory: Defining the Genre* (Ithaca: Cornell University Press, 1979).

2. The edition referred to throughout will be: *Les Ruines, ou Méditation sur les Révolutions des Empires*, introduction by Jean Tulard (Geneva: Slatkine Reprints, 1979). Volney's work was translated into English as early as 1792. Between 1792 and 1804 there were twelve re-editions of the translation, and *Les Ruines* became an important source of inspiration for the English Romantics. Mary Shelley's monster, it will be recalled, is moved by Volney's melancholy reverie. For an account of the critical reception of the work see Jean Gaulmier's *L'Idéologue Volney 1757–1820: Contribution à l'Histoire de l'Orientalisme en France* (Geneva: Slatkine Reprints, 1980).

3. The French edition of Winckelmann's treatise appeared in 1799 under the title *De l'Allégorie, ou Traités sur cette matière; par Winckelmann, Addison, Sulzer, etc. Recueil utile aux Gens de lettres, et nécessaire aux Artistes* (Paris: Chez H. J. Jansen, An VII de la République). All English translations in this text, unless otherwise indicated, are my own.

4. The commentator is presumably either Addison or the Berlin academic, Sulzer but it is not really clear which of the two it is. The title page indicates their names along with Winckelmann's as co-authors of "treatises" that appear in the volume. However, only brief remarks, not treatises, are appended (without indication of authorship) to Winckelmann's longer essay.

5. *Encyclopédie méthodique, ou Dictionnaire raisonné des arts et des métiers, une société de gens de lettres* (1751; rpt. New York: Pergamon Press, 1969). The initials at the end of the articles "Allégorie" and "Allégorique" indicate that their author was the Abbé Mallet.

6. Quoted from a manuscript source (Fl C IV Seine I, Archives nationales) in Mona Ozouf, *La Fête révolutionnaire: 1789–1799* (Paris: Gallimard, 1976). The English translation is from *Festivals and the French Revolution*, tr. Alan Sheridan (Cambridge: Harvard University Press, 1988), 211.

7. Quoted in Anthony Vidler, *The Writing of the Walls: Architectural Theory in the Late Enlightenment* (Princeton: Princeton Architectural Press, 1987), 161.

8. Quoted in Ozouf, *La Fête*, 86–87. The English translation is from the Sheridan translation, cited above, 71.

9. Lynn Hunt, "Engraving the Republic: Prints and Propaganda in the French Revolution," *History Todayy* 30 (1980): 11–17, on 14. Hunt expands upon the thesis of this article in the chapter "Symbolic Forms of Political Practice," in *Politics, Culture, and Class in the French Revolution* (Berkeley: University of California Press, 1984). See also her "Hercules and the Radical Image in the French Revolution," in *Representations* 1 (1983): 95–117. Hunt makes the point, as does Agulhon, that as the Revolution took a more radical turn and became more violent, the Republic came to be represented by a male allegorical figure (for example, Hercules).

10. Maurice Agulhon, *Marianne au combat: l'Imagerie et la symbolique républicaines de 1789 à 1800* (Paris: Flammarion, 1979).

11. Hunt, *Politics*, 62.

12. Joan Landes, *Women and the Public Sphere in the Age of the French Revolution* (Ithaca: Cornell University Press, 1988), 159.

13. Marina Warner, *Monuments and Maidens: The Allegory of the Female Form* (New York: Atheneum, 1985), xix–xx.

14. Quoted in Ozouf, 86. English translation, 70.

15. David's project is described in detail by Judith E. Schlanger, "Le Peuple au front gravé," *L'Enjeu et le débat* (Paris: Denoël/Gonthier, 1979).

16. Schlanger, "Théâtre révolutionnaire et répresentation du bien," *Poétique* 22 (1975): 268–83, on 279.

17. Hans Ulrich Gumbrecht, "Persuader ceux qui pensent comme vous: les fonctions du discours épidictique sur la mort de Marat," *Poétique* 39 (1979): 363–80. Angus Fletcher makes the connection between allegory and epideictic discourse in *Allegory: The Theory of a Symbolic Mode* (Ithaca: Cornell University Press, 1964): "Allegory belongs ultimately in the area of epideictic rhetoric because it is most often used to praise and condemn certain lines of conduct or certain philosophical positions" (121).

18. Gumbrecht, 380.

19. Furet, *Penser la Révolution française* (Paris: Editions Gallimard, 1978); Huet, *Rehearsing the Revolution: The Staging of Marat's Death 1793-1797*, tr. Robert Hurley (Berkeley: University of California Press, 1982); Landes, see especially the chapter, "The New Symbolic Politics."

20. Michel Foucault, *The Order of Things: An Archaeology of the Human Sciences* (New York: Vintage Books, 1973), 63.

21. De La Harpe, *Du Fanatisme dans la langue révolutionnaire, ou de la persécution suscitée par les barbares du dix-huitième siècle contre la religion chrétienne et ses ministres* (Paris: Chez Chaumerot Jeune, 1821).

22. Quoted in Hunt, *Politics*, 91-92.

23. Hunt, *Politics*; see especially the chapter, "Symbolic Forms of Political Practice."

THE PLOT IN A DREAM AND DREAMS OF A PLOT
The Lessons of Occasional Allegory

Deborah Ann Jacobs

Proclaiming "post-Renaissance allegory" an oxymoron, some critics of allegory theory insist that the seventeenth century marked the demise of allegory as a form.[1] Others, such as Angus Fletcher, offer solace to scholars of later literary periods, redeeming "modern" (seventeenth-twentieth century) allegories by treating allegory not as a genre but rather as a symbolic mode, omnipresent in all art forms throughout all periods of human history. Other theorists have adapted Fletcher's ideas where necessary, using them to explain the transmutation of allegory so notable in the "modern" era as a natural evolutionary process which occurs in any mode that survives over a long period of time.[2] While critics are correct in noting that "modern" allegories differ from classical and Renaissance allegories,[3] attempts to define and describe the nature and extent of these differences progresses slowly. Efforts to develop a comprehensive theory of allegory have been hindered by two complex yet surmountable adversities: 1) by the imprecision with which "allegory" has heretofore been defined, and 2) by the large number of "modern" allegorical texts which must be examined before some critic succeeds in discerning a definitive pattern in the transmutations they implement and exemplify. Overcoming these obstacles demands a thoughtful and methodical examination of "modern" allegorical texts.

The text I have chosen for consideration, *The Plot in a Dream; or, the discoverer in Masquerade*, is representative of the "modern" allegorical text, the kind that sends many Renaissance critics of allegory and its theory into paroxysms of denial. Admittedly, it differs dramatically from classical and Renaissance allegories, yet it patently possesses allegorical elements. Furthermore, because this text is an occasional piece, it offers insights into allegory not immediately apparent from other kinds of "modern" allegory. I have identified four areas of concern in which *The Plot in a Dream* epitomizes the problems and paradoxes of an allegory that embraces both antiquity and contemporaneity: 1) the allegorical text as an idiosyncratic expression of one or more pre-texts; 2) the allegorical text as evidence of the existence of a privileged language community; 3) distancing devices commonly associated with allegory; and 4) interpretive problems associated with allegorical texts. Examining the ways in which these allegorical elements find expression in *The Plot in a Dream,* I will argue that this text is a "modern" allegory, and as such offers insight both into allegory and its function as a modernizing mode.

The Plot in a Dream; or, the discoverer in Masquerade in A Succinct Discourse and Narrative of the late and present Designs of the Papists against the King and Government was first published in 1681 under the pseudonym Philopatris, a pseudonym frequently employed during the period 1678–1683 when Charles II's Restoration government faced the greatest challenge to its authority. Ostensibly a re-presentation of the Opposition's version of the events of the Popish Plot, the lightly-veiled allegory operative in this text serves not to veil but rather to highlight the text's relationship to the events of the Plot which had so ordered Englishmen's lives for the previous three years. The author undermines his or her alleged posture by having the text's protagonist, Philopatris, offer his revelations to the audience as a verification of Plot events as described by the Plot's "discoverer," Titus Oates. Philopatris, however, freely confesses the source of his inspiration: dreams!

As critics from C. S. Lewis to Michael Murrin and Clifford Gay have noted, allegory from the seventeenth century on lacks a classical pre-text.[4] Although *The Plot in a Dream* lacks a classical pre-text, it is clearly based upon a pre-text; in fact, it shows evidence of being based on a large number of pre-texts that probably included the vast majority of the pamphlets, broadsides, ballads, news sheets, popular trial accounts, and books dealing with the

Popish Plot which flooded the London market during the three years that preceded its composition.

The dialectical dialogue that critics are currently engaged in questions whether allegory must be based upon a *classical* pre-text, or whether any work based upon one or more *pre-texts* is potentially allegorical. The veil of allegory, which Murrin insists is so essential to the truly allegorical text,[5] functions in this work to cover the author's didactic message, but not his subject. Veiling of characters and places here ranges from the obvious and heavy-handed drapery to featherdusting.[6] Characters, places, and events are so thinly disguised that no one even remotely familiar with the persons and events of the Popish Plot would fail to recognize the persons or places they are meant to represent. Thus, the allegory operative in *The Plot in a Dream* does not operate as a veil; rather, it highlights the text's message by situating the reader within the context in which the author's message is being delivered. This, I propose, is the function of any allegory's pre-text: to situate the audience within the context in which the author's message is to be delivered.

One of the more problematic concerns shared by critics interested in allegory theory involves the question of whether allegory posits the existence of a privileged language community. Murrin, for example, insists that although the allegorist addresses a large audience for the purposes of entertainment, the truth the allegorist reveals has been reserved for a "privileged circle."[7] Murrin follows other critics in identifying the allegorist's role with that of the prophet who "address[es] the many but succeed[s] with the few."[8] While Murrin's assessment may be in keeping with the hierarchically arranged world view operative in the Renaissance, it proves totally inadequate to explain allegory as it has been practiced.

Fletcher, on the other hand, insists that the allegorical mode is "hierarchical in essence,"[9] but acknowledges that allegories are often "symbolic power struggles."[10] Allegory has proved far more serviceable to would-be revolutionaries such as Langland and Bunyan than to more conservative writers who have supported existing governments. And the work Murrin identifies as an "apogee in the history of allegorical rhetoric,"[11] may have confirmed the validity of Elizabeth I's government, but one would be remiss in not noting that its author composed it in the midst of the chaos of sixteenth-century Ireland. Allegory's alleged ability to posit the existence of a privileged language community is further undermined by the literal meaning of the Greek words from which the modern word descends, which, Miller reveals, means

> to speak figuratively, or to speak in other terms, or to speak of other things in public, from the Greek *allegorein*, *allos*, other, plus *agoreuein*, to speak (in public), from *agora*, an assembly, but also the marketplace or customary place of assembly.[12]

Such a public, social emphasis implies that the message of allegory is intended for widespread consumption.

Allegory, as practiced by the author of *The Plot in a Dream*, flatly denies the existence of a privileged language community. The introduction to this work, allegedly written by "the Bookseller," promises, as Murrin insists all allegory does, to entertain the many. The difficulty with this work, the "Bookseller" insists,

> will not lie in reading it out, but laying it aside, having once made an entrance into it: And when thou has read it once, not to read it again, wishing you could read it in a moment, and yet be always reading it.[13]

This "Bookseller," however, insists that the truths the text offers are available, in varying degrees, to all readers of the volume:

> If thine eyes be shut, this Vision will open them; if open, it will delight them. What thou seest in it, or by it intended, but defeated; designed, but discovered; let it excite thy praises to that God, Whose ALL-SEEING eye beholds, and whose INfiNITE POWER AND WISDOM bounds the RAGE, and baffles the Counsels of these wicked ACHITOPHELS.[14]

The "Bookseller" divides the audience into two all-inclusive groups. Those whose "eyes are shut" are promised enlightenment for perusing the text. Those whose "eyes are open" receive pleasure, for, being in an enlightened state when they first approach the text, members of this group will appreciate fully the moral lesson which the text has to impart. The text, however, offers sustenance to all, and it does so by offering Opposition rhetoric to support the Royalist position concerning the validity (or rather lack thereof) of the Popish Plot.

Critics of allegory theory have taken great pains to identify, categorize, and account for distancing devices and their functions in allegorical texts. Distancing devices represent stock features of allegorical texts and include things such as 1) the journey (usually to a strange world), 2) a distortion of time or space, and 3) an incorporation of commentary and interpretation into the action. After discussing how each of these distancing devices finds expression in *The Plot in a Dream*, I will demonstrate in the closing section, dealing with interpretive problems in allegorical texts, how each of these distancing devices must be taken into consideration when interpreting this particular allegorical text.

The journey, as Gay notes, is a rich and readily malleable metaphor, a means of expressing complex movement, an effective means of enacting textually the "transformation" the allegorist is interested in effecting.[15] Allegory is a literature of reform, and reform demands movement. The allegorist envisions a world transformed and employs the journey as a means not only of revealing to the reader the world as it could be but also of suggesting to the reader that he or she, too, may take this journey.

Philopatris, the protagonist in *The Plot in a Dream*, journeys not once but many times, to many different places. His first journey, a journey he repeats later in the text, is to Strombolo, the volcanic island situated in the Mediterranean Sea upon which is located, Phileroy [read: Titus Oates] reveals, the entrance way to hell. Philopatris also journeys to London, to Whitehall, to Oxford, and to some type of limbo in which he encounters and discourses with various individuals who lost their lives as a result of the Popish Plot.[16] All these journeys, however, evince a common feature—they are psychological journeys only. None of the journeys occurs in actuality; each is a dream reported by Philopatris.

A second distancing feature commonly found in allegorical texts is a distortion of time or space. In *The Plot in a Dream*, such distortions are expressed in terms of the protagonist's ability to travel by means of his imagination. Philopatris's ability to ignore temporal and spatial constraints, furthermore, increases proportionately as the plot develops. Philopatris's first dream, a visit to Strombolo and then to London, takes up almost the first one-third of the 285-page text. In the final two-thirds of the text, Philopatris's travels throughout London and other parts of England through the agency of his dreams increase in both frequency and forcefulness. By the end of the text, Philopatris's immunity to temporal and spatial constraints elevates the protagonist to superhuman or perhaps even dæmonic status among mere mortals. Witness, for example, how Philopatris brags of the rapidity of his return to London after witnessing the dissolution of the Oxford Parliament:

> The SENATE being dissolved, and the SENATORS all in a bussle preparing for a departure, my nimble GENIUS outstript the greatest hast they could make, and lodged me again in fansie at LONDINOPOLIS, before any of them could be one foot on the Road towards it.[17]

Throughout the text, Philopatris remains subject to his ecstasies which, as the narrative progresses, become increasingly forceful. Philopatris becomes the helpless pawn of his own imagination. For instance, Philopatris dreams of seeing the five Lords (that is, the five members of the House of Lords Titus Oates accused of conspiring to overthrow the government) taking part in a conference with Ignatian Provincial General Paul Oliva [referred to as Paulus d'Oliva]. The sight of the priest, Philopatris reveals, so fills him with rage that he wishes to attack the Ignatian physically. Philopatris's desires, however, are thwarted by his fancy, which rushes him to the safety and comfort of his own home.[18]

Critics have long noted allegory's tendency to incorporate commentary and interpretation into its narrative.[19] In *The Plot in a Dream* authorial commentary usually comes in the form of remarks made by the protagonist, Philopatris. These remarks, in turn, often function as a means of reminding the reader of how absurd Titus Oates's claims appear to the rational mind. In the following example, Philopatris wonders why Roman Catholics should engage in the kind of plot Phileroy (that is, Titus Oates) describes:

> To suppose any such Intestine Monsters lurking amongst our selves, that should go about to disturb that blessed Peace and Tranquillity we enjoy, were to conclude men Enemies to their own good, as well as their Countrey's in whose welfare they are joynt-sharers.[20]

At other times, commentary and interpretation effectively create aesthetic distance by injecting humor into the situation being described. For example, in one vision Philopatris returns to Strombolo to witness the final judgment of the five Jesuits. These priests (who were executed upon the testimony of Titus Oates and William Bedloe) await trial in a purgatorian courtroom. Philopatris looks on as the five Jesuits beg the Pope to make use of the keys to the kingdom which allegedly dangle from his girdle. The Pope apologizes, explaining that the lock has been changed and that his key no longer fits. The Jesuits, the Pope insists, will have to wait until his Holiness gets a new key, a statement which Philopatris counters with the following couplet:

> *Which* Key *His* Viccarship *will find*
> *When* Rome *turns honest, or the* Devil *blind*.[21]

The execution of these five priests, apparently, proved particularly emotionally trying to Englishmen. First, the Jesuits were put to death before the largest crowd yet assembled for the execution of any of the alleged plotters. Secondly, each of the priests calmly denied his guilt upon the scaffold. Gavan, in particular, offered an eloquent farewell.[22] Thirdly, the execution was interrupted by the arrival of a pardon, signed by Charles II, but contingent upon the priests confessing to the crime of which they stood convicted. All five priests refused to accept the pardon. Although the sentence handed down called for quartering of the priests' bodies while they still lived, the executioner allowed each of the priests to expire before mutilating their bodies.[23]

Critics have long been fascinated by the interpretive complexities presented by allegorical texts. Quilligan claims allegory's complex system of signification defeats would-be explicators and in the final analysis reveals more about the explicator than about the text explicated.[24] Murrin insists allegorical texts are open to at least seven levels of interpretation.[25] Gay finds the multiplication of interpretive possibilities to be the essence of allegory. Teskey views allegory as a form concerned with the generation of meaning, a form which forces readers to discover some meaning from the text.[26]

In *The Plot in a Dream*, most (although certainly not all) interpretive difficulties are readily overcome by a careful reading of the text, for such a reading reveals authorial prejudices. Bent upon exposing Titus Oates [Phileroy in the text]; Anthony Ashley Cooper, the first Earl of Shaftesbury; the House of Commons; and radical Protestant sectarians, the author of *The Plot in a Dream* uses every available opportunity to undermine reader confidence in these individuals, groups, or institutions. Five times Phileroy [Titus Oates] is identified with or as the Devil.[27] Furthermore, errors which the protagonist Philopatris makes recall errors Oates made, errors which led Englishmen to question Oates's veracity as a witness. For example, although Oates claimed to be familiar with Sir George Wakeman, Queen Catherine's physician, whom Oates testified was paid to poison Charles II, Oates proved unable to recognize Wakeman in court. Oates brushed this error off as due to fatigue and poor candlelight, but Oates's protestations met with only partial success. Mocking Oates's failure, Philopatris fails to recognize his "old Friend **PHILEROY**" when he first encounters Phileroy on Strombolo.[28]

The author also expresses his contempt for Anthony Ashley Cooper. The first Earl of Shaftesbury, the man whom many credit with managing Plot witnesses, receives but one direct mention within the text, but that reference takes the form of the unflattering diminutive, "little **EARL ANTHONY**."[29]

Determined to expose the part which members of the House of Commons played in the continuation of the Popish Plot, the author wittily avoids any direct mention of Commons. But the author manages to reflect adversely upon this House of Parliament. There is an old English proverb, found in variant forms in Chaucer's *Squire's Tale*, Shakespeare's *The Tempest*, and Webster's *The Devil's Law Case*, that states, "He should have a long spoon that sups with the Devil." And in England, large serving spoons are referred to as "commons" because they are used "in common" by all diners.[30] Combining these two elements, the author, in a dialogue between Philopatris [the protagonist] and Phileroy [Titus Oates], succeeds in chastising the House of Commons. The author manages this feat in the following way. Intent upon showing Philopatris the entrance to hell, Phileroy leads him up to the volcano's mouth. On the way, the following exchange tales place, which, for clarity's sake, is presented in dialogue form:

> Philopatris: No question but the entertainment must be extraordinary where the **DEVIL** is the **HOST** and his **IMPS** the **SERVITOURS**; but if we come to Table with him, I hope we shall have long Spoons to eat our broth with.
>
> Phileroy: I know not...what length your Spoons are of; but I will ingage your Commons shall be short enough.[31]

Satire is the author's weapon of choice to express disapproval of radical Protestants. When Phileroy first tells Philopatris that Roman Catholics are plotting to overthrow the government, Philopatris expresses skepticism:

The Plot in a Dream *and Dreams of a Plot* 249

> The Experience of now above twenty years, has confirmed us, that there hath no such **PLOTS** or attempts on their parts been attempted.³²

Although Charles II's Restoration government had faced no Roman Catholic plots, numerous radical Protestant plots had been exposed, particularly in the early years of the Restoration. Aping Opposition rhetoric, Phileroy [Titus Oates] insists that no Protestants ever plotted against the King, that all such alleged plots were committed by Roman Catholics dressed up as Protestants. Roger L'Estrange exposed the ludicrous nature of this oft-repeated radical Protestant defense when he declared,

> No man is so senseless as to imagine that the King was *depos'd, pursu'd, rob'd, taken, condemn'd and put to death* by a hundred thousand Priests in Vizors.³³

Although anxious to expose members of the Opposition for their part in the Popish Plot, the author of *The Plot in a Dream* expresses no sympathy for Roman Catholics. Catholics come off as clowns, the pitiable, benighted victims of their own superstitions. Blame for Catholic indiscretions, however, is laid upon the higher members of the clergy, who are presented as deceivers of the laity and of the ordinary priests. This emphasis upon ranking clerical culpability is apparent when the five Jesuits swear to Rhadamanthus, the dæmonic magistrate who resides over the purgatorian court, that they will lie in any court or upon the scaffold if necessary. Rhadamanthus chastises the priests for believing in the lies offered to them by their superiors:

> Ho, ho, ho, you are pure **SPIRITUAL VILLAINS** a-faith, to think, because you can cheat the world with your lyes and **EQUIVOCATIONS**, that you can cheat the **ALMIGHTY**, who is **TRUTH** it self; or dare to provoke his angry Vengeance with a dying Falshood; or did you think your **CHEATING VICCARS DISPENSATIONS** could reach to the other **WORLD**? or that **HEAVEn** would renew them? **POOR SOULS!** how miserably are you cheated!³⁴

Although attention to these authorial prejudices enables the critic to begin the interpretive process, only a consideration of the ways in which the author deftly balances reader sympathies through the employment of distancing devices enables the critic to complete the interpretive act. As noted earlier, three distancing devices—1) the journey, 2) distortion of time or space, and 3) incorporation of commentary and interpretation into the narrative—employed in *The Plot in a Dream* prove of significance in interpreting this text. Examining each of these devices in turn, I will reveal how the author uses each to modify critical response to his story.

Although the protagonist of *The Plot in a Dream* seems to journey extensively, he only dreams that he travels; the events he witnesses, events which he offers as proof of the validity of Phileroy's [Titus Oates's] tales, are not events at all, but dreams. The text's author goes to elaborate lengths to assure that the reader understands that Philopatris's dreams come to Philopatris when the protagonist is in a sleeping state.[35] For example, Philopatris introduces the dream dealing with Sir George Wakeman's trial in the following manner:

> My friend **PHILEROY**...began to rouse me up by plucking me by the Elbow, and saying, What, are you asleep? A **WAKE=MAN**, Here is no **RARE SHOW** a coming; No, no, said I, **PHILEROY**, I am not asleep; though I lyed in that, for I was asleep all this while; but however at this time, I fancied my self awake, only got into a **BROWN STUDY**, out of which being thus roused by **PHILEROY**, I opened mine Eyes again.[36]

Repeatedly, the author calls attention to the sleeping state of his narrator, and this emphasis suggests the importance of this information to the proper interpretation of the text. Witness another of the many times in which Philopatris confesses to being asleep:

> In a little time I fancied we [Philopatris and Phileroy] fell asleep; but what strange whimsies are there in dreams; for alas I was asleep all the while, yet my fancy in this **PARENTHETICAL SLUMBER** ran into new fancies, dreams within dreams, like the **PETROPOLITAN PLOTS**, one within another. Well, as I fancied I slept, so I fancied I waked again in the morning.[37]

Clearly, Philopatris's state of consciousness when receiving his inspirations is not coincidental to the story. Philopatris's inspirations arrive during his dreams, yet those inspirations are identical to Titus Oates's informations. Setting this up as a logic problem reveals the following:

If: A= Philopatris's inspirations, and
B= Dreams, and
C= Titus Oates's informations, then
the following becomes apparent:
A=B and A=C, therefore, C=B

Titus Oates's informations are dreams.[38]

As noted earlier, it is through Philopatris's dreams that distortions of time and space occur. As *The Plot in a Dream* progresses, Philopatris's dreams increase both in frequency and in forcefulness. Philopatris's helplessness, his inability to control his ecstasies, creates a situation in which he (and the reader) become trapped within the imaginative process. The reader, along with Philopatris, senses Philopatris's helplessness. Although Philopatris presents his dreams as beyond his control, in the short poem closing the text Philopatris vows, if necessary, to continue his dreaming:

My Dream is out, I wish the Plot were so,
And that my Dreaming might no further go:
But if provok'd by these designing men,
'Tis ten to one but I shall dream again.[39]

Only through this closing threat does the author reassert authorial control over the text.

The incorporation of commentary and interpretation into the narrative enables the author of *The Plot in a Dream* to accomplish two things. First, through commentary and interpretation the author grounds his audience; he forces them to view reality as the author wishes them to view it. Secondly, textual commentary and interpretation distance the reader from the emotional issues with which the text deals.

For three years preceding the composition of *The Plot in a Dream*, the English government was held hostage while Titus Oates and his fictions ruled London. Through Philopatris's dreams, the author of *The Plot in a Dream* succeeds in re-creating the nightmare-like quality of this national ordeal. Caught in a nightmare, England's only hope was to awaken. By presenting Titus Oates's tale as a dream, the author seeks to awaken his or her countrymen.

Thus, the text's allegory has been made subservient to the text's didactic message. This in no way lessens the importance of the allegory. The allegory situates the reader within the context (that is, within the Popish Plot) in which the message is being delivered, and situating the reader, in turn, proves necessary to a proper comprehension of the text's message.

NOTES

1. See, for example, Michael Murrin, *The Veil of Allegory: Some Notes Toward a Theory of Allegorical Rhetoric in the English Renaissance* (Chicago: University of Chicago Press, 1969), 197.

2. Clifford Gay, *The Transformations of Allegory* (London: Routledge & Kegan Paul, 1974), 6; and Edwin Honig, *Dark Conceit: The Making of Allegory* (Evanston: Northwestern University Press, 1959), 3.

3. Murrin, *Veil*, 14.

4. Murrin, *Veil*, 99; Gay, *Transmutations*, 5.

5. Murrin, *Veil, passim*.

6. The author uses several techniques to develop character names directly from the names of the historical personages those characters represent. For example, some names of people and places are Latinized (Ezeral Tonge becomes Dr. Tongus; Thomas Knox, Knoxius) or translated directly into French (Fr. Whitebread becomes Fr. Blanc=pain; the Whitehorse Tavern, the Blanc Cheval). In other instances, syllables or letters switch places to alter slightly the person to whom the author refers (Lord Stafford is referred to as Lord Fordstaff; Pickering, Ringepick; Gaven, Vanga; Harcourt, Courthar; William Bedloe, Capt. Lobed; and Stephen Dugdale, Dagdule). London becomes Londinopolis; England, Albonia; and Ireland, Bogland. Roman Catholics are Petropolitans and members of the Church of England are Protesto-Petropolitans. Other individuals are identified either fully or in part by a description of the job he or she performs (Lord Treasurer Danby is referred to as the Grand Cashier; Judge Edmund Berry Godfrey is Edmond, a worthy Magistrate). Little or no attempt is made to alter the name of other characters (Fr. Strange is referred to as Fr. Strange; Philopatris, however, mocking Titus Oates's mistake, proves unable to decide upon Fr. Strange's Christian name).

7. Murrin, *Veil*, 15

8. Murrin, *Veil*, 18.

9. Angus J. S. Fletcher. *Allegory: The Theory of a Symbolic Mode* (Ithaca: Cornell University Press, 1982), 22.

10. Murrin, *Veil*, 23.

11. Murrin, *Veil*, 167.

12. J. Hillis Miller, "The Two Allegories," in *Allegory, Myth, and Symbol*, ed. Morton W. Bloomfield, 356.

13. Philopatris, pseud. *The Plot in a Dream: or, the discoverer in Masquerade, in A Succinct Discourse and Narrative of the late and present Designs of the Papist against the Kind and Government* (London: 1681), A₄ᵛ.

14. *Plot*, A₅ʳ.

15. Gay, *Transformations*, 26–33.

16. The limbo to which Philopatris journeys is not the limbo described by the Roman Church. There are neither children nor pagans wandering about. This limbo resembles more the Druid limbo, an earthly plane such as that in which Shakespeare's elder Hamlet awaits, hoping that his son's revenge of his death will release the Danish monarch, freeing him to journey to his final resting place.

17. *Plot*, 278.

18. The passage involved is worth quoting at length: "I now...imagined to what they tended, which filled me with such a rage against the DEVIL in a COWLE, THE IGNATIAN, that I had certainly fell upon him and beat him; but, that the IMPETUS of my fancy at his very time hurrying me away form their compaany [sic], broke off my revenge, and placed me again in my own house, where I became more troubled and discontented than I was before." The passage serves two purposes: First, it cautions the reader concerning the power which the imagination can hold over the individual. Secondly, it offers a mocking excuse to explain why the "Four Ruffians" Oates insisted had been sent to assassinate Charles II never initiated an assassination attempt.

19. Gay, *Transformations*, 23; Fletcher, *Allegory*, 317–19.

20. *Plot*, 10–11.

21. *Plot*, 193.

22. Copies of the priests' final speeches, printed and distributed throughout London, seriously alarmed the Opposition, which attempted, unsuccessfully, to counter the effect of these papers by reminding Englishmen that the priests had been found guilty in a court of law. See Jane Lane, pseud., *Titus Oates* (London: Andrew Dakers, 1949), 200.

23. *Plot*, 198–201.

24. Maureen Quilligan, *The Language of Allegory: Defining the Genre* (Ithaca: Cornell University Press, 1979), 24.

25. Murrin, *Veil*, 101-2.

26. Gordon Teskey, "From Allegory to Dialectic: Imagining Error in Spenser and Milton," in *Publications of the Modern Language Association*, 101 (1986): 9–23.

27. *Plot*, 3, 5–6, 7, 10, 95–96.

28. *Plot*, 9.

29. *Plot*, 263.

30. *The Compact Edition of the Oxford English Dictionary* (Oxford: Oxford University Press, 1971), II: 2978.

31. *Plot*, 19.

32. *Plot*, 11–12.

33. Roger L'Estrange, *An Answer to the Appeal From the Country, to the City For the Preservation of His Majesties Person, Liberty, Property, and the Protestant Religion* (n. p., n. d.), 18.

34. *Plot*, 201.

35. Although I am unable to provide a definitive link between this text and Thomas More's *A Dialogue of Comfort Against Tribulation*, this strategy, of highlighting Philopatris's state of consciousness when his revelations arrive, suggests that the author may have been thinking of More's text. In Book II, chapter 18 of More's work, Anthony and his nephew, Vincent, engage in an epistemological debate in which they attempt the discern the difference between divine revelation and dæmonic inspiration. Anthony insists that the difference between the two is the same as the difference between information received in the waking state (divine revelation) and information received while asleep (daemonic inspiration). See Thomas More, *A Dialogue of Comfort Against Tribulation*, tr. Leland Miles (Bloomington: Indiana University Press, 1965), 112–14.

36. *Plot*, 91.

37. *Plot*, 109–10.

38. And, if, as I have suggested, this text may, with validity, be read back against More's text, Titus Oates's information are thus revealed as daemonic inspirations.

39. *Plot*, 285.

ALLEGORY IN MINOR RESTORATION THEATRICALS
Anti-Papist Rhetoric and Propaganda

Connie Capers Thorson

The Restoration of Charles II to the throne of England in 1660 was a source of both great relief and great enthusiasm for the English populace: Charles II was supported by the majority of the people, and the excesses of the Commonwealth were submerged in a wave of national unity. The fear of the Roman Catholic Church and any monarch who belonged to or supported it was, however, still widespread, and public displays of anti-Papist feeling were not uncommon. As the events of the Popish Plot unfolded in 1678, public demonstrations against the Pope and the Roman Catholic Church were even more prevalent and became national celebrations with a carnival atmosphere. The disclosure of the purported plot to put a Papist king on the throne generated chauvinistic passion that provided the impetus for many events in the next four years. The creative literary output and the journalistic investigative reporting generated by this furor, not surprisingly, reflected the concern over Roman Catholicism felt by the society as a whole. Throughout the period, until the Glorious Revolution brought the Protestants William and Mary to the throne, this seemingly irrational anxiety was expressed not only in street processions and pageants but also in minor theatrical presentations with the same themes though with less theatrical grandeur.

Allegory is a frequently overlooked element in these pieces of street drama. While the religious and political events of the Restoration period, especially the Popish Plot era, were often presented in nearly literal terms, they were nevertheless allegorical in that they represented more general anti-Catholic ideas. These theatrical events and productions deflate the opinion held by some literary historians, for instance Quilligan and Macniece, that allegory languished during the era. The intellectual basis or content of allegory (the focus for some modern commentators on allegory) may not be easily observed in the theatricals because they were aimed at a primarily unsophisticated viewer, but the rhetorical nature of allegory can be because rhetoric examines the effect on the audience first. The powerful rhetorical nature of the anti-Papist theatricals, together with their propagandistic intent, clearly establishes the importance of allegory in the expanded canon for the period.

Alan Roper draws distinctions between the use of the terms "parallels" and "applications" and the term "historical allegory" in the Restoration, stressing the elusive nature of "historical allegory."[1] "A parallel signified authorial intent: authors draw parallels, readers make applications" (40). Applications explain the ready understanding the viewer or reader has of the political events and personages being presented in the street or on the stage. It is true, indeed, that the anti-Papist theatricals allowed the viewer to create political meaning through collaboration with the spectacle, just as Roper asserts that "literary meanings are created by readers in collaboration with texts" (31). Because we are dealing with events designed for presentation rather than for reading (though reports and even texts were printed), allegory, applications, and parallels can, in concert, strengthen our understanding of the rhetorical and propagandistic nature of anti-Papist theatricals. Particularly useful is one of Roper's explanations of what parallels could do: "parallels aimed to blacken by association and only incidentally celebrated by association. They shared with satire the purpose of attack upon a present object and aimed to show its full depravity by arguing its correspondence with an example of agreed depravity from the past or, sometimes, a present polity" (41). No more apt description could be found for the intended purpose of the Pope burnings and other anti-Papist events.

The most unusual and the most intense of the anti-Papist allegories in the Restoration were the Pope-burning processions. The artistic nature of their rhetoric—that is, their essentially non-verbal but elaborately costumed concern with spreading propaganda against the Roman Catholic Church—was unusual because it did not rely on written or spoken language to convey its meaning. The rhetoric of the presentation had a major visual impact on the audience. Pope burnings were an attempt to sway the mob to a political position or to reinforce their belief in that position after the Restoration, the position being that a Roman Catholic monarch would spell the end of England. This nearly wordless allegory is at least as close to visual art as it is to literature, and it may owe more to or depend more on the kind of responses that people make to the visual arts than to the printed word, though there are parallels between the two responses. The elaborate costumes used in many of the processions made living art of the nearly wordless passage of the procession and had an impact on the viewer (reader) that encouraged the allegorical interpretations and political applications the producers were after.

Maureen Quilligan describes the reading process as proceeding "linearly, in a word by word fashion, but allegory often institutionalizes this fact by the journey or quest form of the plot, journeys which are, furthermore, extremely episodic in nature." It would be more precise to say therefore that allegory works horizontally, rather than vertically, so that meaning accretes serially, interconnecting and criss-crossing the verbal surface long before one can accurately speak of moving to another level 'beyond' the literal."[2] While Quilligan focuses on the importance of language to allegory, her exposition of the horizontal nature of allegory applies quite readily to the non-verbal spectacle of the Pope-burning processions and, in fact, helps to clarify the allegorical nature of the entire event.

Often Pope-burning processions were staged on the anniversary of the Gunpowder Plot and helped to commemorate the apprehension of Guy Fawkes in 1605 before he and his Roman Catholic conspirators could blow up the Houses of Parliament. John Evelyn has entries, in his *Diary*, for Gunpowder Plot commemorations in no less than thirty-seven different years, showing that staged irreverence was well liked and received by the mob and at least significant enough for him to comment on thirty-seven times. Evelyn records a description of a particularly important Pope burning on November 5, 1673: "This night the youths of the Citty burnt the *Pope* in *effigie* after they had made procession with it in greate triumph; displeased at the D: (the Duke of York) [later James II] altering his Religion, & now marrying an *Italian Lady* &c."³ John Miller notes in *Popery and Politics in England 1660–1688*, "On 5 November [1673] there were more bonfires and more popes burnt in effigy than there had been for thirty years"⁴ Sometimes the "Guy" himself was burned along with the paper effigies of the popes and other religious figures, giving the Gunpowder Plot celebrations a theatrical aura of their own primarily because of the spectacle involved.

Miller provides some specific details about a few of the popes burned at later events: "on 17 November 1676 and 1677 a larger pope, with devils whispering in his ear, carried in a chair by several persons, was burned at Temple Bar...Persons of quality provided drink for the common people...On 5 November 1678 several expensive popes were burned, the best being at Temple Bar" (184). The impact of the allegorical representation of the Pope burnings cannot be over estimated. The frequency of the burnings fed the passion of the people for ritual, while the costumes and effigies of identifiable clerics heightened the allegorical representation of the events. The burnings offered the populace a kind of socialization of a ritual and led to the fervent politicization of anti-Catholic feeling. This demand for public ritual culminated at the height of the Popish Plot controversy with Pope-burning processions on November 17, 1679, 1680, and 1681 in celebration of Queen Elizabeth's accession to the throne (and perhaps in glee over the anniversary of the death of the Catholic Queen Mary). Miller posits that the reviving of celebrating her accession with Pope burnings "was one expression of the fears aroused by the religious and political leanings of the court; the veneration of Elizabeth implied a condemnation of her successors" (74). Nevertheless, of the theatrical nature of the Pope burnings Miller comments, "But for all that [the fear of the court] they remained a national festival, a pageant, a ritual, an entertainment. Ale and wine flowed freely. In 1679 a room at Temple Bar to watch the show cost £10: it was, after all, a remarkable spectacle" (184). And the allegorical representations in these processions served to work the crowd into a frenzy of delight at the spectacle and a storm of support for the Protestant backers of Charles II. Even such an important writer as John Dryden bowed to their popularity, though he looked down on the vulgar appeal of such spectacle, when he tried to bolster the appeal of his play, *Oedipus*, in the Epilogue:

Charm! Song! and Show! a Murder and a Ghost!
We know not what you can desire or hope
To please you more, but burning of a Pope.[5]

The most important of the Pope burnings, not because it was the most elaborate but because it was the first of the elaborate displays that occurred for three years in a row on the same date, was probably the one that took place on November 17, 1679 in London.[6] Montague Summers credits Elkanah Settle with being "the chief engineer and mechanician of the Pope-burning pageants."[7] Settle is also accepted as the author of a good extant account of such a pageant, "London's Defiance to Rome, a Perfect Narrative of the Magnificent *PROCESSION*, and Solemn Burning of the *POPE* at Temple-Barr, Nov. 17th, 1679. (*Being the Coronation-Day of that Never-to-be-forgotten Princess, Queen ELIZABETH.*) With a Description of the *Order*, Rich *Habits*, Extraordinary *Fire-works*, *Songs*, and General *Tryumphs* attending that Illustrious *Ceremony*."

Settle's account of the procession is brief, but meaty. He begins his narrative with praise for the "Match-less Virgin-Queen" whose memory has not faded even though it has been decades since her reign. It is her "Solid and Heroick *Vertue*" that made her such a great queen: "How fresh and glorious does her memory shine this day, with all *True Englishmen?*"[8] The reference to "true" Englishmen clearly establishes Settle's propagandistic stance in his account of the procession. He praises her "*Zeal* for the *Protestant Religion*" and cautions other monarchs not to make changes (1). Her coronation remains commemorated with a celebration:

> To render which more *Illustrious*, A Number of Worthy *True Protestant Gentlemen*, taking notice of the Insolence of the Papists, who, after all the Late *Miraculous Discoveries* of their several Hellish Conspiracies...were pleased, *this Year*, to prepare a more Extraordinary *Representation*, to Express their *Own* and the *Citie*, indeed the *Whole Nations* [sic] Defiance, and Just Detestation of *Popish Idolatries*; an *Entertainment* so *seasonable*, so *Orderly* Manag'd, and so Universally Joyn'd in, and *Applauded*, That we could not but think it fit to give the World a *Brief*, and *True Account* thereof; the rather, to Correct some False, and Imperfect relations hereof the Truth being as follows. (2)

It is, of course, the celebration of English ritual that Settle is interested in preserving with his detailed description, and it is from his description that the allegorical nature of the pageant really becomes evident.

The route of the procession took it through the streets of London from Moorgate through Algate to Leaden-Hall-Street through Cheapside ending at Temple-Bar. Settle's description clearly represents the linear progression of the procession which, in this case, the viewer experiences. It is this horizontal progression that impacts the viewer's understanding just as when Maureen Quilligan asserts that for the reader "meaning accretes serially." It is the horizontal, episodic progression or journey that constructs the allegory of the event.

The viewers standing on the streets of London watching the procession are *in* the event as Maureen Quilligan asserts they need to be in allegory. (254) With the event happening all around and growing in fervor as the procession brings more and more important personages into view, the viewers understand the most they can from the allegorical representations of the religious figures in the procession. The viewers are so caught up in the ritual playing out in front of them that they cannot be objective about it. Of course, it is this non-objective response that the organizers—the True Protestant Englishmen—want the mob to have. The allegorical representations enable the unlettered person as well as the sophisticated and literate viewer to feel the swell of chauvinistic pride from the procession and the event it supposedly commemorates—the accession of Queen Elizabeth. These processions were an attempt to sway the mob to a particular political position or reinforce their belief in that position.

It is easy to see how the long procession with its realistic representations of religious abstractions (generic priests, bishops, and especially the cardinals and the Pope etc.) could sway the mob, especially one warmed on a cool fall evening with plenty of free ale. The characters are specific only in so far as they represent particular members of religious orders, but they do not normally represent particular named people. Settle continues his account of the event by specifically relating the order and number of the costumed participants, beginning with the whistlers who cleared the way, a man ringing a bell and crying out for people to remember Justice Godfrey, and a dead body representing Godfrey "carry'd before a Jesuit in Black, on Horseback, in like manner as he was

Allegory in Minor Restoration Theatricals 261

carry'd by the Assassins to *Primrose Hill*."[9] Next "came a Priest in a Surplice, with a *Cope* so Embroider'd with Dead *Bones, Skeletons, and Skulls*, and the like, giving *Pardons* very Plentifully to all those that should *Murder* Protestants, and Proclaiming it *Meritorious*" (2). Following close behind were a priest in black, 4 Carmelites in white and black, 4 grey friars, 6 Jesuits with bloody daggers, musicians, 4 bishops, 4 more bishops, 6 cardinals, the Pope's doctor "with *Jesuites* Powder in one hand, and an Urinal in the other" (3), two more priests, and finally the Pope.

Sir William Waller, a whig justice of the peace, collected Catholic vestments, relics, and books for use in the Pope-burning processions, all of which added a note of authenticity to the spectacle.[10] The elaborate costumes and accouterments made the allegorical representations seem authentic—none more so than the Pope himself. Settle describes the Pope in lavish terms:

> *Lastly*, The P*ope* in a lofty glorious *Pageant*, representing a Chair of State, covered with *Scarlet*, the Chair richly Embroidered and Fringed, and bedeck'd with Golden Balls and *Crosses*; At his Feet *a Cushion of State*, and two *Boys* in Surplices with White Silk Banners, and *Bloody Crucifixes and Daggers*, with an Incense-Pot before them, *Censing* his Holiness, who was arrayed in a splendid *Scarlet Gown*, lined through with *Ermin*, and richly daubed with Gold and Silver Lace; on his Head a *Tripple Crown* of Gold, and a glorious Collar of *Gold and precious Stones*, *St. Peters Keys*, a number of *Beads, Agnus Dei's*, and other Catholick *Trumpery*. At his back, his Holinesses Privy Counseller (The *degraded Seraphim*) Anglice the *Devil*, frequently Caressing, *Hugging*, and Whispering him, and ofttimes instructing him aloud to destroy His Majesty; to forge a *Protestant Plot*, and to *Fire the City* again, to which purpose he held an *Infernal Torch* in his hand. (3)

Not only did the costumes and other regalia increase the viewer's ability to identify the religious personage in his view; they made the event real. They also added to the linear progression of the event because they became more elaborate as the procession made its way through the streets. Settle, as master of these revels, writes that the Privy Counseller both whispers to and speaks aloud to the Pope, thereby introducing at least some spoken, though probably unheard, rhetoric to the basically speechless procession. The entire procession was accompanied by hired porters and volunteers carrying thousands of torches. Settle says that "there could not be fewer than *Two hundred thousand* Spectators" all of whom were "expressing their *Abhorrence* of Popery with continual *Shouts* and Exclamations" (3).

At Temple-Bar the procession and the mob were greeted by fireworks. The Pope was brought before the four statues at Temple-Bar—those of King James I, Charles I, Charles II, and Queen Elizabeth. The Queen held a shield with the motto *"THE PROTESTANT RELIGION AND MAGNA CHARTA"* (3). Entertainment by song followed, with one part representing the Cardinal Norfolk and the other the people:

Cardinal   *From* York to London *Town we come,*

Norfolk.   *To talk of* Popish Ire,
                To Reconcile *you all to* Rome
                And prevent Smithfield Fire.

Plebs.   *Cease! Cease thou* Norfolk Cardinal,
                See yonder stands Queen Bess,
                Who sav'd our Souls from Popish Thrall,
                O Queen Bess, *Queen* Bess, *Queen* Bess.

                Your Popish Plot *and* Smithfield Threat,
                We do not fear at all,
                For Loe! beneath Queen Besses *feet,*
                You fall, *you* fall, *you* fall.

                Now God preserve Great CHARLES *our King,*
                And eke all Honest *men*;
                And Traitors all *to Justice bring,*
                Amen, Amen, Amen. (4)

Though Queen Elizabeth and King Charles are not depicted in the moving allegory of the Pope burning, their statues are at Temple-Bar, and they become, at this point, part of the allegory of the scene with the singing of the song. The words of the song predict what will happen to the Pope—indeed he will be burned right here for Elizabeth and Charles to see and to share with the

Allegory in Minor Restoration Theatricals 263

crowd. The parallels drawn and applications made in this scene reinforce the allegorical and rhetorical intensity of the event.

All the while a large bonfire was being built nearby, and when it was ready the Pope "was decently *Toppled* from all his Grandeur into the Impartial Flames" (4). Settle imagines that the great shout at this moment must have been heard as far away as Scotland, France, and Rome. Only at the burning point does Settle mention the word "Effigie" (4), reinforcing that the whole is an allegory of pretty sizeable proportions, played out with living depictions of hated ideas and religious constructs until the bitter end. While this theatrical presentation is obviously different from the written forms that most readers have learned is acceptable for allegory, it is, nonetheless, allegory at its most essential level.

The correlation between the linear progression of the Pope-burning procession and the linear progression of the mass in earlier centuries must not be overlooked in the discussion of the allegorical nature of the Pope burnings. Additionally it must be noted that the reading public, which was growing in size throughout the period, had access to dozens of tracts of all kinds that described the rituals of the Roman Catholic Church.[11] As early as the ninth century Amalarius, Bishop of Metz, wrote allegorical interpretations of the Mass. O. B. Hardison asserts,

> "Of particular interest are the assertions [of Amalarius] that it [the Mass] appealed to the *simpliciores*...Already in 853 there is a suggestion that allegorical interpretation can be appreciated by the illiterate and semi-literate, for whom historical details and theological subtleties are meaningless. The need of the *simpliciores* for a vivid, dramatic understanding of the Roman rite inevitably increased as the separation between the clergy and the laity became more pronounced and as the language of the Church became ever more remote from the vernacular."[12]

The same assertions hold true for the Pope burnings, though the historical and political details and theological subtleties were not nearly so obscure for the seventeenth-century viewer. The organizers were sure that the crowds would be emotionally involved with the processions because of what we now understand as their allegorical nature, and we should assume that the organizers realized, at least to some extent, the impact the allegorical representations would have on the viewers of such organized political propaganda. The allegorical elements of the processions helped the members of the crowd to interpret for themselves exactly what the propagandists wanted them to, while the sophisticated, educated viewer could enjoy the allegorical representations as they would any other dramatic production. The linear progression and allegorical nature of the mass and the pope burning kept the viewer focused on one segment of the procession at a time, building the emotional involvement of the crowd into a frenzy released in exaltation at the climax.

Hardison maintains that Amalarius interprets the mass as a dramatic presentation with the participant clergy playing particular roles and with a plot—one that progresses linearly from the birth of Christ through his death and resurrection (39). It is this linear progression that is important for the later Pope burnings. Later, instead of glorifying the life of Christ, with the ultimate joy of his resurrection, the Pope burnings glorified the death of the Pope after a linear progression, not on the high altar, but through the streets of London. The irony of the similarities between the Mass and the Pope burning is delicious for the propagandists, the producers of the procession, who finally use fire to cleanse and the death and non-resurrection of the Pope as the ultimate irony.

Played against the naturally "happy" or comic ending of the mass when Christ is resurrected, the ending of the Pope burnings is also happy or comic because the Pope dies. In fact, the crowd, fortified with ale and thoroughly involved in the procession of the Pope, would experience a comparable cathartic ebullience that the participants in the mass did. This parallel was not lost on the stagers of the Pope burnings. The Pope burning intensified the role playing that was always important in the mass—particularly so on feast days such as Corpus Christi, Ascension, or Pentecost.[13] Another interesting point that Hardison makes deals with the rememorative nature of the Mass. "From beginning to end, but especially during the Canon and Communion, the Mass is a rememorative drama depicting the life, ministry, crucifixion, and resurrection of Christ. Although other elements vary according to the ingenuity of the interpreter, rememorative allegory is always present" (44). In many of the same ways the Pope burnings were also rememorative dramas, though the ends were different. The representation of Sir Edmund Berry Godfrey, for example, was designed to raise the ire of the crowd with memories of the heinous crimes committed against him. Explicitly depicted and described in a broadside called "The Solemn Mock Procession of the POPE

Cardinalls Jesuits Fryers etc: through the City of London November the 17th 1680"[14] were the tableaux or pageants (small floats with various religious personages and banners with lettered explanations on the sides). These pageants were supposed to make the viewer remember all the atrocities and specious ideas the Roman Catholics were trying to spread in England. The commentary on the broadside oozes with propaganda designed to inflame those who read it after the fact. It was these allegorical representations in what surely was intended to be an allegorical send up of the mass that made the political assertions the producers of the event desired.

London was not the only town or city in England to have Pope-burning processions. Though most of those staged in the provinces were not so magnificent as the ones in London, they were enthusiastically received by the populace. "In 1679, Abergavenny protestants became sufficiently daring to attempt the town's first 'pope-burning' with predictable consequences of murder and mayhem. Cwm was raided, the catholic school at Hereford was closed, and priests began going to the scaffold. The priest hunter Waller [the judge who collected vestments] was active in the area."[15] In the Narcissus Luttrell manuscript collection at All Souls College, Oxford, the unidentified newsletter writer reports the following:

> London. 31 Jan 1681/0 [sic] The Students of ye University of Edinburgh in Scotland did on the 25th of December last, burn the Effigies of ye pope just before the palace there; & the provost of y^t City not being so forward to hinder it (as was desired) that party gave out that ye students should say that they would burn the provosts house for his being busy in kindling the same, the better to colour y^{eir} own designs, since wch ye Provost's house hath been burnt down; but it is supposed to have been done by the popish party in that Citty, however ye Students have suffered for the same, for they are all banished 15 miles out of ye Citty & ye university broke up.[16]

Even as late as 1714 *The Flying Post* printed a letter from Chichester in which was described in great detail a Pope burning staged on October 20 in celebration of King George's coronation. In the same issue there are reports of somewhat less spectacular processions in Liverpool, Trowbridge in Wiltshire, and Frome in

Somersetshire. It is obvious that whenever the possibility of a Roman Catholic's becoming king was seen as a serious threat by the crowd, as it was in 1714 when there were rumblings of the Pretender's return, Pope burnings were staged as a sure way to boost the Protestant sentiments of the crowd. The entwining of propaganda with the allegorical nature of these events was always certain to awaken the political passions of the people and ensure the continued support of the Protestant King.

The Pope-burning processions had more allegorical significance in the effect of their pageantry as a whole than in the individual representation of each participant, though each person did parallel some distinguishable member of religious mythology. Some of the lesser known, less elaborate anti-Papist presentations, such as *The Converted Fryar: or a Defiance to the Church of Rome* (1673), did, however, depend on the representation of the individual rather than the pageantry of the whole. This monologue "was acted in the Pallace-Yard at Westminster on Saturday the 8th of this instant March 1672."[17] The pamphlet recounted the actions of a Capuchin friar who converted to Protestantism. Then, "having sent for some Fagots, and procured Fire, he took his *Beads*, a *Crucifix*, some Popish Mass-Book his *Cowls* and the whole Habit of his Order, and there very reverendly [sic] Burnt them in the presence of a numerous Crowd" (7). For the average viewer of such a theatrical event, the burning of the various accouterments of a member of a Roman Catholic religious order had significance of a particular kind. That significance was allegorical in nature because the accouterments stood for attitudes, idolatries, and superstitions that the English Protestant viewer found abhorrent. Additionally, the visual effect of the burning reinforced the propaganda that the use of allegorical representation was supposed to support. The burning cleanses the friar, allowing him to atone for his previous sins of membership in and support of the Church of Rome.

The few words of this theatrical were used only to reinforce the visual or main event of his "rare Burnt offering" (7), but the published account of this event allowed the author to take advantage of the opportunity for including biting attacks on the Church and its idolatries, a sympathetic account of the life of the friar, and the hope that others will follow this monk's lead to heighten the propagandistic intent of his narrative. The allegorical nature of the event as it actually happened is intensified for the reader by the rhetoric of the narrative because it sets the mood and the tone of the event. It prepares the reader mentally for the full impact of the burning of the Capuchin's religious trappings as he openly testifies for all to see that he is now a good Church of England man. It lets the reader be a participant *in* the event much as he is in the Pope-burning processions.

In 1680 a theatrical titled *The Coronation of Queen Elizabeth, with the Restauration of the Protestant Religion: or, The Downfal of the POPE* was staged in August at Bartholomew Fair and again in September at Southwark Fair, according to the puff on the title page. Though evidently never presented in the legitimate theatre, the printed version of the play asserts that the play was received "With great Applause, and Approved of, and highly Commended by all the *Protestant Nobility, Gentry* and *Commonalty* of *ENGLAND*, who came to be Spectators of the same."[18] At the Restoration in 1660, first Bartholomew Fair and then Southwark Fair had been lengthened to 14 days.[19] This bit of information is important because it means that many people really did have the opportunity to watch this play. Its popularity may be further confirmed by reference to it in a poem about events at the fair, "Bartholomew-Fayr," published in *A Choice Compendium; or, An Exact Collection of the Newest, and most Delightful Songs*, 1680/81:

> Here's that will Challenge all the Fayr,
> Come buy my Nuts, Damzens, my Burgamy Pears;
> Here's the Whore of Babylon, the Devil and the
>   Pope,
> The Girl is just a going on the Rope.[20]

In the section "To the Protestant Reader" the author says that he is publishing the play because it gained great applause, because it "*lay open the Cruelties and Villanies of* Rome, *more to the Life, than they have been exposed since the beginning of this late horrid and most barbarous Plot*", because he thought that "*many who saw the Play, were not of such profound Capacities, as to let it make a firm Impression upon their Memories*", and because he wanted to expose "*the purity of our Religion, and the gross Absurdities and Cruelties of the* Pope *and Church of* Rome, *in their proper Colours*" (1). Again, the simplicity of the crowd is pointed out as a reason for the presentation, and, in this case, the language takes on an importance not seen in the street. It becomes the vehicle for the propaganda against the Church of Rome.

The plot of the play revolves around a scheme by the Pope and the Devil to assassinate Queen Elizabeth and return England to the Papist camp. A secondary plot involves a nun (Dulcementa) who is debauched by the Pope and murdered by her father (Moricena), a Cardinal, who is then killed by the Pope. The plot to murder Elizabeth is foiled, of course, and after he murders the Cardinal, the Pope flees to England on the advice of the Devil and in his company.

Though the viewer can make applications with historical events throughout the play, it is in Act III that the most persuasive allegorical elements enter to reinforce the anti-Papist rhetoric that has gone before. After the Devil has told the Pope that the Pope is now the slave of Lucifer, a stage direction appears in the printed version: "[*The Scene suddenly draws off, and discovers Hell full of Devils, Popes and Cardinals, with the Ghosts of* Moricena *and* Dulcementa *wounded: To them the Devil enters*]" (19). The Pope is horrified at the scene! At this point a voice from behind the scene sings

> *Where, where's the Pope:*
> Answer. *Come to die in a Rope.*
> Or his Breath expire, by the flames of hot fire.
> To meet the just Plagues that his sins do
>   require. (19)

As some of the crowd members who support the Queen enter the scene, a voice from above tells them that the man they have taken is the Pope. They leave the stage, carrying the Pope on their shoulders, wearing his miter and other accouterments, to take him to the bonfire lit to celebrate the defeat of the Spanish Armada. They approach Queen Elizabeth to ask permission to burn the Pope. Her General wants to know where they will get a Pope, and Tim responds, "O, we have a Pope, a lusty Pope, a strapping Pope, a Rumping Thumping Pope, a Pope that will fry like Bacon, an't please you" (22). Giving her permission, Elizabeth advises that they be discreet. The crowd leaves with the Pope, and the play ends with dancing.

Discovering Hell and all of its occupants to the audience, having the Devil and the Pope as characters in the play, presenting the mob members wearing the Pope's miter and robes, allowing the Pope to be burned at Temple-Bar—all these allegorical elements helped to make the viewers part of the action while they were drawing the applications the author intended. Producing the plays at the fairs allowed for the involvement of the viewers in ways similar to their involvement in the Pope-burning processions. They could identify the allegorical characters and could join in the shouting and hoorahing in significant ways.

Rome's Follies, Or the Amorous Fryars, A Comedy was, according to the title page, "lately Acted at a Person of Qualitie's House."[21] While the printed version of the play was advertised in the *Impartial Protestant Mercury*, 30 December 1681–3 January 1681/82,[22] it was, evidently, never acted on the legitimate stage, perhaps because it would have been difficult to produce or perhaps because it has almost no redeeming literary merit. Certainly Papist bashing at its utmost, this play sacrifices any dramatic integrity it might have hoped for to a nearly ritualistic and allegorical exposé of the excesses of the Roman Catholics.

Florimel, Marforio, and Father Turbin form a love triangle. When Marforio finally catches Florimel being unfaithful to him with Turbin, he appeals to the Pope. The Pope makes excuses for one of his own and pardons the lovers. They leave the stage. The plot that has controlled the action to this point just stops, but the play goes on.

Although the anonymous author has exposed the commonly accepted excesses of the priests and the Pope throughout the first three quarters of the play, he cannot resist piling on vitriolic propaganda against the Roman Catholics, even though the plot has in no way prepared the audience or the reader for this unlikely twist in the plot. The Pope asks Odcroff, a Jesuit, to conjure up the Fathers of the Church, and following a great bolt of lightening the ghosts of Clement I, Boniface VIII, Gregory III, and Innocent III appear. At this point in the action, most of the audience would apply the knowledge that, as Jerzy Limon explains in a discussion of Thomas Middleton's *A Game at Chesse* (1624), "blessed souls cannot return to earth as ghosts: this is the ability of damned souls only."[23] In turn, each of these Popes recounts the major accomplishments of his Papal reign. Innocent, for example, tells the current Pope,

'Twas I brought in Auricular Confession.
What Godly Plots have by that Art been made
To turn and destroy poor Maiden Heads? (54)

In response to the current Pope's wanting to know how long Rome will hold power over men, another ghost enters the scene. Pope Joan excoriates the male Popes, accusing them of ignoring her reign and calling it a fable.[24] She recites a litany of the Popes' abuses of the religion and of their followers. Pope Joan's final speech makes reference to the many accoutrements that reinforce the allegory of the anti-Papist theatricals before making a prediction:

> Our Church is on such weak Foundations laid,
> As long it cannot stand―――――――
> 'Tis built on Medals, and on Cowls of Monks,
> Nuns-hoods, and Censers, Disciplining Whips,
> Chains, Cords full of Knots, and Images,
> Bonnets of various Colours, Sandals, Cloggs,
> Pantoffles, and Miters Pontifical,
> Cardinals Hats, Vails Hypocritical,
> Green Hats, and Girdles, Bulls, Relicks of Saints,
> Sophistry, and Books of Controversie.
> All these, and many more, which I could name,
> Are the great Props t'uphold the mighty Frame.
> It stands but shiv'ring, and a solid Gale
> From *Albion*, will make proud *Rome* bewail.

With this pronouncement, which would have been met with great enthusiasm and approbation from the viewers, Pope Joan exits. The other Papal ghosts exit after a dance by four devils.

The viewers were, if the title page is to be believed, probably fairly literate. They would have known that the sentiments of the drama were expressed to appeal to their anti-Papist views, and they really did not have need of a litany of excesses recited by the ghosts. The reader of the printed version would have drawn the same applications as the viewer, though the viewer had the added advantage of seeing the ghosts in their papal costumes and the devils dancing. All of these recitations do, however, reinforce the allegorical nature of the play, supplying the viewer/reader with reinforcement for the applications he makes. The naming of the ghosts acted as a similar reinforcement, because, though more specific in nature than in many allegories, the ghosts have names that offer at least vague associations with the hated past for the Protestant audience. In 1681 the viewer/reader was ready to interpret any anti-Papist production as a condemnation beneficial for the state. While plays such as *Rome's Follies* did not have the spectacular impact of the Pope burnings on the viewer and while they did rely more, though not entirely, on spoken rhetoric, the result or effect desired was always the same—the viewer/reader response was of the utmost importance, and it was reinforced by the use of allegorical elements.

Many people in the seventeenth century were firmly convinced that the Papists were a serious threat to the protestant succession in England. They were eager to believe in the Plot exposed by Titus Oates, for example, and used it as an excuse for expressing their anti-Papist sentiments in a variety of ways, including all kinds of printed propaganda, street processions, and minor theatricals. The allegorical nature of Roman Catholic liturgy, ritual, and pageantry lent itself to allegorical representation in these productions and strengthened the political propaganda that the organizers of the various events were purveying. In many ways the use of allegory allowed the propagandists to represent the impossible as a method of reinforcing their anti-Papist ideas to an accepting audience. The rhetorical nature of allegory—that is, the effect of the allegory on the viewer/reader—was used by the producers of the theatricals and events to influence the thought and conduct of the viewer/reader. The allegorical elements of the various theatricals present simple yet direct lessons for the semi-literate or illiterate viewer to share in. Those who would impose stringent rules for allegory miss the point of its being something that makes the story intelligible to the common, unlettered man. Expanding the canon to include such minor theatricals as the Pope burnings and *Rome's Follies* broadens what should be viewed as allegory in the period and dispels many contentions about the static nature of allegory in the Restoration.

NOTES

1. Alan Roper, "Drawing Parallels and Making Applications in Restoration Literature," *Politics as Reflected in Literature*, Papers presented at a Clark Library Seminar 24 January 1987 (Los Angeles: William Andrews Clark Memorial Library, University of California, 1989), 31.

2. Maureen Quilligan, *The Language of Allegory: Defining the Genre* (Ithaca: Cornell University Press, 1979), 28.

3. John Evelyn, *The Diary of John Evelyn*, ed. E. S. de Beer (Oxford: Clarendon Press, 1955), IV: 26.

4. John Miller, *Popery and Politics in England 1660–1688* (Cambridge: Cambridge University Press, 1973), 131.

5. John Dryden, *The Works of John Dryden*, ed. Maximillian E. Novak, vol. 13 (Berkeley: University of California Press, 1984), 215.

6. For a detailed and factual description of the broadsides and accounts of the Pope-burning pageants for these years, see Sheila Williams, "The Pope-Burning Processions of 1679, 1680, and 1681," *Journal of the Warburg and Courtauld Institutes* 21 (1958): 104–18.

7. Montague Summers, *A Bibliography of the Restoration Drama* (1934; New York: Russell & Russell, 1970), 110.

8. Elkanah Settle, *London's Defiance to Rome*, [s. l.] [s. d.] [1].

9. Sir Edmund Berry Godfrey (1621–1678) was murdered some time between 12 and 17 October 1678. Because of the Popish Plot scare, the mob immediately assumed that the Roman Catholics had killed Godfrey. The murder was never solved, though several men were hanged for it. *DNB*, vol. VIII, 31–35.

10. Tim Harris, *London Crowds in the Reign of Charles II: Propaganda and Politics from the Restoration until the Exclusion Crisis* (Cambridge: Cambridge University Press, 1987), 104.

11. Many tracts and other pamphlets published throughout the Renaissance and Restoration were designed to explain and expose what were commonly called the excesses of the Roman Catholic Church. Daniel Brevint wrote *Missale Romanum, or The Depth and Mystery of Roman Mass. Laid open and Explained, For the use of both Reformed and Un-reformed Christians*, which was printed at the Theater in Oxford, 1673. Printed in 1682 for an anonymous "Minister of the Gospell [sic]" and sold by Tho. Parkhurst was the interesting *No Popery, or A Catechism Against Popery: Wherein The Heretical Doctrins, Idolatrous Worship, and Superstitious Practices of the Roman Church Are Briefly yet Plainly Refuted, and the Protestant Principles Proved by Testimonies of Holy Scripture, and Evidence of Reason*. Various important Bishops of the Church of England also published pamphlets and sermons against the Church and its rituals—William Lloyd, Bishop of Worcester, Edward Fowler, Bishop of Gloucester, John Cosin, Bishop of Durham, Thomas Barlow, Bishop of Lincoln, to name a few.

12. O. B. Hardison, Jr., *Christian Rite and Christian Drama in the Middle Ages: Essays in the Origin and Early History of Modern Drama* (Baltimore: Johns Hopkins Press, 1965), 39.

13. What O. B. Hardison says on this point reinforces the parallels between the mass and the Pope burning: "The initial emphasis on expectation—the sense that the Messiah is coming and will soon be not only among us but united with us—is admirably calculated to express (or engage) the emotions of the participants. The congregation is immediately involved in the drama in the role of the Chosen People longing for fulfillment of prophecy. On certain feast days this role-playing is intensified by explicitly

mimetic actions: on Palm Sunday, for example, there is a formal procession with palms—identifying the congregation with the crowds who welcomed Jesus into Jerusalem—and hymns of praise echoing the Gospel accounts of his entry" (46).

14. This broadside was printed in London for Nathaniel Ponder, Jonathan Wilkins, and Samuel Lee.

15. Philip Jenkins, "Anti-Popery on the Welsh Marches in the Seventeenth Century," *The Historical Journal*, 23 (1980): 275–93. For a good description of the Pope burning at Abergaveny, see "The Popes Down=fall, at Abergaveny, or A true and perfect Relation of his being carried through the Fair in a solemn Procession with very great Ceremony. Also, How he was Burnt, with several Popish Books and Relicks lately taken out of St. *Xaverius*'s Colledge near that place," printed in London for T. C. and N. L. in 1679.

16. Narcissus Luttrell manuscript collection, All Souls' College, Oxford University, ms # CLXXI, leaf 133^r. This volume is titled in Luttrell's hand "State Affairs from Jan. 1678/9 unto Feb. 1681/0 [sic] being a Collection of News Letters many of wch contain diverse false stories, & scandalls, wch were then going in those times."

17. "The Converted Fryar: or a Defiance to the Church of Rome, As it was acted in the Pallace-Yard at Westminster on Saturday the 8th of this instant March 1672. By one of her late Sons an Eminent Capuchin, Who being happily Converted to the Protestant Religion; Did then, and there publickly Burn his Beads, Crucifixes, Agnus Dei's, Rosary, Mass. Book, Cowl, Habit, and other Popish Knacks, in Detestation of their ridiculous Idolatries," London, Published for general information by W. P. Philopratest, Printed for H. B., 1673 (probably 1672).

18. *The Coronation of Queen Elizabeth, with the Restauration of the Protestant Religion: or, The Downfal of the POPE* (London: Printed for Ben. Harris, at the Stationers Arms under the Piazza in Cornhil, 1680).

19. Summers, *A Bibliography of the Restoration Drama*, 17.

20. *The London Stage 1660–1800*, Part I: 1660-1700, ed. William Van Lennep (Carbondale: Southern Illinois University Press, 1965), 288.

21. *Rome's Follies, Or the Amourous Fryars, A Comedy* (London: Printed for N. Noxell, 1681).

22. *The London Stage*, Part I, 1660–1700, 300. Alfred Harbage, the *Annals of English Drama 975–1700* (Philadelphia, University of Pennsylvania Press, 1904) 144-45, has similar information.

23. Jerzy Limon, *Dangerous Matter: English Drama and Politics in 1623/24* (Cambridge: Cambridge University Press, 1986), 111.

24. The story of Pope Joan has been treated by several authors, among them Elkanah Settle and Emmanuel Royidis (Royidis's *Papissa Joanna* has been translated from the Greek by Lawrence Durrell). Legend has it that she was a very learned woman who, disguised as a man, rose through the hierarchy of the Church to become Pope John

VIII. She was discovered after more than two years in office when she delivered a boy child in the streets of Rome and both died. Her biography is included in Platina's *Lives of the Popes*.

POLITICAL ALLEGORY IN THE LATER PLAYS OF JOHN GAY

Janet Wolf

A year after the premiere of *The Beggar's Opera*, Arbuthnot sent a letter to Swift expressing amusement at the idea that their friend had written a play considered political dynamite.[1] "The inoffensive John Gay," he wrote, has become "the terror of ministers."[2] And Gay's reputation as a satirical writer ever since then has been mixed; he has never been considered an angry and heavy-hitting satirist like Swift and Pope. Several recent critics have downplayed the political satire in his most famous play as random and incidental. Both Robert Hume and William McIntosh have suggested that the satire in *The Beggar's Opera* is directed more against abuses in general—widespread avarice or corrupt lawyers, for example—than at specific targets in contemporary politics.[3] Very little attention has been paid to the political satire in his other works, except for a careful study by Edwin Graham of the second series of *Fables*, in an article which established that Gay was fully immersed in the topical satire of his day.[4] Graham felt, however, that the second series of *Fables* were anomalies in Gay's work, exceeding even *The Beggar's Opera* in the harshness of their political attack.[5]

This paper will establish that *The Beggar's Opera* and the second series of *Fables* are not anomalies in Gay's late work, and that in his four last plays, Gay includes attacks on Walpole that are pointed, especially in their use of politically charged language, and draw on anti-Walpole allegories in common use in the Opposition press.

Polly (1728) was banned by the Lord Chamberlain, and the prevailing opinion today is to wonder why, in spite of Lord Hervey's assessment that the sequel to *The Beggar's Opera* was "less pretty, but more abusive"[6] than the original. Even John Fuller, Gay's most recent editor, finds it more innocuous than its predecessor, and it is generally thought that Walpole was being overly sensitive when he banned it.[7]

Walpole knew exactly what he was doing. *Polly* is even more daring than *The Beggar's Opera.*

As in *The Beggar's Opera*, several characters represent Walpole in a method William Schultz calls "rotating satire."[8] One of these is Ducat, the nouveau riche planter who "buys" Polly (ostensibly as indentured servant, but in reality as a mistress), and who boasts that he has "a fine library of books that I never read" and "a fine stable of horses that I never ride...I build, I buy plate, Jewels, pictures, or anything that is valuable and curious, as your great men do, merely out of ostentation." This would immediately have reminded the audience of the extravagant display of wealth by Walpole, the Great Man, at Houghton, his accumulation of what one satire calls "pictures, palaces, and plate."[9] The scene in which Ducat buys Polly from the procuress Diana Trapes may refer to current gossip that Lady Mary Wortley Montagu had procured Maria Skerrit for him and that Maria was being paid handsomely for her services. The account in Hervey's *Memoirs* puts it plainly:

> Sir Robert Walpole at this time kept a very pretty young woman, daughter to a merchant, whose name was Skerrit, and for whom he was said to have given (besides an annual allowance) £5,000 by way of entrance money.[10]

Hervey later relates that the Queen wondered how Walpole could derive any satisfaction from the relationship knowing that it was only his money, and not his physical attractiveness, that had gained Miss Skerret's favors.[11] The same idea comes up in a 1731 anti-Walpole satire, *Sir Robert Brass; or, the Intrigues, Serious, and Amorous; of the Knight of the Blazing-Star.* The hero, Sir Bob,

> Affects to talk of his Amours,
> And boasts of having ruin'd Scores
> While all who hear him bite the Lip

And scarce with Pain their Laughter keep,
That he should think, so dull his Pate is
Threescore a Fav'rite with the Ladies
Whilst well they know 'tis golden Show'rs
Gain both his Creatures and his W———s.

Another character representing Walpole is Di Trapes herself. Trapes makes the equation between herself and a corrupt politician explicit when she rationalizes betraying Polly.

> I now and then betray and ruin an innocent girl. And what of that? Can I in conscience expect to be equally rich with those who betray and ruin provinces and countries? In troth, all their great fortunes are owing to situation; as for genius and capacity I can match them to a hair; were they in my circumstances they would act like me; were I in theirs, I should be rewarded as a most profound penetrating politician,

she maintains, and then sings

> In pimps and politicians
> The genius is the same;
> Both raise their own conditions
> On others guilt and shame.

This is more than an attack on corrupt politicians in general. The pimping politician was a common anti-Walpole slur, occurring in *The Craftsman*,[12] in Gay's own fables ("the first in favour's pimp the first"[13]), in his last ballad opera *Achilles*, and in the fourth book of *Gulliver's Travels*. Gulliver's Houyhnhnm master tells him

> He had heard indeed some curious Houyhnhnms observe, that in most herds there was a sort of ruling yahoo...who was always more deformed in body, and mischievous in disposition, than any of the rest. That this leader had usually a favourite as like himself as he could get whose employment was to drive the female yahoos to his kennel...But how far this might be applicable to our courts and favourites, and ministers of state, my master said I could best determine.[14]

The same pimps and politicians slur occurs in a scene in which three of Macheath's band of pirates are bragging about their vocations and recounting to each other the steps by which they rose to their present stations. One of the pirates, Laguerre, got his start in the world as "pimp to a man of quality." This scene is riddled with other recognizable anti-Walpole insults. "Our profession is great, brothers," says another pirate, Hacker, using that word, "great," which was always associated with Walpole, because of his corpulence as well as his power and position. Hacker made his fortune as footman to a gamester and worked at his master's profession, and the third pirate, Capstern, began as a drawer, and both cheated his master and cheated for him "as a dutiful servant." Finally, "Ambitious...of a gentleman's profession," he too became a gamester.

The scene contains barbs aimed at Walpole's ambition and his precipitous rise to success from commoner status. Walpole is variously represented in satires as a former coachman, or porter, or just "poor as church mouse."[15] All Opposition satires agree that he acquired his power, status, and wealth by dishonest means, or as one satirical ballad puts it, "By Fraud, by Rapine, or by Stealth."[16] A favorite anti-Walpole nickname was "the Gamester," or "the Norfolk Gamester,"[17] bestowed for what the Opposition perceived as his skill in "playing the game of statesmen," and in "packing the cards."[18] The servant who cheated his master and cheated for him was a common figure in anti-Walpole allegory (often, as we will see, Walpole is depicted as a corrupt steward who cheats his master and tenants alike).

The best evidence there is to counter the commonly accepted view that *Polly* is a harmless piece of generalized rather than topical satire is the fact that both Peachum and Macheath are, in *The Beggar's Opera*'s sequel, finally brought to justice. All fictional anti-Walpole allegories, whether they be lyrical dream visions like *The Dream from Mist* (1729) and Bolingbroke's *The Vision of Camilick* or raucous ballads like "B—b, Take Care Lest Your Crib be Bilk'd," exhibit wish-fulfillment in ending with the downfall of the Walpole avatar, or a prediction that the minister's time has almost come. Predicting the overthrow of the tyrant not only represents wishful thinking for the Opposition but provides not-very-subtle warnings to the minister. In *The Dream from Mist*, the man who resembles a brass statue (another Walpole nickname was Brazen or Brazen Face) with the claws of a harpy makes Britannia dance on a tightrope after stealing her treasure, but at the end of the allegory is bound and led away. *The Vision of Camilick* ends when the man with the "sneer" and "face bronzed over with a glare of confidence" runs out of money to bribe followers and falls to the ground, bereft of his power.

Tales of wicked ministers or favorites who came to bad ends were always popular; one, on Wolsey, closes with

> Attend, ye Courtiers, though with Power elate;
> Be warned by his example, shun his Fate.[19]

The Craftsman had genuine news and advertisements mixed in with Opposition satire, but one notice which was clearly not genuine advertises playing cards for children: "political cards" "Proper for New-Year's gifts to Children of Quality and Distinction,"

> describing, in beautiful and instructive prints, the terrible, tragical Ends of *wicked ministers* in all Ages and all Nations; viz *Sejanus*, the Favourite of the Emperour *Tiberius*, dragged about the streets of *Rome* as a publick Spectacle of horrour and detestation...The Earl of Strafford on a Scaffold, with his head off...The Knez Menzikoff doing Penance for his wicked and insolent Administration, in a little Hutt in the Deserts of Siberia, feeding on Bear's flesh and wild Chestnuts, etc.

The Yahoo chief minister mentioned earlier ends in disgrace that is described in terms at least as colorful:

> This favourite is hated by the whole herd, and therefore, to protect himself, keeps always near the person of his leader. He usually continues in office until a worse can be found; but the moment he is discarded, his successor, at the head of all the yahoos in the district, young and old, male and female, come in a body, and discharge their excrements upon him from head to foot.

There are numerous anti-Walpole satires that develop a hunting metaphor (probably because of Walpole's known fondness for fox hunting), and they all end with ominous warnings to the minister. In the 1731 mock-heroic *The Hunting of the Stag*, the stag warns the hero, Sir Ribbon (whose name is derived both from "Robin" and from Walpole's pride in his garter ribbon), that the stag too was once great and feared by the rest of the "herd," but now is abandoned by his followers and at bay, and the time will come when the same fate will befall Walpole; the land will rise to avenge itself against him. Swift, in his poem "On Mr. Pulteney being Put Out of the Council," represents Walpole as a hare trying vainly to escape from hounds. He flees to the underworld, only to meet Cerberus, the hound with three heads, and then tries the heavens, only to come face to face with Sirius, the dog star. Swift ends the poem by reminding Walpole that he is too fat even to *think* of escaping by fleeing to the heavens.

Because of the "Gamester" nickname, many anti-Walpole satires develop gaming metaphors, and they also end with ominous warnings. "The Norfolk Game of Cribbidge" ends, "No Gamester so long did continue in play" and "B—b, Take Care" predicts

> And soon he will be call'd upon
> His Crib be bilk'd, himself undone.

What must be among the last of the anti-Walpole ballads to compare Walpole to a sharper, written in 1742, the year of his fall, is entitled: "Bob Booty's Lost Deal, or, the Cards Shuffled Fair at Last."

Sometimes the warning is expressed in the satire's title itself; for example, a ballad, "The Statesman's Fall, or Sir Bob in the Dust," or another play which was censored, *The Fall of Mortimer*.

Peachum, of course, had been seen as a Walpole figure in *The Beggar's Opera*. At the beginning of *Polly*, Polly gives Di Trapes the news of her father's death:

> He was in too much haste to be rich. I wish all great men would take warning. 'Tis now seven months since my Papa was hang'd.

As John Loftis has said, even "the dimmest wit"[20] in the audience wouldn't have missed this allusion to Walpole. Macheath, another Walpole figure, is executed by the Indians at the end of *Polly*, and just to make sure the audience doesn't miss the point, the final chorus repeats the frequent theme of the Opposition:

> Justice long forbearing,
> Power or riches never fearing,
> Slow, yet persevering,

Hunts the villain's pace.

The idea that Justice is slow but inevitable is also found in the play's epigraph, from Horace: "Rarely does vengeance, though with halting gait, fail to overtake the guilty," and is echoed in other Opposition satires. It comes up at the close of the ballad "B—b, Take Care Lest Your Crib be Bilk'd":

For Vengeance, tho' she moves not fast,
Will catch unwary Knaves at last.

The second verse of *Polly*'s chorus is sung by the Second Indian (and I mention this only because I find the idea of all this anti-Walpole satire coming from the mouths of Caribbean Indians delightfully incongruous), and it states another Opposition theme, that when Walpole falls, even his supporters will desert him:

What tongues then defend him:
Or what hand will succour lend him?
Even his friends attend him,
To foment the chace.

A typical anti-ministerial satire reads: "After this, all the little Parasites, who were, but now, his profess'd Creatures, are loudest and most bitter in their Cry against him,"[21] and another, "At the name of your successor, those crowds that attend your levee will vanish like spirits at the dawn of day."[22]

Even Macheath obligingly helps to point the lesson, cheerfully accepting his fate. "Ambition must take its chance. If I die, I die in my vocation." This is followed by an air in which he lists other professions who run risks and take their chances—for example, the soldier. And then, interestingly, rope-dancers:

The men, who with adventrous dance,
Bound from the cord on high,
Must own they have the frequent chance:
By broken bones to die.
Since rarely then
Ambitious men
Like others lose their breath;
Like these, I hope,
They know a rope

> Is but their natural death.

Walpole is frequently associated with popular entertainments like puppet shows, magic shows, and circuses. A mock-advertisement in *The Craftsman* for June 13, 1728 announces "Signior Roberto Presto Truffarello," who will perform card tricks and magic tricks (consisting mostly of conveying the audience's money from its own pockets into his) and who has brought along a tumbler and rope dancer for his show in Westminster (see the tightrope dancing in *The Dream from Mist*). To the modern reader, a more familiar instance of the Walpole-as-acrobat allegory is the episode of the rope-dancers in *Gulliver's Travels*, with Flimnap the Treasurer, who could "cut a caper on the strait rope, at least an inch higher than any other lord in the whole empire," and who had once narrowly missed a broken neck from a fall.

Macheath's idea that the rope is a natural death for men of ambition also recurs frequently in Opposition satire. *The Norfolk Congress*, a satire on Walpole's extravagant entertainments at Houghton, ends with this prayer, a mock-blessing on the squire and his company:

> Make them hang together in Unity and A-Cord
> and let all the People say, Amen.

And a 1730s ballad ends

> Sir Robert his merit or interest to shew
> Laid down the red riband to take up the blew.
> By two strings already the knight has been tried
> But when twisted at Tyburn the third will decide.

Another theme that recurs in anti-Walpole allegories is that to show mercy to a wicked or corrupt minister is to endanger the country. "They who spare the Guilty, hurt the Innocent" says an anti-Walpole piece in *The Craftsman*.[23]

> It would be Weakness...rather than Mercy, it would be Madness rather than good Nature, to pardon the Man, who would have destroy'd our Constitution

says a character in the 1735 satirical play *Court and Country*. Macheath makes a not-very-convincing plea for mercy (he wonders why he is being denied the ordinary forms of British justice, like a routine right to bribe witnesses, judge, and jury). But the Indian King is adamant, and sends Macheath off to be hanged for the good of the country:

> Let justice then take her course...Mercy too obliges me to protect my country from such violences. Immediate death shall put a stop to your further mischiefs.

Gay claims innocently in the "Preface" that his attack is general and not specific, but it was a favorite ploy of the Opposition to accuse the Government of twisting words to find libelous meanings where none was intended. Thus, they could have it both ways: they could write satire against Walpole and simultaneously ridicule him for his paranoia in thinking that all general satire was directed against himself. If he took it personally whenever someone mentioned bribes or corruption, he must have a guilty conscience. This is a theme in some of Gay's *Fables*, and is the subject of his later satire on the suppression of *Polly*, *The Rehearsal at Goatham*. Two months after the suppression of *Polly*, a letter appeared in *The Craftsman*, ironically praising the Government's decision. It begins by accusing *The Craftsman* of unjustifiably seeing political satire in *The Beggar's Opera*.

> It cannot be denied indeed that some *general Strokes* of political Satire are scatter'd up and down in the Piece...But I believe I may defy the warmest Enemy of that *diverting Opera* to prove that the Character of MACHEATH in general was either designed by the *Author*, or understood by the *Audience*, in any other Sense than as a just Representation of a notorious Malefactor in *low Life*, till you directed their Views *higher*, and apply'd his Satire to *some Persons* in Authority.

This is, of course, perfectly absurd, since everyone, including Walpole, recognized right away that he was being attacked in *The Beggar's Opera* (there is the famous anecdote that everyone in the theatre turned toward Walpole's box to watch his reaction to the lines "When you mention vice or bribe, 'tis so pat to all the tribe, each cries that was levelled at me"). The letter writer goes on to say that he hopes to squelch unwarranted rumors about the opera's sequel. Among these are rumors that in the play "Macheath is transported, turns *Pyrate*, becomes *Treasurer* in a certain Island abroad, proves *corrupt*, and is sacrificed to the Resentment of an *injured people*." The letter writer (who signs himself "Hilarius") says this is utterly false and malicious, for Macheath is not a treasurer or in fact a public official at all. That he is executed is true, but "surely there can be no great Crime in bringing a notorious Offender to condign punishment abroad, who hath had the good Fortune to escape so long at Home." Walpole, of course, was chancellor of the Exchequer. By denying that *Polly* contains any satire against what Hilarius describes as "one of the greatest and most virtuous men in the Kingdom," he draws our attention to it, and reiterates the Opposition obsession that Walpole should be, would be punished. Fuller has pointed out that "Hilarius" is a translation of the word "gay" and thinks that Gay may have written the letter himself.[24]

The Opposition got a lot of mileage out of the suppression of *Polly*, for it helped to prove what they had been claiming all along about the Walpole administration's tyrannical disregard for freedom of expression. Among others who got involved in the hubbub that followed was Colley Cibber. He was suspected of having used his influence to block the production of *Polly* in order to ensure the success of his own *Love in a Riddle*, and the Opposition doubled its attacks on him. *The Craftsman* accused him of cutting from plays passages that might be offensive to the government, and ironically suggested that the government establish a Protestant Index of plays too dangerous to be performed.[25] Walpole did have the last laugh here, when he invoked the Licensing Act in 1737.

But as Fuller points out, the initial furor over the play's suppression couldn't have been consoling to Gay, who as a playwright wanted to see a play of his on the boards again.[26] For his next stage piece, Gay played it safe, and revived his-fifteen-year old comedy *The Wife of Bath*, in which, he wrote to Swift, he had not so much as mentioned the word corruption. His last three plays return to political satire. *The Rehearsal at Goatham* spoofs the whole *Polly* affair, and both *Achilles* and *The Distress'd Wife* have unmistakable Walpole figures. But in both of these plays, the political rhetoric tends to be clustered around these figures, who are dramatically interesting but minor characters, and one wonders if this was done so that their scenes could be easily detachable to avoid censorship. In *Polly* he had not been so careful.

The Distress'd Wife, whose exact date of composition is unknown (sometime between 1729 and 1732) and which was not staged until 1734, two years after Gay's death, deals with a termagant social climber who almost ruins her husband financially. At the end of the play, he forces her away from London to their country estate. There, it is assumed, away from the temptations of town life, she will of necessity become frugal, moderate, and rational. At the end of the first act (scene 7), the husband is warned by his tenants that his steward is robbing both him and them, and he is finally, in the last act, induced to leave London to care for his hereditary estate when he discovers that the steward has advanced his wife large sums of money.

The corrupt steward's robbing a deceived master and resentful tenants alike was a common symbol for Walpole's abuse of an innocently credulous king and angry British people. This allegory, which occurs in several early issues of *The Craftsman*,[27] is most fully developed in the anonymous pamphlet *The History of the Norfolk Steward*,[28] and is developed in a 1731 poem from Swift to Gay himself: "To Mr. Gay, On His Being Steward to the Duke of Queensbury." In this poem Swift contrasts the honest steward he knows his friend Gay will be to that other steward, the corrupt one, the "bloated minister"[29] who enriches himself at the expense of king and nation. A family-servant metaphor is also developed in Fielding's 1731 *Grub Street Opera*, which resembles slightly and may in fact have influenced Gay's play. In Fielding's play, Walpole is represented by the butler, Robin, and the King and Queen by a Welsh landowner and his wife. The husband, like Gay's husband, is oblivious to the fact that his servants are stealing him blind. Implicit in these allegories in which King, first minister, and country are compared to landowner, steward or servant, and tenants or family, respectively, is the charge that the King has neglected the hereditary estate for which he is responsible. By focusing the attack on a servant, the Opposition could attack Walpole without attacking the King directly, although they do warn the King that his irresponsibility is hurting him in the long run. Or as Swift puts it in his poem to Gay,

> The people with a sigh their taxes bring
> And cursing Bob, forget to bless the king.

A recurring theme in all anti-Walpole satires is that he has amassed great wealth at public expense, as evidenced by his palatial Norfolk mansion.[30] In *The Distress'd Wife*, Trenchwell, the farmer who brings the petition from the angry tenants, asks his master, Sir

Thomas Willit, "By what Means, think you, hath he purchased all those fine Tenements round you?" (1.7.20–23)

Another recurring theme in anti-Walpole attacks is Walpole's close relationship with Queen Caroline. Many of these satires suggest that Walpole stayed in power so long because of Caroline's protection of him. For example, the 1734 ballad "The Game of Chess Versify'd" says that the Queen's protection enables the Knight to be more powerful than the King:

> When he is guarded by the Queen,
> What dreadful Slaughter then is seen!
> And very often, horrid Thing!
> This Knight does then Check-mate the King.

The ballad, "B—b, Take Care Lest Your Crib be Bilk'd," (1734) is more bawdy in its implication of exactly what the relationship of queen and minister was:

> But when Occasion did present,
> He then would palm a Queen;

The 1734 ballad "Appius Unmask'd" sums up the perception of many—

> Most people are surprized
> At this dull 'Squire's Rise;
> And say he ne'er did merit it,
> By being over-wise.
> So, take it, Sir, for granted
> A Friend at Court had he,
> Nor mind what People call her,
> For a Friend she'll ever be.

In Fielding's *Grub Street Opera*, when Robin is told that his rival, the coachman, is about to inform against him, he responds, "I am too well with Madam to fear any mischief he can make with Master."[31] Gay had alluded to Walpole and Caroline's friendship in *The Beggar's Opera*, when Mrs. Peachum, out of gratitude, protects Bob Booty, another recognized Walpole avatar:

> What of Bob Booty, husband? I hope nothing bad hath
> betided him. You know, my dear, he's a favorite

customer of mine. 'Twas he made me a present of this ring.

In *The Distress'd Wife*, the steward appeals to the wife for help when he thinks he may be caught. At the end of the play, the husband intercepts the following letter, which confirms his decision to return to the country to look after his estate:

Madam, Your Ladyship must protect me from the Information of Trenchwell, or the Money I have advanc'd to you from time to time must all be brought to Account—In short, Madam, my Affairs are in such Confusion, that unless I receive a satisfactory Letter from your Ladyship the very next Post, I shall be oblig'd to make the best of my Way to Calais. (5.4.33–43)

Up until his last plays, Gay had been genial toward women. When he did write the kind of anti-feminist satire which seemed almost a compulsory exercise for an eighteenth-century satirist, he had been much less bitter than his contemporaries.[32] For sheer bitchiness, the wife in *The Distress'd Wife* out-Noah's wifes Noah's wife. Lady Willit is a hot tempered spendthrift gambler, who is abusive to everyone in her household, from her husband and female relatives on down to the servants. In one painfully unfunny scene, she humiliates a dependent relative, an impoverished young female cousin, by forcing her to empty her pockets while Lady Willit takes an inventory of the contents. When she finds a letter, she has no scruples about reading it. The scene is reminiscent of the pocket-searching in Book I of *Gulliver's Travels*, generally interpreted as an allegory of the 1715 Committee of Secrecy. Gay himself had his mail opened after *The Beggar's Opera*. That a political interpretation of Lady Willit's tyrannical abuse of her power is intended can be assumed from a more obvious reference later in the play to invasions of privacy under the Walpole regime. Sir Thomas notes that the letter from Survey, the steward, to Lady Willit has been opened, and wryly comments, "The Curiosity or Fears of Mankind are prodigious," and his merchant friend Barter replies, "'Tis a Grievance that is become so general, that no Particular will take it upon him to complain" (5.4.24–28).[33] The wife is fiery tempered, suggesting satirical references to George II. She is also a compulsive gambler, which may simply be one of the stock attributes of a society woman in a standard eighteenth-century misogynist portrait (see *Guardian* essays #120 and 174 and Swift's *Intelligencer* #4). But her gaming may also be intended as a poke at Walpole, "the Gamester." In short, the vicious Lady Willit may be a composite of representations of the Queen, the King, and Walpole.

If Lady Willit does represent Walpole, the satiric method is similar to the "rotating satire" in *The Beggar's Opera* and *Polly*, where a number of different characters represent Walpole. But in *The Distress'd Wife*, the most obvious Walpole representative is the steward, whom Gay surrounds with the argot in which the Opposition had couched its abuse of Walpole. One is "Great"; Farmer Humphrey encourages Trenchwell to tell Sir Willit all he knows about Survey, the steward, by saying, "Be a Rogue never so Rich and Great, 'tis the part of an Honest Man to detect him". (1.7.12) Another word associated with Walpole is "Knave," because the knave is the inevitable third member in the trinity of king, queen, and knave, and because of the Walpole-as-gamester nickname. In "The N—r——k Game of Cribbidge" (1734), Walpole's strategy is described as follows:

> Be that as it will, he did oft' play the KNAVE,
> By which many Games at a Pinch he did save

which could mean either that Walpole acted the knave, or played the knave in his hand. Humphrey goes on to say of the steward, "A Knave, before he is found out, is proud and insolent" (Walpole's insolence was also legendary, earning him the "Brazen" nickname). Another word associated with Walpole is "job" (that is, "racket") referring generally to his corrupt practices and particularly to his involvement in the South Sea Bubble and stockjobbing.[34] Stockjobbing was synonymous with fraud, and stockjobbers were regarded as worse than sharpers who cheated an individual gamester, for stockjobbers had banded together in a confederacy to cheat the entire nation.[35] One suspects, however, that the main reason the word "job" got attached to Walpole was that it rhymed so nicely with "Bob," "fob," and "rob." In the satirical poem *Verres and his Scribblers*, the Walpole figure amasses his huge fortune, consisting of "Mannors, Pictures, Palaces, and Plate,"

> By selling, quartring, palming, private jobbing
> Reversions, Places, Pensions, publick robbing.

In *The Distress'd Wife*, Trenchwell tells Sir Thomas, "He never had any Thing to transact with any one Tenant, but he had a private Job of his own." (1.7.21)

The scene in which Survey is exposed echoes the anti-Walpole steward allegories in other ways. In *A Supplement to the Norfolk Congress*, the Walpole figure is warned that the tenants might appeal to the landlord. We have seen at the close of *Polly* the recurring theme in Opposition literature that honest, true-born Englishmen have a moral obligation to get rid of the minister, and this is echoed when Humphrey encourages Trenchwell to tell Sir Thomas the truth: "'tis the part of an Honest Man to detect him." That plain hardworking farmers are the ones who expose the steward is also important, for part of the fiction of *The Craftsman* is that the authors represent country, as opposed to court interests.[36] The Craftsman of the paper's title is Walpole, the crafty man, but also poor Will Briton who is excluded from the benefits of Walpole's personal prosperity.[37]

The most obvious anti-Walpole satire occurs in this single brief scene. Although the steward is a pivotal figure in the action of the play, he never appears on stage. Was making him an important character with no lines an attempt to forestall censorship?

Other allusions to anti-Walpole rhetoric occur later in the play, in Act 4, scene 16. A lord named Courtlove is trying to help one of Lady Willit's friends seduce the honest merchant, Barter. Courtlove suggests to Barter that having connections at court might help him in his business, and that "great fortunes" have been made with the help of men in power. Barter vehemently objects to this eighteenth-century equivalent of insider trading, pointing out that such practices enrich a few at the expense of thousands, and uses the language in which the Opposition had inveighed against stockjobbing.

> 'Tis the most fraudulent, the most pernicious Gaming, under a more specious Denomination: and those who practice it, disgrace the Profession of a Merchant.

The "great fortunes" which are offered to Barter could well be a reference to the South Sea Bubble, when Walpole and the royal family were accused of using privileged information to sell out before the crash came. Barter also accuses Courtlove of setting a bad example for the lower classes, who are punished for their greed and avarice while the rich are not. The scene is a pastiche of many anti-Walpole themes: the identification of stockjobbing with gaming, the benefits to the nation of free trade ("In gaming," says Barter, "one man's gain is t'other's ruin; but commerce is for the mutual advantage of both"), the harmful potential for control by a minister of the price of stocks, the immense fortunes made and great losses suffered as a result of the South Sea Bubble, and the idea that men of rank and privilege are immune from prosecution for their misdeeds.[38]

Lady Willit's extravagance and her conviction that being in debt is *de rigeur* for people of fashion may also have political overtones, especially when Barter, in the closing lines, moralizes about her sins:

How much we hazard by superfluous cost!
In ev'ry debt some liberty is lost.
He then whose fortune and expense agree
Is wise and great; for he alone is free.

The national debt, perceived as a threat to English independence, was a major preoccupation of Opposition criticism of the Walpole ministry.[39] Criticism of extravagance and indebtedness is the first theme in Gay's *Polly*, occurring in the opening lines.

Achilles, Gay's last ballad opera, which was about to go into rehearsal at the time of Gay's death in 1732, and which was also staged posthumously, in 1733, tells the story of Achilles' stay at the court of Lycomedes, where his mother Thetis has hidden him, disguised as a girl, to escape the Trojan War. Achilles loses no time in undeceiving Deidamia, the king's daughter, about his true nature (by the time the play opens, he has already managed to get her pregnant) but he is also subjected to a rape attempt at the hands of the king, who is egged on by his minister. Any reference to a corrupt minister in the 1730s would be understood to mean Walpole, and the pimping minister or prostitute minister was also a common anti-Walpole slur, occurring, as we have seen, in *Polly*, frequently in *The Craftsman*, and in Gay's *Fables*.

As in *The Distress'd Wife*, Gay directs his attack against the minister rather than the king. King Lycomedes is culpable, but Achilles reminds him that his biggest mistake is being overly susceptible to flattery by a minister who does not have his best interests at heart, and that the king is capable of reform. As he does in *The Distress'd Wife*, Gay surrounds the Walpole avatar with the Opposition argot: "Great," "Knave," and "Screen." This last had been applied to Walpole in various forms, like "Screen-Master General" and "Bobby the Screen," since the South Sea Bubble. In Air XXI, Achilles calls the minister "the greater Knave," and in Air XXIV, Achilles sings to Lycomedes,

> How unhappy are the Great,
>   Thus begirt with servile Slaves!
> Such with Praise your Reason cheat
>   Flatt'rers are the meanest Knaves.

And after the rape attempt, Achilles predicts that the minister will "trump up a horrid Conspiracy to skreen his own infamous Practices" (2.6.3). The word trump suggests the card-playing metaphor applied to Walpole, and the word was in fact used in a 1730 satirical ballad "On Colonel Francisco, Rape-Master General of Great Britain," about Colonel Chartres, a known rapist[40] whom Walpole had saved from the gallows: "Ay, and Bobby the Screen too was put to his Trumps."

I have noted that every anti-Walpole allegory ends with the downfall of the minister. Gay's *The Distress'd Wife* and *Achilles* follow the same pattern of wishful thinking. In both plays the Walpole representative is exposed, humiliated, and turned out of office. The steward, Survey, fears that he might have to escape to France, the same fate predicted for Walpole in the ballad "Appius Unmasked":

> Now having Friends about him
> Strange Things the Knight has done;
> Which some do say he'll swing for,
> Or else to France must run.

Both plays express the themes of *The Beggar's Opera*, that "the world is all alike" and that corruption is not confined to any particular level of society but found in all classes, and that in fact the upper classes, who should be setting an example for the lower classes, are worse than the lower classes and are corrupting the rest of the nation. This too is a theme of *The Craftsman*, set out in the first issue: "as for the corruptions of servants, I can look upon them in no other light than as a natural consequence of the corruptions of those in a higher sphere." When Sir Thomas in *The Distress'd Wife* expresses surprise at the peculations of his steward,

Trenchwell remarks, "Knavery, Sir Thomas, is not confin'd to London. We are not so ignorant of the Way of the World" (1.7).

Also an important theme in *The Beggar's Opera* is that while rich and poor are all alike, only the poor are punished for their crimes. In *The Distress'd Wife*, Barter tells Courtlove, "Common Charity obliges those of your Rank to show clear and conspicuous Proofs of Honour and Disinterestedness; for whenever you are mean and mercenary, the Vulgar are hang'd for following your Example" (4.16). In *Achilles*, Achilles tells the minister who has just offered him a valuable ring in exchange for sleeping with the King, "Was you not a Man of Quality, was you not a Favourite, the World, my Lord, wou'd call you a Pimp, a Pander, a Bawd, for this very honourable Proposal of Yours" (2.1.33).

Polly, *The Distress'd Wife*, and *Achilles* are very different from each other—*Polly* is a ballad opera with domestic farce and romance, including some noble savages, *The Distress'd Wife* is a middle class comedy of manners, and *Achilles* is another ballad opera with elements of travesty and farce—but all three works demonstrate that Gay was fully involved in the political discourse of the time. He was influenced by Opposition rhetoric, and he in turn contributed to it.

Awareness that Gay was in the thick of the mudslinging directed against Walpole should lead us back to *The Beggar's Opera*, to see how often the satire there becomes particular and topical as well as general and social. It has long been recognized that at least five different characters represent Walpole (Macheath, Peachum, Lockit, Filch, and Bob Booty), and that the entire play insists that members of the government are no better than highway robbers. One wonders if there are other pointed allusions that have been overlooked. For example, negative comments about gamesters are common in the play. Are they Gay's indictment of a social vice, or are they attacks on *the* Gamester? Another example of political satire may be Peachum's complacent assumption that any crime is justified by his own self-interest, and that his interest and the public interest agree, which seems a direct echo of Opposition attacks on Walpole's smug self-satisfaction.[41]

After the suppression of *Polly*, Gay wrote an allegory of the affair, *The Rehearsal at Goatham*, in which an itinerant puppet master has his show banned because a group of narrow-minded magistrates think his play contains personal libels directed against them. Among their objections is that the first initial of the heroine's name is the last letter in the name of the town's mayor.

Any student of the topical satire of the period runs the risk of sounding like these hypersensitive magistrates. A common charge against the Walpole government was that it ferreted out political meanings where none was intended. On the other hand, this charge was a screen for the satirists, who loved to satirize Walpole while simultaneously satirizing Walpole's perfectly justified suspicion in seeing personal satire, directed against him, everywhere.[42]

Likewise, there is a fine line in this period between political, topical satire, and general, social satire. Satirists could and did take refuge in the defense that they were only attacking corruption in general, and that it was certainly not their fault if the shoe happened to fit a certain statesman. As Lockit in *The Beggar's Opera* sings, "if you mention vice or bribe, 'tis so pat to all the tribe,/Each cries, 'that was levelled at me.'" Or as Gay puts it in a Fable which appeared in *The Craftsman*[43]

> Shall not my Fable censure Vice
> Because a Knave is over-nice?

The Opposition maintained that Walpole was not only a symptom of, but also partly the cause for, the venality and corruption in the society—that he was the spring from which much of the corruption flowed, that society was what it was because of Walpole.

Perhaps Gay was more affable and congenial, less angry and bitter than Swift and Pope. But there can be no doubt that he was fully immersed in both the social *and* political satire of his day.

NOTES

1. Research on this paper was begun during a William Andrews Clark Memorial Library Fellowship, summer, 1986. The author wishes to thank Henry Goodman and Simon Varey for their assistance.

2. *Correspondence of Jonathan Swift*, ed. Harold Williams (Oxford, 1963), III: 325.

3. William A. McIntosh, "Handel, Walpole, and Gay: The Aims of *The Beggar's Opera*," *ECS* 7 (1974): 415–453; Robert D. Hume, *The Rakish Stage* (Carbondale: University of Illinois Press, 1983).

4. Edwin Graham, "John Gay's Second Series, the *Craftsman* in Fable." *Papers in Literature and Language*, 5 (1969): 17–25.

5. A more recent article by J. A. Downie, "Gay's Politics," in *John Gay and the Scriblerians* edited by Peter Lewis and Nigel Wood (London and New York: Vision Press and St. Martin's Press, 1988) takes a welcome step in the right direction by acknowledging that Gay had a political viewpoint.

6. Romney Sedgewick, ed., *Some Materials Towards Memoirs of the Reign of King George II* (London, 1931; rpt. New York: AMS Press, 1970), I: 98.

7. John Fuller, "Introduction" to *John Gay: Dramatic Works*, (Oxford, 1983), I: 53. All quotations from Gay's plays are from this edition.

8. William Eben Schultz, *Gay's Beggar's Opera* (New York: Russell and Russell, 1923), 197.

9. *Verres and his Scribblers* (London: 1732).

10. I: 86.

11. II: 421.

12. See, for example, #30.

13. References to Gay's poetry are to the edition of Vinton A. Dearing and Charles E. Beckworth (Oxford: Oxford University Press, 1974).

14. *Gulliver's Travels*, ed. Herbert Davis (Oxford: Basil Blackwell, 1965).

15. For the coachman, see *Craftsman*, #1; for the porter, *Sir Robert Brass* and "B—b, Take Care, Lest your Crib be Bilk'd"; for the churchmouse, "The N——R——K Game of Cribbidge, or, the Art of Winning All Ways."

16. "B—b, Take Care, Lest your Crib be Bilk'd."

17. A 1734 anti-Walpole ballad collection is called *The Norfolk Gamester*, with the subtitle, *Or, the Art of Managing the Whole Pack, Even King, Queen, and Jack.*

18. *Craftsman*, #231.

19. *Craftsman*, #93.

20. John Loftis, *The Politics of Drama in Augustan England* (Oxford: Clarendon Press, 1963), 97.

21. *Craftsman*, June 7, 1729.

22. *The Life of Mr. Robin Lyn* (London: 1729).

23. *Craftsman*, June 7, 1729.

24. "Cibber, The Rehearsal at Goatham, and the Suppression of Polly," *Review of English Studies* n. s. 13 (1962): 125–134.

25. *Craftsman*, March 8, 1729.

26. *"Introduction," Dramatic Works*, 57.

27. Numbers 25 (3 March, 1727) and 30 (20 March, 1727). Both of these are by Bolingbroke.

28. 1728. Later included in Volume III of the bound edition of *The Craftsman*.

29. *The Complete Poems of Jonathan Swift*, ed. Pat Rogers (New Haven and London: Yale University Press, 1983).

30. See, for example, *The Norfolk Congress.*

31. Edited by Edgar V. Roberts. Lincoln: University of Nebraska Press (Regents Restoration Drama Series).

32. See, for example, his "To a Lady on her Passion for Old China," where criticism of the woman's misplaced priorities is tempered by the poet's criticism of the rest of mankind's obsessions, and by the startling recognition of the injustice of the eighteenth-century woman's status as property in the last two lines:

>And woman's not like china sold,
>But cheaper grows in growing old.

33. Carolyn D. Williams in "The Migrant Muses: A Study of Gay's Later Drama" (in Lewis and Wood, *John Gay*) notes the political implications of this later scene.

34. See Pope's adaptation of Donne's Fourth Satire: "Who makes a Trust, or Charity, a Job,/And gets an act of Parliament to rob?"; Swift's "The Character of Sir Robert Walpole"; "A Jobber of Stocks by retailing false news"; and *Craftsman*, #9.

35. Daniel Defoe, *An Anatomy of Exchange Alley* (London: 1719).

36. Simon Varey, *Henry St. John, Viscount Bolingbroke* (Twayne: Boston, 1984), 34.

37. See the close of *The Norfolk Congress*.

38. See in particular *Craftsman* #114.

39. Isaac Kramnick, *Bolingbroke and his Circle* (Cambridge: Harvard University Press, 1968), 40–44, 70–71. See Book II of *Gulliver's Travels* and *Craftsman* ##12, 15, 19.

40. Yvonne Noble thinks that the rape scene in *Achilles* refers to the Chartres scandal ("Sex and Gender in Gay's *Achilles*," in Lewis and Wood, *John Gay*).

41. See, for example, *The Norfolk Congress*: "Who is there that doth not rejoice at the Plenty that is within his Palace? for he hath strewed Plenty over the face of the Land."

42. See *Craftsman* #18; Gay's first Fable in the Second Series; and *Crambo-Satyricon! or, a Learned Poetical Paraphrase on the Christ-Cross Row* (London: 1731).

43. Simon Varey, "John Gay: A Contribution to *The Craftsman*," *Etudes Anglaises*, T. XXIX, No. 4 (1976): 579–82.

Part III

REPRESENTATIONS

Texts, Talks, Tales

KNOWLEDGE, POWER, ALLEGORY
Swift's *Tale* and Neoclassical Literary Criticism

Neil Saccamano

As we learn in its "Preface," Swift's *A Tale of A Tub* owes its existence to the political crisis of modernity initiated by Hobbes's *Leviathan*. "[T]ossing and sporting with the *Commonwealth*" and with "all other Schemes of Religion and Government," the *Leviathan* spawned a brood of "formidable Enquirers" whose dangerous "canvasing and reasoning" the satire's modern author hopes to deflect from political institutions to his own inconsequential literary text.[1] In presenting the *Tale* as a reaction to the continuing political aftershocks of the *Leviathan*, Swift singles out Hobbes as a particularly nefarious modern writer and thereby justifies the satiric reduction of his opponent's philosophy to a theory as "empty," "noisy," and "given to Rotation" as the diversionary tale itself (40). Yet despite Hobbes's adversarial position in Swift's satire of modernity, the *Leviathan* formulates one crucial condition of right reason that Swift would also grant. "Metaphors," the *Leviathan* warns, "are like *ignis fatui*; and reasoning upon them is wandering amongst innumerable absurdities; and their end, contention, sedition, or contempt."[2] To found the science of politics, Hobbes, like the Royal scientists and empirical philosophers after him, had to be certain that his analysis would not yield merely a paper whale. A blind reasoning upon rhetorical figures would disperse knowledge into "innumerable absurdities," and the multiplicity of such empty figures would inevitably give rise to the very "sedition" political science seeks to prevent or overcome. In the *Tale*, of course, Swift dramatizes exactly this epistemological error in the specious reasoning of the modern wit and virtuoso, who unwittingly confounds the material and the spiritual, the literal and the figurative. The parody provides an immanent critique by exhibiting the failure of modern learning to meet the condition of knowledge it set itself; moderns might there confront the horrifying image of their blind reproduction of non-knowledge. And in Swift too, though it is not perhaps as immediately entailed as in Hobbes, such confusion ends with a fractious, sectarian public destroying social order.

That the failure to avoid the interference of rhetorical figures in the realm of cognition should end in a threat to public order is a historical commonplace. When Pope writes in the *Dunciad* that Dulness "sees a Mob of Metaphors advance,"[3] he merely exemplifies the tendency, pervasive in the Augustan period, to link the literary or linguistic and the social, ethical, or political. If the effect of literary disorder is popular "contempt," then Pope's figure of figures is a metonymy: multiple, mixed metaphors do not just resemble but produce mobs or, in a further turn, are produced by mobs (of commercial writers). But whether Pope's figure is exclusively metaphorical or metonymic—and these terms describe two dominant ways of relating the literary and the extraliterary: by analogy or homology, on one hand, and by reflection or causality, on the other—the problematic character of the linkage recedes before the forging of the link by the figure. Since, as Hobbes feared, figures can conceal themselves in the cognitive work they perform, the coupling of the literary and the social may come to have the self-evidence and necessity of a natural event. There can be no contingency in this relation, no chance that it may not happen; moreover, that both the literary and the extraliterary are linked *in* the literary text, *by* a linguistic operation, can present no cognitive difficulties. Yet while the problematic character of this linkage may recede, it does not disappear. Because Swift's *Tale*, in particular, also acknowledges the epistemological complications introduced by rhetorical figures, especially the difficult figure of allegory, this text encourages a more critical analysis of the commonplace Augustan alignment of the literary and the social, ethical, or political. Through an analysis of allegory in the *Tale*, then, we shall be able to assess the stakes of this alignment as it occurs not only in

Swift's satire, but in literary criticism on allegory by other Augustan or neoclassical writers.

II

The misapprehension of figures may not appear in the *Tale* to lead as immediately as in the *Leviathan* to seditious consequences because Hobbes's anxiety about reasoning becomes there, perhaps what it always was, an anxiety about reading. After all, the success of the *Tale* as a diversionary ploy depends on its ability to take the place of politics for the formidable Hobbesians and to engage them in interpreting an allegory instead of reasoning on the state. To deflect the destabilizing effects of political cabals, the "Grandees of *Church* and *State*" shrewdly employed a modern Cabbalist, one of those "*Grubaean* Sages" who always use "Types and Fables" in their art. The commissioned work rivals the productions of that ancient Cabbalist Homer—"he design'd his Work for a compleat Body of all Knowledge Human, Divine, Political, and Mechanick" (127)—and *The Hind and the Panther* of a fellow Grubaean: the *Tale* is a "faithful Abstract drawn from the Universal Body of all Arts and Sciences" (38), imbued with the "sublime Mysteries" (54) worthy of a "Divine Treatise" (124), and fully comprehensible only by "*Verè adepti*" (114) and the "devout Brother[s] of the *Rosy Cross*" (187). But this peculiar allegorical tub also carries in tow the political issues for which it acts as decoy. "Reformation of Church and State," Dryden remarked in the preface to *Religio Laici*, "has always been the ground of our Divisions in *England*";[4] yet one element of the *Tale*'s diversion consists precisely in an allegorical narrative of reformation. This shortening of the towline would not necessarily endanger the ship if, however, the satire did not also figure inquiries into the grounds of political authority as questions concerning textual authority and interpretive legitimacy. As Philip Harth has noted, the *Tale*'s allegory of reformation may be distinguished from other similar parables insofar as, in this work, "the differences between the Church of England and the Catholic Church...and those with Puritanism all turn upon the question of the proper standard of Christian belief and practice and the correct method of interpreting this standard."[5] To confirm that the textual decoy cannot contain and may even exacerbate the political threat, we need only recall that the narrator digresses on madness as the cause of "The Establishment of New Empires by Conquest; The Advance and Progress of New Schemes in Philosophy; and the contriving, as well as the propagating of New Religions," in an attempt to explain the extraordinary doctrines and practices of the Aeolists, the religious sect to which Jack's reformed interpretive procedures give rise (162). In the *Tale*, interpretation is not exempt from power relations but implicated in social struggle and political unrest.

Allegory plays a prominent role in the *Tale*, but not primarily because Swift aims simply to reaffirm the traditional literary values threatened by the progress of modernity and thus satirically "anatomizes the causes of the end of an allegorical age," as Maureen Quilligan has put it;[6] to the extent that Swift and other Augustans share certain tenets of modernity, which we will soon elaborate further, the *Tale* defends a notion of allegory based on distinctly modern formal and epistemological criteria that justify its right to survive in the modern age. Rather, allegory has prominence because the multiple commentaries that this literary mode has traditionally been presumed to sanction are figured as acts performed by socially constituted readers, disclosing or promoting their interests. The proliferation of radically diverse interpretations of an allegory raises particularly vexing epistemological questions concerning how text and commentary constitute themselves as independent entities, where the boundary between them may be located, and how the specific nature of their relation may be determined. And these questions may compel a demand for the justification or legitimation of every interpretive claim in cognitive terms. But when reading is considered a socially determined activity of readers, the epistemological problematics of allegorical interpretation carry with them a political urgency.

In response to the semantic multiplicity attributed to allegory, critics have often relied on an opposition between knowledge and power in order to specify the relation of readers to texts. Quilligan, here again, may serve as an example: the *Tale*'s allegorical satire of interpretation confirms for her the distinction between "actual" allegory and an "imposed" allegory that reduces the act of interpretation to merely the exercise of a reader's power. For Quilligan, allegorical interpretation can supply no knowledge of allegory because it confuses the meanings posited by readers with those presented by the text: "Allegories do not need *allegoresis* because the commentary, as [Northrop] Frye has noted, is already indicated by the text." Refusing or unable to acknowledge that allegories are self-contained totalities that in effect already interpret themselves, allegorical interpreters simply expound "meanings not originally intended" and suppress those manifestly communicated by allegorists.[7] With the help of such formal-intentional criteria as wordplay and personification to provide knowledge of allegory in an argument from "design" (that of the text and its author), mistakes about the meaning of an allegory become possible, but only as a consequence of the character of the reader—or, more precisely, of those other, imposing readers.

In this particular way of negotiating the epistemological difficulties of reading allegory, semantic multiplicity results solely from the apparently avoidable mistakes committed by powerful readers. But as Werner Hamacher has remarked, an explanation of allegorical polysemy that resorts to some failure or flaw of the interpreter is not the only one available: "It is one of the trivia of literary criticism that every text is open to an illimitable abundance of interpretations, applications, and reactions; but most crucially, this manifold of interpretive possibilities does not indicate a lamentable insufficiency of the interpreters that could be healed in a messianic moment; rather, it is a structural effect of the constitution of language itself that every project of literary criticism must take into account."[8] If a text cannot limit its possible meanings or unify them within a determinate field or horizon, then polysemy must be considered an irreducible linguistic effect that does not depend on the interpretive power of certain kinds of readers. In fact, a linguistic account of semantic multiplicity unsettles the ability of all readers to know the difference between knowing and forcing meaning: we cannot tell for sure what the text itself "does" (as if on its own or by its author's will), and what we "do" to it (as if on our own and against its will). When assessed in terms of the paradoxes of passivity and activity implied by this account of polysemy, the identification of reading as an act continuous with ethical or political acts becomes a metaphorical operation seeking to avert the disturbing epistemological consequences of a specifically linguistic problem.

Eighteenth-century literary and critical texts do not provide a systematic analysis of semantic multiplicity as "a structural effect of the constitution of language itself." But they do allow for just this possibility and even articulate some of its more distressing implications for literary knowledge. Swift's *Tale* broaches the epistemological difficulty, as always, with a vengeance. Perhaps its most concise formulation occurs in a passage from §X in which the modern author identifies an extravagant polysemy with allegory as the literary genre produced in the "Republic of *dark* Authors":

> For, *Night* being the universal Mother of Things, wise Philosophers hold all Writings to be *fruitful* in the Proportion they are *dark*; And therefore, the *true illuminated* (that is to say, the *Darkest* of all) have met with such numberless Commentators, whose *Scholiastick* Midwifry hath deliver'd them of Meanings, that the Authors themselves, perhaps, never conceived, and yet may very justly be allowed the Lawful Parents of them: The Words of such Writers being like Seed, which, however scattered at random, when they light upon a fruitful Ground, will multiply far beyond either the Hopes or Imagination of the Sower. (186)

Working with what could be called a paternal model of literary meaning, the narrator here challenges its categories of legitimation and demonstrates the paradoxical logic entailed in any account of polysemy that denies the pertinence of the distinction between knowledge and power. To understand the peculiar logic necessary to explain such effects as the troping of darkness as illumination in this very passage, we have to analyze the analogies closely. In the first analogy, the author-father inseminates the mother-text which, with the mediation of the midwife-commentator, gives birth to meaning. But the potential innumerability of these meanings, the possibility of their mutual incompatibility and their incoherence within a single semantic field, makes questionable any recourse to an author's seminal act of conception as the origin of linguistic effects. Authors have "never conceived" the meanings "deliver'd" of words. If linguistic production is figured in terms of human reproduction in a juridically organized society, then authors must always be pronounced the "Lawful Parents" of all textual signification. With the analogy to husbandry, however, the entire question of legitimation no longer has any bearing because it is the fertile soil that multiplies the seed in apparent indifference to the sower's design and juridical status. If the fruitfulness of words as seeds depends on the ground's fertility, then words may be scattered blindly, at random, without a unified and unifying intention, and still multiply. Writing thus becomes not the insemination but the dispersal or dissemination of meaning, and polysemy no longer indicates the imposing power of readers but discloses something essential about the constitution of language itself.

The logic of linguistic scattering is not rigorously maintained in this passage, however, because the analogies tend to figure commentary as the natural and necessary culmination of the text, as if interpretation were not as subject to the contingency of scattering as the text whose meaning it claims to deliver. As simply part of an organic process, commentary brings to fruition what was already anticipated by the text, if not by its author. When the author of the *Tale* declares that his own work will nurture various commentaries that "will be all, without the least Distortion, manifestly deduceable from the *Text*" (185), he certainly denies recourse to the notion of a reader's will to power as the violent origin of interpretive differences by insisting on the evidentiary ground of every commentary; but if words are seeds, then a text should have a determinate, limited signifying potential and should command a process of development, a history of interpretation, that moves toward its end with a certain predictability and coherence. The analogies to natural reproduction thus conflict with the contingency of commentary: reading produces a potentially illimitable number of ends which are all ascribed to the text, but the figure of generation or germination implies that texts should issue in certain, but not any and all, effects. Since the analogies assume that some immanent orientation of a text governs the unfolding of its meaning, the linguistic scattering that displaces the author as the origin of meaning is ultimately replaced by the natural continuity of fruitful commentary and textual seeds.

Despite its naturalization of literary meaning as a process of generation or germination, this passage from the *Tale* does explicitly challenge any determination of allegory that seeks its legitimation by distinguishing acts of cognition and imposition. As a result, it constitutes a threat and provokes an apprehensive editorial gloss: "Nothing is more frequent than for Commentators to force Interpretation, which the Author never meant" (186). The editorial note reinstates authorial intention as the fertile ground of textual meaning and reaffirms an ethical account of interpretive differences. Of course, nothing prevents us from reading this comment in terms of the remarks on which it comments; instead of simply manifesting the proper meaning of the satiric passage it glosses, the note can be read as the attempt to deliver a satiric meaning perhaps never conceived by the author—which would not, according to the peculiar logic of delivering meaning in that passage, make it any less (or any more) just or proper. But if we insist on taking the note to indicate Swift's understanding of allegorical interpretation in the *Tale*, then allegoresis entails for Swift an ethics of interpretation as the illicit exercise of force. Allegoresis does not suggest cognitive complications; it is merely an act of violence against the authority of authorial intention and the rule of textual evidence. And, as we have already noted, once allegorical interpretation is thus construed, it can become consonant with political activity.

The strategy of responding with force to the cognitive difficulties encountered in reading recurs throughout Swift's *Tale* and, as we shall see, in some of the more influential critical discourses on allegory during the period. The allegorical narrative of reformation in the *Tale* will allow us to describe more precisely the dynamics between an epistemology and an ethics of reading. For in this narrative the satire bases its ethical critique of interpretation on a specific formal-intentional model of a text that could give literary knowledge to those readers disposed to seek it candidly. This model is, of course, the "plain" text. As Hans Frei has explained, the philological and critical notion of the plain text was not limited to a certain kind of biblical exegesis but made possible a "*general* hermeneutics" in the eighteenth century: "No matter what the privileged, singular truth of the Bible, the meaning of the texts as such could be understood by following the rules of interpretation common to all written documents." The point of departure for understanding the Bible, merely one group of texts among others, was the assumption of the primacy of the literal sense as grammatical and intentional, not typological and providentially historical. This assumption does not expel rhetorical figures from a text, such as metaphor narratively extended to allegory; it simply demands that these figures show themselves as such and that their figured meaning be plain. The consequence of such a general hermeneutics for the Bible in particular was to render suspect its authoritative mediation of history: as documents written by individuals and in languages having their own specific histories, the Biblical texts were themselves historicized by philological criticism and were judged, instead, in terms of their own problematic referential status. At best, the Bible could "simply verify [historical events], thus affirming their autonomy and the fact that they are in principle accessible through any kind of description that can manage to be accurate." The more general consequence of this enlightened philological criticism was the suspension of belief, by the end of the century, "in layers of meaning in a single text—literal, typological, and spiritual or mystical."[9]

The plain text is a hermeneutic desideratum because, in ensuring the possibility of cognition, it would render interpretation unnecessary. Hence, in the *Tale*'s allegorical narrative of reformation as an interpretive event, the modern author must insist on this premise of legibility: the father's will "consisted wholly in certain plain, easy Directions" (190). However ironized his pronouncements elsewhere in the satire, the narrator's testimony here must be credited if reading is to provide knowledge of its object. Moreover, the legibility of the text precludes any epistemological difficulties so that the allegorical narrative of reformation as the allegory of interpretation can have an ethical plot. Since the will needs no interpretation, any allegorical reading of it can be construed as merely a forcing of meaning. In fact, interpretation as such abuses and perverts in the frame of this paradigm because the testament is claimed to be identical to its author's "will." The traditional figure of the will for the biblical texts, also employed by Dryden in *Religio Laici*, does not just stress the juridical significance of the document. Since the testament is a set of imperatives, a linguistic expression of the author's volition, interpretation—or misinterpretation, for these amount here to the same—can only be, in turn, an act of transgression. To read this testament is to know the father's commands; free to act on this knowledge, readers should respond in a morally proper way and obey the word. The "correct method of interpreting" the text, recalling Harth, is thus not to interpret it at all. As "will," the plain text eliminates the open semantic field of a linguistic utterance and endows reading with an immediacy of cognition equivalent to perception. Once a text becomes a self-evident object of knowledge, it can then supply a standard by which to determine ethically the deviance of interpretation. Hence the allegory of interpretation in the *Tale* narrates a filial rebellion: Peter apparently *knows* the meaning of the text; he willfully violates it. Of course, since Martin and Jack, despite signs of resistance, initially accede to Peter's commentary and seem to mistake his interpretive power for knowledge, the ethical plot is stalled at the very beginning—the father's will appears to the younger brothers indistinguishable from Peter's will. Nonetheless, interpretation in the narrative has not just an ethical but a theological significance to the extent that its gratuitousness is both the legacy and the repetition of the Fall, the first act of disobedience against the father's evident will.

With the possibility of cognition assured by the plain text of the will, the allegorical narrative of interpretation as a series of transgressions can unfold apparently without complication. The moments comprising this narrative are well known; I need only indicate their trajectory here. In their desire "to comply with the Modes of the World," with those "Fashions perpetually altering" (89), the brothers, led by the "Scholastick" Peter (89), perform a number of interpretive maneuvers with the text which eventually render it superfluous, merely a pretext. Peter fragments the will into scattered words, syllables, and letters; he uses philology to amend orthography; he treats testimony concerning the author's intent as authoritative commentary on the text; and, of course, he discovers what one of his brothers calls "unnatural and impertinent" meanings of terms in their "*Mythological* and *Allegorical* Sense" (88). In the end, Peter locks up the text out of sight and usurps the authority of the father: declaring himself "*Monarch of the Universe*" (115) and issuing commands in his own name, the interpreter becomes the author; the son, a father to his brothers. A schism between the brothers occurs, of course, with the recovery of the text itself, "by which [Martin and Jack] *presently saw* how grosly they had been abused" by Peter's interpretive tyranny (121; my emphasis); but they realize their previous misreading of the text only retrospectively and by re-reading this same text. Jack then opposes Peter's self-serving operations on the will with absolute fidelity to its word: he never "let slip a Syllable without Authority from thence" (191). The text itself, though, cannot prevent him from "working it into any Shape he pleased" (190). If Peter's reading of the will transgresses it out of self-interest and a will to power, Jack's similarly transgressive reading derives paradoxically from his scrupulous obedience and consequently requires a different explanation. Both brothers force interpretation, but one believes he knows and simply follows the text's directives. As in the passage on word-seeds analyzed earlier, the solution to this problem is the "Fruitfulness of [Jack's] Imagination," which blindly, unknowingly overpowers the text by "fixing Tropes and Allegories to the *Letter*, and refining what is Literal into Figure and Mystery" (189, 190). The disposition of the reader explaining such powerful interpretive effects is madness, the psychological limit of ethics, the condition wherein readers know not what they do.

Through the paradigm of the plain text, the allegorical narrative can ascribe a heterogeneous polysemy to ethical or ultimately psychological causes; but in affirming this paradigm, the *Tale* leaves suspended the question of the criteria by which the literal or figurative mode of a text could be determined with assurance instead of merely assumed to be evident. Although of the utmost urgency for understanding the dizzyingly ironic and parodic *Tale* itself, this question is suspended because, if it were explicitly posed, the *Tale* would lose its satiric victims. To consider the mistaking of commentary for text or the confusion of literal and figurative language as linguistically conditioned effects is to hinder the satiric impulse to locate blame in persons performing ethically and socially objectionable actions. Taking seriously this consideration in assessing the *Tale*, we can view Swift's satiric parody as allegorical in another sense: in dramatizing textual interpretation as if it were an avoidable use of force, the *Tale* allegorically figures epistemological problems of language in an ethical, psychological, and ultimately social and political narrative. The satire acknowledges the possibility that interpretive differences may be an inevitable linguistic effect by allegorically displacing them in an ethical account of reading. Although this allegorical displacement, itself a linguistic operation, may be equally inevitable once the literary and the social are linked, the ethical or (broadly) ideological determination of semantic multiplicity may nonetheless be read as merely figurally resolving an epistemological problem. Indeed, Jack bears the brunt of Swift's satire because he figures the very possibility of not being able to know with certainty the difference between knowing and forcing and hence the difference between text and commentary—a possibility already raised by Martin's and Jack's acquiescence in Peter's interpretive practices, well before the recovery of the text and the ensuing reformation. For such a reader, success is inseparable from failure; as Samuel Butler remarked of Jack's literary predecessor Hudibras, "His Notions fitted things so well,/That which was which he could not tell."[10] And if this doubt cannot be settled but only displaced, then madness is no longer a pathological state but an allegorical emblem of the epistemological predicament of reading.

III

Although the complicated rhetorical tactics of Swift's *Tale* render suspect its narrator's affirmation of the indisputable legibility of any text, the desire that linguistic entities be immediate objects of cognition nonetheless organizes the critical discussions of allegory by Swift's contemporaries. The plain text, as Frei remarked, is the model of a general hermeneutics encompassing all written documents. In the literary criticism of the period, one finds an insistent normative demand for "claritas" over "difficultas," as Ronald Paulson has argued,[11] a demand for the construction of literary works on an empirical model of language as merely a medium of visibility. However, this perceptual model ensures textual cognition in a curious way. If knowledge of a text is menaced by the semantic multiplicity resulting from the force of interpretation, then literary texts should themselves no longer risk reading; reading should be a mode of seeing, readers should become spectators, and texts, especially allegorical ones, should have the supposed self-evidence and formal coherence of visual objects. The Augustan or neoclassical period does not prohibit the production of allegory; it stipulates a rhetorically perspicuous form of allegory that also permits past literary works to be legitimated by enlightened literary modernity. To be sure, early eighteenth-century critics denigrated the allegories of Spenser and Ariosto, as well as the emblematic tradition of medieval and Renaissance Christian moralizing of the ancients; but they promoted an enlightened notion of allegory based primarily on personification as the most effective formal technique to manage both semantic multiplicity and the interpretive power held responsible for it.

The neoclassical strategy of legitimating allegory may be more easily specified through its treatment of the allegorical enigma. In *The Arte of English Poesie*, where duplicitous and dissembling *allegoria* is figured as "the chief ringleader and captaine of all other figures," Puttenham had reserved a place for one species of allegory under "covert and darke speaches" called enigma or riddle, "of which the sence can hardly be picked out, but by the parties owne assoile [solution]."[12] The enigma is the zero degree of allegory: it suggests or promises a meaning that it defers to some indefinite future. Not just baffling to readers, such covert speeches elicit "gealous opinions and misconstructions," as Spenser remarked to Raleigh; since these dark conceits may be "doubtfully construed," they yield diverse commentaries.[13] But, as we have already noted in the *Tale*, the "misconstructions" that Spenser seeks to avoid by declaring his intentions to Raleigh are characteristic of allegorical reading. In her discussion of the transformation of Malbecco into the allegorical personification "Gealousie," Patricia Parker has observed: "This collapse of phenomenon and meaning reveals by contrast the more devious ways of signification in Spenser's poem. Meaning too has a meantime, a gap which provides a fertile field for 'error'...'Meaning' is deferred in order to leave room for the crucial act of reading, which does not necessarily lead to a single end."[14] Of course, reading must be teleological to the extent that it seeks in meaning its own culmination and end, as "Gealousie" fills and fulfills Malbecco and thus concludes his narrative history. Since only those seeking to know could doubtfully construe, the deferral alone of meaning conditions both the allegorical narrative and the interpretive wandering of its readers. To read is to "err" (*errare*); the gap between phenomenal form and meaning makes reading possible but only as deviation from truth. And insofar as this gap is constitutive of linguistic representation, neither the figure of "Gealousie" nor any literary mode or way of signification can close it. Enigmatic allegory does not need to leave room for reading, since reading will necessarily find room for itself in the meantime, despite the forms prescribed it.

Early eighteenth-century critics, however, proscribed enigmatic allegory precisely because they considered it the literary form or rhetorical figure that deferred meaning and thereby opened a space in which the interpretive power of readers could be deployed. In identifying this dark conceit with the semantic multiplicity attending reading, these writers could hope to eliminate error or doubt by banishing it from a normative taxonomy of styles or genres based on the paradigm of perceptual cognition. "An Allegory, which is not clear, is a Riddle," John Hughes asserted in *An Essay on Allegorical Poetry*, "and the Sense of it lies at the Mercy of every fanciful Interpreter." Such "perplex'd and dark" fables, Hughes warns, will lead to the kind of commentary Francis Bacon provided on "the Heathen Mythology" in *The Wisdom of the Ancients*: "his Interpretations are often far fetch'd, and so much at random, that the Reader can have no Assurance of their Truth."[15] Formally marking the limit of textual intelligibility, the allegorical enigma comes to figure the epistemological risks of reading itself, in contrast to seeing.

Personification, on the other hand, becomes an essential formal index of allegory in neoclassical literary discourse. In an influential essay, Bertrand Bronson described the appeal of this figure: "It obviates the inconvenient necessity of an initial reading to discover significance. It anticipates and prevents doubt of intention...Where the artist's meaning—in the sense of intellectual ideas—is clear and unambiguous, and where also the focus of his attention is beyond the world of physical phenomena, he will instinctively employ the device of named abstractions in allegorical configurations."[16] In the context of the neoclassical epistemology of literary forms, however, personification seems less the "instinctive" result of a specific artistic process than a tactical maneuver: it obviates the necessity of reading, preventing "doubt of intention." This is, at least, the promise of the figure, if not what it actually accomplishes, and the reason neoclassicists turned to it in their normative evaluation of allegory. For allegorical personification makes meaning visible but only in a recognizably figurative way. Allegory, according to Addison, transcribes "Ideas out of the Intellectual World into the Material" and thus makes manifest the truths of the understanding; yet since such truths, for the enlightened critic, can never exist phenomenally, allegorical personifications are always only "Imaginary Persons," merely figures or fictions, paper persons.[17] Allegorical personifications thus constitute signals by which authors indicate the rhetorical status of their texts and direct their readers' understanding; they buttress the formal-intentional frame of literary knowledge and its attendant ethical account of polysemy. Seized upon as *gardes-fou*, personifications restrain readers from wandering in a text at the peril of losing themselves in its enigmas. As Richard Blackmore explained in his preface to *Prince Arthur*, allegory may be "well enough accommodated to the *present* Age" only to the extent that the figural mode of the text can be "presently discern'd"; and "when *Vices* and *Virtues* are introduc'd as *Persons*," the reader "sees it immediately to be an *Allegory*."[18] Through personification, then, a text can show itself in the blink of an eye to be what it is and thereby avoid the semantic errancy of reading.

In accommodating allegory as personification to the modern age and consigning enigmatic allegory to the extravagant Renaissance, neoclassical writers sought to establish their literary-historical identity in epistemological terms. Their modernity depends on this banishment of a constitutively deviant reading and the literary forms sanctioning it to a past that should not survive; as long as contemporary and accommodable older works adhere to the perceptual model of signification, readers who do not willfully or madly blind themselves could undoubtedly apprehend the text. The powerful readers held responsible for semantic multiplicity in this period thus figure the intolerable continuation of the cognitive difficulties of what should be the past. These fanciful or fruitful interpreters are anachronisms to be expelled from the present. Yet the continued need for critical vigilance and expulsion is a sign of stress in neoclassical epistemology. Like the figure of personification by which it attempts to save allegory, neoclassical literary knowledge is a promise and, as such, it only anticipates what it claims to have accomplished—the supersession of reading and its mediations.

The problems with taking literary form as an epistemological ground can be elaborated by briefly recalling neoclassical discussions of epic and allegory. One of the main aims of this formalist criticism is to distinguish clearly the rhetorical modes of these genres. But the attainment of this goal is complicated by the question whether a literal narrative—"fram'd of real or historical Persons, and probable or possible Actions," as Hughes puts it—can also convey an allegorical, figurative sense. To resolve this question, Hughes, for one, discriminates between two forms of allegory in a tripartite generic schema: first, there is the self-sufficient, historical epic of Homer, which provides only practical exempla; then, there is Virgil's similarly self-sufficient narrative of Aeneas which, however, also figuratively presents a "Parallel" political story concerning the reign of Augustus; and, finally, there is the allegory that "may more properly challenge the Name"—those "visionary and romantick" narratives that violate verisimilitude and literal or historical reference. In one respect, allegory proper seems the least problematic of these three kinds of discourses insofar as it is properly allegorical. Disentangled from archaic enigmatic allegory, this proper allegory poses no difficulties precisely because it "often assembles things of the most contrary kinds in Nature, and supposes Impossibilities" such as vices and virtues personified: in this genre, "it is impossible for the Reader to rest in the literal Sense, but he is of necessity driven to seek for another Meaning under these wild Types and Shadows."[19] Proper allegory formally "drives" the reader; if the fable does not employ personifications or otherwise make itself immediately "transparent, to shew the moral Sense," it must nonetheless deliver the "clear and intelligible" meaning it alerts the reader to seek. The "Grotesque Invention" displayed by these works constitutes the propriety of allegory because it assures the reader that the text is, in truth, an allegory.[20]

By excluding allegorical enigma as a category, Hughes can supply through this schema the formal conditions of literary knowledge and can, of course, ethically account for a reader who, like the *Tale*'s narrator, would turn "the whole Writings of Homer into an Allegory": this deceitful alchemist of an "Expositor...proceeds in his Operations like a *Rosycrucian*, and brings with him the Gold he pretends to find." But the intermediate genre of the "Parallel" suggests the irreducibility of the epistemological complications of reading. For, while Hughes insists that the figurative meaning of a narrative must be discernible—he criticizes Tasso for the belated allegorizing of his epic—Virgil "has avoided the making it plain and particular, and has thrown it off in so many Instances from a direct Application, that his Poem is perfect without it."[21] How, then, can one formally tell an epic from a parallel, if both are self-sufficient narratives with no monstrous personifications disturbing their verisimilitude and thereby signalling another sense? In his "Remarks on *Prince Arthur*," John Dennis, on the other hand, conflates epic and allegory. He supposes that "An Epick Poem is a Discourse invented with Art, to form the Manners by Instructions disguis'd under the Allegory of Action," and argues that Virgil, like all epic poets, feigned not a particular, historical action but a "general Action [only made] singular by the imposition of [proper] Names."[22] And for Blackmore, too, epic action is both verisimilar and allegorical: epic "Action must be related in an *Allegorical* manner" and must consist of a self-sufficient narrative, a literal sense, "besides another *Metaphysical* or *Typical* Sense." Affirming that "Nothing is more necessary than *Probability*," "no Rule more chastly to be observed" in allegorical epic,[23] Blackmore, like Dennis, admits the possibility that a literary text may be allegorical even without formal devices by which its double sense could be undoubtedly known.

The identification of allegory and epic in Blackmore and Dennis and the unannounced parallel of literal and allegorical sense in Hughes are symptomatic of the failure of a taxonomy of literary forms to supply the conditions necessary to distinguish knowledgeable from powerful readers. The suspension of textual knowledge—in the meantime of reading—continually recurs, and it affects even the supposedly most immediately obvious figure of allegorical personification. Although Dennis's definition of epic in effect repudiates the possibility of literal or historical reference, it suggests that the status of personifications cannot be assured. If heroic agents are only "Poetical Persons, to which Particular Names are assign'd," remaining "at the bottom Universal and Allegorical,"[24] then every proper name in an epic is already a personification. It was to prevent such indistinction that Addison, whom Hughes followed, sought to restrict personification in epic and to define it as the peculiar mark of an allegorical mode of writing that could be accommodated to the present age. "Emblematic Persons," he writes in "The Pleasures of the Imagination," properly belong to a kind of poetry that does not copy nature but makes "new Worlds of its own." Since these imaginary beings violate the rule of probability essential to epic, they must never become agents in its narrative. As he had previously explained in his famous remarks on Sin and Death in Milton, personifications are permissible in epic only as clearly recognizable poetic similitudes—"in short Expressions, which convey an ordinary Thought to the Mind in the most pleasing manner, and may rather be looked upon as Poetical Phrases than allegorical Descriptions."[25] These "short Allegories" may be included in epic because:

> It is plain that...[they] are not designed to be taken in the litteral Sense, but only to convey particular Circumstances to the Reader after an unusual and entertaining Manner. But when Such Persons are introduced as principal Actors, and engaged in a Series of Adventures, they take too much upon them and are by no means proper for an Heroic Poem, which ought to appear credible in its principal Parts.[26]

Yet despite Addison's stress on narrative credibility as the reason for prohibiting personifications from becoming "Actors," what worries him is that these allegories not "designed to be taken in the litteral Sense" may in fact be mistaken by (other) readers for actual persons. Personifications are inappropriate in epic less because they violate probability than because they may be granted literal, historical referents in accordance with the probability of the action. Instead of confirming the distinction between literal and figurative modes of signification, personifications, as Steven Knapp has also argued, can "spread, as if by contagion, to other, ostensibly more 'literal' agents."[27] Thus Addison's preference for what Patricia Spacks calls "*controlled* personifications"[28] in epic indicates the critical need to prevent the "error" of reading by restraining the movements of these figures. For such mobility threatens to confound not just metaphors of persons in a text with the persons who read the text, but also historical narrative with fictional narrative. Yet the text itself cannot establish or maintain this division, as Addison's remarks on Homer suggest. While Homer's "allegorical Persons" might be allegorical or figurative to enlightened Christians, the Greeks themselves were "Heathens" who superstitiously mistook these poetic persons for "real Deit[ies]."[29] If the rhetorical mode of persons in a text cannot be guaranteed, then modern Christians remain susceptible to the mistakes attributed to heathens, and, consequently, lose the epistemological foundation of their historical identity. Perhaps the past has not yet passed but lives on in the age of enlightened literary modernity.

IV

Superstitious Greeks, Rosicrucian expositors, lunatic modern authors, tyrannical Catholic exegetes, deluded Puritan zealots—such is the diverse but still select list of those other, imposing readers possessing or possessed by "converting Imaginations" on whom early eighteenth-century writers inevitably fixed responsibility for the failure of a literary text to say unequivocally what it means and to show immediately what it is. The continued proliferation of commentaries indicates the irrepressible persistence of semantic multiplicity, despite the attempt to confine it to a style or genre, to an enigmatic kind of allegory, and then banish such unenlightened literary forms to the past. In the dispersal of a text into potentially innumerable meanings, neoclassicists were confronted with the possible error of all commentary and thus with a challenge to literary knowledge; these other readers are the horrifying doubles of their own possible non-knowledge and perhaps their ignorance of this non-knowledge itself. The ethical and, at the limit, psychological account of reading as an interpretive act merely displaces the epistemological difficulties posed by literary texts and justifies the exclusion of those powerful interpreters as a way of instituting or confirming a legitimate community of readers. Knowledge falters only when jostled, never because literary texts might constitute epistemologically unstable ground.

Yet, for all their antagonism in neoclassical discourse, knowledge and power stay in touch. As I have tried to show, while Augustans or neoclassicists account for allegorical polysemy by distinguishing knowledge from imaginative power, literary texts never prevent their own abusive manipulation by readers; in fact, they disturb the assurance of readers who claim to know the difference between cognition and imposition. Moreover, imposed allegory has the scandalous ability to pass successfully for knowledge of a text with other readers and, in the limit case of madness, with the allegorical interpreters themselves, who know not what they do—"A strong Delusion always operating from *without*, as vigorously as from *within*" (171), according to the *Tale*. The possibility that allegoresis might impose on readers by simulating allegory—a possibility which is necessary to explain formally the acceptance of diverse commentaries and a history of interpretation—also points to the force that knowledge is expected to exercise. Since reading or reasoning upon rhetorical figures is believed to entail social consequences, knowledge cannot be without power. Knowledge should have the power to eliminate or halt the forcible production of multiple meanings by imposing readers. Like delusion, its double, knowledge has to operate as vigorously without as within the reader: it should, in this period, maintain public order. Although the ability to see the evident rhetorical status of a text might save readers from becoming Rosicrucians who bring with them the goods they pretend to find, the findings of knowledgeable readers will nonetheless obey a moral or political imperative.

Dryden's defense of Roman Catholic hermeneutics in *The Hind and the Panther* provides one instance of a politics of reading based on the strict social determination of interpretive acts. Since in this account reading always performs, however deliberately or delusively, some social function or dysfunction, the challenge to knowledge posed by the semantic multiplicity of the Bible entails a loss of disciplinary or regulatory power. Rejecting the model of the plain text, Dryden concedes that readers of the Bible cannot see what they should see because the entire text is, in effect, an enigmatic allegory: "And what one Saint has said of Paul,/*He darkly writ*, is true apply'd to all."[30] Although he wavers in his explanation, Dryden for the most part attributes the genesis of diverse commentaries and interpretive communities not to the transgressive acts of interested readers but, rather, to the rhetorical character of language which the text can by no means limit or exclude: "As long as words a diff'rent sense will bear,/...The word's a weathercock for ev'ry wind" and hence "The most in pow'r supplies the present gale."[31] This assertion that textual meaning is conditioned by the troping or turning of the "weathercock" word denies the possibility of distinguishing cognition from imposition, yet it does so by turning all meaning into the effect of an impositional act. Dryden suffers no anxiety because he can affirm his knowledge that knowledge of the text is posited and therefore impossible: all meaning is interested, the ideological effect of "the most in pow'r" or those aspiring to greater power. Since the epistemology of reading had been all along in the service of ethics and politics, Dryden resolves the problem of semantic multiplicity by relying, in Hobbesian fashion, on the arbitrary authority of a sovereign power instituted to quell contention—the "pow'r supreme,"[32] of the Pope and his Councils, to which all interpreters should submit for pragmatic reasons. With literary knowledge definitively out of the question, the social determination of the literary requires in this case that some ethical imperative or politically correct goal constitute the motive and standard of interpretive practice.

By affirming, in contrast, the formal and intentional criteria of textual meaning, Swift and the neoclassical writers on allegory (as well as the Dryden of *Religio Laici*) face a dilemma. While the possibility of literary knowledge should still confirm ethical or political principles, readers must only find, not force, this confirmation. The possibility of knowledge may well depend on the prior disposition or ethos of readers (for Augustans, their candor or common sense), but this ethical condition of reading should not thoroughly determine knowledge itself. Reading should of itself, disinterestedly, serve practical ends. Its potential regulatory effects must not become ends for the sake of which reading takes place; such an instrumental or prejudicial notion of reading would once more reduce knowledge to a stratagem of power, thereby precipitating the institution of some supreme power to adjudicate equally grounded or ungrounded interpretive claims. The truth of both text and commentary should have as immediate and necessary a force as reason does among the Houyhnhnms: "Neither is *Reason* among them a Point problematical as with us, where Men can argue with Plausibility both Sides of a Question; but strikes you with immediate conviction; as it must needs do where it is not mingled, obscured, or discoloured by Passion and Interest." It is this force of knowledge on which Gulliver relies when he says the truth of his *Travels* "immediately strikes every Reader with Conviction" and will initiate a moral reformation among the Yahoos.[33] Of course, it is also precisely the possible ironic, figurative sense of the apparently mad Gulliver's utterances that indicates the problematical character of reason "with us" and suspends both the cognitive foundation of reading and the unforced force of knowledge that should simultaneously expose and overpower the imposing force of interest or passion.

V

The allegorist, according to Walter Benjamin, by no means avoids "that arbitrariness which is the most dramatic manifestation of the power of knowledge." "Any person, any object, any relationship can mean absolutely anything else" because, for the allegorist, an entity is "incapable of emanating any meaning or significance of its own; such significance as it has, it acquires from the allegorist."³⁴ Detached and unelaborated as they must be here, Benjamin's remarks nonetheless stress the need to consider allegorical writing and reading in terms of the interplay between power and knowledge. For Benjamin, the secularizing impulse of modernity defers any absolute instance of meaning to another time and place, leaving behind a disparate collocation of mere objects (including letters, syllables, words and the persons deploying them) whose existence, devoted to death, is a matter of indifference. But it is because spirit does not live in the natural world—and allegorical personifications, for Benjamin, attest to the non-immanence of spirit—that knowledge of that world becomes possible. Only on the condition that entities emanate no meaning of their own can they be given a conventionally constituted meaning by the allegorist. Knowledge thus becomes inseparable from an act of power that bestows meaning on dead objects, and yet this knowledge also knows its own arbitrary, impositional character; the allegorical knowledge of knowledge as power cannot avoid the arbitrariness of its self-reflection, the contingency of its self-reference.

Aiming in effect to limit contingency, the distinction between allegory and allegoresis is symptomatic of a modern or enlightened conflictual response to power. Rosemond Tuve, from whom Maureen Quilligan takes this distinction, betrays such conflict in a comment on one interested or deluded allegorical reader: "Who would forbid Paul his allegory of Hagar, or Jerusalem, 'the mother of us all' in Galatians 4, because Genesis knew nothing of the second covenant?" Tuve herself, of course, should "forbid" Paul's allegorizing transgression and appropriation of the Judaic text: "The intelligence revolts from the idea that great writings have no life of their own but must eternally...be killed and offered up as sacrifices to conceptions and values currently attractive, then with difficulty brought back to life, to be re-sacrificed to another reigning notion of the profound and the significant."³⁵ In narrating the history of allegorical interpretation as a series of gruesome acts of sacrificial violence performed by the highpriests of those "Fashions perpetually altering" (in Swift's phrase), this passage hopes to manage semantic multiplicity by dramatizing an ethical struggle of enlightened culture against the forces of barbarism. The horror or revulsion at such "killing" wards off the knowledge of knowledge as power that Benjamin unsentimentally emphasized when he asserted that "Criticism means the mortification of the works";³⁶ yet the horrifying spectacle of sacrifice itself suggests a violent response to those other mortifying interpreters. Perhaps by acknowledging the problematic entanglement of knowledge and power can critics forestall the scenarios of polarization, debasement, and exclusion staged to legitimate a community of enlightened readers of allegory.

NOTES

1. Jonathan Swift, *A Tale of a Tub*, ed. A.C. Guthkelch and D. Nichol Smith (Oxford: Clarendon Press, 1958), 40, 39. All citations of the *Tale* are from this edition and, hereafter, will be included in the body of my text.

2. Thomas Hobbes, *Leviathan*, ed. C.B. Macpherson (Hammondsworth: Penguin Books, 1968), 116–17.

3. Alexander Pope, *The Dunciad*, in *The Poems of Alexander Pope*, ed. John Butt (New Haven: Yale University Press, 1963), I: 67.

4. John Dryden, *Religio Laici*, in *The Poems and Fables of John Dryden*, ed. James Kinsley (Oxford: Oxford University Press, 1970), 281.

5. Philip Harth, *Swift and Anglican Rationalism: The Religious Background of "A Tale of a Tub"* (Chicago: University of Chicago Press, 1961), 19.

6. Maureen Quilligan, *The Language of Allegory: Defining the Genre* (Ithaca: Cornell University Press, 1979), 137.

7. Quilligan, *Language of Allegory*, 30, 31.

8. Werner Hamacher, "LECTIO: de Man's Imperative," tr. Susan Bernstein, in *Reading de Man Reading*, ed. Lindsay Waters and Wlad Godzich (Minneapolis: University of Minnesota Press, 1989), 189.

9. Hans Frei, *The Eclipse of Biblical Narrative: A Study of Eighteenth and Nineteenth Century Hermeneutics* (New Haven: Yale University Press, 1974), 55–56, 4. See Everett Zimmerman's *Swift's Narrative Satires: Author and Authority* (Ithaca: Cornell University Press, 1983), 41–50, for a useful discussion, following Frei, of the new philological-critical hermeneutics in relation to the *Tale*. See also Jay Arnold Levine's "The Design of *A Tale of a Tub* (with a Digression on a Mad Modern Critic)," *ELH* 33 (1966): 198–227, for Swift's anti-critical position and his attack on Richard Bentley, and Ronald Paulson's *Theme and Structure in Swift's Tale of a Tub* (New Haven: Yale University Press, 1960), for Swift's satire of Bentley's historical analysis of language.

10. Samuel Butler, *Hudibras*, ed. John Wilders (Oxford: Clarendon Press, 1967), I: 1: 139–40.

11. Ronald Paulson, *Emblem and Expression: Meaning in English Art of the Eighteenth Century* (Cambridge: Harvard University Press, 1975), 48–57.

12. George Puttenham, *The Arte of English Poesie* (Kent, Ohio: Kent State University Press, 1970), 197, 198.

13. Edmund Spenser, *Poetical Works*, ed. J.C. Smith and E. De Selincourt (London: Oxford University Press, 1965), 407.

14. Patricia A. Parker, *Inescapable Romance: Studies in the Poetics of a Mode* (Princeton: Princeton University Press, 1979), 99.

15. John Hughes, *An Essay on Allegorical Poetry*, in *Critical Essays of the Eighteenth Century, 1700–1725*, ed. W.H. Durham (New Haven: Yale University Press, 1915), 101.

16. Bertrand H. Bronson, "Personification Reconsidered," *ELH* 14 (1947): 169.

17. Joseph Addison, *The Spectator*, ed. Donald F. Bond, 5 vols. (Oxford: Clarendon Press, 1965), 3: 577, 573.

18. Richard Blackmore, "Preface to *Prince Arthur*," in *Critical Essays of the Seventeenth Century, 1685–1700*, ed. J. E. Spingarn, 3 vols. (Oxford: Clarendon Press, 1908–1909), 3: 238.

19. Hughes, *Allegorical Poetry*, 91–92.

20. Hughes, *Allegorical Poetry*, 94, 100, 92.

21. Hughes, *Allegorical Poetry*, 101–2, 92.

22. John Dennis, *The Critical Works*, ed. Edward Niles Hooker, 2 vols. (Baltimore: Johns Hopkins Press, 1939–43), I :55, 57.

23. Blackmore, "Preface to *Prince Arthur*," III: 237, 238.

24. John Dennis, *The Critical Works*, I: 58.

25. Addison, *Spectator*, IV: 573; III: 337.

26. Addison, *Spectator*, III: 338.

27. Steven Knapp, *Personification and the Sublime: Milton to Coleridge* (Cambridge: Harvard University Press, 1985), 59.

28. Patricia Meyer Spacks, *The Insistence of Horror: Aspects of the Supernatural in Eighteenth-Century Poetry* (Cambridge: Harvard University Press, 1962), 135.

29. Addison, *Spectator*, III: 337.

30. John Dryden, *The Hind and the Panther*, in *The Poems and Fables*, II: 344–45.

31. Dryden, *The Hind and the Panther*, I: 462–67.

32. Dryden, *The Hind and the Panther*, II: 102.

33. Swift, *The Prose Works*, ed. Herbert Davis, 14 vols. (Oxford: Basil Blackwell, 1939–1968), XI: 267, 8.

34. Walter Benjamin, *The Origin of German Tragic Drama*, tr. John Osborne (London: NLB, 1977), 184, 175, 184.

35. Rosemond Tuve, *Allegorical Imagery: Some Medieval Books and Their Posterity* (Princeton: Princeton University Press, 1966), 220, 221.

36. Benjamin, *German Tragic Drama*, 182.

THE VISIONARY SCENE
Vision and Allegory in the Poetry of Pope

Dustin Griffin

As Pope's career began in the first decade of the eighteenth century, there seems to have been something of a minor fashion among poetasters of the day for poems cast in the form of allegorical visions or prophetic dreams, poems such as *The Vision, or a Prospect of Death, Heav'n, and Hell. With a Description of the Resurrection and the Day of Judgment* (1702), *The Vision, An Allegorical Dream* (1705), and *The Vision of Mons. Chamillard Concerning the Battle of Ramilies* (1706). Defoe, interested in the supernatural and always on the lookout for literary opportunity, capitalized on the fashion in his *Vision* (1706). In the same year Thomas Neale gave the subtitle *The Vision* to an imitation of the prophecy of Rome's future greatness in the sixth book of the *Aeneid*—a prophecy that Pope himself later imitated. Whether Pope knew these poems is uncertain, but he clearly knew the mode, and in particular knew and imitated Elizabeth Rowe's *The Vision* (1704).[1] The "vision" remained a part of the available literary vocabulary, appearing frequently in the *Spectator* papers and even as late as Johnson's mid-century *Vision of Theodore*.[2]

Pope himself was evidently drawn to the mode, especially in the years 1711 to 1715, when he wrote *The Temple of Fame*, *Messiah*, *Windsor Forest*, and *The Rape of the Lock*. In a note to the *Temple of Fame* (subtitled "A Vision"), he makes clear what he meant by "visionary" poetry:

> A strict Verisimilitude is not requir'd in the Descriptions of this visionary and allegorical kind of Poetry, which admits of every wild Object that Fancy may present in a Dream, and where it is sufficient if a moral Meaning atone for the Improbability.[3]

The *Temple* is written, he observed in the prefatory note, "in the manner of the Provencal Poets, whose works were for the most part Visions, or pieces of Imagination, and constantly descriptive." "Vision" for Pope combines "imagination"—something seen by means of fancy or dream—and what he would later call "pure Description" (*Epistle to Arbuthnot*, 148)—a strong pictorial element. He told Joseph Spence that he had once had "some thoughts of writing a Persian Fable; in which I should have given a full loose to description and imagination."[4] In these same early years he was also reading and translating Homer. We may speculate that the young Pope, steeped in the *Iliad* and *Odyssey,* was drawn by the oracles, prophets, and frequent visionary appearances of the gods to the Greek heroes—he regularly used the words "vision" and "visionary" to describe such appearances in the Homeric translations—and sought to create a modern equivalent for that larger antique world.

Although it is a critical commonplace (originating with the poet himself) that Pope's poetical career may be divided into two parts, a "Romantic" phase up to about 1717 ("fancy's maze"), followed by a "satiric" phase in which the poet "stoop'd to Truth," it is my argument that Pope remained interested in poetic "visions" throughout his career, and that he may appropriately be thought of as a "visionary" poet, in some precise ways that we have not yet adequately recognized.[5]

It is understandable why we have not looked for a "visionary" side of Pope's work. The major reason, perhaps, is that (despite our very high current estimate of his importance) we have focused narrowly on his achievement in satiric and didactic forms, and have disregarded some major areas of his work, and in particular those areas—like the heroic—in which he was carrying on an older tradition. Second, we generally assume that "visionary" poets belong to the next age. "Visionary" is an epithet we routinely apply not to Augustan but to Romantic poets, where it has become something of a cliche. To redirect attention to a visionary element in Pope is not to install him as a pre-Romantic member of the "visionary company." Pope is "visionary" in a different sense. The Romantic poet, as M. H. Abrams usefully summarizes, typically makes a distinction between "optical" and "imaginative" seeing, between the "outward" and the "inner" eye. The inner eye, in Romantic poetry, sees unity rather than fragments, sees inner forms rather than outward shapes. To see the world with the inner eye of what Blake calls "Vision" is to create a new earth and new heaven.[6] By contrast, Pope inherited a taste for dream vision and allegory (derived from a reading of medieval poetry). He neither makes a firm distinction between inner and outer eye, nor claims that the visionary poet's "new world" is always higher in ontological status or value.[7] Indeed, he sometimes presents that "world" as frankly unreal, the product of a playful or even a diseased imagination. Third, if we look for visionaries in the eighteenth century, we have tended to turn toward the poets of the mid- and late-eighteenth century. Patricia Meyer Spacks's influential *The Poetry of Vision* (1961) taught a generation of readers to think of Thomson, Collins, Gray, Smart, and Cowper as the century's poets of prophetic, allegorical, and emblematical "vision."[8] To look for a "visionary" side to Pope might help us see why Pope remained of great interest to the poets of mid-century who set out deliberately to explore an "unreal scene" of "visions wild." Although we ordinarily think of Collins as a poet who gave a looser rein to his fancy than did Pope, he may be a more Popean poet than we have considered. He may have found in Pope a model not only for his own early eclogues and epistles, and the delicate atmosphere of his elegies, but for his allegorical odes themselves.

II

Pope's interest in poetic "visions"—his sense of both their power and their danger—can perhaps be traced back to his own accounts of how his poems took their *origin* in moments of intense "vision." The young Pope left a number of suggestive remarks about the nature of his own creative process, particularly during the years of his first great poetic achievement, 1712–1714, when he published *Messiah*, *The Rape of the Lock*, and *Windsor Forest*, and began working on his translation of Homer. Of his modern interpreters, Maynard Mack has most effectively pointed the way here. He twice cites a 1712 letter in which Pope describes his profound creative withdrawals from the quotidian world:

> Like a witch, whose carcase lies motionless on the floor, while she keeps her airy sabbaths, and enjoys a thousand imaginary entertainments abroad, in this world, and in others, I seem to sleep in the midst of the hurry, even as you would swear a top stands still, when 'tis in the whirl of its giddy motion. 'Tis no figure, but a serious truth when I say that my days and nights are so much alike, so equally insensible of any moving power but fancy, that I have sometimes spoke of things in our family as truths and real accidents, which I only dreamt of; and again when some things that actually happened came into my head, have thought (till I enquired) that I had only dreamt of them.[9]

Two years later, while working on the Homer translation, Pope writes of "withdrawing his thoughts as far as he can, from all the present world, its customs and its manners, to be fully possessed and absorbed in the past."[10] About the same time he speaks of the disciplined passivity that precedes inspiration: "I have been lying in wait for my own imagination this week and more, and watching what thoughts of mine come up in the whirl of fancy."[11]

In a state which Pope calls "Reverie,"[12] the poet at work, moved only by "fancy," envisages another world in imagination and then attempts to capture it in words:

> We grasp some more beautifull Idea in our Brain, than our Endeavours to express it can set to the view of others; and still do but labour to fall short of our first Imagination. The gay Colouring which Fancy gave to our Design at the first transient Glance we had of it, goes off in the Execution; like those various figures in the gilded Clouds, which while we gaze long upon, to separate the Parts of each imaginary Image, the whole faints before the Eye, & decays into Confusion.[13]

The fading of the bright vision merges, in the mind of the verbal artificer, with the fading of a painter's materials, or the decay of a poet's very medium. The familiar passage in the *Essay on Criticism*, "and such as *Chaucer* was, shall *Dryden* be" (483), though primarily a lament about the impermanent nature of the "failing" English language, seems mixed in Pope's mind with that other fading of the poet's "beautifull Idea":

> So when the faithful *Pencil* has design'd
> Some *bright Idea* of the Master's Mind,
> Where a *new World* leaps out at his Command,
> And ready Nature waits upon his Hand;
> When the ripe Colours *soften* and *unite*,
> And sweetly *melt* into just Shade and Light,
> When mellowing Years their full Perfection give,
> And each Bold figure just begins to Live;
> The *treach'rous Colours* the fair Art betray,
> And all the bright Creation fades away!
>   *(Essay on Criticism,* 484-93)

Like the rapt sibyl who at length falls from her trance, or Miss Blount, whose "vision" of London "sceptres, coronets, and balls" vanishes, and leaves her in "lone woods, or empty walls" *(Epistle to Miss Blount, on her Leaving the Town, after the Coronation),* the poet suffers an inevitable lapse from imagination to reality.

The traditional figure for that apparently eternal prompting of vision is the muse, and as Maynard Mack long ago pointed out, Pope "never discarded the Muse, either the conception or the term."[14] The muse appears throughout Pope's career, from his earliest pieces of "pure description" to his latest pieces of satiric "sense." In the light of Pope's remarks about the inspiring power of "fancy," we should perhaps not take as mere convention his repeated invocations and celebrations:

> Ye sacred Nine! that all my Soul possess,
> Whose Raptures fire me, and whose Visions bless.
>   *(Windsor Forest,* 259-60)[15]

The muses are the source of the poet's "visions." Their "Rapture" and "Fire" become for Pope synonyms of the poet's *vivida vis.* The young poet who would imitate the mighty dead hopes to catch "some Spark of your Celestial Fire" *(Essay on Criticism,* 195). When he reads a great writer like Homer he catches something of the "fire" and the "rapture" that animated him.[16] "Fire" is an essential attribute of every great poet.[17] But Pope is aware that poetic "fire" is no guarantee of poetic merit. It can also animate dullards to produce bad poetry. With "Fire in each eye, and Papers in each hand," bad poets swarm raving over the landscape *(Epistle to Arbuthnot,* 5). The sight of Dulness' past and future, says Father

Settle to the sleeping Cibber, will "fire thy brain" (*Dunciad* III: 66). The trance-like reverie that characterizes the moment of creation can likewise be grotesquely parodied by the droning dunce:

> Still humming on, their drowzy Course they keep
> And lash'd so long, like Tops, are lash'd asleep.
> False Steps but help them to renew the Race,
> As after Stumbling, Jades will mend their Pace.
> What Crouds of these, impenitently bold,
> In Sounds and jingling Syllables grown old,
> Still run on Poets in a raging Vein,
> Ev'n to the Dregs and Squeezings of the Brain;
> Strain out the last, dull droppings of their Sense,
> And Rhyme with all the Rage of Impotence!
> *(Essay on Criticism, 600–609)*

To describe the dull poet Pope uses precisely the same figure—the sleeping top—that he used eighteen months later to describe his own creative rapture. But the dunce's reverie needs to be forcibly prolonged. The creative flow has become constipated (like the later poet who "strains from hard-bound brains eight lines a year"—*Epistle to Arbuthnot*, 182). "The Rage of Impotence" looks ahead to another bad poet, Bays (or Cibber) in the *Dunciad* who sinks into his own miscreating brain:

> Sinking from thought to thought, a vast profound,
> Plung'd for his sense, but found no bottom there,
> Yet wrote and flounder'd on, in mere despair,
> Round him much embryo, much abortion lay,
> Much future Ode, and abdicated Play;
> Nonsense precipitate, like running Lead,
> That slip'd thro' Cracks and Zigzags of the Head;
> All that on Folly Frenzy could beget,
> Fruits of dull Heat, and Sooterkins of Wit.
> (I: 18–26)

If we recall Pope's description of his own apparently effortless and motionless reverie, we see that Cibber's failing is not that his brain is overheated but that it is not heated enough ("dull Heat"), not that he presumes to be "inspired," but that he writes in the absence of inspiration.

The Visionary Scene

Elsewhere in the *Dunciad*, however, Cibber errs in the other extreme, and illustrates another misuse of the trance that produces visionary poetry. As Cibber lies asleep on Dulness' lap, he is curtained with "Vapors blue" and sprinkled with "Cimmerian dew":

> Then raptures high the seat of Sense o'erflow,
> Which only heads refin'd from Reason know,
> Hence, from the straw where Bedlam's Prophet nods,
> He hears loud Oracles, and talks with Gods:
> Hence the Fool's Paradise, the Statesman's Scheme,
> The air-built Castle, and the golden Dream,
> The Maid's romantic wish, the Chemist's flame,
> And Poet's Vision of eternal Fame.
>   (III: 5–13)

The passage is primarily designed to suggest that Cibber is a brainless lunatic, visited by delusions which he mistakes for oracles, His "Raptures" only measure his distance from "Sense" and "Reason." His "Vision," as Pope note says, is thus intimated to be "no more than the chimera of a dreamer's brain" (III: 5–6n). More deeply, I think, the passage serves as a reminder of the dangers of poetic rapture. There is no functional difference between Cibber's dream and Pope's creative submission to the power of fancy. The apparently anomalous line about the "Poet's Vision of eternal Fame" suggests that Cibber's dream is in fact not utterly different from the dream of all poets. Though Pope's note pretends that his "Vision" must be false "and not a real or intended satyr on the present Age, doubtless more learned, more enlightened, and more abounding with great Genius's...than all the preceding," it is in fact at least partly true. The passage is not proof of Pope's rationalistic suspicion of rapture, enthusiasm, inspiration,[18] and vision, or evidence that he prefers a poetic based on sense and reason. It serves rather as Pope's recognition of the irrational element in poetic creation, and the risks he runs as he attends the visitation of his muse.

III

If inspiration came to Pope in a "whirl of fancy," he sought ways (particularly in his early career) to indulge and preserve the visions of fancy. Again he was aware of the risks involved. It was only too easy, Pope must have known, to write an allegorical vision. A poet need do no more than set the scene and introduce a figure who promptly falls asleep or is visited by a "vision." If visions are so readily and so mechanically manufactured, then readers are not likely to take them seriously. Another risk is that, like any poet who wanders too long "in Fancy's maze," the visionary may lose all touch with "truth." It is with a sense that allegorical poetry needs a defense before the best contemporary judges that Pope wrote the prefatory note to *The Temple of Fame*, subtitled "A Vision," his first major poem in the mode.

Pope's primary means to make *The Temple of Fame* acceptable to a polite modern audience is to keep the allegory clear and to restrain his invention from indulging in irrelevant or fantastic details.[19] Although the poem appeals to our visual sense, it is primarily, as Pope notes, an "Intellectual Scene" (to be apprehended, that is by the intellect) in three phases. Pope begins with static and formal architectural description of the Temple itself (imagined as a grand baroque "Pile," with columns, gates, pillars, frontispiece, and sculptured architrave). In the second phase he describes the troops who petition the Queen of Fame in a ritualized drama of procession, supplication, and response. In the first two phases the *mode* of the description might be called quasi-realistic; that is, Pope describes a wholly and self-consciously imaginary scene, but presents it as if it might have taken place or been represented on a stage. Chaucer's fantastic Gothic is modernized into baroque and Palladian, but more important Chaucer's "trivial Circumstance" and "little Particularities" (Pope's note) are omitted in the interest of regularity and probability. Pope's concern for verisimilitude leads him to defend his famous simile of "Zembla's Rocks" as compatible with "Probability and Nature" and "agreeing with the Accounts of our modern Travellers."

The Temple itself has all the solidity of a real building. Within the Temple the groups of petitioners advance, speak, and are spoken to in plausible fashion. Rarely does Pope make use of dream logic that the genre of allegorical vision permitted. The laws of probability remain in effect. Solid forms retain their shape, with one significant exception. The Goddess Fame seems at first little taller than a cubit, but swells the more the poet gazes at her, "Till to the Roof her tow'ring Front she rais'd" (261). Actors make conventional entrances and exits, except for one troop who seek fame for ill deeds. With some justice, these phantom tyrants sink into Night (355).

For the most part the scene changes are deliberate and logical (first the west front of the Temple, then the east; first the interior friezes, then the central shrine), though for major changes the architectural solidity becomes more fluid. As the goddess herself swells, "With her, the Temple ev'ry moment grew,/And ampler Vista's open'd to my View,/Upward the Columns shoot, the Roofs ascend,/And arches widen, and long Iles extend" (262–265).[20] After the last group of petitioners is dismissed, "some Pow'r unknown/Strait chang'd the Scene, and snatch'd me from the Throne" (419–20). Such moments anticipate the phantasmagoria of the *Dunciad*, where Dulness reigns "in clouded majesty" (I: 43), and her "ample presence fills up all the place" (I: 217), where spectres appear and disappear as in a dream. But in their relative infrequency such moments in *The Temple of Fame* also suggest Pope's modest and restrained beginnings in fantasy.

Only in the third phase of the poem, the description of the whirling Mansion of Rumour, does the scene lack architectural solidity. The site of the mansion is "uncertain"; of its appearance we are told little more than that its doors are numberless. We no longer have sense of physical setting, for the actors "pass, repass, advance, and glide away" (464), more like spirits than representatives of flesh and blood creatures.

In its basic "verisimilitude," then, *The Temple of Fame* is an allegorical vision designed to appeal to an enlightened audience.[21] Pope goes further and provides a clear "moral meaning." Even though Chaucer's poem breaks off abruptly, Pope ends by returning to the dreaming poet:

While thus I stood, intent to see and hear,
One came, methought, and whisper'd in my Ear;
What cou'd thus high thy rash ambition raise?
Art thou, fond Youth, a Candidate for Praise?
(497–500)

The poet answers modestly by measuring the uncertainty, dangers, and costs of fame, and asks the goddess to "grant an honest Fame, or grant me none!" (524). The passage, Pope notes, is based on a "hint" in the third book of Chaucer's poem, but Pope remodels it: "In Chaucer, he only answers 'he came to see the place,'" while Pope "more naturally" makes it the conclusion of his poem "with the addition of a Moral to the whole" (497n). Chaucer's poem, he seems to have felt, had no explicit moral meaning. Pope further reclaims the wild visions of fancy for his critical age by ending his poem on a firmly moral note.

Messiah, written at the same time as *The Temple of Fame*, allowed Pope to explore the possibilities of another species of visionary poetry.

> No more shall Nation against Nation rise,
> Nor ardent Warriors meet with hateful Eyes,
> Nor Fields with gleaming Steel be cover'd o'er;
> The brazen Trumpets kindle Rage no more:
> But useless Lances into Scythes shall bend,
> And the broad Faulchion in a Plow-share end.
>   (57–62)

The words are closely adapted from Isaiah and thus in some sense not Pope's own, as his notes point out. The very singer of the poem, furthermore, is curiously separated from the composing poet. Although Pope begins by invoking the "Nymphs of Solyma" and the Old Testament seraphim in his own voice, he interpolates an Isaiah-like unnamed "Bard," who sings the rest of the poem:

>   O Thou my Voice inspire
> Who touch'd Isaiah's hallow'd Lips with Fire!
> Rapt into future Times, the Bard begun.
>   (4–6)

This interpolation is without precedent in Virgil, who sings his own song, or Milton, whose *Nativity Ode* Pope seems here to echo. Pope's prophecy, then, for all its apparent rapture, can be seen as a careful and tentative experiment, an attempt perhaps to reproduce the Pindaric note of Dryden's celebrative odes in the more restrained measure of the heroic couplet, the meter Pope adopted for all his prophetic visions.

One grammatical feature of *Messiah* is worth pointing out, to show that Pope was already at this early date experimenting with what would later become a common feature in his prophetic poetry, the complex manipulation of verb tenses. The prophet projects present hopes and fears into the future, and may either choose to depict future events as vividly present (what Pope's Twickenham editors call the "prophetic future tense" (I: 106), or present events as future, foretelling "from what we feel, what we are to fear" *(Dunciad*, III: 337)—or in this case to hope. Here, Pope modulates from future tense ("The Steer and Lion at one Crib shall meet," 79) to an understood future that has the effect of a present ("And harmless Serpents lick the Pilgrim's Feet," 80), to the "prophetic perfect" which carries an even stronger sense of present time, as in the final lines of the poem: not "Thy Realm for ever [shall] last," but "Thy Realm for ever lasts." So too he moves from prophecy (foretelling the future) to vision (seeing the future as present) to exhortation (urging the future to appear as the present),[22] which itself verges on exclamation.[23] By varying tense and mood here (and in the *Dunciad*) Pope avoids the tiresome repetition of future auxiliaries and the static quality of a scene set at a remote distance, and keeps the poem from falling into mere narrative. The poet himself can become an active presence in the poem, addressing the characters he depicts, or exclaiming at the wonders of the scene.

Windsor Forest (1713) marks a significant development in Pope's visionary poetry. In the poem Pope again draws on Virgil and on Isaiah.[24] But here the grand prophecy with which *Windsor Forest* concludes is secularized and is adapted to English commercial circumstances. In his mercantile prophecy Pope combines a vision of future triumph adapted in part from the 60th chapter of Isaiah and Virgil's second *Georgic* and an allegorical set-piece of the imprisoning of Discord and her allied evils, based on passages from the *Aeneid* and the third *Georgic*. In his "sacred eclogue" *(Messiah)* Pope had prophesied the rise of "Imperial Salem":

> See barb'rous nations at thy Gates attend,
> Walk in thy Light, and in thy Temple bend,
> See thy bright Altars throng'd with prostrate Kings,
> And heap'd with Products of Sabaean Springs!
>   *(Messiah*, 91–94)

In his secularized georgic the city becomes "two fair Cities" (of London and Westminster) and the "Products" not gift offerings but the fruits of British commerce. Although it is economic and military power that Pope celebrates, that power is still endowed with spiritual attributes:

> There mighty Nations shall inquire their Doom,
> The World's great Oracle in Times to come;
> There King's shall sue, and suppliant States be seen
> Once more to bend before a British Queen.
>   *(Windsor Forest,* 381–384)

Even the mercantile reality is discreetly disguised through the rhetorical heightening available in the visionary mode. The wealth of British merchants is nothing so material as cargo accumulating on London's docks or even epically magnificent "spoils." Rather it is the spontaneous tribute of an animate world offering Thames what is only his due:

> For me the Balm shall bleed, and Amber flow,
> The Coral redden, and the Ruby glow,
> The Pearly Shell its lucid Globe infold,
> And Phoebus warm the ripening Ore to Gold.
>   (393–96)

As Pope's heavenly scene closes, he concludes the vision with a brief glimpse of hell. The evils which had beset England throughout her history are gathered and symbolically purged. Although Pope is indebted to Virgil for the language,[25] it is perhaps Milton's visions of evil at last recoiled on itself, "Self-fed, and self-consum'd,"[26] that prompted his final scene in "deepest Hell":

> Exil'd by Thee from Earth to deepest Hell,
> In Brazen Bonds shall barb'rous Discord dwell:
> Gigantick Pride, pale Terror, gloomy Care,
> And mad Ambition, shall attend her there,
> There purple Vengeance bath'd in Gore retires,
> Her Weapons blunted, and extinct her Fires:
> There hateful Envy her own Snakes shall feel,
> And Persecution mourn her broken Wheel:
> There Faction roar, Rebellion bite her Chain,
> And gasping Furies thirst for Blood in vain.
>   (Il: 413–422)

Why should Pope change the mode of his description from a recognizable if visionary Thameside to an allegorical underworld? Perhaps, having determined to close the vision with evil in chains, based on Virgilian precedent[27] or on iconographic tradition,[28] Pope wanted to avoid a lengthy and particularized fantastic scene. Having seen to it that his chief villains, the Norman despots, had been fittingly and divinely punished,[29] he took advantage of the economy offered by allegory and chose to report concisely on the fate of Discord, whom "great Anna" had, with even greater economy, simply bid "cease." Pope's scene is largely static, as if he were here describing sculpture less "living" than that which adorns the *Temple of Fame*, perhaps because he wants to emphasize Discord's utter defeat. The lines clearly anticipate a similar scene of symbolic confinement in the *Dunciad*:

> Beneath her foot-stool, Science groans in Chains,
> And Wit dreads exile, Penalties, and Pains,
> There foam'd rebellious Logic, gagg'd and bound,
> There, stript, fair Rhetoric languish'd on the ground.
> His blunted Arms by Sophistry are born,
> And shameless Billingsgate her Robes adorn.
> (*Dunciad*, IV: 21–26)

The passage in *Windsor Forest* has been unjustly depreciated in favor of lines from the *Dunciad*, described by one critic as "drama rather than a set of attitudes," in which definition and response now depend "more on action than on descriptive evocation."[30] While it is true that Pope tends to rely on descriptive epithets to do his work for him ("barb'rous Discord," "hateful Envy," etc.), much of the sense of stasis comes from Pope's relatively inert verbs (dwell, attend, retires) in the first part of the passage. In the latter part, however, Pope's abstractions enact their own punishment, raging in impotence or in self-torture. Verbs become more energetic (roar, bite, thirst) and the scene displays the kind of wit and density that characterizes the lines from the *Dunciad*. Pope was later to become more expert at animating abstractions in allegory. But by 1713 he had already given an impressive sample of what he could do in this branch of visionary poetry. What he was not yet ready to do, however, is to prophesy in his own voice. Perhaps the most significant aspect of the prophecy in *Windsor Forest* is that it is put in the mouth of Father Thames. Still clinging to pastoral modesty, Pope leaves to others—to Granville and to a mythological river god—the loftiest prophetic strains. Just as the visionary dream in *The Temple of Fame* is as much Chaucer's as it is Pope's, and the glorious prophecy in *Messiah* is Virgil's and Isaiah's, so in this first fully independent visionary poem Pope still prefers to speak through another.

In the five-canto *Rape of the Lock* (1714) Pope increased his visionary repertoire. Again he makes use of dream vision, although the "Vision" that appears to Belinda is modeled not on medieval dream-vision but on classical epic. Again Pope uses allegory to describe a scene of vexed and tormented passion, but the Cave of Spleen is his first extended psychological landscape. For the first time too Pope uses the visionary mode to explore and revel in a purely imaginary realm, the airy element of the sylphs, who "sport and flutter in the Fields of Air" (I: 66). Each "vision" in the poem is part of the delicate supernatural machinery added to the original two-canto poem. The visionary world is kept distinct from the world of human actions and responsibilities.

Ariel's appearance to the sleeping Belinda in the beguiling form of a "Morning-Dream"—the first "vision" in the poem—simultaneously invokes a Homeric world, where epic heroes are instructed or warned before a critical encounter, and confirms conventional assumptions about female self-indulgence and frivolity. This visionary appearance, Pope assures Arabella Fermor in the prefatory letter to her, is wholly "Fabulous," a merely fanciful invention for the skeptical amusement of wits and ladies. Ariel's subsequent marshaling the "lucid squadrons" of sylphs is equally "fabulous," an opportunity for the creation of a fantasy world of air, light, and color:

> Some to the Sun their insect-Wings unfold,
> Waft on the Breeze, or sink in Clouds of Gold,
> Transparent Forms, too fine for mortal Sight,
> Their fluid Bodies half dissolv'd in Light.
> Loose to the Wind their airy Garments flew,
> Thin glitt'ring Textures of the filmy Dew;
> Dipt in the richest Tincture of the Skies
> Where Light disports in ever-mingling Dies
> While ev'ry Beam new transient Colours flings,
> Colours that change whene'er they wave their Wings.
>   (II: 59–68)

Here is a visionary poetry tied not to political celebration, to prophecy, or to allegory, but to the pure and gratuitous exercise of the imagination, the kind of "fanciful & Imaginary" description he would later recommend to Judith Cowper. It is as if Pope had set out to re-imagine Milton's world of immaterial spirits, who may assume "what Sexes and what Shapes they please." Where Milton emphasizes the morally "spirituous and pure" nature of the angels and their intuitive intelligence, Pope's diminutive creatures are aestheticized; the emphasis falls on their fluidity of form, their transience, their evanesence.

When Pope imagines the penalties to be imposed if a sylph failed in his duty—

> Be stopt in Vials, or transfixt with Pins;
> Or plung'd in Lakes of bitter Washes lie,
> Or wedg'd whole Ages in a Bodkin's Eye:
> Gums and Pomatums shall his Flight restrain,
> While clog'd he beats his silken Wings In vain.
>   (Il: 126–30)

—much of the delicate wit comes from the paradoxical idea that "Fluid Bodies" might be fixed or confined, and from the simultaneous aggrandizement of the toilette and diminishing of the sylphs. The effect is partly what we are accustomed to call mock-heroic, but the special Popean quality of the passage derives from the fastidious imagining of a fantasy world of domestic torture.

The Cave of Spleen, one of Pope's best-known unreal scenes, combines several different visionary elements. Pope begins with an allegorical tableau in the Temple of Spleen, the Queen attended by Pain, Megrim, Ill-nature, and Affectation. The fantastic scene is at the same time a recognizable social setting, the levee of a fashionable lady receiving visits in bed. At the center of the episode, however, Pope suspends his externalized allegorical description and inhabits the disordered and hallucinating minds of the splenetic:

> A constant Vapour o'er the Palace flies;
> Strange Phantoms rising as the mists arise;
> Dreadful, as Hermit's Dreams in haunted Shades,
> Or bright as Visions of expiring Maids,
> Now glaring Fiends, and Snakes on rolling Spires,
> Pale Spectres, gaping Tombs, and purple fires:
> Now lakes of liquid Gold, Elysian Scenes,
> And Crystal Domes, and Angels in Machines.
>   (IV: 39–46)

The scene is pure fantasy, though Pope's readers would have considered such visions appropriate to melancholic imaginations, and would have recognized that he had borrowed much of his fantastic imagery from contemporary stage spectacle.[31] Pope clearly thought such spectacles absurd, but must have also found them visually compelling, to judge by his recreation of them here and in the *Dunciad*.[32]

Not only do the splenetic see visions, but they also imagine themselves transformed "to various Forms," living teapot, pipkin, and goose-pie. As he would do later in the *Dunciad*, Pope here associates poetic creativity ("Pow'rful Fancy") with displaced or perverted sexual currents (Spleen can give the "Poetic" as well as the "Hysteric" fit; "Men prove with Child," and maids turn bottles). In this respect the Cave of Spleen is a forerunner of the Cave of Poverty and Poetry and of Cibber's "monster-breeding breast" in the *Dunciad*. In each instance Pope imagines a dark and gestative womb-like scene of misbirths and "wild creation." Although the grotesquerie of the Cave of Spleen serves primarily satiric ends, it is tempting to suspect that in such fantastic grottoes Pope is also exploring the "whirl of fancy" that was for him the first stage in poetic composition. When we remember that Pope often spoke of the muse as his only spouse and poems as his only offspring, we may not find it surprising that he should see poetic creativity as a species of sublimated sexuality.[33]

IV

The poetic "vision" has an obvious potential for satiric application, as Opposition writers in the 1730s did not fail to notice. The "dreaming" poet may call up a scene in which venality corrupts a court, in pointed parallel to an evil minister.[34] It comes as no surprise that the visions in Pope's late satires have a distinctly satiric dimension. But they don't wholly forsake "pure Description" for "sense," and we cannot simply say that in his later career Pope harnessed his visionary impulse to the service of his morality or his satire. To examine Pope's fanciful poems with care is to discover that for him throughout his career the "barrier" between moral sense and visionary description, like the barriers between sense and thought, or sense and nonsense, is a "nice" one. This is not to say that we can make no distinctions between the visions in the early poems and those in the later poems. On the contrary, vision in the later poems tends to be assigned not to hermits, expiring virgins, splenetic hypochondriacs, dreamers, or mythological creatures, but to the poet himself in his own person and voice. Visions are presented not as illusions, dreams, or manifest fantasy but as distorted or exaggerated versions of reality. The rapt prophecies of "Golden Days" in the early poems tend to be supplanted in the later ones by apocalyptic visions of a "Saturnian" age of Lead.[35] As the world of economic and political greed and rapacity seemed to him absurd, irrational, nightmarish, and surreal, Pope drew on allegory and visionary fancy to describe it and (perhaps ultimately) try to contain it.

The *Dunciad* is Pope's great visionary poem.[36] It includes allegorical tableaux, prophecy, scenes of pure fantasy, and psychic scenes that take place within heads of the dunces. Not only does the *Dunciad* include all the types of visionary poetry with which Pope had earlier experimented, it also in some sense by allusive parody assimilates those poems. The earlier *Temple of Fame* reappears as a "temple of infamy." The arrival of the "Light Himself" in *Messiah* becomes the extinction of all light. The confinement of Discord in *Windsor Forest* reappears as the confinement of Science, Wit, Logic, and Rhetoric; and the Cave of Spleen is transformed into the Cave of Poverty and Poetry. The *Dunciad* is Pope's most thoroughgoing exploration of vision, its delights as well as its dangers.

The dunces figure foremost as visionaries in the bad sense of the term. Their poetry, as I noted earlier, is born from impotent floundering inside their own brains (I: 115–26) or from the rapturous trance that over-flows the seat of sense (III: 1–6). Poems begin in the womb-like chaos of the Cave of Poverty and Poetry. Their natural history extends from bastardy ("genial Jacob" serves as father to the "nameless Somethings") to miscegenation (Tragedy and Comedy "embrace," farce and Epic "get a jumbled race"). From unnatural birth emerges a poetry that ignores or perversely transforms nature:

> Here gay Description Aegypt glads with show'rs,
> Or gives to Zembla fruits, to Barca flow'rs;
> Glitt'ring with ice here hoary hills are seen,
> There painted vallies of eternal green,
> In cold December fragrant chaplets blow,
> And heavy harvests nod beneath the snow.
> (I: 73–78)

False visionaries, the dunces are consistently linked with raving lunatics (the Cave of Poverty and Poetry is near Bedlam Hospital—I: 29n), with breeders of monsters (I: 108, III: 252), and finally with mental anarchy that appears to make a "new World" (III: 241, IV: 15) unknown in Nature but in fact through the power of its Word attempts only to "uncreate."

In another sense, of course, the poem's visionary is Pope himself. It is he who stages the allegorical pageants at the beginning of Book IV (as the repeated invocations remind us—IV: 1–8, 619–26) and who imagines the dark and luscious bower of the "Mud-Nymphs" that lies beneath the "unconscious stream" of Fleet Ditch (III: 304, 331–43). The sleeping Cibber has a prophetic vision of Father Settle who reveals the past and future triumphs of Dulness, but it is in fact the "easy wing" of Pope's fancy that conveys the prophecy. Thus Pope can spontaneously indulge and deny the vision, revel in a world of dream and dismiss it as "no more than the chimera of the dreamer's brain" (III: 5–6n).

The *Dunciad* is Pope's most anarchic flight of fancy, his most imaginary scene. But even here the visionary poet, as a reminder of his own sure grounding in truth, makes his fantasy only a distorted or exaggerated version of contemporary reality. Pope's own footnotes to the poem continually remind a reader not only of the historical Alexander Pope but of the historical reality of the dunces and their follies. Thus when the prophecy in Book III is at its most fantastic—

> Hell rises, Heav'n descends, and dance on Earth,
> Gods, imps, and monsters, music, rage, and mirth,
> A fire, a jig, a battle, and a ball,
> Till one wide Conflagration swallows all.
> (III: 237–240)

—Pope's note drily intrudes: "This monstrous absurdity was actually represented in Tibbald's Rape of Proserpine." When forests unnaturally "dance,"

> the rivers upward rise,
> Whales sport in woods, and dolphins in the skies;
> And last, to give the whole creation grace,
> Lo! one vast Egg produces human race.
> (III: 245–48)

Pope draws on the pantomimes staged by Rich and performed by Cibber, and provides documentary evidence for the basis of his fantasy: "The history of the forgoing absurdities is verified by [Cibber] himself," in words quoted from the *Apology* (III: 266n).

The near alliance of the fantastic and the real is perhaps the keynote of Pope's later visionary poetry. The *Dunciad* is the major example but Pope found an outlet for his visionary impulse in other poems with more "realistic" settings. The ending of the "Epistle to Burlington," for example, rises into the visionary mode, The final paragraph begins as exhortation to Burlington to carry out his own building projects and to promote public works:

> You too proceed! make falling Arts your care,
> Erect new wonders, and the old repair...
> Till kings call forth th' Ideas of your mind,
> Proud to accomplish what such hands design'd,
> Bid Harbors open, public Ways extend,
> Bid Temples, worthier of the God, ascend.
>   (Il: 191–92, 195–98)

As the passage proceeds, what Pope exhorts Burlington to do is as it were accomplished while he speaks. Several imperative verbs (proceed, erect, bid, repair) can at the same time be taken as indicatives (with "you" understood).[37]

The visionary poet now beholds what he first summoned, just as kings "call forth" the ideas in Burlington's mind. The sense of verbal magic (words make things happen) is accentuated as Pope literalizes the king's "bidding" into a magician's command which is answered instantly by the world of nature and inanimate objects:

> Bid the broad Arch the dang'rous Flood contain,
> The Mole projected break the roaring Main;
> Back to his bounds their subject Sea command,
> And roll obedient Rivers thro' the Land;
> These Honours, Peace to happy Britain brings,
> These are Imperial Works, and worthy Kings.
>   (199–204)

Strictly speaking, the repeated "Bid" is governed by "Till" (195) and describes a series of desired future actions. But "Till" tends to be forgotten as the passage shifts from prospect to prophecy. By the end the grammar reflects not a desired future but an accomplished present: not the hopeful "[till] These Honours, Peace to happy Britain *bring*," but the declarative "These Honours, Peace, *brings*."

Characteristically, however, Pope's future does not lose touch with the historical present in which arts are unfortunately "falling," in part because the present king has neglected his public duty. It takes only a minor adjustment for Pope to slip from the satiric into the visionary mode. Thus earlier in the "Burlington" poem, Pope contemplates the destruction of Timon's villa. Timon's tasteless and unnatural display will one day be swept away, as Nature magically takes her revenge:

> Another age shall see the golden Ear
> Imbrown the slope, and nod on the Parterre,
> Deep Harvests bury all his pride has plann'd,
> And laughing Ceres re-assume the land.
>   (173-6)

A fertile landscape is traditionally "smiling" but Pope turns metaphor or allegory into a tiny mythological narrative by making Ceres laugh, as if in scorn, at Timon's folly.

Thus, in the "Epistle to Bathurst," Pope abruptly shifts from contemporary London and notoriously mean Peter Walter to a vision of general corruption, by means of a "wizard" who inexplicably appears and prophesies "our fate":

> At length corruption, like a gen'ral Flood,
> (So long by watchful Ministers withstood)
> Shall deluge all; and Av'rice creeping on,
> Spread like a low-born mist, and blot the Sun;
> Statesmen and Patriot ply alike the Stocks,
> Peeress and Butler share alike the Box,
> And Judges job, and Bishops bite the town,
> And mighty Dukes pack cards for half a crown.
> See Britain sunk in lucre's sordid charms,
> And France reveng'd of Anne's and Edward's arms!
>   (137-146)[38]

The "wizard" usefully permits Pope to shield himself by shifting the satiric burden of attack onto other shoulders and into a dark future that is at the same time a recurrence of the ancient corruption swept away by an earlier Deluge. But the disappearance of the future auxiliary verbs after line 139 makes prophecy of future and memory of ancient decline blend into satire against present corruption. As in *Messiah*, what is predicted has already arrived.

A similar vision appears at the climax of the *Epilogue to the Satires*, but in this poem Pope more daringly emerges to speak in his own voice. Characteristically, Pope mingles modes. Though the poem begins as conversation, it rises into fervent argument in defense of virtue, shifts into allegory, and then back into a heightened present. "Vice" mounts a "Tribunal" and "sees pale Virtue carted in her stead" (149–150). The lines that follow continue to present what Vice "sees":

> Lo! at the Wheels of her Triumphal Car,
> Old England's Genius, rough with many a Scar,
> Dragg'd in the Dust! his Arms hang idly round,
> His Flag inverted trails along the ground!
> Our Youth, all livery'd o'er with foreign Gold,
> Before her dance; behind her crawl the Old!
> See thronging Millions to the Pagod run,
> And offer Country, Parent, Wife, or Son!
> Hear her black Trumpet thro' the Land proclaim,
> That "Not to be corrupted is the Shame."
> (151–60)

Pope's grammar is aptly ambiguous. The first verbs—"dragg'd" and "hung"—are apparently governed by the earlier "sees." Vice *sees* England's Genius "Dragg'd in the Dust," *sees* his "arms hang idly round." At line 154 grammar begins to shift. Vice as our seer recedes and we get the clearly declarative "trails" rather than "[sees] His Flag trail." By line 157 ("See thronging Millions...") Pope has subtly but clearly shifted modes, from allegorical description of what Vice sees, to an aroused warning in his own voice. Now *he* beholds the scene, and urges us to "See all our Nobles begging to be Slaves!/See, all our Fools aspiring to be Knaves" (163–4). The visionary mode here enables Pope to present with great rhetorical heightening—and perhaps with greater security from government reprisal—a bitterly satiric picture of Walpole's England. The scene is at once the allegorical unreal and the historical present.[39]

Visionary prophecy and satire are never far apart in the later Pope. Just as the longed-for and predicted arrival of a golden age or of a Messiah is joyously proclaimed as present in the early Pope, so in the later poems events anticipated in ominous prophecy can suddenly appear in the present. The shifts from visionary future into present in the *Epistle to Bathurst* and the *Epilogue to the Satires* are only local versions of the "Completion of the Prophecies" that Pope accomplishes in the fourth book of *The Dunciad*. In its three-book version the arrival of Dulness herself is merely a "Vision," planted in the "raptur'd" brain of Theobald by Father Settle, that finally flies "thro' the Ivory Gate" of false dreams. Scriblerus notes—recalling Pope's words to Judith Cowper—that "all such imaginations" are merely "wild, ungrounded, and fictitious" (1729 ed., III: 337n.). But his note also reminds us that what the prophetic poet "says shall be, is already to be seen, in the writings of some of our most adored authors." In the four-book *Dunciad*, of course, the lines in which the prophet "sees" the arrival of Dulness ("She comes!") are transferred from the end of the third to the end of the fourth book. No Scriblerian note appears in 1743 to tease us about the truth or wildness of the vision; no "Ivory Gate" tells us it is merely fictitious. Satire and visionary prophecy converge.

Many readers continue to think of the conclusion of the fourth book as Pope's gloomy admission of defeat: dulness buries all. The visionary poet does not wake from his fearful dream and return us to a reassuringly normal world, still safe for wit and poetry and Pope. But if we remember the mode of dream vision in which Pope is working—and which he is here re-inventing—we have another way of reading the dark conclusion. Traditionally, visions come to a sleeping poet. Perhaps, however, the true visionary is not the poet who falls asleep, but the one who wakes while others sleep.

As the dunces begin to fall asleep at the end of Book II, Dulness asks "If there be man, who o'er such works can wake" (II: 372). No dunce is able to hold out, but Pope carefully notes that the recording poet remains awake: "Why should I sing, what bards the nightly Muse/Did slumb'ring visit, and convey to stews?" (421–2). The whole of the third book is Pope's vision of what takes place within Cibber's sleeping brain. Perhaps the visionary fourth book only recapitulates, in allegorical form, what had already taken place in the dunces' brains. If that is the case, then the apocalyptic conclusion to the poem only represents the mental extinction of the dull. The visionary poet, armed with "Ulysses' ear" and "Argus' eye," defies Dulness' power and sits "Judge of all present, past, and future wit."[40]

The visionary mode served Pope well throughout his long career.[41] In his early years visionary poetry represented a distinct species of descriptive verse in which a poet might legitimately indulge his fancy and still please a polite audience. In later poems Pope found the mode useful as rhetorical heightening, as an economical means of representing action as emblem, as a means of exploring psychological depths and recesses. To see with a prophetic or an allegorical eye was for Pope yet another way of attaining wider vision, moving from part to whole. An enlightened poet might not, like Milton, soar into the mythopoeic realm, or like Homer call up a world in which supernatural powers regularly intervened in human affairs. But we make ourselves deaf to Pope's appeals if we imagine that he substituted for Miltonic or Homeric amplitude a world wholly answerable to "reason" and "correctness." Pope found in the indulgence of fancy a means of evading the bounds that seemed (to Warton and others) to limit his verse to the world of "modern manners...familiar, uniform, artificial, and polished."[42] Fully aware of the risks of deploying poetic vision—from the mechanical false sublime to the self-indulgent raptures of a would-be genius—Pope found in the visionary mode a means of observing with an eye both engaged and detached the world of Sir Plume and Sir Balaam, Cibber and Walpole, Great Anna and the Great Anarch.

NOTES

1. See the Twickenham Edition of Pope's poems (New Haven: Yale University Press, 1951-1969), II: 178. All quotations from Pope are from this edition. Later poems in the visionary mode include Samuel Croxall's *The Vision* (1715) and *The Temple of Love. A Vision* (1717), by a "Mr. Lock." For bibliographical details, see David Foxon, *English Verse, 1701-1759* (London: Cambridge University Press, 1975).

2. Fielding was especially attracted to the form in prose. Examples include his pamphlet, *The Opposition: A Vision* (1741), and nine other dream visions attributed to him by Battestin, from early contributions to the *Craftsman* (1736) to later numbers of his own *Covent-Garden Journal* (1752). See Martin Battestin, *New Essays by Henry Fielding* (Charlottesville, 1989), 160–61.

3. Pope's note to 53–60.

4. Joseph Spence, *Observations, Anecdotes, and Characters of Books and Men*, ed. J. M. Osborn (Oxford: Oxford University Press, 1966). He later recommended to Judith Cowper the "Pieces of the old Provencal Poets, which abound with Fancy & are the most amusing scenes in nature" *(Correspondence*, ed. George Sherburn (Oxford: Oxford University Press, 1955), II: 202–3.

5. Frederic Bogel, in *Acts of Knowledge: Pope's Later Poems* (Lewisburg: Bucknell University Press, 1981), uses the term "visionary" to refer to a tendency to abstraction, Olympian detachment, lofty denunciation, and a traditional *contemptus mundi*. I want to restrict the term to its eighteenth-century meanings: prophecy, allegory, and conscious flights of fancy.

6. *Natural Supernaturalism: Tradition and Revolution in Romantic Literature* (New York: Norton, 1971), 341–2, 375–7.

7. *Natural Supernaturalism*, 390.

8. Despite the reminder in Spacks's later book that the *Essay on Man* displays an "almost obsessive concern with 'seeing.'" See *An Argument of Images: The Poetry of Alexander Pope* (Cambridge: Harvard University Press, 1971), 42.

9. To John Caryll, 5 December 1712, in *Correspondence*, I: 163. Mack quotes the letter in his Introduction to the Twickenham Edition of Pope's Homer and again in *The Garden and the City* (Toronto: University of Toronto Press, 1969).

10. *Correspondence*, I: 240.

11. *Correspondence*, I: 213.

12. *Correspondence*, I: 125.

13. *Correspondence*, I: 135. For a richly suggestive discussion of the ways his grotto may have served Pope as "accessory to his Muse," see Mack's "The Shadowy Cave," in *The Garden and the City*, 41–76.

14. In "The Muse of Satire," *Yale Review*, 41 (1951), repr. in *Satire: Modern Essays in Criticism*, ed. R. Paulson (Englewood Cliffs: Prentice-Hall, 1971), 193.

15. See *Windsor Forest*, 237–38; *Essay on Criticism*, 128–29; *Epilogue to the Satires*, 223.

The Visionary Scene

16. "It is to the strength of this amazing Invention we are to attribute that unequalled fire and rapture, which is so forcible in Homer, that no man of a true poetical spirit is master of himself while he reads him" ("Preface to the *Iliad*"). Mack compares an earlier letter to Ralph Bridges *(Correspondence,* I: 44). See Mack's introduction to the Homer in the Twickenham Edition.

17. Horace sings "with Fire" *(Essay on Criticism,* 659) and Longinus is blest "with a Poet's Fire" (676). Dryden's fire is "native" and Corneille's "noble" *(Epistle to Augustus,* 274).

18. Pope's praise of Shakespeare is that his poetry was "Inspiration indeed: he is not so much an Imitator, as an Instrument, of Nature; and 'tis not so just to say that he speaks from her, as that she speaks thro' him" *(Preface to Shakespeare).*

19. Much of the fantastic material in Chaucer—for example, the talking eagle—was omitted.

20. The enlargement of the goddess and the temple are both found in Chaucer.

21. Dennis, however, who had no sympathy for this kind of poetry and seems not to have known Chaucer's *House of Fame,* denounced the *Temple of Fame* as a "feverish and delirious" dream. For his rationalistic (and rather wooden) critique of the poem's unnaturalness and improbability, see his "Observations upon The Temple of Fame," in Dennis's *Critical Works,* ed. Edward Niles Hooker (Baltimore: Johns Hopkins University Press, 1939–1943), III: 138–50.

22. "Oh spring to Light, Auspicious Babe, be born," *Messiah,* 22.

23. "See nodding Forests on the Mountains dance,/See spicy Clouds from lowly *Saron* rise," 26–27.

24. See Maynard Mack, "On Reading Pope," *College English* 7 (1946): 263–73; and *Twickenham Edition* I: 141–44.

25. Wakefield compared *Georgics* III: 37–39 and *Aeneid* I: 293–96. For a broadly similar allegorical scene of gathered evils, one might compare the famous vestibule of Hell in *Aeneid,* VI: 273–81.

26. *Comus,* 592–6, where evil shall be "in eternal restless change/Self-fed." See also *Paradise Lost* X: 629–40, on the final cleansing of the world by God's hell-hounds, which will at last be sealed up in hell forever: "Then heaven and earth renewed shall be made pure."

27. In the third *Georgic* Virgil describes a temple to Caesar adorned with statues and relief sculptures representing the hero's victories, the conquering peoples, and cowering Envy *(Invidia).*

28. Was Pope perhaps thinking of religious allegorical painting, in which the damned are commonly portrayed in bondage at the bottom of the canvas? A Magdalen College altarpiece, described in Addison's Latin poem, *The Resurrection,* tr. Nicholas Amhurst, shows (at the top) Christ in glory, with the saved, and (at the bottom) the dead arising

from their graves while an avenging angel herds sinners into the flames of hell. Or was he perhaps thinking of secular allegorical painting, in which a mighty king triumphs over his fallen enemies?

29. William I and his son William Rufus both died while hunting. See *Windsor Forest*, 79–84. Pope perhaps hesitates to pursue his other villains, murderers of Charles I, since justice for the Stuarts might have exposed his Jacobite sympathies.

30. Spacks, *An Argument of Images*, 139. To make her point about the relative stasis of the scene from *Windsor Forest*, Spacks quotes only 413–18, omitting the more "active" (and *Dunciad*-like) lines, in which Faction "roars," Rebellion "bites her chain," and so forth.

31. Twickenham Edition, II: 186–7.

32. *Dunciad* I: 55–70, 115–26.

33. *Correspondence* I: 243, 292, 293; II: 227; IV: 169, 364.

34. For an account of one such vision, see *The Vision of Camelick* (see Mack, *The Garden and the City*, 120–21).

35. See also the "Saturnian days of Lead and Gold," *Dunciad*, IV: 16. I leave out of account the *Essay on Man*, much of which is written in what one might call the physico-theologico-visionary mode. At many points, particularly in the first epistle, Pope as it were climbs a Pisgah Mount to give a visionary description of the ordained scheme of the universe (I: 207–8, 233–34, 267–68). Joseph Warton found the end of Epistle I "transcendently sublime" *(An Essay on the Genius and Writings of Pope*, 4th ed. [1782], II: 77). Ironically, it is in such intuitions of the unity of all life, in this quintessentially "Augustan" poem, that Pope comes closest to the visionary Blake.

36. This element has received some attention in John Sitter's *The Poetry of Pope's Dunciad* (Minneapolis: University of Minnesota Press, 1971), which considers the poem as an "allegorical vision" (80). Sitter's book first drew my attention to the way Book IV serves as a parody of *The Temple of Fame*.

37. "Be" in 194 remains an imperative. The process is not complete.

38. Pope's note to the passage suggests that the "prophecy" (his word) is a parody of Blunt's own declamations "against the corruption and luxury of the age."

39. As James Osborn has shown, Vice is a thinly-disguised representation of Molly Skerrett, the whore whom Walpole raised to be his wife. "Pope, the Byzantine Empress, and Walpole's Whore," *Review of English Studies* n.s. 6 (1955): 372–82.

40. For a more extended discussion of the poet's triumph, see Dustin H. Griffin, *Alexander Pope: The Poet in the Poems* (Princeton: Princeton University Press, 1978), 217–77.

41. Spence reports that on his deathbed Pope saw what he called a "vision": "'What's that?' [Pope asked] pointing into the air with a very steady regard, and then looked down on me, and said with a smile of great pleasure, and with the greatest softness, 'Twas a vision.'" Spence, *Observations*.

42. *An Essay on the Genius and Writings of Pope*, 5th ed. (London: 1806), II: 401.

"EMBODY'D DARK"
The Simulation of Allegory in *The Dunciad*

Veronica Kelly

Read from within the tradition in literary criticism that has designated allegory as the genre of transcendence and that reads in the later texts of allegory our loss of that high moment, the allegory of Pope's *Dunciad* must seem to be perversely entangled in local histories.[1] The triumphal procession of Dulness from Smithfield to the court, where Chaos and Night enter to conclude the poem, entails the poem's passage through the details of its own genesis in the back streets of obscure controversy. As the readers of *The Dunciad* are forced back from the hermeneutic imperative of allegory into one fact-finding, historical digression after another, the "particular allusions infinite..." (*The Dunciad*, "Martinus Scriblerus," 346) of this historical satire bleed the poem's allegory of its different, "transumptive" narrative force.[2] Like the allegorical figures held captive by Dulness at the beginning of Book IV, the narrative allegory of *The Dunciad* seems to be "in Chains," "gagg'd and bound" by minute history. (*Dunciad* IV: 21–23). Even the apocalyptic allegory of the poem's close—where the light of civilization is subsumed by the expanding darkness of man's "native anarchy"—appears to be thematically at odds with its status as an allegorical utterance, the poem's radical self-implosion negating allegory's referential gesture towards something before and beyond its own language.

This tension between allegory and history is partially alleviated by the typology through which the poem structures its collection of otherwise ephemeral information. Settle, Blackmore, Mist, Curl, and the other dunces and duncely events that complicate *The Dunciad*'s footnotes are all types of Cibber and of his reign. They serve as necessary antecedents to his incarnation of Dulness and to the establishment of Dulness's empire. Through this typology the poem retrospectively organizes the dunces into a "meaningful" narrative history: we see that history crest its final generation when the father Settle guides the son Cibber through the visionary underworld of Book III. But while this parodic version of providence can rationalize Cibber's reign, it stops short of explaining the tropological relation between the two major figures of the poem, Cibber and Dulness, or of finally resolving the conflict between history and allegory which is focused in the relation of those two figures to each other. Far from easing the tension between contesting genres, the relation between Cibber and Dulness—who are both mother and son and king and queen—places incest at the tropological "center" of the poem, as the event most instrumental in bringing the poem's demonic productions—its abortions, miscegenations, mutating genres, and miscellanies—to their anti-climax in anarchy.

One effect of the reach of incest in Pope's poem is to direct us away from the purely literary historical work of determining the poem's genre—of deciding whether it is or is not an allegory—and toward an analysis of the questions that are put to the category "genre" by the poem.[3] It is clear, for example, that the incest between Cibber and Dulness subsumes its immediate satiric moment to become the zero-point of the poem's preoccupation with difference and sameness, a preoccupation exemplified in the measured but unstable antitheses of the poem's rhymed couplets.[4] More emphatically, incest is the other of genre, the same-difference against which family histories, including the genealogies written for literary history, erect their standards of type and kind. We see these standards destabilized throughout *The Dunciad*, where types, categories and kinds—as numerous as they are—are fragmented and ephemeral, appearing as the momentary effects of a generalized zeugma. The poem displays whole orders of literary forms becoming unviable, reversing—in each of these failures—the logic that establishes formal or familial integrity through the repudiation of incest.[5] The sheer number of these genealogical failures, and the rising unimportance of any individual one, urges us to read the conflict among genres in *The Dunciad* not as a problem to be resolved (is this an allegory or isn't it?) but as an instrumental diversion that allows the poem to complete its other, regressive motion, in which providential order is un-made through the failure of genre's initial, unacknowledged separation from incest. Such a reading gives us a context for the poem's enigmatic finale, where the fact that the end comes as irresistible sleep just doesn't seem to take apocalypse seriously enough. In that initial separation, incest will have been defined by genre as unspeakable and unfigurable and therefore outside history. What we see in *The Dunciad* is the failure of this exclusion with the return of incestuous possibilities in reproduction and in representation, possibilities that appear, as they must within genre, as the end of history. For reasons that will become clear, *The Dunciad* plays incest as a crisis in the allegorical register. We can look at that crisis—and at the status of allegory in it—as an index both to the specific historical contexts within which incest complicates the notion of kind in *The Dunciad* and to the difficulty or unreadability that the poem produces in the place of ideally delineated genre.

The dispensation of genre is, especially in Pope, always attached to the myth of a patrilineal succession. While this remains true in *The Dunciad*, patriarchy's grip on the poem has seemed to critics to be threatened by the gleeful affect of the poem's misrule and its power to implicate the poet himself in its ultimately apocalyptic lapse of control and decorum. The centrality of incest misruled by the goddess Dulness submits the poem's desire for the patrimonies of literary heritage to the irony of genre's own definitive separation from incest. The story of genre's initial contamination by incest figures prominently in the labyrinthine genealogy provided in the poem's "critical apparatus." There, although Scriblerus produces the requisite classical lineage for the poem, proclaiming "the first Dunciad" to be "the first Epic poem, written by *Homer* himself, and anterior even to the Iliad or Odyssey" (343), he can secure Homer's literary paternity for the later *Dunciad* only by positing "the first Dunciad" as a lost original: only, that is, by reversing paternal time and deriving the father from his offspring. This reversal is not in itself surprising: the use of retrospect to name the father is not only a familiar feature of patriarchal logic, but such a reversion is not in itself antithetical to the writing of allegory, which shares patriarchy's preoccupation with a mythic anteriority. But Scriblerus *tells* us that the paternal name "Homer" marks an originary absence in the sight of which he labors, through literary taxonomy, to produce the pure generic line that would secure the father with the father's name. Thus, while critics have argued that great poems, like great sons, name themselves (and their genres) by taking the paternal place, Scriblerus displays the confounding of the lineage and the father. This display, more than either the fact or fantasy of usurpation, constitutes the Scriblerian satire on the law of genre. It operates to withhold satire's conventional high moral ground from the poem's readers by giving the poem, and its protagonist Cibber, not sorrow but satisfaction in sleeping with the mother.[6]

The overt coupling of satisfaction and maternal incest breaks the analogy between patrilineal family order and representation. When Scriblerus announces that the poem will "imitate...that which is lost," he contaminates the claims of succession in representation with a pre-history that appears, in language, as nonsense. At the same moment, incest appears within literature's patrilineal order as a disruption in the rubric of mimesis: how can something that is lost be imitated? But *The Dunciad* not only disrupts the order of mimesis, with its insistent separation of the true from the false representation. The display of reproductive transgressions in the poem increasingly exceeds the satire's ability to force their concealment. In its zany account of *The Dunciad*'s succession to epic status, the Scriblerus satire produces an excessive pleasure that renders *The Dunciad* unaccountable to the conventionally satiric norms of guilt and reform. Its unruly language and its participants, the dunces, continuously manage to escape the backlash that critics anticipate from (or want to establish as) Pope's paternal displeasure.[7] One part of the thesis of this paper is that incest assumes allegorical form in *The Dunciad* and takes the name "Dulness." It is also part of the complicated interpretive history of *The Dunciad* that the presence of the allegorical figure "Dulness" has failed to convince us that the poem is "truly" allegorical. But our disagreement on this point may simply register this: that in the representational economy of the poem, incest returns within genre precisely as allegory's susceptibility to simulation.[8] What this essay ultimately hopes to show is why such simulations appear in *The Dunciad* as dark bodies.

II

The scene defining Cibber's incest with Dulness occurs as a parody of the Christian "light metaphysic" in which the soul descends through darkness in its approach to the light of divine illumination.[9]

Its more particular allusion is certainly Milton's invocation to "holy Light" in Book III of *Paradise Lost*, where the poet describes his poetic journey in terms of a reascent from darkness to light:

> Thee I re-visit now with bolder wing,
> Escap't the *Stygian* Pool, though long detain'd
> In that obscure sojourn, while in my flight
> Through utter and through middle darkness borne
> With other notes than to th' *Orphean* Lyre
> I sung of *Chaos* and *Eternal Night*,
> Taught by the heav'nly Muse to venture down
> The dark descent, and up to reascend,
> Though hard and rare...
>   (*Paradise Lost* III: 13–21)

Whereas Milton speaks from within the "cloud...and ever-during dark" of his blindness, but calls upon "Celestial Light" to "Shine inward" and in his mind "there plant eyes," "all mist from thence/Purge and disperse, that I may see and tell/Of things invisible to mortal sight" (III: 53–55), Cibber's address to Dulness celebrates her very power to obscure: "O! ever gracious to perplex'd mankind,/Still spread a healing mist before the mind;/And lest we err by Wit's wild dancing light,/Secure us kindly in our native night" (*Dunciad* I: 173–6). In Cibber's prayer to Dulness, the divinely inspired mind, isolated by blindness and yet even so illuminated, returns shrouded in an unmediating mist, its effort to attain prophetic sight by traversing the distinction lux/lumen in poetic song translated downward into the increasingly solid incarnations of darkness: "Nonsense precipitate, like running Lead,/That slip'd thro' Cracks and Zig-zags of the Head" (I: 123–4). This same substitution of the opaque for the luminous appears in Cibber's yearning for "our native night," though here, as in Cibber's recognition scene with Dulness, the allusion broadens to include that topos whereby the association of the metaphysics of light with Aristotle's doctrine of natural place opens out onto the geography of an allegorical journey.[10]

In the incest scene of *The Dunciad*, when Cibber is translated from his garret to Dulness' cave below Bethlehem Hospital, the cosmology of allegorical correspondences supported by the distinction between earthly and heavenly light and motivated in narrative by the desire to travel the distance of that difference descends with him into an urban geography which Pope portrays as dark and self-centered, a city-scape converging to the point where degrees of difference are subsumed to identity:[11]

> Her ample presence fills up all the place;
> A veil of fogs dilates her awful face:
> Great in her charms! as when on Shrieves and May'rs
> She looks, and breathes herself into their airs.
> She bids him wait her to her sacred Dome:
> Well pleas'd he enter'd, and confess'd his home.
> So Spirits ending their terrestrial race,
> Ascend, and recognize their Native Place.
>   (I: 261–8)

The events narrated in these lines, Dulness's mock-pentecostal ascent and Cibber's translation to her Dome, pretend to move us between one "place" and another. Two perfect rhymes, "place"/"face" and "race"/"Place," frame this passage, reinforcing our sense that it narrates movements that complete part of a larger, providential journey. But these perfect rhymes are themselves enclosed by the repetition "place"/"Place," a reiterative sound-image that negates what narrative would order in time as progress and genealogy by collapsing chronology into the prior relation of identity. Moving us from "place" to "Place," where the only change is not different but bigger, the form of these lines implies that there is no anywhere else. This metrical convergence is replayed in the characterization of Cibber and Dulness. The first "place," Cibber's garret, seems to function rather conventionally as a metonymy—the garret signifying his persona as a hack writer—but the poem transgresses the distance of that figure (the hack writer is not actually a garret) to identify Cibber with the range of his omnivorous "eye" as it takes in his room. Through the most obvious of puns (I/eye), Cibber's self becomes identical with the range of his vision. He treats this visual space as part of his own body, alternately populating and devastating it, littering it with his failed productions ("Round him much Embryo, much Abortion lay") and cannibalizing the objects of his perception ("How here he sipp'd, how there he plunder'd snug,/And suck'd all o'er, like an industrious Bug"). Passing through him, the objects of Cibber's sight become parts of his body. That the space occupied by the now extended body of Cibber is also occupied by Dulness, whose "presence fills up all the place" when she comes to comfort him, transforms the allusive "movements" of Cibber and Dulness into mere rhetoric: the best that narrative can do to figure their unspeakable identity.

The downward counter-movement of the passage elaborates this perfect spatial identity of Cibber and Dulness as incest: Cibber descends to the Dome of Dulness, recognizes it as his "home," and resumes his residence in the subterranean womb that, in *The Dunciad*, corresponds to the "Native Place" sought by heavenly souls travelling in search of their true country. Cibber's descent to Dulness's "Dome," then, narrates both his "apotheosis" into her consort and his return, as son, to her womb. The poem figures this translation as a progress, narrating the mutually informing coalescence of Cibber's perceiving self and his mother Dulness's womb as a bilateral change of location. Although narrative shape is compromised by the incestuous exchange it recounts, narrative here preserves its outline as the story of origin and destination—but only long enough to be brought down by the claims made by alternative stories issuing from the verbal and visual innuendo playing on the periphery of these couplets: from the claim, for example, that Dulness impregnates Cibber (she swells his head), or that, in his return to the Dome, Cibber fathers his enlarged self on his mother Dulness. The familial relations marked out in these competing genealogies sacrifice linear to centripetal and retrograde motions, at once collapsing the narrative line and incarnating in Cibber and Dulness an encyclopedia of incestuous possibilities. Caught, as it were, in every act, Cibber and Dulness emerge as co-present and mutually engendering, able to sex, arouse and gestate each other within a present tense organized as contrapuntal variations on the same-difference.

This analysis of incest in Pope's poem suggests that what is experienced by readers of *The Dunciad* as a conflicted "tension" between history and allegory may instead be a relaxation of the countervalences that support the allegorical mode, a relaxation of the kind of textual architecture that theorists of allegory have described as a structure extrapolated on the bias between temporal and spatial paradigms.[12] Whereas these theories show us that the language of allegory traverses the difference between diachrony and synchrony, progression and hierarchy, narrative and meaning, *The Dunciad* shows us the followers of Dulness spiraling to an inertial point where "None want a place, for all their Centre found" (IV: 77). The poem thematizes its un-making of allegorical structure in images of gravity and of the vortex, such as this one describing the influence of Dulness over her crowds:

> The gath'ring number, as it moves along,
> Involves a vast involuntary throng,
> Who gently drawn, and struggling less and less,
> Roll in her Vortex, and her pow'r confess.
>   (IV: 81–84)

The relaxation of allegorical structure proceeds in *The Dunciad* as a sophisticated demolition, revealing what we see as allegory in the poem to be something like the suspended image of an imploded building, held briefly aloft by the blast in the instant that it collapses itself. In his invocation to Chaos and Night at the beginning of Book IV, the poet identifies allegory as the internal force that will bring the poem down. What he asks of "dread Chaos" and "eternal Night" is that the unfinished poem itself might occupy the virtual temporality of a suspended image:

> Yet, yet a moment, one dim Ray of Light
> Indulge, dread Chaos, and eternal Night!
> Of Darkness visible so much be lent,
> As half to shew, half veil the deep Intent.
> Ye Pow'rs! whose Mysteries restor'd I sing,
> To whom Time bears me on his rapid wing,
> Suspend a while your Force inertly strong,
> Then take at once the Poet and the Song.
>   (IV: 1–8)

Like an imploding building, *The Dunciad* presents us with a recognizable but uninhabitable structure: it writes an allegory that cannot be read. Whereas Milton, in his blindness, is "Taught by the heav'nly Must to venture down/The dark descent, and up to reascend,/Though hard and rare," *The Dunciad* strikes its readers blind—not of course with an excess of revelatory light, but with the "darkness visible" of the inert material sign. By severing the read from the written sign, the poem replaces the temporal recursions of allegory—where, in the time of signification, desire contests meaning—with an instant of recognition that isolates and completes, leaving allegory with nothing else and nowhere else to mean. If, for example, we apply to *The Dunciad* one critic's suggestion that allegory unfolds from within the misprisions of narrative and meaning, that it goads its reader into opening a route through a semiotic territory on a search that generates meanings by being about that generation, we find that the incest of Cibber and Dulness has foreclosed the explanatory power of the term "generation" itself.[13]

The precision with which incestuous reproduction turns allegory against itself in *The Dunciad* recalls Paul de Man's often quoted definition of allegory as a genre that consists "in the *repetition*...of a previous sign with which it can never coincide, since it is of the essence of this previous sign to be pure anteriority,"[14] for the situation of allegory in *The Dunciad* is defined by the fact that Dulness and Cibber do coincide and that their incestuous marriage generates not repetition but sufficiency in the poem. This sufficiency is centered in Dulness, whose "presence fills up all the place." Thus while the figure of Dulness puts the face of allegory on the poem, the effect of her "presence" negates allegory's elaboration as meaning that "lie[s]...precisely in its non-coincidence with itself, [in] its failure to simply *be*—a failure that obliges it not only to meaning, but to meaning something else, somewhere else—*allos agoreuein*."[15] We have already seen how the recognition of Cibber and Dulness eradicates allegory's "somewhere else." The loss of this otherness before the presence of Dulness is dramatized in the absence of melancholy in Cibber and the dunces. In the sheer exuberance of their projects, their games and their grievances, in their eagerness to embrace the "me" and "now," the dunces display an exact indifference to the magisterial influences of loss and origin, to the trace of "pure anteriority" that binds allegory to the temporal and marks it with melancholy.[16] If the poem can make a lament, then, it is necessarily the second-order lament of black comedy: not for the lost origin, but for the loss of that loss. The "play" of the poem's language, like the games of the dunces, closes down differences, giving language a sort of magical but deadly acuity that collapses word and thing, history and event, meaning and reference. The formally constructed progress of the poem thus makes the "inertia" of dulness more and more inescapable until, with the etymological implosion of the poem's close, the all encompassing yawn of Dulness—"the long solemn Unison," "Wide, and more wide"—conjures up the figure of Chaos, whose name derives from the Greek verb meaning "to yawn."[17] With this yawn, we readers are drawn into the dark body of Dulness herself.

III

Incest, darkness, and the sufficiency of the same-difference: in these structures *The Dunciad* not only inverts the metaphysics of light but produces the effect of allegory through the reflexive structure of that inversion. *The Dunciad* reiterates the movement of Miltonic allegory, described by D. C. Allen as "a downward descent of knowledge, a revealing of suprarational information that enabled the humble learner to ascend" (179), only to "reveal" that this allegorical form is unfounded either in resemblance or in the extra-referential guarantees of Idea or Revelation. This formal self-sufficiency (which might as accurately be called the form of self-sufficiency), and its manifestation in the poem as the figure of Dulness, refers *The Dunciad*'s allegory to the theological tradition of accommodation. Seventeenth-century proponents of accommodation argue that God reveals himself to man through a mediating or symbolic vocabulary that is suited (accommodated) both to man's limited comprehension and to his need for redemptive knowledge. Defining scripture as a supplement to human incapacity, the theory of accommodation makes God's word readable by allegorizing it: only the ability to read that divine allegory offers escape from human dulness. In 1615, for example, Thomas Wilson writes that:

> An hand is applied to God to signifie his working power, an eye to signifie his knowledge, an heart, his will; a foot, his presence or government, winges, his care and protection, a mouth, his word and commandement, a finger, his might, a soule put for the essence of God, nostrils, for his indignation. Because our dulness to conceive the thinges of God is so great as wee cannot perceive them, but by comparisons drawne from the thinges of men, for this infirmity of our understanding, the Scripture very often speaketh of invisible thinges by visible, and shadoweth spirituall, by corporall. This rule striketh against the errour of the Anthropomorphites which fashion unto God the shape and nature of a man, upon mistaking such scriptures, as attribute to him the members and actions of a man.[18]

For Wilson, "our dulness" is a register of what we cannot perceive and cannot know about God, and the vocabulary of accommodation provides him with the allegorical conceit through which, "by comparisons" with the "corporall...thinges of men," language can allude to the imperceptible world of the spirit. When theories of accommodation such as Wilson's call on allegory to supplement our understanding so that we can "conceive the thinges of God," they identify language's failure to speak literally of God with the human body's failure to perceive God directly. This analogy allows the body anatomized in language to become the vehicle for allegory within theories of accommodation, which use the fact that anatomized bodies once lived to imply that their allegories will, someday or somewhere else, literally speak of God. Thus it is in images of the body that the semiotic play of lack and supplement produces allegory in the texts of accommodation. When Wilson enumerates God's characteristics by analogy to bodily parts, he would subordinate language's failure to refer a "heart" to "his will" or "a foot" to "his presence" both to the completed body that is implied by a partial list of anatomized body parts and to that body's former organic life. Through this temporal chiasmus (which prevents accommodation's "comparisons" from being simply analogies), the anatomized body's former life becomes its resurrection in allegory's future life as God's presence to language.

But allegory here does not only supply an approach to divinity: much of its work in Wilson's text is to ward off "the errour of the Anthropomorphites," to insist that the future of allegorical illumination is not now. As an exegetical method, accommodation uses allegory both to counter and to preserve the failure of human perception and of its languages, which in this tradition can never comprehend the divine in the present of perceiving or of reading without reducing it to the merely instrumental status of a body or a text. The apology for accommodation in *Theologicall Rules* resists this "errour" by taking the starkest possible allegorical form as two parallel lists that propagate because they are not equivalent: because they set the desire to speak of God against the propensity of physical images to replace the ineffable qualities they would convey.

It is as an effect of a small alteration in the relations among these components—allegory, accommodation and the body—that the supplemental structure of accommodation is turned into the vision of sufficiency put forward as incest in *The Dunciad*. In the 1695 *Essay Concerning Human Understanding*, Locke applies the doctrine of accommodation to the "language" of perception. Having derived knowledge from perception—from the gleanings of hands and feet, nostrils and eyes—Locke describes the foundational referentiality of the smallest component of knowledge, simple ideas, in these terms:

> Simple *Ideas*, which since the Mind...can by no means make to it self, must necessarily be the product of Things operating on the Mind in a natural way, and producing therein those Perceptions which by the Wisdom and Will of our Maker they are ordained and adapted to. From whence it follows, that *simple* Ideas *are not fictions* of our Fancies, but the natural and regular productions of Things without us, really operating upon us; and so carry with them all the conformity which is intended; or which our state requires: For they represent to us Things under those appearances which they are fitted to produce in us: whereby we are enabled to distinguish the sorts of particular Substances, to discern the states they are in, and so to take them for our Necessities, and apply them to our Uses. (IV.iv.4)

Here Locke anchors an epistemology that continually threatens to devolve onto the ephemera of sense perception by relieving simple ideas of any necessity to refer to things. Simple ideas need not refer because they carry with them the requisite, divinely intended conformity: the "Things" they "represent" are accommodated to our senses just as holy scripture is accommodated to our understandings.

We can surmise that Locke uses accommodation's exegetical method in the *Essay* to exorcise all the possible skepticisms (representationalism, theatricality, neo-platonism) introduced into it with the "appearances" of simple ideas. But for our analysis, the motivation for Locke's rhetoric is of less importance than its effect: that this transfer of an exegetical rhetoric from exegesis into a new discourse of human physiology doesn't occur without some alterations rebounding from the new context onto the genre—in this case allegory—that permits the transference. We see the *Essay* recycle allegory, re-working it to answer the utilitarian demands of a new semantic field. In this new field, Locke's allusion to accommodation grounds his epistemology on a postulated conformity which works not as difference between two orders, as it does in the allegorical accommodations of exegesis, but as the sufficiency of the understanding's presence to itself. The tests arising in allegory out of textual difference ("a foot" referred to "his presence") are supplanted by the empirical tests of "our Necessities" and "our Uses," suggesting that whatever piece of information serves a useful purpose has been rightly and completely perceived. And as knowledge is accommodated to the right perceptions of the body, allegory descends into the body, where it quietly rides the line between perceptions and ideas. With this descent, the body ceases to be instrumental to allegory—to be its pivotal image—and becomes instead its site, in the way that the page had been up to that point. The new paradigm of usefulness contains allegory in the body but denies that it is there, for what is precisely not useful to this new configuration of ideas and the senses are those vertiginous relays of inside and outside, perception and apperception, that define empiricism's foundational narrative—its account of "images of the body"—as allegory.[19] To counter the anti-foundational implications of that allegory, the *Essay* tries to separate the receptive from the perceived body, to bring the body as the source of images under the rubric of common sense (we all see it that way), and to manage the body-as-image through "scientific" codifications of physical character, such as physiognomy. This denial that allegory has taken up residence in the empirical body means that while the myriad and cross-referencing journeys traced by perception across the body may be experienced as allegory, they cannot be read that way. In *The Dunciad* this embodied allegory is figured not, as it is in Locke, as a useful sufficiency, but as a justified dulness.

IV

My argument to this point indicates that the incest of Cibber and Dulness is an analogue in the narrative and metaphoric structures of *The Dunciad* for the sufficiency that accommodation, applied by Locke to the first or simplest perceptions, invests in the body and in its epistemology. The incest of Cibber and Dulness mimics the logic of accommodated perception, an epistemology that is itself—the analogy suggests—incestuous: for once dulness is justified, the semantics and the semiotics of the senses coincide, and what perception can mean becomes indistinguishable from how it means what it means. *The Dunciad* writes that convergence as the end of history, defining the uneventful end of this same-difference as the body fully incarnated into its self-evidence. That "dark" identity—exemplified by the transfigurations of Cibber's body—is not patrilineal but simulational, "produced as the law that complicates all series, causing them to return within each one as the course of compulsion."[20] My reading of the troubled identity of genre in *The Dunciad* has shown that the trouble arises because incest, both confusion and source of genre, returns within genre as allegory's susceptibility to simulation. In *The Dunciad* this susceptibility takes shape as the questionable "allegory" of Dulness. A broader reading of the poem, by placing this issue in the context of the intersection between seventeenth-century exegesis and Enlightenment epistemology, shows *The Dunciad* dramatizing the return of simulation within empiricist epistemology, where it is both the confusion and the source of mimesis in the perceptual field. The poem dramatizes this return as the body's susceptibility to allegory. These homologies imply that, for the first half of the eighteenth-century and in the wake of a new perceptually-oriented epistemology, allegory may function primarily to register as a crisis the newly elevated body's susceptibility to simulation.

The games of Book II, for example, not only parody the tradition of epic contest but use the dunces' contending bodies and their visions to conduct an elaborate send up of allegory as immanent signification. Throughout the games, as the dunces scramble for meaningless prizes, we begin to suspect that the elusive prize is meaning itself. Although we experience these games as parody, the participants remain blissfully unaware of the way the text is embarrassing them. Their satisfaction—which is secure and even utopian—rests on and also indicates Dulness's power to endow the body as prize with the immanent signification promised but always deferred by narrative allegory. As readers of a parody, we see that bodies so endowed lack the provocative ambiguities of dualism (that dream navel of the Enlightenment and of its theories of representation) and that they cannot sustain the syntax of allegorical elaboration. Where for the dunces Dulness "heals" the body's difference from itself as representation, we see an uproarious satire on the dunces' greed and stupidity. To the participants of the games it doesn't matter whether the body is a phantasm or an organism, a representation or a mammalian machine; because the body has subsumed form and meaning to itself, no one even notices these variations as differences. Different manifestations of the human aspect are merely equivalent indications of the body's repletion in form.

Perhaps the best example of Dulness's power to purge the body and allegory of their complicated textuality occurs in the competition between stationers, when Dulness places a simulated "Poet's form" before the rivals Lintot and Curl:

> All as a partridge plump, full-fed, and fair,
> She form'd this image of well-body'd air;
> With pert flat eyes she window'd well its head;
> A brain of feathers, and a heart of lead;
> And empty words she gave, and sounding strain,
> But senseless, lifeless! idol void and vain!
> Never was dash'd out, at one lucky hit,
> A fool, so just a copy of a wit;
> So like, that critics said, and courtiers swore,
> A wit it was, and call'd the phantom More.
>   (II: 41–50)

From the perspective of epistemology and its history, we can see that the illusion that Dulness constructs of "well-body'd air" satisfies the sight of Lintot and Curl because More and the sight of More must be indistinguishable within an philosophy that grounds itself in the phantoms of sense perception. That problematic foundation appears here as a utopian, even transcendent correspondence between the visibility of Dulness's playful holograph of More and the vision of More received by the stationers. The thoroughly ridiculed worthlessness out of which the phantom is made—the quite conventional air, feathers, and empty words—would identify this passage as an example of social satire, verbally acute but limited in scope, if it were not for the fact that those very features, all pieces of the poem's "allegory" of Dulness, are transformed by and for the enthralled "critics" into More himself. In this miniature apotheosis, both allegory and the body depart their material vehicles and ascend, translated, to Dulness.

The fact that the "phantom More" is a professional plagiarist thus not only satirizes the publishing industry's anemic scruples, but emphatically perfects and so destroys allegory's characteristic preoccupation with past texts by gathering all possible allusions in this present and full realization of an all-inclusive Author.[21] In the face of this prankish millennium, only the poem's fragmented allegorical diction, in which allegory persists as the relic of history, attests to the fate of the real, historical body.

In this sequence, then, the stationers try to grasp onto the figure "More" as their "Prize" in a parodic realization of allegory's desire for the prize that is immanent meaning, the unification of form and content in a perfected text. As readers of, rather than participants in, the games, we see that the perfected text is a simulation. The "copy" which Dulness forms is "just" not because of the verisimilitude with which it represents the person "More" but because its supposed original denies the very distinction between original and copy. Where an ebullient plagiarist—or the physiology of sense perception or a xerox machine—produces origin, form is self-justifying. Indeed, "the phantom More" has neither interiority nor an original but "contains a positive power which negates *both original and copy, both model and reproduction.*"[22] At the moment of the game's beginning, when Curl and Lintot forget the stakes involved in representation to pursue the "phantom More," that memory lapse completes allegory's teleology. The ridiculous situation that this puts allegory in—it completes centuries of literature in credulity—leads to Pope's insistence that the body under simulation is in crisis. For Pope this seems to be primarily an aesthetic crisis, in which the fear that perception cannot distinguish an original from a copy serves mainly to emphasize the horrendous aesthetic chaos that results when perception cannot differentiate among copies. The pressing danger here is not that the real Alexander Pope will be confused with an imposter Pope but that "Pope" will be set aside for "Cibber." The poem reestablishes hierarchy between original work and plagiarism by setting allegory in a crisis that mirrors the perceived crisis of the simulated and simulating body. Having produced an analogy between the material aspects of allegory and the body—between the socio-historical world in which allegory works and the perceptual world of the body—the poem sacrifices both by reducing them to the vapid but complete consensus of the stationers.[23] In the duncely games, the phantom More corroborates the perceptual community of "our dulness"; the critics and courtiers who "call'd the phantom More" perform an act of perceptual consensus that both names and summons, recognizes and creates More.

The visionary verses of Book III and Cibber's "new world" illustrate again and on a more global scale the poem's preoccupation with the work of accommodated perception as simulacrum.[24] As Settle opens the future to Cibber, an ambiguity of syntax has Cibber viewing his "mental eye":

For this, our Queen unfolds to vision true
Thy mental eye, for thou hast much to view
   (III: 61–62)[25]

What unfolds to Cibber in subsequent lines as the spread of the power of Dulness over the globe is a narrative extension of the principles of self-sufficiency that govern Cibber's mind, an allegorization of Cibber's way of seeing. Carrying the logic of sufficient perception to its conclusion, the poem universalizes his justified dullness. This is what happens when Cibber's vision of his own "mental eye" becomes the fate of the world: as Cibber's guide explains to him "are these wonders, Son, to thee unknown?/Unknown to thee? These wonders are thy own" (III: 273–4). Cibber's vision—the introspection by which his "mental eye" takes shape as the "Embody'd dark" of global war and ignorance—is an example of how, in the context of accommodated dulness, perceived meanings begin and end and are justified within the terms of their own perceptual systems.

> Joy fills his soul, joy innocent of thought;
> "What pow'r, he cries, what pow'r these wonders wrought?"
> "Son; what thou seek'st is in thee! Look, and find
> Each Monster meets his likeness in thy mind."
>   (III: 249–52)

The Dunciad narrates the equation of knowledge and the body, or "our Dulness," as the universalizing of Cibber's point of view. The progress of Dulness occurs within the perceptual landscape of the "Cibberian brain" (I: 218) which, in its interactions with Dulness, becomes the condition of the poem. In Book I, Cibber, despairing of the duncely cause and the ignoble fates of his works, nonetheless proclaims his own enduring centrality:

> What then remains? Ourself. Still, still remain
> Cibberian forehead, and Cibberian brain.
>   (I: 217–18)

While it is possible to say of this passage that Cibber, making one of his last waking remarks, experiences the solipsist's self-affirmation, it is also true that Cibber as a volitional individual fades from the poem just as (and because) his point of view is universalized.[26] Chosen, crowned, and transported to the Dome of Dulness, Cibber undergoes an apotheosis that transforms him from the paragon of self-absorption into the informing principle of a "new world" that operates through him but without his intervention. As the perceptual "reality" of the Cibberian self fades to a background snore, it becomes the founding "reality" of *The Dunciad*. While Cibber experiences a solipsistic moment, that solipsism is only what *The Dunciad* narrates as the first, nostalgic experience of the perceptual system functioning as a simulacrum—a simulacrum that "includes within itself the differential point of view, [so that] the spectator is made part of the simulacrum which is transformed and deformed according to his point of view."[27] Cibber's vision in Book III "seemeth to embrace the whole world" because Cibber has embraced Dulness and now both he and the world begin to appear as reversible, phantasmatic effects of his perceptions. Cibber doesn't figure in Book IV, that is he doesn't appear as a character and he doesn't take any action, because—with the restoration of Dulness's empire—the Cibberian point of view has become general, the particular psychological location of the "Cibberian brain" (I: 218) having been transformed into a landscape of "Cimmerian gloom" (IV: 352). Cibber's "brain" thus becomes the place and occasion of the poem and his apotheosis into a universal condition issues in the kingdom of dullness. As Cibber disappears, so does solipsism's nostalgia for true representation. The disappearance of Cibber repeats as narrative the general genealogical paradox of the poem and of the duncely world: as Cibber fades, sleeping, deeper and deeper into the background of *The Dunciad*, the Cibberian mind becomes the semiotic ground against which the triumphant pageant of his mother, Dulness, occurs.

The profane cosmology of Cibber's "new world," which is articulated through the poem's parodic allusions to the divine cosmology in *Paradise Lost*, satirizes an epistemology that substitutes the accommodated text of perception for the divine word. The fate of reference in the kingdom of Dulness is determined by two aspects of the Cibberian cosmology: it is a universe that revolves around the "Embody'd dark" of human presence or self-identity and it is created out of the theater of Cibber's perceptual world. The movement by which the poem's satiric interest in theater gives way to a dramatic structure parallels the gradual movement by which Cibber's consciousness gives way to dream-vision and finally to the dark sleep of Dulness. What emerges from the confluence of self-identity and theatricality in the Cibberian cosmology is the very peculiar allegory of Dulness—the allegory of the simulation of allegory.

In that allegory, the end of a world is not necessarily the end of the world. While "Pope" must disapprove of the dunces and all their works in order to protect his and our investment in poetic authority, *The Dunciad* celebrates justified dulness insofar as it breaks the order of representation. This affirmation can happen because Dulness functions in the poem neither as a divine nor as a demonic similitude, but as a simulation; she is not a shadow of truth, but the aspect of "our dulnes," a figure for the fullness of human presence. She is thus not a representation but an effect—and our analysis of some aspects of *The Dunciad*'s historical moment reveal her to be the effect of the perceiving body functioning as the simulacrum. This is, of course, where her allegory fails to establish itself as true allegory, and why she is condemned as Dulness. But it is also where Dulness and *The Dunciad* succeed to their strange, ambivalent modernity. We can say that in *The Dunciad* the reign of the Goddess Dulness and the apocalypse that she ushers in recount the loss of divine authority and its replacement by an epistemology that generates idolatrous simulations in the image of its own parameters. Dulness herself is the allegorical figure for that "embody'd dark," just as she is mother to all of the poem's dunces. Beyond that, she faces the English empiricist epistemology with its consequences: *The Dunciad* is what will come to be because, after Locke, perception (our dulness) functions as a simulacrum against which not even the violence of satire can reassert the distinction between the true and false representation and with it literature's patrilineage. But whatever questions about the poem these arguments can settle, Dulness continues to display for us—in the contagious play of language and of the dunces—that the empirical body is susceptible to simulation. One of the lingering consequences of empiricism has been that perception, and with it reading, continue to be subjected to the ends of usefulness. To read Dulness is to read the criteria of usefulness as part of empiricism's repression of the simulacrum that always abides with its epistemology. It is also to understand that theories that claim to meet those criteria merely remake empiricism, reissuing its patrilineage under a new guise to adjudicate, once again, the good and true from the unworthy bodies. Dulness offers her readers no such useful vantage. In *The Dunciad*, our dulness appears in the form of an allegory, and—in the accommodated world of Cibberian perspective—the form is replete. Thus while we cannot doubt that Dulness is an allegory, we would be dunces if we did not doubt it.

NOTES

1. Alexander Pope, *The Dunciad* in *The Poems of Alexander Pope*, ed. James Sutherland (London: Methuen & Co., 1943). All subsequent references to *The Dunciad* will be to this edition and will be cited parenthetically in the text.

2. My use of the term "transumptive" here refers to Edwin Honig's discussion of Dante's "Letter to Can Grande" in *Dark Conceit: the Making of Allegory* (Hanover and London: University Press of New England, 1959), 4.

3. In his own discussion of "generic confusion" in the poem, John E. Sitter traces critical dissatisfaction with the status of genre in *The Dunciad* as far back as John Dennis's early remarks on the inactivity of Cibber as the poem's "epic" hero. See John E. Sitter, *The Poetry of Pope's Dunciad* (Minneapolis: University of Minnesota Press, 1971), 6–50.

4. In his excellent "Dulness Unbound: Rhetoric and Pope's *Dunciad*," Fredric Bogel discusses the ambiguous "kinship" structures in Dulness' genealogy in the context of his argument that the poem not only describes but enacts "the subversion of difference and thus of meaning." *Publications of the Modern Language Association* 97 (1982): 844–55.

5. Because the incest taboo legitimates resemblance within representation by defining acceptable difference in terms of or as small alterations in the same, forms of difference (the ill-suited and mismatched: promiscuity, miscegenation, bad taste) produce not more but fewer possibilities in *The Dunciad*, suggesting that especially those who persist in mixing tragedy and comedy or in seeking love too far outside their kind will come to incest and entropy.

6. On the law of the law of genre, see Jacques Derrida: "It is precisely a principle of contamination, a law of impurity, a parasitical economy. In the code of set theories, if I may use it at least figuratively, I would speak of a sort of participation without belonging—a taking part in without being part of, without having membership in a set. With the inevitable dividing of the trait that marks membership, the boundary of the set comes to form, by invagination, an internal pocket larger than the whole; and the outcome of this division and of this abounding remains as singular as it is limitless." Derrida alludes to incest on 78. "The Law of Genre," *Critical Inquiry* 7 (1980): 55–81.

7. In *The Argument of Images*, for example, Patricia Meyer Spacks completely subordinates the problematic happiness of the dunces to Pope's corrective prerogative: "In *The Dunciad*, the poet's authority is final; the poet-perceiver can achieve and render a complex understanding of truth." *The Argument of Images: The Poetry of Alexander Pope* (Cambridge: Harvard University Press, 1971), 112.

8. On simulation see especially Gilles Deleuze, "Plato and the Simulacrum," tr. Rosalind Krauss, *October* 27 (Winter 1983), 45–56. This is an excerpt from *The Logic of Sense* (New York: Columbia University Press, 1990).

9. See D. C. Allen, "Milton and the Descent to Light," *Milton: Modern Essays in Criticism*, ed. Arthur E. Barker (Oxford: Oxford University Press, 1965): 177–95; and Joseph Anthony Mazzeo, "Light Metaphysics, Dante's 'Convivio' and the Letter to Can Grande della Scale," *Traditio* 14 (1958): 191–230. Aubrey Williams writes generally

and comprehensively about "the inversion of Christian themes and situations in the *Dunciad*" in his *Pope's Dunciad: A Study of its Meaning* (Baton Rouge: Louisiana State University Press, 1955).

10. Joseph Mazzeo gives a good account of Aristotle on motion and place in "Light Metaphysics," 218–19. Aristotle discusses natural place in *De Caelo*, 3.2 and 4.3–4. The *Dunciad*'s critical apparatus cites Plato's account of the immortality of the soul in ostensible homage to Lintot's editions.

11. In the empire of Dulness, the comparative is merely rhetorical. An example of this is Dulness's review of her offspring in Book I, where "In each she marks her Image full exprest,/But chief in BAY's monster-breeding breast" (I: 107–8).

12. Elaborating on a Jakobsonean model of language, Joel Fineman describes allegory as "the poetical projection of the metaphoric axis onto the metonymic, where metaphor is understood as the synchronic system of differences which constitutes the order of language (*langue*), and metonymy as the diachronic principle of combination and connection by means of which structure is actualized in time in speech (*parole*)." Joel Fineman, "The Structure of Allegorical Desire," *Allegory and Representation, Selected Papers from the English Institute* (Baltimore: The Johns Hopkins University Press, 1981), 31.

13. I am here paraphrasing part of an argument put forward by Gordon Teskey in "From Allegory to Dialectic: Imagining Error in Spenser and Milton," in *PMLA* 101 (1986): 9–23.

14. Paul de Man, "The Rhetoric of Temporality," in *Blindness and Insight* (Minneapolis: University of Minnesota, 1971), 207.

15. Stephen Melville, *Philosophy Beside Itself* (Minneapolis: University of Minnesota Press, 1986), 125.

16. Cibber *is* melancholy at the opening of the poem, when he builds a pyre for his under-appreciated literary works, but that is before he invokes Dulness and is translated to her dome. It is again in "The Rhetoric of Temporality" that de Man argues that "the prevalence of allegory always corresponds to the unveiling of an authentically temporal predicament" (206). Both his argument and my own here draw off Walter Benjamin, *The Origin of German Tragic Drama* (London: NLB, 1977).

17. *The Oxford English Dictionary* traces chaos to the Greek "any vast gulf or chasm, the nether abyss, empty space, the first state of the universe," from the verb stem "to yawn, gape."

18. Thomas Wilson, *Theologicall Rules: To Guide Us in Understanding and Practice of Holy Scriptures*, by T. W. Preacher of the Word (London, Printed by Edw. Griffin for Fran. Burton, 1615), 22–23. Part of this passage is quoted by C. A. Patrides in "Paradise Lost and the Theory of Accommodation," *Texas Studies in Language and Literature* 5 (1983).

19. For a discussion of allegory and its relation to the difference inherent in phrases which simultaneously express the subjective and the objective genitive relation, see Joel Fineman, "The Structure of Allegorical Desire," in *Allegory and Representation*, 26–60.

20. Gilles Deleuze, "Plato and the Simulacrum," 53.

21. The idea that allegory involves a creative commentary on previous texts is a commonplace of theoretical work on allegory. Maureen Quilligan argues that each allegory constructs itself through revisionary allusions to what she calls "threshold texts." See her *The Language of Allegory: Defining the Genre* (Ithaca and London: Cornell University Press, 1979): 51–64. In Paul de Man's work, this idea recurs as allegory's "discovery of a truly temporal predicament" ("The Rhetoric of Temporality," 222).

22. Deleuze, "Plato and the Simulacrum," 53.

23. Of the materialism of allegory, Michael Murrin writes "Allegory is intimately associated with the society in which the poet writes; it demands human participation and must be explicable in human terms." *The Veil of Allegory: Some Notes toward a Theory of Allegory in the English Renaissance* (Chicago: University of Chicago Press, 1969).

24. Angus Fletcher discusses the idea that "kosmos" is "the essential type of an allegorical image" in his *Allegory: The Theory of a Symbolic Mode* (Ithaca and London: Cornell University Press, 1964): 108–46.

25. Pope introduces this ambiguity into the lines from Milton:

>   ...but to nobler sights
> *Michael* from *Adam's* eyes the Filme remov'd
> Which that false Fruit that promis'd clearer sight
> Had bred; then purg'd with Euphrasie and Rue
> The visual Nerve, for he had much to see.
>   (*Paradise Lost* XI: 411–15)

26. On Cibber and solipsism, see David B. Morris, *Alexander Pope: The Genius of Sense* (Cambridge: Harvard University Press, 1984): "All centers on Cibber's solipsistic answer to the riddle that he poses to himself as he contemplates the ruin of his fortune and career: 'What then remains?' His answer constricts the world to his own dimensions, recreating reality in his image" (288); and Patricia Meyer Spacks, *An Argument of Images*: "That solipsism which is assumed by such later poets as Eliot to be a necessary condition of life seems to Pope a symbol of the ultimate evil" (94).

27. Deleuze, "Plato and the Simulacrum," 49.

GUARDIAN #39
Berkeley's Allegory of Mind

Peter Walmsley

With the shift of genre between *A Treatise concerning the Principles of Human Knowledge* (1709) and the *Three Dialogues between Hylas and Philonous* (1713), Berkeley showed his willingness to experiment with form and to employ the literary in the service of philosophy. In dialogue he was free to dramatize a conversion to immaterialism, and to develop ironies and emotional appeals constrained by the philosophical treatise's closed deductive method. When, in 1713, Berkeley came to London to publish the *Three Dialogues*, he was admitted by the leading writers of the day as an equal, a man of letters. Pope presented him with a copy of *Windsor-Forest*, and Addison found a place for him in his own box on the opening night of *Cato*. But the highest mark of favor was Steele's invitation to contribute to *The Guardian*, and Berkeley took the opportunity to continue the literary exploration begun with the *Three Dialogues*. We can now attribute fourteen *Guardians* to Berkeley, and these show him taking advantage of the small canvas of the daily paper to attempt a range of modes and forms.[1] He was already well familiar with the repertoire of the genre as it had been shaped by Addison and Steele. He had subscribed to the first octavo edition of *The Tatler* in 1710, and his letters show that, like everyone else, he made *The Spectator* part of his daily diet in Dublin. He seems to have been particularly impressed by Addison's *Spectators* on the imagination; Philonous's long rhapsody on the sublimities of the heavens in the second of the *Three Dialogues* is full of verbal echoes of *Spectators* ##412 and 420. While in London in 1713 Berkeley read *The Examiner*, the organ of the Tory ministry, and *The Guardian*, sending copies of both papers back to his friend John Percival in Dublin. In an accompanying letter he remarks how the weekly *Examiners* "are written by some new hand, and much better than formerly; I speak not with regard to party debates, but to the style and spirit, which is all we moderate sort of men mind in those sort of papers" (*Works*, VIII: 59). In another letter to Percival he praises Steele's "peculiar delicacy and easiness of writing" (*Works*, VIII: 63). So even before he started to contribute to *The Guardian*, Berkeley had a growing appreciation for the style and conventions of the new daily paper—valuable knowledge, for *The Guardian* aimed to capitalize on *The Spectator*'s winning formula, and Berkeley would certainly have been encouraged by Steele to fit the mold. In *Guardian* #98, Addison describes the paper as a "Nursery for Authors" where the literary talents of younger writers could be put to public trial (*Guardian*, 349). Berkeley was one initiate who acquitted himself with honour; Steele writes that his contributions "are often inserted in the *Guardian* without Deviation of one Tittle from what he sends me" (*Guardian*, 324).

The range of Berkeley's *Guardians* is impressive. Some show a philosopher's predilection for orderly debate—in #55, for example, he announces that he will be "polemical," and proceeds first to expound and then refute Shaftesbury's main ethical arguments. Both this essay and #83, where Berkeley attacks free-thinkers for their "Short-sightedness," are proving grounds for the sustained apologetic satire of *Alciphron* (1732). In two other papers, ##62 and 70, Berkeley imitates Addison's "essays" on places in London, letting a sight or an incident trigger a chain of open and spontaneous reflection. But of all his contributions the most imaginative and ambitious are *Guardians* 35 and 39, the latter particularly as it adopts the mode of moral allegory that Addison worked to revive in *The Spectator*.[2] In both ##35 and 39, Berkeley writes to Nestor Ironside as Ulysses Cosmopolita, a young man who, having completed his grand tour, has recognized that he needs some learning as ballast for his polite education. He tells how this need was met by a French virtuoso who presented him with a box of philosophical snuff. This snuff has the virtue of releasing the soul from the body, and so lets Ulysses visit the pineal glands of philosophers, there to catch the "sublime Ideas and comprehensive Views" as they rise in their minds (*Guardian*, 145). This remarkable conceit is not original to Berkeley, but is borrowed from

Gabriel Daniel's *Voyage to the World of Descartes*,[3] and Berkeley acknowledges the debt when in *Guardian* 35 Ulysses notes that he got the snuff from Daniel's nephew. But Berkeley's purposes with the snuff prove very much his own. Daniel's *Voyage* is a mock travel book, the snuff permitting him to leave his body to visit the world that Descartes' spirit is building on the other side of the moon. His design is an easy introduction to the principles of Cartesian philosophy, enlivened by the fantasy of interplanetary travel and by light satire on the vanity of philosophical sects. While in the opening of *Guardian* 35 Berkeley shows his appreciation of Daniel's satire on Cartesian mental physiology with its choice of the pineal gland as the earthly habitation of the soul, the concerns of his own satire are quite different and more immediate. And where Daniel uses his freedom from the body to voyage to imaginary philosophical worlds, Berkeley chooses to enter other minds. In #35 Ulysses relates how he found improvement in the pineal glands of philosophers and mathematicians, but confesses too that his attention wandered:

> Nor was it an unpleasant Entertainment, sometimes to descend from these sublime and magnificent Ideas to the Impertinences of a Beau, the dry Schemes of a Coffee-House Politician, or the tender Images in the Mind of a young Lady. (*Guardian*, 145)

Here Berkeley hints at the comic possibilities of his snuff conceit, and, in Scriblerian fashion, scientific readily slides into sexual curiosity. The remainder of the essay is devoted to a moral anatomy of a man of pleasure, a character torn between violent passions and a dull, nagging remorse. In this psychological analysis, Berkeley owes nothing to Daniel but much to *The Spectator*, where many essays adopted similarly privileged vantage points to display the inner lives of various urban types. In ##275 and 281, for example, Mr Spectator dreams of dissecting first the head of a beau and then the heart of a coquette, finding both to be cluttered with the trivial objects of their daily lives but empty of thought and feeling.

Both the mode and the focus of Berkeley's satire shift, however, in *Guardian* 39, where Ulysses recounts his visit to Anthony Collins's pineal gland during the composition of *A Discourse of Free-thinking*. The *Discourse*, published shortly before Berkeley's arrival in London, had won Collins instant notoriety.

Disturbed by the deistical tendencies of its argument, Berkeley visited Collins's haunt, the Grecian Coffee-house, only to overhear blatantly atheistical talk from members of Collins's coterie.[4] He recognized then the danger that Collins posed—that the religious skepticism propounded in the *Discourse* was, in fact, designed as an introduction to atheism. The force of this recognition invigorates Berkeley's satire. Where *Guardian* 35's examination of the spiritual condition of the man of pleasure remained distanced and somewhat abstract, #39 is a vivid and fantastic allegory narrating Collins's mental degeneration from a harmless idiot to an enemy of religion. Collins's mind is rendered as a chaotic mansion whose rooms Ulysses visits, encountering personifications of Collins's prejudice, vanity, and atheism. *Guardian* 39 is remarkable, however, not only as it reveals Berkeley's powers as a imaginative writer and a satirist, but for the way it shows him discovering in allegory new possibilities for his own philosophical discourse. The paper seems, on one hand, to violate his central metaphysical tenets of the immateriality and invisibility of the soul, and to contradict his warnings about the dangers of metaphors that describe the soul in terms of sense experience. Yet Berkeley finds in the conventions of allegory a way of depicting the spiritual that avoids metaphor's conflation of mind and body. Moreover, the process of allegorical reading enacted in *Guardian* 39 reflects Berkeley's own beliefs about the process of interpreting sense experience. In practicing allegory as it was revived by Addison in his periodical papers, Berkeley discovers a mode deeply sympathetic to the rhetorical needs and intellectual priorities of his own epistemological discourse.

II

In his early writings Berkeley seems to have a clear apprehension of the nature of spirit and is emphatic in distinguishing mind from the fleeting world of "ideas":

> A spirit is one simple, undivided, active being: as it perceives ideas, it is called the *understanding*, and as it produces or otherwise operates about them, it is called the *will*. Hence there can be no idea formed of a soul or spirit: for all ideas whatever, being passive and inert...cannot represent unto us, by way of image or likeness, that which acts. (*Works*, II: 52)

Mind is pure activity, and cannot be represented by ideas which are, for Berkeley, "visibly inactive" (*Works*, II: 51). Mind is, moreover, a unity, and while Berkeley speaks of such conventional mental faculties as the understanding, will, memory and imagination, he recognizes that these distinctions are merely nominal. He does not clarify, however, how it is that we do know mind, and his definition seems at odds with his own epistemological method, not least with his denunciation of abstraction.[5] And this view of mind is as troublesome for Berkeley's rhetoric as for the consistency of his immaterialist system, for the metaphysical writer is obliged to dramatize mental life. He admits in the *Principles* that "ideas," those vivid pictures which validate and illuminate so much of his argument, cannot be permitted to represent our processes of thought:

> nothing seems more to have contributed towards engaging men in controversies and mistakes, with regard to the nature and operations of the mind, than the being used to speak of those things, in terms borrowed from sensible ideas. For example, the will is termed the *motion* of the soul: this infuses a belief, that the mind of man is as a ball in motion, impelled and determined by the objects of sense, as necessarily as that is by the stroke of a racquet. (*Works*, II: 107)

Here Berkeley recognizes that our inevitably metaphorical discourse about spirit is dangerously misleading and must be carefully restrained, lest it open the way for a reductive, mechanical conception of the mind's activity.

Berkeley's predecessors shared this anxiety about depicting the mental. Locke too objected to "lively metaphorical Representations" in philosophy, and he showed how enthusiasts are led astray when they adopt "the Metaphor of seeing and feeling" to describe their spiritual experiences.[6] And although Locke is more attracted to corpuscular explanations of sense experience than Berkeley, he sees just as clearly that such accounts are little more than romances. He readily admits the absurdity of explaining the phenomenon of light as the effect of "a Company of little Tennis-balls, which Fairies all day long struck with Rackets against some Men's foreheads."[7] Any talk of our sense experience must be kept distinct from speculation about its unknown mechanical causes. It has, of course, long been recognized that Locke's rhetorical postures have little to do with his rhetorical practice,[8] and this is nowhere more true than in his metaphors of spirit. In Books I and II of the *Essay* he does not hesitate to speak of mind as inhabiting space, relying on traditional architectural metaphors to substantiate his view that knowledge is first a matter of accumulating innumerable simple ideas of sense, and not of referring to a few transcendent innate ideas. Locke's diction emphasizes the storage of ideas in the mind: the child's mind is an "empty Cabinet"; a "stock" of ideas is "convey[ed] into the mind" by the senses; and the memory is nothing but "the Store-house of our *Ideas*."[9] More playfully, he will argue that if the organs of sense

> or the Nerves which are the Conduits, to convey [ideas of sense] from without to their Audience in the Brain, the mind's Presence-room (as I may so call it) are any of them so disordered, as not to perform their Functions, they have no Postern to be admitted by; no other way to bring themselves into view, and be perceived by the Understanding.[10]

Ideas, in this strain, become so many lodgers in the mind's mansion, dozing peacefully until called upon to attend the understanding, or, indeed, until "rouzed and tumbled out of their dark Cells, into open Day-light, by some turbulent and tempestuous Passion."[11] Locke also wishes to emphasize the mind's activity—he frequently paints the dangers of intellectual laziness—and so describes the understanding as the builder as well as the lord of its mansion. Sense, he tells us, is "the Groundwork, whereon to build all those Notions" which we need in the course of life.[12]

Although Locke's models for thought and representations of mind were influential in the genesis of immaterialism, Berkeley is altogether a more disciplined philosophical writer, and much more wary of metaphor.[13] Though like Locke he employs the pervasive metaphor that thought is sight, speaking of ideas as "clear and distinct," he nowhere gives mind the same spatial presence in the *Principles* and the *Three Dialogues* that it had in Locke's *Essay*. Berkeley's talk of "in the mind" and "without the mind" is necessitated by his refutation of the materialists' external substance, but has for him more to do with the provenance of ideas than with the mind's dimensions. Even the verbs he favors to describe the understanding's activity, "perceive" and "consider," are metaphorically dead. Berkeley is attracted, however, to another strain of imagery in the *Essay*. Locke's empiricism found support in Aristotle's metaphor of the *tabula rasa*, and so Locke described the child's mind as a "white Paper," and elsewhere likened both the memory and the senses to a wax tablet on which ideas, or their material archetypes, are stamped.[14] In the same vein Locke spoke of how our memories fail with age:

> our Minds represent to us those Tombs, to which we are approaching; where though the Brass and Marble remain, yet the Inscriptions are effaced by time, and the Imagery moulders away.[15]

Berkeley too speaks of ideas as "imprinted on the senses" (*Works*, II: 41 and 53), but in so doing has more in mind than the mechanical process of inscription which seems the point of Locke's usage. Berkeley consistently uses a linguistic analogy to describe sense experience: "visible ideas are the language whereby the governing spirit, on whom we depend, informs us what tangible ideas he is about to imprint upon us, in case we excite this or that motion in our own bodies" (*Works*, II: 59). Again, "the connexion of ideas does not imply the relation of *cause* and *effect*, but only of a mark or *sign* and thing *signified*" (*Works*, II: 69). Berkeley goes on to suggest that simple ideas of sense are in some ways like letters: a very few signs combined in regular ways can be used efficiently to signify a vast range of effects. Throughout the *Principles* God is spoken of as the "Author of Nature," and natural law becomes the "grammar" of our sense experience.

William H. McGowan has shown how Berkeley's development of Locke's inscription metaphor makes it consistent, granting the language of ideas an author.[16] God wins a role in our lives as he "speaks" directly to our minds, without the encumbrance of an intervening material substance. Indeed, in *Alciphron* Berkeley admits that language is the most persuasive evidence of the presence of another spirit. Alciphron tells Euphranor "that nothing so much convinces me of the existence of another person as his speaking to me. It is my hearing you talk that, in strict and philosophical truth, is to me the best argument for your being" (*Works*, III: 148). Moreover, by insisting on our roles as readers of the world, Berkeley keeps his metaphor in the realm of the human, avoiding mechanical models of thought. This linguistic analogy likewise insists on the agency of the human spirit which, as sign reader, finds itself much busier, much more the author of its own world even than Locke's builder. Berkeley shows that in our simplest sense experience, far from simply presenting a wax surface, our minds are at work decoding the world. Appropriately, then, mind reveals itself in Berkeley's writing not as place or image but as voice, as language user. With the prominent and questioning "I" of the *Principles* and the interplay of voices in the *Three Dialogues*, Berkeley shows us mind engaged in what he sees as its fundamental and characteristic activity, ordering experience through language.

III

At the opening of *Guardian* 39, Berkeley reifies Collins's mind, adopting for the first time the conventional image of the mind as a mansion:

> On the 11th Day of *October* in the Year 1712, having left my Body locked up safe in my Study, I repaired to the *Grecian* Coffee-house, where entering into the *Pineal Gland* of a certain eminent *Free-thinker*, I made directly to the highest part of it, which is the Seat of the Understanding, expecting to find there a comprehensive Knowledge of all things Humane and Divine; but, to my no small Astonishment, I found the Place narrower than ordinary, insomuch that there was not any room for a Miracle, Prophesie, or *Separate Spirit*.
> This obliged me to descend a Story lower, into the Imagination, which I found larger, indeed, but Cold and Comfortless. I discovered *Prejudice* in the Figure of a Woman standing in a Corner, with her Eyes close shut, and her Fore-fingers stuck in her Ears; many Words in a confused Order, but spoken with great Emphasis, issued from her Mouth. (*Guardian*, 156–7)

In this passage Berkeley realizes Collins's mind as a domestic interior, rendering each faculty as a different story and even remarking on how "Cold and Comfortless" he finds Collins's imagination. But even as Berkeley literalizes, reviving the dead metaphor of narrow-mindedness, he introduces another distinct level of meaning. Collins's understanding is too cramped "for a Miracle, Prophesie, or *Separate Spirit*," objects we have never before thought of as demanding floor-space. The disjunction demands allegorical reading; the features of the domestic mindscape are clearly figures of Collins's religious thought, here particularly the *Discourse*'s insinuations that all miracles are impostures.[17] The allegory becomes more insistent with the personification of Prejudice "in the Figure of a Woman." The phrase renders Prejudice's already dubious ontological status even more tenuous, and her grotesque posture demands that she be read as an emblem, not a character. Everything about the trope advertises the distance between vehicle and tenor, concrete and abstract, sensible and spiritual.

As Prejudice speaks, her words condense into a mist through which Ulysses watches, as in a *camera obscura*, the thoughts that pass in Collins's mind. A horrific tableau appears through the gloom—Ulysses sees a fortified castle with a tower, "filled with Racks and Halters," surrounded by the "scattered bones of men," and "garrisoned by certain Men in Black, of Gigantick Size, and most terrific Forms." But as Ulysses moves closer, penetrating the distorting medium Collins's prejudice, the scene undergoes a metamorphosis:

> The Castle I found to be only a Church, whose Steeple with its Clock and Bell Ropes was mistaken for a Tower filled with Racks and Halters. The terrible Giants in black shrunk into a few innocent Clergymen. The Dungeons were turned into Vaults designed only for the habitation of the Dead, and the Fortification proved to be a Churchyard with some scattered Bones in it, and a plain Stone Wall round it. (*Guardian*, 157)

With this scene Berkeley reveals the true intent of Collins's *Discourse*, which attacked the authority of the Church under a specious plea for "free-thought" and promulgated a conspiracy theory of religion. But Berkeley also probes Collins's psyche, offering a satiric history of the origins of his contempt for the clergy. Collins is the victim of an irrational association of ideas; from a sight of bones lying in a churchyard he invested the clergy with all his fears of death, turning them into agents of destruction.

Drawn by a loud noise, Ulysses descends a story lower to find "a Mob of Passions assembled in a riotous manner." Of these Vanity soon takes charge, offering to lead an attack on the black giants in the imagination. But first she rummages the magazine of Collins's memory for arms:

> Away posted *Vanity*, and I after her, to the Store-house of Ideas; where I beheld a great number of lifeless Notions confusedly thrown together, but upon the Approach of *Vanity* they began to crawl. Here were to be seen, among other odd Things, Sleeping Deities, Corporeal Spirits, and Worlds formed by Chance, with an endless Variety of Heathen Notions, the most irregular and grotesque imaginable. And with these were jumbled several of Christian Extraction; but such was the Dress and Light they were put in, that they looked little better than Heathens. There was likewise assembled no small number of Phantomes in strange Habits, who proved to be Idolatrous Priests of different Nations. (*Guardian*, 157)

Elaborating here Locke's image of a sudden passion rousing ideas from their sleep in memory's dark cells, Berkeley explores the incoherence of Collins's thought—his reliance on ancient authorities in matters of religion, his frequent *ad hominem* employment of Christian notions against Christianity, his constant allusions to the conduct of pagan priests. The scene rapidly deteriorates as these notions, under the command of Atheism and Vanity, form ranks and charge into the imagination. The image is that of madness's mingling of faculties, and as Ulysses scrambles to free himself from this carnivalesque rebellion from belowstairs, the layers of satiric allegory are captured in a pun: "I, for my Part, made the best of my Way, and re-entered my own Lodging." Ullyses's spirit returns to his own rooms and his own body, but also to his own more orderly intellectual house. Here again, Berkeley draws attention to the doubleness of his allegorical discourse.

Guardian 39 displays many of the features that characterize Scriblerian satire, not least its method of humiliation through the domestic and its implication of the subject in the larger forces of mutability and chaos. Yet most evocative and engaging are its physicality and energy, qualities which make *Guardian* 39 successful allegory as well. Berkeley makes Collins's thought immediate and accessible through place and action. Ulysses is not simply a reader of tableaux but a participant as he explores the recesses of Collins's mind. But, at the same time, the mental anarchy Berkeley depicts destabilizes the vehicle of the allegory. Metamorphosis prevails: monsters become clergymen and lifeless ideas mutate first to "crawling" reptiles and then to phantom warriors. The scene is shifting, offering a bewildering clutter of images which lacks coherence and dramatic autonomy. Like the story of the coats in *A Tale of a Tub* or the domestic squabbles in Arbuthnot's John Bull pamphlets, Berkeley's allegorical vehicle is obviously concocted. So as much as Berkeley successfully renders the abstract concrete, his disjointed literalization keeps the focus of the allegory clearly on the tenor. Transcendent reading is further encouraged by his self-conscious use of personification. Indeed the three cruces of Berkeley's drama involve the revelation and naming of the three motives in Collins's thought—Prejudice, Vanity and Atheism. Where Berkeley had rejected spiritual metaphors for their conflation of subject and analogue, he finds in allegory's sustained disjunction of tenor and vehicle a means for talking about mind without muddling the spiritual and the sensible.

Critics and theorists of allegory in the present century have found the mode rich in radical ironies. J. Hillis Miller dwells on its covert expression of esoteric truths: "What the allegory reveals at the same time it hides, since the more visible and audible it is to ordinary eyes and ears, the more accommodated it is to limited vision, and therefore the less directly representative of the secrets it would tell."[18] Reading allegory for Miller involves an "oscillation" from flesh to word and word to flesh. Ellen Douglass Leyburn, writing earlier but in a very similar vein, celebrates allegory's "indirection" and "deliberate dissimulation," and even though writing of Augustan allegory, she argues that personification in its explicitness is foreign to allegory's essential method.[19] Berkeley and his contemporaries, however, seemed as interested in allegory's possibilities for moral instruction as for sustained irony. Writing in part at least in the emblem tradition, they regularly turned to personifications in symbolic settings when they wanted to explore the human psyche, as with Pope's cave of Spleen or Addison's allegories throughout *The Spectator*, which deal most often with virtues, vices, and passions. But as Addison strives to resurrect allegory as a mode of moral and spiritual discourse, he is conscious in his critical writings of how personification can undermine the mimetic purposes of art. Sin and Death, "empty and unsubstantial Beings," violate the "Probability" of Milton's history with their evident immateriality.[20] In his *Spectators* on the imagination, Addison includes allegory with the "*Faerie way of Writing*" as one in which the author "quite loses sight of Nature."[21] As "a Scheme of Thoughts traced out upon Matter" allegory denies art's dependence on the natural.[22] So not only does allegory turn customarily on psychological subjects, it consistently privileges thought over sense. This view of a hierarchy of meanings in allegory asks that we read through the physical to the spiritual.

Allegory, then, lets Berkeley dissect for public view Collins's confused intellectuals, and yet also preserve mind as transcendent. In *Guardian* 39 Collins's mental house and its crazed inhabitants clearly stand as signs of an invisible, spiritual condition. The reified mind that Berkeley had so carefully eschewed in his philosophical writings finds a place in the essay's satiric allegory. But the metaphysical metaphor that Berkeley does permit himself to use in the *Principles* and the *Three Dialogues*—that the world is God's book and that language stands as a sign of mind—also has a place in the allegory. Indeed, allegory's attention to the process of reading, to the relation between sign and signified, permits Berkeley to explore the implications of his chosen metaphor and to consider again what it is to read.

Words and their meanings are themselves a recurrent concern of the essay. Ulysses, a confirmed modern, is, like Swift's index learner, eager to avoid the tedium of reading. The philosophical snuff appeals to him as mechanical short-cut to knowledge. But Ulysses becomes, despite himself, a reader of the scenes in Collins's mind. And it is as a "Spectator" of text in its ideal form that he writes *Guardian* 39, showing "the original Formation or Production of a certain Book in the Mind of a Free-Thinker," and disclosing the "secret Manner and internal Principles by which that Phaenomenon was formed" (*Guardian*, 146). Ulysses's "philosophical" turn of phrase here casts Collins's *Discourse* as a material object, the product of a mechanical operation. Berkeley again confounds text and mind when at the end of his adventure Ulysses returns to our world:

> *Vanity* had no sooner led her Forces into the Imagination, but she resolved upon storming the Castle and giving no Quarter. They began the Assault with a loud Out-cry and great Confusion. I, for my Part, made the best of my Way, and re-entered my own Lodging. Some time after, inquiring at a Bookseller's for *a Discourse on Free-thinking*, which had made some Noise, I met with the Representatives of all those Notions drawn up in the same confused Order upon Paper. (*Guardian*, 158)

The "loud Out-cry" made by the army of Collins's notions becomes the "Noise" made by the town about his book, and the grotesque notions become words on paper, "drawn up in the same confused Order." *Guardian* 39, then, stands as both an anatomy of Collins's psyche and a reader's guide to the *Discourse*. On the pages of the *Discourse* we meet the "Representatives" of the notions we have "seen" in *Guardian* 39. The allegory effects the conflation of mind and text that Swift plays upon so tirelessly in the *Battle of the Books*.

Of all modes, allegory is, perhaps, the most self-consciously literary as it plays with signs, encoding tenor within vehicle. In *Guardian* 152 Addison stresses that much of pleasure of allegory lies with our appreciation of the wit and originality of the conceit; new and surprising subjects are best, especially those "appearing difficult to have been thrown into emblematic Types and Shadows" (*Guardian*, 497). This creative self-consciousness is nowhere more evident than in personification, where something which has a purely nominal existence like *vanity* is given a sensible human form. Berkeley draws our attention to this play between word and idea when Ulysses spies Atheism standing among the ranks of Collins's notions:

> I could, nevertheless, observe that they all agreed in a Squinting Look, or Cast of their Eyes toward a certain Person in a Masque, who was placed in the Center, and whom by sure Signs and Tokens I discovered to be *Atheism*. (*Guardian*, 158)

Here the tenor of the allegory dissolves as Ulysses seems unable to depict Atheism in her mask. He can only assure us that he had "sure Signs and Tokens" as to her identity. At this moment of allegorical breakdown, Berkeley shows the ultimate impossibility of reaching Collins's motives through his text alone. Collins had, in fact, repudiated atheism in the *Discourse*.[23] Without the secret knowledge Berkeley gleaned when eavesdropping in the Grecian, the hermeneutic path to the true intent of the *Discourse* is blocked.

Allegory, then, with its stylized, exploded view of signifier and signified, permits Berkeley to analyze the possibilities of reading mind through text. While *Guardian* 39 treats text as a mirror of mind, it also raises the spectre of language's deceits—that Collins's agenda is in part masked by his rhetoric. Such contradictions had, in fact, troubled Berkeley in his earlier writings. In the Introduction to the *Principles* he recognized that word and idea have become united by long habit, so much so that the separation Locke strives for in Book III of the *Essay* seems impossible. Here he entreats his reader "to make my words the occasion of his own thinking, and endeavour to attain the same train of thoughts in reading, that I had in writing them" (*Works*, II: 40). His worry in the *Principles* is that we will get caught in queries about particular terms, when meaning lies beyond, in "the scope and tenor and connexion of a discourse" (*Works*, II: 63). Berkeley's apparent uncertainty here about the adequacy of his language as a medium for his own thought is partly explained if we reconsider his central metaphor of the world as God's language and how this informs his understanding of word and idea.

As a system of signs, Berkeley's physical world is contingent upon mind—God's mind as he "speaks" through our senses, and our minds as we make meaning from passive ideas of sense. I've suggested that allegory proved a particularly amenable mode of discourse to Berkeley for its subordination of the sensible to the spiritual. When in the *Principles* he describes the appropriate hermeneutics of the world, he asks for allegorical reading, reading that learns to transcend the literal at all points. Berkeley complains that too often we get mired in the text of the world. In our preoccupations with mechanical causes in natural philosophy we behave like grammarians, obsessed with linguistic rules rather than meaning, with efficient rather than final causes:

> We should propose to our selves nobler views, such as to recreate and exalt the mind, with a prospect of the beauty, order, extent, and variety of natural things: hence, by proper inferences, to enlarge our notions of the grandeur, wisdom, and beneficence of the Creator: and lastly, to make the several parts of Creation, so far as in us lies, subservient to the ends they were designed for, God's glory, and the sustentation and comfort of our selves and fellow-creatures. (*Works*, II: 89)

Only by reading rhetorically, for the character and intentions of the author, do we find the meaning and value of the text. These concerns are paramount in Berkeley's reading of Collins's *Discourse* in *Guardian* 39. By recreating Collins's purposes and state of mind in the act of writing, Berkeley is able to disclose the dangers posed by the subversive text. Berkeley, like Swift, is sensitive to the deceits of language and the dangers of excess in allegorical reading. But *Guardian* 39 reveals that for Berkeley all reading, whether of texts or of the world, is essentially allegorical, a search for intentions, for spiritual narratives encoded in stories about the world.

NOTES

1. A. A. Luce assigned twelve *Guardians* to Berkeley: ##27, 35, 39, 49, 55, 62, 70, 77, 83, 88, 89, 126; see *The Works of George Berkeley, Bishop of Cloyne*, ed. Luce and T. E. Jessop, 9 vols. (London: Nelson, 1948–1957), VII: 178, and his "Berkeley's Essays in the *Guardian*," *Mind* 52 (1943): 247–63. In his edition of *The Guardian* (Lexington, KY: University of Kentucky Press, 1982), John Calhoun Stephens adds #58 to the list (p. 28), but despite the fact that it toys with the theme of Berkeley's #49, the evidence for the attribution is scant. David Berman has accepted #69, on the grounds that it is attributed to Berkeley by his friend the American philosopher Samuel Johnson, in his review of T. E. Jessop's *A Bibliography of George Berkeley*, *Hermathena* 125 (1978): 70, and the case is strengthened by Kenneth P. Winkler, "The Authorship of *Guardian* 69," *Berkeley Newsletter* 7 (1984), 1–6. Finally, Berman marshals substantial evidence for including #130; see "Did Berkeley Write *Guardian* 130?," *Berkeley Newsletter* 5 (1981): 10–13. The two essays to be discussed here, ##35 and 39, were attributed to Berkeley by his son in 1765. The long postscript to #39 was, however, written by Steele; see E. J. Furlong's "How Much of Steele's *Guardian* #39 Did Berkeley Write?," *Hermathena* 89 (1957): 76–88. All further reference to Berkeley's writing will cite Luce and Jessop's *Works*, with the exception of the *Guardian* papers, for which Stephens's edition will be used.

2. "As some of the finest Compositions among the Ancients are in Allegory, I have endeavoured, in several of my Papers, to revive that way of Writing, and hope I have not been altogether unsuccessful in it"— #501, *The Spectator*, ed. Donald F. Bond, 5 vols. (Oxford: Clarendon Press, 1965), IV: 275. Both here and in #524 Addison remarks on the popularity of allegorical papers with readers and contributors.

3. Daniel's *Voyage*, first published in Paris in 1690, made two editions in its English translation (1692 and 1694). Bolingbroke, whose reading of Descartes is clearly influenced by Daniel, ranks the *Voyage* with *Don Quixote* as "the two most ingenious satirical romances that were ever written"; see *The Works of Lord Bolingbroke* (1844; rpt. London: Cass, 1967), IV: 115n.

4. For Berkeley's allusions to this encounter and its influence on *Alciphron*, see my *The Rhetoric of Berkeley's Philosophy* (Cambridge: Cambridge University Press, 1990), 123–5.

5. Berkeley's less than satisfactory suggestion, elaborated in the second edition of the *Principles*, that while we do not have an "idea" of mind, we can have a "notion" has generated a growing body of critical speculation, including recently Daniel E. Flage's *Berkeley's Doctrine of Notions: A Reconstruction based on his Theory of Meaning* (London: Croom Helm, 1987).

6. *An Essay Concerning Human Understanding*, ed. Peter H. Nidditch (Oxford: Clarendon Press, 1975), 676, 700.

7. *Essay*, 424.

8. Studies of the paradoxes of Locke's positions on language include Paul de Man's "The Epistemology of Metaphor," in *Critical Inquiry*, 5 (1978–1979), 13–30, and John Sitter's "About Wit: Locke, Addison, Prior, and the Order of Things," in *Rhetorics of Order/Ordering of Rhetorics in English Neoclassical Literature*, ed. J. Douglas Canfield and J. Paul Hunter (Cranbury, NJ: University of Delaware Press, 1990), 137–57. Most direct of all was Montaigne, resurrected in Prior's "A Dialogue between Mr: John Lock and Seigneur de Montaigne" (written 1719), who tells his opponent "you make similes while you blame them"; see *The Literary Works of Matthew Prior*, ed. B. Wright and M. K. Spears, 2nd ed. (Oxford: Oxford University Press, 1971), I: 625.

9. *Essay*, 55, 101, 105, 150.

10. *Essay*, 121.

11. *Essay*, 152–3.

12. *Essay*, 118.

13. See John Richetti, *Philosophical Writing: Locke, Berkeley, Hume* (Cambridge: Harvard University Press, 1983), 157.

14. *Essay*, 81, 151, 363.

15. *Essay*, 152–3.

16. "Berkeley's Doctrine of Signs," in *Berkeley: Critical and Interpretive Essays*, ed. Colin M. Turbayne (Minneapolis: University of Minnesota Press, 1982), 235–6.

17. *A Discourse of Free-thinking, Occasion'd by the Rise of a Sect call'd Free-thinkers* (London: n.p., 1713), 19–24.

18. "The Two Allegories," in *Allegory, Myth, and Symbol*, ed. Morton W. Bloomfield (Cambridge: Harvard University Press, 1981), 358.

19. *Satiric Allegory: Mirror of Man* (New Haven, CT: Yale University Press, 1956), 2–7.

20. #273, *The Spectator*, II: 563–4.

21. #419, *The Spectator*, III: 570.

22. #421, *The Spectator*, III: 577.

23. *Discourse*, 104–7.

INDEX

INDEX

This index is intended as a compendious, not an exhaustive, guide to persons, texts, and themes mentioned in this book. To avoid redundancy and superfluity, those works, authors, or issues that serve as the principle topic of an essay are indexed only at their first occurrence within that essay. These same items are, however, indexed for all occurrences in other essays concerned mainly with other topics. Terms that appear throughout the book, such as "allegory" or "metaphor," are elided from this index. Notes are indexed only when they add substantial information to the text.

Abrams, M. H., 325
Ackermann, William, 199
Accommodation, 360–63
Adams, Hazard, xiii
Addison, Joseph, 55, 77, 81, 121n20, 237n4, 314–315, 373, 374, 376, 383; *Cato* 373, 387n1; "Faerie way of Writing" 383
Admiral De Fonte, 207, 211
Aesop, 177
Agulhon, Maurice, 225, 238n9
Akenside, Joseph, 82; *The Pleasures of the Imagination*, 82
Allegoresis, xiii, 22, 23, 35, 41, 68n1, 99, 302, 306, 319
All Souls College, 265
Allen, Don Cameron, 360
Alpers, Svetlana, 121n19
Althusser, Louis, 142
Altick, Richard, 82
Amalarius, Bishop of Metz, 263
Andrews, Lancelot, 191
Anteriority, 359
Arbuthnot, John, 383; John Bull pamphlets, 383
Arianism, 54
Ariosto, 206
Aristotle, 355
Arnold, Matthew, 76; "Empedocles on Etna," 76; *Poems* (1853), 76; "Sohrab and Rustum," 76
Atheism, 385
Attenuated semiosis, 50, 65
Aubrey, John, 193
Augustine, St., 23
Ault, Donald, 125n60

Bachelard, Gaston, 133
Bacon, Sir Francis, 311
Barlow, Thomas, Bishop of Lincoln, 272n11
Barthes, Roland, 112, 135
Bartholomew Fair, 267

391

Bastille Day Festival, 224 ff.
Batteaux, Charles, 72n28
Battestin, Martin, 346n2
Baudrillard, Jean, 150
Bayle, Pierre, 140
Bedloe, William, 252n6
Beer, John, 80, 120n15
Behn, Aphra, 33, 195; *Oronooko*, 33
Bell, A. Colquhuon, 164
Bender, John, 121n19
Benjamin, Walter, 76, 100–101, 119n5, 318–19, 371n16; *Ursprung des deutschen Trauerspiels*, 76
Bentham, Jeremy, 82, 93; Panopticon project, 82
Berkeley, George, 176, 191, 193, 373 ff.; *Alciphron*, 374; *Three Dialogues between Hylas and Philonous*, 373 ff.; *A Treatise Concerning the Principles of Human Knowledge*, 373 ff.
Berman, David, 387n1
Bernheimer, Charles, 119n5
Bethlehem Hospital, 355
Biblical commentary, 23
Blackmore, Richard, 82, 314, 352; *Creation*, 82
Blackwell, Thomas, 4, 10, 13 ff.; Cool and flashy myth, 13; *Enquiry into the Life and Writings of Homer*, 10 ff.
Blair, Robert, 175
Blake, William, xi, 4, 18 ff., 82, 172, 191, 325; "The Crystal Cabinet," 75 ff.; *An Island in the Moon*, 82; *The Marriage of Heaven and Hell*, 4, 18 ff.
Bloom, Harold, 80, 120n15
"B—[o]b, Take Care Lest Your Crib be Bilk'd," 286
Bogel, Fredric, 346n5, 370n4
Boileau, Nicolas, 223; *Le Lutrin* 223

Bolingbroke, Henry St. John, Viscount, 278, 387n3; *The Vision of Camilick*, 278–279
Boniface VIII, Pope, 269
Booth, John, 217n63
Bowen, Margarita, 215n41
Bradbury, Charles, 175–6; *Cabinet of Jewels*, 175–6, 177, 179
Brathwait, John, 192, 199; *The Ladies Love-Lectvre*, 192
Brevint, Daniel, 272n11; *Missale Romanum*, 272n11
Brisman, Leslie, 105
Broberg, Gunnar, 168n18
Bronson, Bertrand, 311
Bruce, Kames, 115; *Travels to Discover the Source of the Nile*, 115
Bunyan, John, xi, xiv, 21, 23 ff., 41, 43, 47, 171, 182, 243; *The Pilgrim's Progress*, 21, 23 ff., 36, 41
Burke, Edmund, 72n29
Butler, Samuel, xiii, 309; *Hudibras*, xiii, 309

C18-L, 214m32
Camera obscura, 81, 82, 86, 88, 381
Carnochan, W. B., 121n19
Caroline, Queen, 286
Cartland, Barbara, 191
Cartography, 193 ff.
Cartouches, 200 ff.
Cary, John, 215n41
Cassirer, Ernst, 10
Catharsis, 264
Chapin, Chester, 212n2
Charles I, King, 262
Charles II, King, 26, 242 ff., 255, 258, 262
Chaucer, Geoffrey, 116, 172, 248, 331–2, 347n19; *The Canterbury Tales*, 116, 172; *The House of Fame*, 331–2; *The Squire's Tale* 248
Cheevers, J., 200; *Mappa Britanniae Septentrionalis*, 200

Choice Emblems, 176-7
Chrétien de Troyes, 171
Cibber, Colley, 28, 284, 329, 338, 341, 345, 352 ff.; *Love in a Riddle*, 284
Cicero, 39n11
Clarke, John, 53-4, 59
Claude glasses, 82
Clement I, Pope, 269
Cole, Benjamin, 177, 182; *Tales and Fables*, 177-9
Coleridge, Samuel Taylor, xiv, 76, 78, 89, 95, 97, 118, 139, 174, 231; *Biographia*, 95, 96; "Christabel," 111; "Dejection: An Ode," 118; "The Eolian Harp," 89; infinite regresses in, 96-97; *The Statesman's Manual*, 78, 108
Collins, Anthony, 375-6, 380-81, 384, 385; *A Discourse of Free-thinking*, 375-6, 381, 385-6
Collins, William, 325
Colonel Chartres, 291
Commentary, 245-6, 302, 372n21; *see also* Biblical commentary; metacommentary
Committee of Secrecy, 287
Commonwealth, 255
Compendious Geographical Dictionary, 206
Condillac, Étienne, 233
Condor, Thomas, 200
Conservatives, 243
Cook, Captain James, 208
Cope, Kevin L., 70n17
Copeland, Aaron, 193
The Coronation of Queen Elizabeth, 267
Corpuscular theory, 377
Cosin, John, Bishop of Durham, 272n11
Costume, 257
Couplets, 352
Court and Country, 283

Cowper, William, xiii, 172, 325; *The Task*, xiii
Cozens, Alexander, 164; *A New Method of Assisting the Invention in Drawing Original Compositions of Landscape*, 164, 166
The Craftsman, 279, 282-5, 289, 292-3
Creative withdrawals, 325
Croce, Benedetto, 10
Crouch, Nathaniel, 181 ff., 197, 206-7; *Admirable Curiosities*, 206-7; *Delights for the Ingenious*, 181 ff.

Dame Allegory, xv
Dampier, Captain William, 164, 166; *Discourse of Winds, Breezes, Storms, Tides and Currents*, 164
Damrosch, Leopold, 120
Daniel, Gabriel, 375, 387n3; *Voyage to the World of Descartes*, 375
Dante, xiii, 28; *Commedia*, 28; *Letter to Can Grande*, 28, 370n2
Darwin, Charles, 167; voyage of the Beagle, 167
Darwin, Erasmus, 82, 122n26; *Botanic Garden*, 82, 122n26
Data retrieval systems, xii
David, 223
Da Vinci, Leonardo, 166
Davis, Lennard, 167
Daly, Peter, 174, 178, 213n16
Danby, Lord Treasurer, 252n6
De Beauzée, Nicolas, 223
Dechristianization, 236
DeFoe, Daniel, 136; *Moll Flanders*, 136, 140; *Vision*, 323
De Fuentes, Bartelme, 207
De Man, Paul, 35, 106, 119n5, 168n9, 191, 359, 388n8
De Meung, Jean, 223; *Le Roman de la Rose* 223
Dennis, John, 314, 347n21;

Prince Arthur, 314
De Quincey, Quatramère, 223
Derrida, Jacques, 95, 141, 370n6
Desaguliers, Jean Theophile, 180
Descartes, René, 81, 375
Description, 324
Didacticism, didactic, 45, 49, 61, 193, 236
Diderot, Denis, 140, 143 ff., 162 ff.; *Encyclopédie*, 143 ff., 162 ff., 223
Difference, 27
Diorama, 82
Distortion of time and space, 245
Doctrine of natural place, 355
Dodsley, Robert, 191, 196; *The Oeconomy of Human life*, 191; *The Preceptor*, 196; see also *London Magazine*
Doeticum, Jan van, 199
Donato, Eugenio, 166
Done, John, 180
Donne, John, 174
Downie, J. A., 294n5
Drake, Sir Francis, 174, 198
The Dream from the Mist, 278–9, 282
Dryden, John, 26, 33, 67, 178, 191, 258, 307, 317–18; *Absalom and Achitophel*, 26; *The Hind and the Panther*, 301, 317; *MacFlecknoe*, 33; *Oedipus*, 258; *Religio Laici*, 307, 317
Duff, William, 57, 59, 64, 68n6
Dugdale, Stephen, 252n6
Dulce et utile, 16
Durrell, Lawrence, 273n24

Edward Scissorhands (movie), 162
Eagleton, Terry, 76
Eidophusikon, 82

Eliot, George, 76
Elizabeth I, Queen, 29, 243, 258, 260, 262; virgin queen, 259
Emblems and emblem books, 173 ff.
Empiricism, 132
Epic, 58, 313–14, 354
Epstein, Julia, 124n46
ESTC (*Eighteenth-Century Short Title Catalogue*), xiv
Euhemerism, 11, 59
Evelyn, John, 177, 179–180, 257; *Diary* 257
Examiner (newspaper), 374

Fable, 14
Fact and facticity, 135
The Fall of Mortimer, 280
Fawkes, Guy, 257
Fermor, Arabella, 336
Ferry, Anne Davidson, 46, 69n11
Festival of the Constitution, 224
Festival of Gratitude and of Victories, 224
Festival of Reason, 224–5
Festival of Republican Reunion, 224
Feyeraben, Paul, 132
Fielding, Henry, xi, xiv, 34, 86, 140, 163, 192, 346n2; *Grub Street Opera*, 285-7; *Jonathan Wild*, 86; *Joseph Andrews*, 36; *Tom Jones*, 140
Fineman, Joel, 116–17, 119n5, 371n12, 371n19
Flage, Daniel E., 387n5
Fletcher, Angus, xii–xiii, 37n2, 42, 68n2, 100–101, 119n5, 173, 231, 232, 241, 243, 372n24; on incompleteness, 100, 173
Flying Post (newspaper), 265
Foley, Margaret, 218n69
Fordham, Sir Herbert George, 215n41
Foreshadowing, 45
Formalism, xiii
Foucault, Michel, 133, 141, 143, 150, 233

Fowler, Edward, Bishop of Gloucester, 272n11
Foxon, David, 345n1
Fraunce, Abraham, 27
Freeman, Rosemary, 174, 213n16
Frei, Hans, 306, 309
Freud, Sigmund, 72n33, 90–91, 93, 101, 123n43, 140–41; and Dora, 141; on compulsivity, 101–102
Frye, Northrop, xii, xiv, 105, 119n5, 120n15, 302
Fuller, John, 276
Furet, François, 230
Furlong, E. J., 387n1

Gallagher, Philip, 71n26
Gallop, Jane, 125n56
Gay, Clifford, xiii, 173, 242, 245, 247
Gay, John, 275 ff.; *Achilles*, 277, 285, 290–92; *The Beggar's Opera*, 275 ff.; *The Distress'd Wife*, 285–8, 291–2; *Fables*, 283, 291; *Polly* 275, ff.; *The Rehearsal at Goatham*, 283, 285; *The Wife of Bath*, 284
Gaulmier, Jean, 237n2
Gaze, 73n36
Gentlemen's Magazine, 54
George I, King, 265
Godfrey, Judge Edmund Berry, 252n6, 260, 264, 272n9
Goethe, Johann Wolfgang von, 18, 97; *Faust*, 97
The Golden Hind (ship), 174, 198
Golden, Morris, 94
Gombrich, Ernst, 85
Guardian (newspaper), 288, 373 ff.
Gumbrecht, Hans Ulrich, 228, 229
Gostling, William, 195; *A Walk in and about the City of Canterbury*, 195

Gower, John, xiv
Graham, Edwin, 275
Grand tour, 132
Gray, Thomas, 325
Gregory III, Pope, 269
Green Berets, 192
Green, Thomas, 72n29
Greenberg, Mark, 124n46
Greenblatt, Stephen, 119n5
Grégoire, L' Abbé, 234–235
Greville, Fulke, 192
Griffin, Dustin, 348n40
Gunpowder Plot, 257–8

Hagberg, Knut, 168n18
Halley, Sir Edmund, 196
Hamacher, Werner, 303
Hardison, O. B., 39n12, 263, 272n13
Harris, Michael, 215n41
Harris, Tim, 272n10
Harth, Philip, 301, 307
Hawkesworth, John, 163
Hawthorne, Nathaniel, 76
Hegel, Georg Wilhelm Friedrich, 164; *Philosophy of History*, 164
Helmsely, Leona, 191
Hensel, Gottfried, 195
Herbert, George, 175
Hervey, Lord, 276
Heydon, John, 194; *Harmony of the World*, 194
Hieroglyph, hieroglyphics, 5, 6, 8–9, 12, 56, 192
Historical allegory, 25, 357
The History of the Norfolk Steward, 285
Hobbes, Thomas, 199, 299–301
Hogarth, William, 77
Holly, Grant, 168n9
Homer, 9, 10–11, 22, 28, 35, 54, 313, 315, 324, 345, 353; *Illiad*, 28, 324; *Odyssey*, 28, 324
Honig, Edwin, xii, 119n5, 370n2
Hooke, Robert 88, 124n49; *Lectures on Light* 88
Hooker, Edward Niles, 347

Horace, 88, 223
Horatian Ode, 223
Horne, Tooke, 69n13
House of Commons, 247
Hughes, John, 52, 54, 56, 63–4, 313–14
Hugo, Father; *Pia Desidera*, 174
Hume, David, 81, 93, 120n18
Hume, Robert, 275
Hunt, Lynn, 225, 236, 238n9
Hunt, Margaret, 214n32
Hurd, Richard, 57
Huet, Marie-Hélène, 230
Husserl, Edmund, 95

Impartial Protestant Mercury (newspaper), 269
Incest, 352 ff.
Irony, 383
Irrationality, 329
Isaiah, 332–3, 336

Jakobsen, Roman, 116; sructural linguistics of, 116
James I, King, 262
James, William, 86
Jameson, Fredric, 94
Je ne sais quoi, 17
Jefferys, Thomas, 216n44
Joan, Pope, 269, 273n24
Johnson, Samuel, xiv, 42, 68n5, 98–99, 112; *Vision of Theodore* 323
Joyce, James, 70n15; *Finnegans Wake* 70n15
Jung, Carl, 49; *Answer to Job*, 49

Kant, Immanuel, 95, 96; principle of self-consciousness, 96
Keach, Benjamin, 191
Kepler, Johannes, 81
Keys, 23
Kilmer, Dorothy, 192
Kitchin, Thomas, 200, 216n44
Knapp, Steven, 42, 56, 68n2, 71n26, 212n2, 212n6, 315

Knoespel, Kenneth, 58–9
Knox, Thomas, 252n6
Korshin, Paul, 46, 68n7
Kristeva, Julia, 73n36
Kuhn, Thomas, 132

Lacan, Jacques, 92–3, 125n56, 142; *Écrits*, 125n56; Méconnaissance, 92
Laharpe, Jean-François, 233; *Du Fanatisme dans la langue révolutionnaire*, 233
Landes, Joan, 226, 230
Lane, Jane (pseudonym), 253n22
Landscape painting, 132
Langland, William, xiii, xiv, 41, 243; *Piers Plowman* xiii, 41
Law, John; Introduces paper money in France, 151
Lawson, Robert, 167n1
Leslie, Charles, 53
L' Estrange, Roger, 249
Levine, Arnold, 320n9
Lewis, C. S., xii, xiii, 172, 242
Leyburn, Ellen Douglass, 383
Licensing Act, 284
Lieb, Michael, 70n14
Light metaphysic, 354 ff.
Limon, Jerzy, 269
Linnaeus, 151; Linnaean taxonomy, 166–167
Lloyd, William, Bishop of Worcester, 272n11
Locke, John, 80, 81, 84, 92, 215n41, 361–3, 377–9, 382; *Essay Concerning Human Understanding*, 80, 361–362, 378–379; Ideas of reflection, 83; *tabula rasa*, 379
Loftis, John, 280
London Magazine, 194, 196, 216n44
Lowes, Jonathan Livingston, 109, 112, 115
Lubac, Pere Henri de, 28n9
Luce, A. A., 387n1
Luttrell, Narcissus; Narcissus Luttrell manuscript, 265

Mack, Maynard, 325, 327, 347n16
Macniece, Louis, xiv, 256
Madsen, William, 69n8
Magdalen College, 347n28
Mallet, Abbé, 237n5
Mandeville, Bernard, xiv
Manichæism, 49
Manipulation of verb tenses, 332–3
Marvell, Andrew, 175
Marxism and Marxists, 173
Mason, Reverend John, 196
Mass (Holy), 263–4
Mazzeo, Anthony, 370n9
Mazzeo, Joseph, 371n10
McGowan, William H., 379
McIntosh, William, 275
MCI Telecommunications, 199
Melville, Herman, 76
Merleau-Ponty, Maurice, 129n114
Metacommentary, 94; *see also* commentary
Methodism 182
Middleton, Thomas, 269; *A Game at Chess*, 269
Mileu, Pean-Pierre, 117
Millar, George Henry, 197, 206; *New and Universal System of Geography*, 197–8, 206
Miller, J. Hillis, 383
Miller, John, 258
Milton, John, 41 ff., 88, 99, 112, 315, 332, 337, 345, 355, 360; *Comus*, 347n26; *De doctrina christiana*, 61; "Lycidas," 52, 110; *Nativity Ode*, 332; *Paradise Lost*, 41 ff., 99, 346n26, 355; *Paradise Regain'd*, 46, 51
Mimesis and the mimetic, 43–4, 354
Mississippi River, 194
Mock-heroic, 337
Modernism and the modern, 132, 241–2
Möll, Hermann, 195
Monmouth, James Scott, Duke of, 26
Monthly Miscellany, or Memoirs for the Curious, 207
More, Thomas, xiv, 254n35; *A Dialogue of Comfort Against Tribulation*, 254n35
Morris, David B., 372n26
Murrin, Michael, 38n5, 60, 68n2, 71n19, 242–3, 247, 372n23
Muse, 327
Myers, Robin, 215n41

Nabokov, Vladimir, 101; *Pale Fire*, 101
Narcissism, 61–2, 65, 73n36
Natural law, 235
Neale, Thomas, 323; *The Vision*, 323
Neo-Platonism, xiv
Newton, Sir Isaac, 81, 82, 84, 89; gravity, 89
Nietzsche, Friedrich, 128n104, 141, 150, 167
Nieuhoff, John, 199; *Travels*, 199–200
Noble, Yvonne, 296
No Popery, or A Catechism Against Popery, 272n11
The Norfolk Congress, 282
"The Norfolk Game of Cribbidge," 280, 288
Norris, Frank, 76
Northwest Passage, 207, 211
Notre Dame (cathedral), xi
Nuttall, A. D., 121n19

Oates, Titus, 242 ff.
Ogilby, John, 199
"On Colonel Francisco, Rapemaster of Great Britain," 291
Osborn, James, 348n39
Ovid, 23, 35; *Metamorphoses*, 23
Ozouf, Mona, 227, 229, 236

Paley, William, 82, 124n48
Panorama, 82
Pantheonization of Marat, 224, 228
Parnell, Thomas, 56
Patrides, C. A., 371
Patrilineality and patriarchy, 353, 363, 369
Paulson, Ronald, 310
Pearl Poet, xiv
Peirce, C. S., 95, 108, 125n68
Percy, Walker, 131; *The Moviegoer*, 131
Pentateuch, 5
Percival, John, 374
Perrin, Jean, 179
Personification, 23 ff., 43 ff., 137, 311–12, 315; defined, 26
Phillips, Michael, 120n17
Physiognomy, 363
Pico della Mirandola, Giovanni, 47; *Heptaplus*, 47
Picus, Josephus, 5
Platina, 274n24; *Lives of the Popes*, 274n24
Plato, 124n51
The Pleasures of Reason, xiv, 208, 211
The Plot in a Dream, 242 ff.
poetic logic, 8, 12
Pope, Alexander, xiii, 150, 178, 300, 323 ff., 351 ff., 373; *The Dunciad*, xiii, 23, 300, 351 ff.; *Epilogue to the Satires*, 343 ff.; *Epistle to Arbuthnot*, 324 ff.; *Epistle to Miss Blount*, 327 ff.; "Epistle to Bathurst," 342 ff.; "Epistle to Burlington," 341 ff.; *Essay on Criticism*, 326 ff.; *Messiah*, 323 ff.; *The Rape of the Lock*, 23, 143, 323 ff.; *The Temple of Fame*, 323 ff.; *Windsor Forest*, 323 ff., 373
Popish Plot, 242 ff.
Popper, Karl, 132

Post-stucturalism, xiv
Praz, Mario, 213
Prefiguration, 49
Pre-texts, xiv, 242–243
Priestley, Joseph, 69n13
Privileged language communities, 242–243
Probability, probable, 58, 314
Prophecy, 323, 344
Prosopopœia, *see* personification
Protestantism, 174, 247, 260, 266
Proverbs, 248
Punning, 85
Purchase, Samuel, 112
Puttenham, George, 310; *The Arte of English Poesie*, 310

Quintilian, xiii
Quilligan, Maureen, xiv, 37n2, 46–47, 68n2, 69n11, 85, 99, 101–2, 199n5, 120n14, 126n75, 172, 173, 191, 221–2, 233, 237, 247, 256, 260, 302, 319, 372n21; on otherness, 99, 102

Radzinowicz, Mary Ann, 69n10
Raine, Kathleen, 80, 120n15
Ramsay, Allen, 191; *Health*, 191
Rationalist conception of language, 9
Ray, John, 215n41
Reagan, Nancy, 171
Reagan, Ronald, 171–2
Realism and realists, 135, 140, 192
Révolutions de Paris (journal), 224
Reynolds, Henry, 4, 77
Rhine (river), 199
Richetti, John, 388n13
Ricour, Paul, 139
Romantics, English poets, 237n2, 324–5
Rome's Follies, Or the Amorous Fryars, 269–71
Rollenhagen, Gabriel, 181; *Nucleus emblematum selectis-*

simorum, 181
Roper, Alan, 26, 38n10, 256
Rorty, Richard, 121n19
Rosicrucianism, 175, 182, 194, 316
Rowe, Elizabeth, 323; *The Vision*, 323
Royalists, 244 ff.
Royidis, Emmanuel, 273n24; *Papissa Joanna*, 273n24
Rules and Maxims for the Conduct of Life, 175
Russell, J. Stephen, 68n1

Schiller, Johann Christoph Friedrich von, 17
Scriblerians, 23, 353–4, 375
Salmon, Mr,. 216n44
Sears Tower (building), xi
Schultz, William, 276
Schwartz, Regina, 59
Schwarzenegger, Arnold, 162
Scientific aesthetic, 132
Settle, Elkanah, 259, 273n24, 352
Shaftesbury, Anthony Cooper, First Earl of, 26, 247–8
Sharrock, Roger, 38n6
Sheiley, Mary, 237n2
Shelley, Percy Bysshe, xiv, 67, 84, 89, 104; "Mont Blanc," 84; "Ode to the West Wind," 90; "Ozymandias," 126n81; *The Triumph of Life*, 104
Shakespeare, William, 248, 347n18; *The Tempest*, 248
Short Circuit (movie), 162
Simonneau, Mayor, 224, 226, 229, 234
Sir Orfeo, 206
Sir Robert Brass, 276
Sitter, John, 348n36, 370n3, 388n8
Skerrett, Molly, 348n39
Smalley, Beryl, 38n9
Smart, Christopher, 325
Smith, Adam, 82, 89; iconographic tradition, 335; impartial spectator, 82; invisible hand, 89
Smith, Bernard, 167n1
Snoek, Jan, 214n32
Socrates, 179
Solipsism, 372n26
South Sea Bubble, 290
Southwark Fair, 267
Spacks, Patricia Meyer, 315, 325, 346n8, 348n30, 370n9, 372n26; *The Poetry of Vision*, 325
Spectator, 81, 323, 373, 374, 375, 383
Spence, Joseph, 324, 348n41
Spenser, Edmund, 3, 28–30, 34, 36, 41, 42, 57, 65, 171, 174, 310; *The Faerie Queene*, 3, 29–30, 36, 41, 43–4, 60; *Letter to Raleigh* 28–30, 36, 310
Stafford, Barbara, 133–4, 167n1; *Voyage into Substance*, 133
Stafford, Lord, 252n6
"The Statesman's Fall," 280
Steele, Richard, 374
Stendhal, 76
Stephens, John Calhoun, 387n1
Sterne, Laurence, 33, 92; *Sentimental Journey*, 33; *Tristram Shandy*, 33, 92–3
Summers, Joseph, 69n12
Summers, Montague, 259
A Supplement to the Norfolk Congress, 289
Swaim, Kathleen, 69n11
Swedenborg, Emanuel, 175
Swift, Jonathan, 23, 29, 33, 99, 124n50, 207, 280, 285, 299 ff., 384, 385; *The Battle of the Books*, 33, 385; *Gulliver's Travels*, 23, 207, 277, 282, 287; Houyhnhnms, 277, 318; *Intelligencer*, 288; "On Mr. Pulteney being Put Out of the Council," 280; *A Panegryical Essay upon the Num-*

ber Three, 124n50; *A Tale of a Tub*, 23, 29–30, 99, 299 ff., 383; Yahoos, 279
Symbol, 18
Synecdoche, 12

Tatler (newspaper), 373
The Terminator (movie), 153
Teskey, Gordon, 247, 371n13
Thomson, James, 82, 112, 175, 325; *The Seasons*, 82
Todorov, Tzvetan, 127n93
Tom Telescope, 82, 121nn22–23
Tonge, Ezeral, 252n6
Transcendentalism, German, 95
Treip, Midele, 70n18
Troost, Linda, 214n32
Trope, 8, 12, 17
Turpentine, 192, 193
Tuve, Rosemund, xiii, 21, 37, 37n1, 37n2, 37n3, 319
Tyacke, Sarah, 215
Type characters, xi
Typology, 45, 49, 352

Van Dyke, Carolyn, xiii, 173
Verres and his Scribblers, 289
Vico, Giambattista, 4, 6, 8, 9, 12, 142–3; *The New Science*, 4, 6, 9, 142
Virgil, 23, 35, 54, 313, 332–3, 335–6, 347n27; *Æneid*, 23, 333; *Georgics*, 333, 347n27
The Vision, An Allegorical Dream, 323
The Vision of Mons. Chamillard, 323
The Vision, or a Prospect of Death, 323
Visionary poetry, xi, 19, 323 ff.
Volney, C. F., 221
Voltaire, 55, 71n25, 140, 223; *Henriade*, 223

Wagner, Richard, 128n104

Wakeman, Sir George, 247, 250
Walker, William, 123n46
Waller, Sir William, 261
Walmsley, Peter, 387n4
Walpole, Sir Robert, 275 ff., 345
Watson, Frederic, 198; *Geographical Dictionary*, 198
Watts, Isaac, 191
Watts, Susannah, 191; *Chinese Maxims*, 191
Wayne, John, 192
Weather Channel, 164
Webster, John, 248; *The Devil's Law Case*, 248
Wharton, Joseph, 348n35
Wharton, Thomas, 191
Whitman, John, 172, 173, 174, 191
William and Mary, 255
Williams, Aubrey, 370n9
Williams, Carolyn, 295n33
Williams, Sheila, 272n6
Wilson, Andrew, 180
Wilson, Thomas, 360–361
Winckelmann, Johann Joachim, 77, 222–3; *Reflections on the Imitation of Greek Works in Painting and Sculpture*, 77
Winkler, Kenneth, 387
Winstanley, William, 191
Wither, George, 180–82, 191, 197
Woodward, David, 216n44
Wordsworth, William, 20, 89, 91, 93, 95, 192; "Intimations," Ode 91, 128n104; *Lyrical Ballads*, 20; *Prelude*, 89, 95

Yeats, William Butler, 18
Young, Edward, 175

Zeno's paradox, 138
Zeugma, 352